THE WEIDENFELD
ATLAS OF
MARITIME
HISTORY

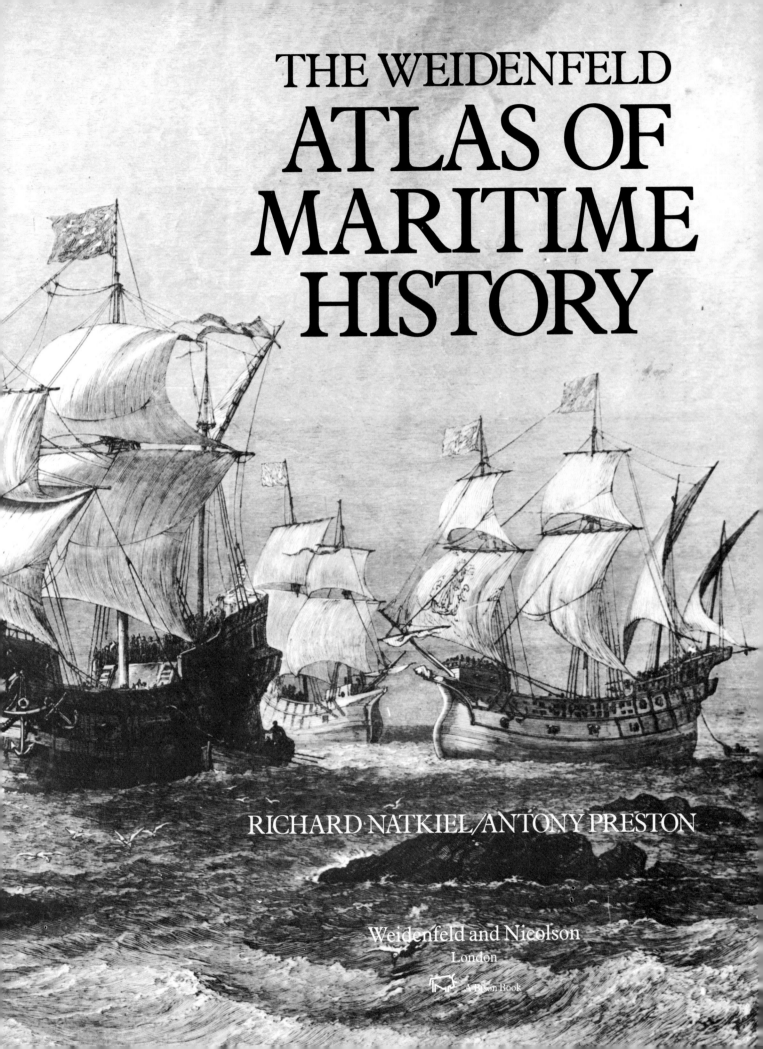

THE WEIDENFELD
ATLAS OF
MARITIME
HISTORY

RICHARD NATKIEL/ANTONY PRESTON

Weidenfeld and Nicolson
London
A Bison Book

Published by
Weidenfeld and Nicolson
91 Clapham High Street
London SW4 7TA

Produced by
Bison Books
176 Old Brompton Road
London SW5

ISBN 0 297 7853 9
Printed in Hong Kong

Richard Natkiel would like to thank his
assistant David Burles for his help in
preparing the maps for this book.

Editor's note. The 24-hour clock has been
used to show times of day in the maps and
text. Different nations introduced the
modern calendar at different times in history
but for the sake of consistency all articles in
this book from the time of the Spanish
Armada in 1588 have used the modern
calendar.

Page 1: The typical trading ship of the
Hanseatic League, the cog, as shown on an
early seal.
Pages 2-3: Magellan during his historic
voyage of discovery through the Straits
which now bear his name.
This page: A German *Konigsberg* class light
cruiser arrives in Britain to surrender along
with the rest of the German fleet at the end of
World War I.

CONTENTS

1 The Ancient World   6
2 The Medieval World   22
3 The Age of Exploration   38
4 The Rise of British Seapower   56
5 The Napoleonic Wars   84
6 Pax Britannica   100
7 World War I   144
8 World War II   172
9 The Modern Era   230
Glossary   251
Index   253
Acknowledgments   256

A Victorian impression of the Battle of Salamis.

THE ANCIENT WORLD

The Phoenicians and Trade in the Ancient World

The Mediterranean was the cradle of Western civilization, and it was maritime trade which spread that civilization throughout the 'known world.' Nobody knows exactly when adventurous traders started to sail to other settlements to barter produce, but we can be certain that as early as 1500 BC the Egyptians had evolved a workable ship with a long central keel. We can also infer from archeological evidence that developments in Crete, Greece and Phoenicia must have taken place at a similar pace, if not in parallel.

Circumstantial evidence points to the development of Egyptian seaborne trade under the protection of Cretan warships. According to Thucydides the Minoan kings of Crete were the first to build a fighting navy, and evidence points to the use of their fighting ships to clear the seas of pirates, so that trade could flourish.

It was the Phoenicians, however, who did most to promote sea trade. From Tyre and Sidon their ships ranged throughout the Mediterranean and even beyond in search of trade. In the Bronze Age Phoenician metalworkers created a demand for tin and copper,

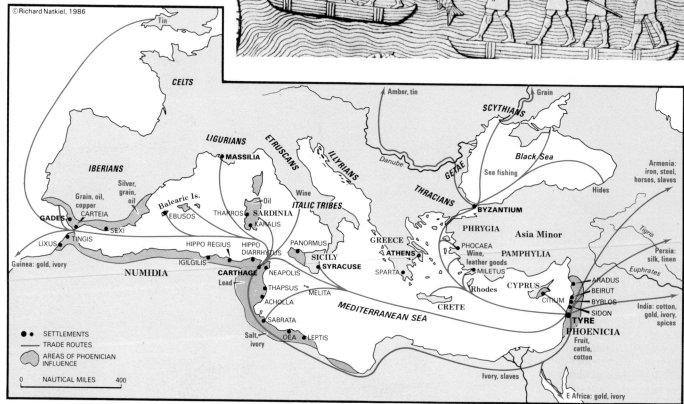

© Richard Natkiel, 1986

CELTS

Tin

LIGURIANS

ETRUSCANS

ILLYRIANS

SCYTHIANS

Amber, tin

Grain

Danube

Black Sea

GETAE

Sea fishing

THRACIANS

Armenia: iron, steel, horses, slaves

Hides

IBERIANS

MASSILIA

Silver, grain, oil

Grain, oil, copper

Balearic Is.

Wine

ITALIC TRIBES

PHRYGIA

Asia Minor

Tigris

GADES

CARTEIA

EBUSOS

THARROS

SARDINIA

Oil

BYZANTIUM

PHOCAEA

Wine, leather goods

PAMPHYLIA

Persia: silk, linen

SEXI

KARALIS

GREECE

MILETUS

Euphrates

LIXUS

TINGIS

HIPPO REGIUS

HIPPO DIARRHYTUS

PANORMUS

ATHENS

ARADUS

Guinea: gold, ivory

IGILGILIS

SICILY

SYRACUSE

SPARTA

Rhodes

CYPRUS

BEIRUT

India: cotton, gold, ivory, spices

NUMIDIA

CARTHAGE

Lead

NEAPOLIS

CITIUM

BYBLOS

THAPSUS

MELITA

CRETE

SIDON

TYRE

ACHOLLA

MEDITERRANEAN SEA

PHOENICIA

SABRATA

Fruit, cattle, cotton

Salt, ivory

OEA

LEPTIS

Ivory, slaves

E Africa: gold, ivory

●● SETTLEMENTS
— TRADE ROUTES
▨ AREAS OF PHOENICIAN INFLUENCE

0   NAUTICAL MILES   400

8

and in exchange commodities from as far afield as Armenia and India were imported.

Two types of ship emerged, the *gaulus* for trading in the Aegean and the Tarshish *hippo*. The latter sailed far to find tin for bronze-making, first to Spain and then to Cornwall and the Scilly Islands. Tarshish ships also reached the Canaries, the Guinea Coast of West Africa, and the Indian Ocean. Ancient writers talk of a canal across the Isthmus of Suez, 3000 years before the present Suez Canal. In about 600 BC one Phoenician expedition claimed to have circumnavigated Africa.

Tyre and Sidon became clearing-houses for trade for three centuries, but Phoenicia never developed into a nation, merely a collection of independent city-states which failed to understand the need to combine against outside enemies. Thus when Nebuchadnezzar King of Babylon attacked them one by one early in the sixth century BC only Tyre was able to hold out. Even though it withstood a 13-year siege, at the end of which only the outer area had fallen, Tyre took many years to regain its position. When it was attacked by Alexander the Great in 332 BC the city was only able to hold out for nine months.

With the end of Tyre came the end of Phoenician supremacy. For a while the major Phoenician settlement on the coast of North Africa, Carthage, kept up the tradition of adventurous trading but the mantle had already fallen on the shoulders of the Greeks.

Above left: Phoenician ships and soldiers fighting in marshy country, from a drawing based on reliefs found at Konyunik and believed to depict episodes in a war between the King of Tyre and the Assyrians.
Right: A Victorian view of Phoenician traders meeting with Britons, by Lord Leighton. A somewhat fanciful depiction perhaps but a clear token of the wide range of the Phoenician seafarers.

Greek Domination of the Mediterranean

The pattern of Greek trade was shaped by colonial coastal settlements which were set up in Italy, Sicily, the South of France, North Africa and the Black Sea. The Black Sea settlements were most important to the prosperity of the Greek trading empire, for they gave access to a wheat-producing area which could feed virtually the whole of Greece. They also provided alluvial gold, and the method of using sheepskins to catch grains of gold being washed down the rivers created the legend of the Golden Fleece.

The legend of Jason and the Argonauts sheds much light on Greek ships and the pattern of trade in the Black Sea. The fact that the *Argo* was a *penteconter*, a relatively narrow-beamed fighting ship of about 80 feet in length, indicates that the distinction between piracy and trade was a fine one in Greek eyes. The Greeks were above all buccaneers, and although many 'round' (that is broad-beamed in relation to their length) cargo-carrying craft were built, the numerous wars between individual Greek city-states and Carthage, Persia and finally Rome led to progressive development of the original galley into a more formidable fighting machine.

The evolution of the galley, with its single bank of oars, into the two-banked bireme and the three-banked trireme has puzzled scholars for centuries. What is quite certain, however, is that references to sixteen banks of oars must be to additional rowers on each oar, not additional decks. Perhaps quadriremes and quinqueremes were built for a while. In a *tesseraconteres* (a reported 40-banked ship) a single oarsman would have to pull a 53 feet long oar, an unlikely combination.

Inevitably there were challengers to Greek sea power. Carthage checked Greek expansion in North Africa in an intermittent series of wars with the Greek colonies in Sicily and southern France and Rome's growing power in Italy prevented any further penetration. The great victory at Salamis in 480 BC freed Greece from the threat of Persian domination, but the greatest enemy was from within. The rivalry among the city-states led to debilitating conflict, and eventually (by 338 BC) Philip of Macedon (father of Alexander the Great) established himself as the supreme overlord. The Greek provinces in southern Italy had been brought under Roman control by around 270 BC and following Rome's hard fought victory over Carthage, Roman influence was soon extended throughout the Eastern Mediterranean also.

The eclipse of the Greek city-states did not mean the end of Greek traders, for their settlements, and the cultural patterns they established, continued to flourish under Roman rule. Rome held Greek culture in such high esteem that it was reluctant to take any steps which would stamp out Greek influence, but what remained was no more than a shadow of the former Greek maritime empire.

Below: **Drawings based on vase paintings of a Greek warship (right) and a merchant vessel (left).**

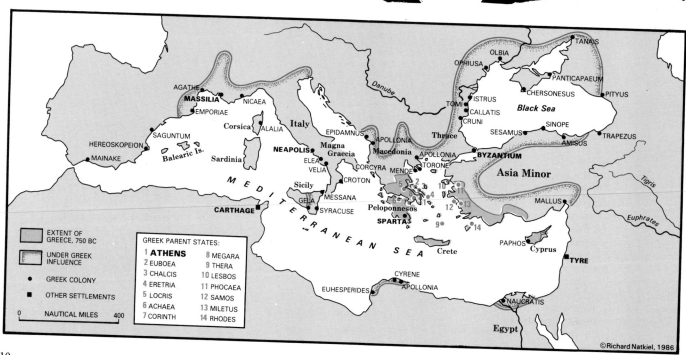

EXTENT OF GREECE, 750 BC

UNDER GREEK INFLUENCE

● GREEK COLONY

■ OTHER SETTLEMENTS

0   NAUTICAL MILES   400

GREEK PARENT STATES:

1 ATHENS	8 MEGARA
2 EUBOEA	9 THERA
3 CHALCIS	10 LESBOS
4 ERETRIA	11 PHOCAEA
5 LOCRIS	12 SAMOS
6 ACHAEA	13 MILETUS
7 CORINTH	14 RHODES

©Richard Natkiel, 1986

The Persian Wars and The Battle of Salamis

The newly created Persian Empire under Cyrus I soon came into conflict with the Greek colonies on the Ionian coast of Asia Minor, but while Cyrus lived the Ionian Greeks were not badly treated by their Persian overlords. Not until the rule of Cambyses (530-521 BC) and Darius I (521-486 BC) did benevolent rule turn to oppression. A revolt was crushed in spite of the support of Athens, and Darius decided to invade Greece to put an end to Athenian meddling.

The first Persian expedition in 492 failed dismally when the Persian fleet was destroyed in a storm off Mount Athos; unsupported from the sea the large Persian army had no choice but to retire across the Hellespont. A second expedition two years later was decisively beaten by the Athenians and their allies on land at the Battle of Marathon.

From these two humiliating reverses Darius learned that he could never defeat the Greeks without a strong fleet to protect his army's flanks, but his plans to launch a third expedition were delayed by internal troubles in his empire. He died in 486 without seeing his plans come to fruition but his successor Xerxes was equally intent on crushing the Greeks.

The third Persian expedition was on a massive scale, with as many as 180,000 men and 750 galleys. To avoid some of the risk of losing the fleet in a storm on the way Xerxes ordered a canal to be dug through the Athos peninsula, a notoriously stormy area. His intention was to capture as many Greek cities as possible to rob Athens of her allies' support. By the spring of 480 BC the entire force was ready to march.

The state of Athens had not been supine since its reprieve at Marathon. The statesman Themistocles had succeeded in persuading the city's rulers to spend their revenues on building a new fleet of 200 triremes. The other 15 maritime city-states also contributed warships, so that the eventual total of the Greeks' combined fleet was about 385 warships. Because of inter-city rivalry it was necessary to put this fleet under the nominal command of the Spartan Eurybiades but effective control remained in the hands of Themistocles.

The master-plan was to engage the Persian fleet as far to the north as possible, in confined waters where it would be hard for them to deploy their full strength effectively. But the might of the Persians seemed irresistible and threatened to frustrate Themistocles' plans. The Persians were, however, held in

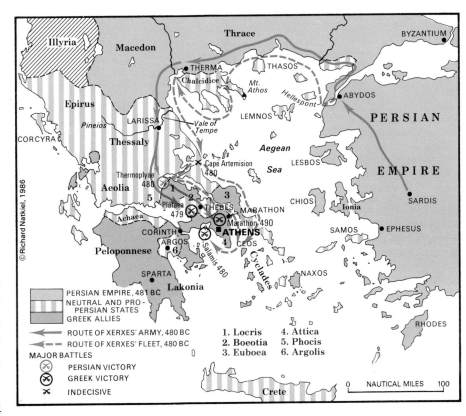

an indecisive sea battle at Cape Artemision, but after the failure to stop the Persians on land at Thermopylae the northern Greek states made their peace with Xerxes, while the southern states withdrew into the Peloponnese, leaving Athens alone.

Themistocles never lost faith in sea power, even at this point of crisis, and persuaded the Athenians to abandon the city and migrate *en masse* to the island of Salamis, which blocks the entrance to the Bay of Eleusis. He planned to lure the Persians into the narrow strait between Salamis and Athens, in order to offset their numerical advantage.

Xerxes played into the Greeks' hands, sending his Egyptian ships to block the western passage between Salamis and the mainland while the Ionian and Phoenician squadrons blockaded the eastern channel to cover his main force advancing up the strait.

The pre-battle movements were complete by sunset on 22 September and next day battle was joined. The Greeks came out in line ahead, curving to the east to form an arc across the strait while a Corinthian decoy force pretended to retire to the north. The right flank was held by Eurybiades with 16

Below: Darius I, King of Persia, twice defeated by the Greeks, from a seventeenth century print.

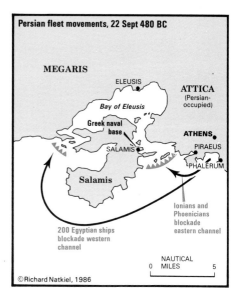

Persian fleet movements, 22 Sept 480 BC

MEGARIS

ELEUSIS

ATTICA
(Persian-occupied)

Bay of Eleusis

Greek naval base

ATHENS

SALAMIS

PIRAEUS

PHALERUM

Salamis

Ionians and Phoenicians blockade eastern channel

200 Egyptian ships blockade western channel

NAUTICAL MILES
0   5

©Richard Natkiel, 1986

The Battle of Salamis, 23 September

Bay of Eleusis

Corinthians 'retreat' to draw Persians into narrow strait

Greek fleet
380 ships
1 Corinthians
2 Athenians
3 Allies
4 Spartans

SALAMIS

PIRAEUS

Cynosura Promontory

Phoenicians

Ionians

Persian fleet
800 ships

Greek fleet inflicts heavy losses on Persians (200 ships) who return to Phalerum.
Greeks lose 40 ships

NAUTICAL MILES
0   2

ships, the center was held by the few remaining allies, and Athenian ships were placed on the left flank. The Persians adopted a clumsy three-line formation which became badly disorganised when it had to reform into columns to pass the island of Psytallia at the entrance to the strait.

Themistocles had calculated his deployment to take advantage of the morning breeze, which whipped up a heavy swell in the narrows. This made the job of maneuvering the larger Persian ships harder, and he now launched his own forces in a series of line abreast ramming attacks. With more room to maneuver the Greeks caused havoc among the already disorganised Persians. The Athenian marines were able to overwhelm the Persian archers and the strongly built Greek ships were able to run alongside and shear off the enemy's oars.

The Persians fought bravely, particularly as they were under the personal eye of Xerxes, seated on his golden throne on the mainland shore, but they could do little to stave off defeat. Fighting aboard the crippled Persian ships continued until sunset, by which time 200 Persian ships had been sunk, the Greeks having lost a fifth as many.

The result was decisive; Xerxes ordered an immediate retreat to prevent his army from being trapped. A token army was left in Greece but this force was destroyed the following year at the Battle of Plataea, a defeat which marked the end of Persian attempts to conquer Greece. Without naval supremacy in the Aegean land operations were not feasible, and Hellenic civilization was saved from the grasp of the Persian Empire. Salamis marked the end of westward expansion of the Persians and ushered in a new era of Greek maritime power in the Mediterranean.

Right: Statue from the temple of Poseidon, god of the sea, at Sounion. The damage to the face of the statue is believed to have occurred during the Persian invasion.
Below: The Greek ships move in to ram at the height of the battle of Salamis.

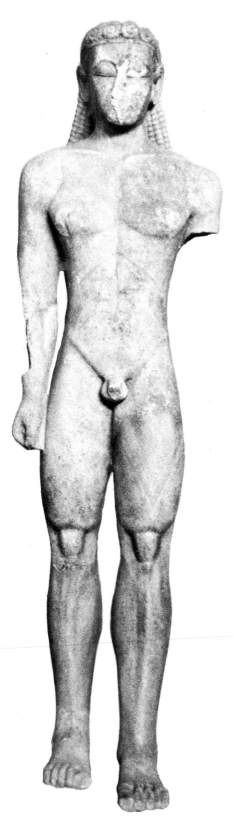

The Peloponnesian Wars

After the defeat of the Persians the leading Greek city-states were clearly Athens and Sparta. Their interests were soon to come into conflict. Between 460 and 446 Athens had won over as allies or subdued many cities in the Peloponnese and central Greece, and although she had been forced to give up these gains under the Thirty Years' Peace of 446, she was regarded as a perpetual threat by the cities in the Peloponnese.

Under the threat of eventual Athenian revenge the city-states of the Peloponnese looked to Sparta for protection. As the most efficient military power on land in Greece Sparta was the natural counterbalancing force to Athenian sea power. By 431 almost all the Peloponnesian cities except Argos and the Boeotian League and others in central Greece had joined the Spartan confederacy.

The first move of the war which then began was made by the Spartans and their allies, who invaded Attica in 431 and laid siege to Athens. Pericles, the Athenian leader, countered by sending a hundred ships to ravage the coast of the Peloponnese, and the invaders were forced to withdraw from Attica when their provisions were exhausted. The following summer they returned but this time they were aided by an outbreak of plague in Athens. Already overcrowded with refugees from the outlying areas, the city

suffered severely but once again the advice of Pericles proved sound, and the invaders withdrew from the plain of Attica for lack of supplies.

Under Phormio the Athenian fleet won a surprising victory at Naupactus in the Gulf of Corinth in 430, defeating 47 Corinthian ships with only 20 by superior seamanship. A second action at nearby Rhium in 429 caught Phormio at a disadvantage, with 77 ships ranged against the same 20 which had fought at Naupactus. At first the Spartans prevailed, capturing nine ships but the Athenians rallied and recaptured all but one of their own ships and captured six more.

The defection of Mytilene from the Athenian cause in the early summer of 428 was a serious blow, for it was the only city among Athens' allies which still possessed a large fleet. The Athenians reacted promptly by investing the rebel city, and when its citizens tried to negotiate terms, executed their envoys to crush the rebellion. The effects of the plague were now being shaken off by the Athenians, and by 425 they were able to take the offensive against the Spartans and their allies.

The first step was to occupy and fortify Pylos. The Spartans were slow to counterattack, and at Sphacteria their attempt to recapture Pylos by land and sea was defeated

Above: **The Athenian military leader and statesman Alcibiades took a leading role in planning the Sicilian expedition of 415.**

by Demosthenes. Athens was now in the ascendant, but in the winter of 424 her army suffered a disastrous defeat at Delium. The Spartans then attacked Thessaly and Thrace, and an Athenian naval expedition under Thucydides failed to relieve Amphipolis. Peace was concluded in 421 but neither side was keen to preserve it.

In the winter of 416-415 a larger expedition was planned by the Athenians against the

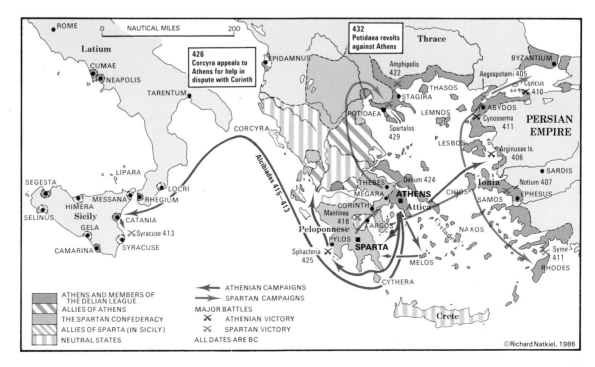

Above: The hard-fought naval battle in the harbor at Syracuse. The Athenian defeat here is regarded as a turning point in the Peloponnesian War.

cities in Sicily allied with Corinth and Sparta. It was ultimately to prove a disaster, when in 413 BC the Athenian commander Nicias and the defenders of Syracuse (which Nicias and his army had captured the previous year) surrendered. The expedition had been undertaken for gain, not strategic advantage, and the loss of an entire army was a deadly blow to Athenian morale. Nor did her allies fail to infer that Athens would no longer be able to coerce them into remaining within the empire. Defections weakened the financial position of Athens, as the flow of tribute and taxes slackened. The growth of the Peloponnesian allies' fleet could not be countered as rapidly as it should, especially as the Spartans were being subsidised by the Persians.

By 411 BC Athens was in desperate straits, and it was clear that her democratic institutions were not suited to the pressures of defeat. Off the harbour of Eretria the Athenians were defeated by a Peloponnesian fleet under Agesandridas, and shortly afterwards the province of Euboea broke into open revolt. The Athenian fleet at Samos had mutinied, and Athens now had neither ships nor crews

to man them. The result was revolution, and the oligarchs were expelled from the city.

The recall of Alcibiades did much to retrieve some gains from the disaster. In the spring of 410 he destroyed the main Peloponnesian fleet off Cyzicus in the Sea of Marmora after luring them out of harbor by pretending to retreat, freeing the grain route from the Black Sea from interference. That fleet would take years to rebuild, and Alcibiades used the time to consolidate the Athenian hold on the cities of Thrace and the Hellespont, and thereby to raise much-needed revenue.

Sadly these victories were thrown away by the misbehavior of the democrats. They abolished the moderate government and substituted 'popular' rule. The citizens of Athens unwisely rejected a Spartan peace offer, which would have retained much of the old empire. Then in 406 they removed Alcibiades from command after a minor defeat.

With Persian subsidies the Peloponnesian fleet now re-emerged as a major force, and it was only defeated with great difficulty at the Battle of Arginusae in 406, said to be the bloodiest battle of the war. Persia now determined to help the Spartans bring the war to a close. The Spartan admiral Lysander was given a large subsidy to build up his strength, but in 405 the bulk of the Athenian fleet was destroyed at Angospotami in the

Hellespont by incompetence or treachery.

The result was inevitable: Athens was surrounded by land and sea and starved into submission in 404. Despite the bitterness of the 27-year-long war Sparta was magnanimous in victory. Instead of being razed to the ground as Sparta's allies, the Corinthians and Thebans wanted, Athens was made a satellite state under an oligarchy. Within a decade Athens had recovered her independence and some of her old strength.

The Punic Wars and the Rise of Rome

As Roman Trade expanded in the Western Mediterranean and Roman power grew in southern Italy it was inevitable that she would come into conflict with Carthage. At first the Carthaginians tried to contain the upstart Latin state by treaties recognising the large Carthaginian trading interests, particularly in Sicily, the first being signed in 508 BC and again in 348 BC. However relations were soured by the presence of Greek colonies in southern Italy, which asked Rome for help in fighting Carthage, and continuing friction eventually led to war in 264 BC.

The first Punic War (the word Punic is derived from Phoenician) lasted 24 years as the Romans and Carthaginians fought for possession of Sicily. The Romans were at first hard put to beat the Carthaginians, being landsmen and good soldiers but not particularly skilled sailors. With typical thoroughness a wrecked Carthaginian quinquereme was copied by the Romans and a fleet of 100 quinqueremes was built, and crews were trained on shore, using dummy rowing benches. When that fleet was wrecked another one was built.

These soldiers turned sailors proved quick learners and inflicted a serious defeat on the Carthaginians at Mylae in 260 BC. Gaius Duilius destroyed the Carthaginian fleet, sinking or capturing more than 40 enemy ships. To commemorate the event a platform for public orators was made in Rome from the bronze rams of captured Carthaginian ships. The Latin word for ram was the word *rostrum* meaning beak, the speakers' platform was known as the rostra and gives us the origin of the modern word for such a platform.

At attempt to carry the war to Carthage failed when an expedition under Attilius Regulus was defeated in 256 BC. To add to Rome's humiliation the fleet was wrecked on its way home, but the Romans grimly rebuilt their fleet and returned to the attack. Being soldiers at heart they devised a method of bringing their military strength to bear against Carthaginian seamanship. A drawbridge or gangplank pivoted from the mast of Roman ships, and known from the long 'pecking' spike designed to attach it to enemy vessels as the *Corvus* or crow, enabled Roman soldiers to board Carthaginian galleys more easily and proved a war-winning weapon.

In 241 BC the Romans won the final and decisive battle at Lilybaeum (otherwise known as the battle of Aegates Insulae) which forced the great Hamilcar Barca to surrender Eryx, the last fortress still in Carthaginian hands. Exhausted by the years of attrition Carthage could only sue for peace, and Rome demanded the virtual surrender of Sicily. Shortly after the peace a mutiny of Carthaginian mercenaries gave the Romans a pretext for renewing hostilities, and as the price of peace they annexed Sardinia and Corsica. This excluded Carthage from all waters west of Italy.

Above: An impression of a Roman galley fitted with the *corvus* and gangplank, from an old French print.

The Second Punic War, which began in 218 BC, was led by Hamilcar's son Hannibal, who longed for revenge on Rome for the humiliating peace signed in 241 BC. His strategy was unorthodox, to catch the Romans off balance but particularly to offset their control of the sea. He transported his army and a 'secret weapon,' war elephants, to Spain, where there was a large and prosperous Carthaginian colony.

The Carthaginians captured Saguntum in 219 and this led to the outbreak of war. Hannibal set off with his army to march to Italy. The march through Southern Gaul took two years, but it accomplished the capture of many important Rome settlements. On 2 August 216 he won a decisive

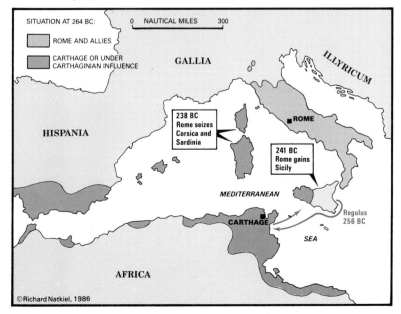

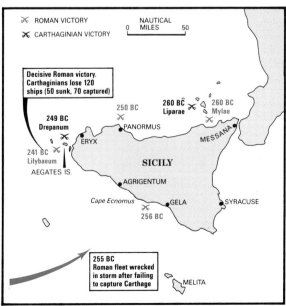

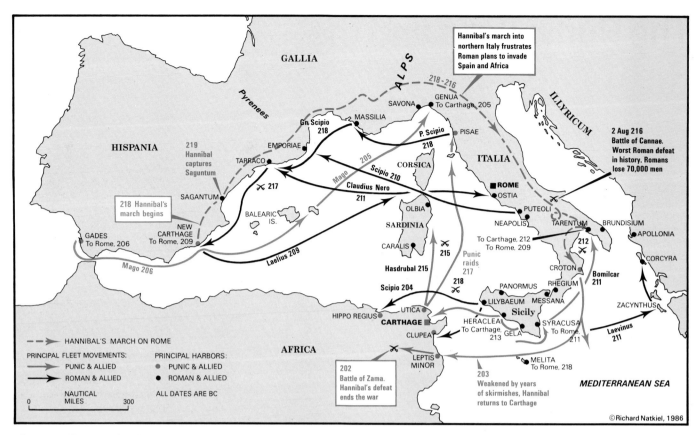

GALLIA

ALPS

ILLYRICUM

Hannibal's march into
northern Italy frustrates
Roman plans to invade
Spain and Africa

Pyrenees

SAVONA
GENUA
To Carthage, 205

218-216

MASSILIA

2 Aug 216
Battle of Cannae.
Worst Roman defeat
in history. Romans
lose 70,000 men

HISPANIA

Gn. Scipio
218

219
Hannibal
captures
Saguntum

EMPORIAE

P. Scipio
218

PISAE

205

Scipio 210

CORSICA

ITALIA

TARRACO

Mago

Claudius Nero
211

ROME
OSTIA

217

SAGANTUM

218 Hannibal's
march begins

BALEARIC
IS.

OLBIA

PUTEOLI

NEAPOLIS

TARENTUM

BRUNDISIUM

NEW
CARTHAGE
To Rome, 209

SARDINIA

APOLLONIA

GADES
To Rome, 206

212

Laelius 209

CARALIS

215

To Carthage, 212
To Rome, 209

CROTON

212

CORCYRA

Mago 206

Hasdrubal 215

218

PANORMUS

RHEGIUM

Bomilcar
211

Scipio 204

LILYBAEUM

MESSANA

ZACYNTHUS

HIPPO REGIUS

UTICA

Sicily

HERACLEA
To Carthage,
213

SYRACUSA
To Rome,
211

CARTHAGE

GELA

Laevinus
211

CLUPEA

HANNIBAL'S MARCH ON ROME

AFRICA

PRINCIPAL FLEET MOVEMENTS:

PRINCIPAL HARBORS:

PUNIC & ALLIED

PUNIC & ALLIED

ROMAN & ALLIED

ROMAN & ALLIED

LEPTIS
MINOR

202
Battle of Zama.
Hannibal's defeat
ends the war

MELITA
To Rome, 218

203
Weakened by years
of skirmishes, Hannibal
returns to Carthage

Punic
raids
217

MEDITERRANEAN SEA

NAUTICAL
MILES

0   300

ALL DATES ARE BC

©Richard Natkiel, 1986

victory at Cannae, slaughtering perhaps as many as 70,000 Roman legionaries, the worst defeat in Roman history. At this point it must have seemed that nothing could stop Hannibal from capturing Rome but the Roman state proved remarkably resilient under stress, and the alliance of Italian cities held firm.

At sea the Carthaginians harassed Roman

trade, and the daring naval commander Mago established a forward base at Minorca (from which Port Mahon takes its name), and succeeded in capturing Genua (Genoa) in 205 BC. But on land the obstinacy of Rome and an adroit use of 'scorched earth' tactics by Quintus Fabius Maximus wore down Hannibal. Only when that army was subdued and expelled could Publius Cornelius Scipio seize the initiative by attacking Carthaginian possessions in Hispania (Spain).

With her Gallic colonies recaptured and the Carthaginians' base in the Iberian peninsula destroyed it was at length possible to take the offensive directly against Carthage,

and in 202 Scipio's forces mustered for the final Battle of Zama. That victory put an end to Carthaginian hopes of dominating the Mediterranean and gave Rome the keys to world-wide power. At the heart of it was Rome's command of the sea. As long as she dominated Mediterranean trade her allies would not desert her, no matter how long Hannibal's army remained at large in Italy. By avoiding disastrous battles with Hannibal after the first defeats, Rome preserved her strength for a counterstroke, and when the time came her naval power enabled her to carry the war to the enemy before he could recover his position.

Below: **The Roman victory over the Carthaginians at Ecnomus in 256, from an eighteenth century print.**

The Battle of Actium

In the power struggle for control of the Roman world which followed the assassination of Julius Caesar in 44 BC, the former allies Octavian and Mark Antony found themselves on opposite sides. Octavian chose as his commander Agrippa, who captured Methone in the Peloponnese and then moved north to Corinth. The strategic aim was to destroy Mark Antony's main force in Epirus, and a logical consequence of this was the need to cut him off from his ally, Queen Cleopatra of Egypt.

Mark Antony had established his camp at Actium, a promontory on the southern side of what is known today as the Gulf of Arta in Greece. By the beginning of September, 31 BC the Romans had mustered a fleet of 400 ships against 230 Egyptian ships. Although outnumbered the Egyptians had larger and heavier vessels which they hoped would be proof against Agrippa's lighter ships.

In the battle which followed the smaller Roman ships proved their worth by outmaneuvering the slower Egyptians. They made little use of ramming tactics but instead they ran alongside, crushing their opponents' oars to immobilize them before boarding. The Egyptian fleet fought bravely, but the squadron under Cleopatra slipped away from the battle to escape to Egypt and when the fleet realised that Mark Antony had deserted them as well the issue was already settled. The remainder of their fleet was surrendered or destroyed.

Actium decided the outcome of the civil war and laid the foundations of the new Roman Empire under Octavian, soon to become known as Augustus, the first Roman emperor. The battle also marked the end of the very large oared fighting ship, for Agrippa's smaller and speedier ships had no difficulty in defeating their powerful opponents. His ships were developed from an lightly-built one- or two-decked Adriatic design known as the 'liburnian', whereas Mark Antony's fleet was made up largely of heavily-timbered multi-banked galleys.

Below: The victor of Actium seen in a later guise as Augustus, the first Roman emperor.

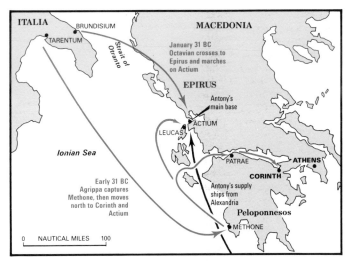

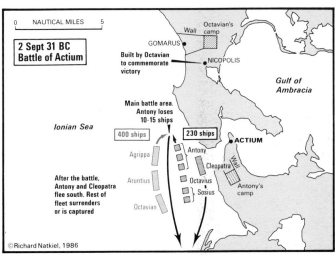

© Richard Natkiel, 1986

The Roman Empire

Octavian and Agrippa's victory at Actium in 31 BC set the seal on Rome's dominion of the Mediterranean. During the next 250 years her galleys kept the *Pax Romana* and allowed her merchant ships to trade to the edges of the known world.

Although Roman rule was harsh it was tempered by a sophisticated code of justice. Pacified provinces were granted citizenship and potentially troublesome neighbors were bought off by alliances and promises of protection. A magnificent network of paved roads linked the Empire and permitted the rapid movement of troops in time of crisis. By sea came the food and luxuries to satisfy the demands of its citizens.

Although there were no revolutionary changes in ship design the lessons of Actium were absorbed. The 'liburnian' was developed, in parallel with heavier galleys. Tactics evolved as land weapons were adapted for use

at sea, and ramming and boarding were supplemented by catapults capable of hurling lead and stone missiles up to 700 yards.

In its original form the 'liburnian' had 25 oars on each side. The larger 'dromon' was up to 150 feet long, with 50 oars in two banks, and was armed with catapults and 'fighting towers' at either end. Merchant ships remained true to the old concept of 'round' (broad-beamed) ships, and all evidence points to a considerable growth in their size during this period. St Paul, for example, was wrecked while travelling in a ship which carried as many as 276 passengers and crew.

The remains of a ship found at Lake Nemi in 1932, if typical of contemporary design, reveal a length of about 240 feet and 47 feet beam. An account by Lucian during the 2nd Century AD talks of a ship about 180 feet long, 45 feet in the beam and a hold 44 feet deep.

Although it has been fashionable to talk of the galley being a fair-weather ship, Roman warships reached Britain and it is known that Agricola led an expedition to Ireland, so the stormy waters of Northwest Europe were familiar to Roman sailors. They were, when

all is said, following in the footsteps of the Phoenicians.

As the center of power within the Empire shifted from Rome to Byzantium the importance of the Western Empire declined. Gradually the legions were withdrawn from the outposts, and, without the protection of the once-powerful Imperial navy, maritime trade succumbed to the depredations of Saxons and Vikings. Conversely maritime trade in the east flourished and the Byzantine navy became a formidable force.

EXTENT OF ROMAN EMPIRE AT 200 AD

PRINCIPAL SEA ROUTES

Timber   PRODUCE AND MATERIALS SUPPLIED TO ROME

0   NAUTICAL MILES   400

Intercontinental Trade in the Ancient World

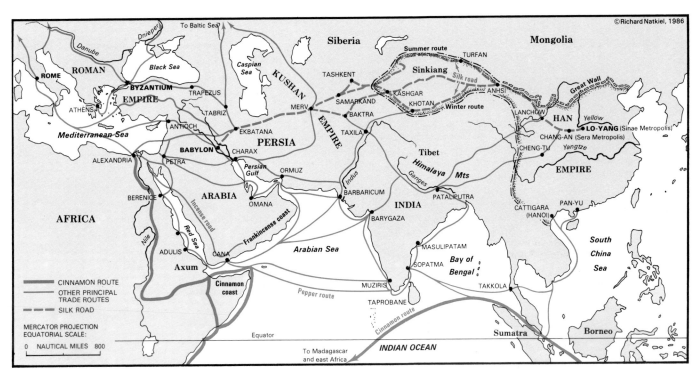

Although Western Asia remained largely unknown to the peoples of the Near East until the 6th century BC, a few economic and cultural contacts existed. After the emergence of Achaemenid Persia the links grew stronger, and by the second century AD there was a lively trade between east and west.

Although the Roman Empire and Han China had no formal links, each nation was aware of the other's existence. Silks and spices were transported by caravan and ship from the east, while gold and silver went from the west by land and sea. Two important 'middlemen', the Kushan Empire and the Parthians in Persia thrived on the tolls, and in return protected trade caravans and travellers.

As many as 120 Greek merchant ships each year maintained a lucrative trade between the Red Sea and India, while Arab ships traded along the northwest coast of India, the Persian Gulf, the shores of Arabia and the coast of modern Ethiopia and Somalia.

The Romans exported manufactures, principally glass, copper, tin, lead, red coral, textiles, pottery and coinage, and in return the East offered incense from Arabia, silks from China, and precious stones, muslin and spices from India. Spices also came from the East Indies and East Africa.

By the beginning of the third century AD the overland trade-routes were under pressure from 'barbarians' to the north, and although the land-traffic did not disappear suddenly there was a perceptible shift to sea trade. Ships carrying as much as 500 tons of cargo could use the monsoon winds to cross the Arabian Sea to India, and when the winds reversed direction in winter they could return laden with goods. The sea-route was much more economical and so the price of silks and spices to the Romans became comparatively low.

The sea-route was of course subject to interference, particularly when disputes among the Arabs disrupted shipping along the Arabian coast, but east-west trade continued to flourish long after the collapse of the Western Roman Empire. Byzantium and the eastern provinces of the Empire continued to be prosperous until the Arab conquest at the end of the sixth century.

Right: An ancient Chinese magnetic compass known to date from at least as early as 235 AD. The compass is designed so that the finger of the figure always points south. The compass is believed to have become known to mariners in the Mediterranean world around 1270.

19

The Maritime Empire of Byzantium

For 200 years after the collapse of the old Roman Empire in the west the new Eastern Empire with its capital Byzantium (renamed Constantinople in 330 AD) maintained Roman traditions and culture from decay. Thereafter the Eastern Empire evolved into a Greek-speaking civilization with its own unique character.

The change from the old Roman culture to the true Byzantine culture became clear during the reign of the Emperor Heraclius (610-641). His reign saw the crushing victory over the Persians at Nineveh in 628 but in spite of the Emperor's triumph over Rome's most formidable rival, the new empire was under attack from the Arabs and Bulgars. Constantinople was besieged twice by the Arabs, in 647-8 and in 717-8, and by the eighth century the Bulgars had penetrated to within 60 miles of the city.

The Arabs took over the old Roman dockyard at Alexandria, enabling them to build an Egyptian fleet to work with the existing fleet of Syria. In 655 Moaviah the governor of Syria decided on a maritime attack on Constantinople, and his combined squadrons inflicted a sharp defeat on the Emperor Con-

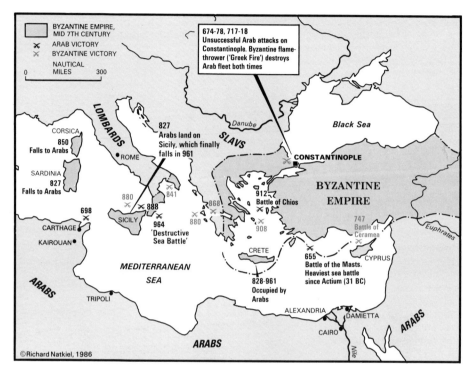

BYZANTINE EMPIRE, MID 7TH CENTURY

✗ ARAB VICTORY

✗ BYZANTINE VICTORY

NAUTICAL MILES 0 — 300

674-78, 717-18
Unsuccessful Arab attacks on Constantinople. Byzantine flame-thrower ('Greek Fire') destroys Arab fleet both times

LOMBARDS

CORSICA
850 Falls to Arabs
● ROME

SARDINIA
827 Falls to Arabs

827 Arabs land on Sicily, which finally falls in 961

698

CARTHAGE ●

KAIROUAN ●

880
888
841
SICILY
964 'Destructive Sea Battle'

MEDITERRANEAN SEA

TRIPOLI

Danube

SLAVS

Black Sea

CONSTANTINOPLE ■

BYZANTINE EMPIRE

868
880
912 Battle of Chios
908

CRETE

828-961 Occupied by Arabs

747 Battle of Ceramea

CYPRUS

Euphrates

655 Battle of the Masts. Heaviest sea battle since Actium (31 BC)

ALEXANDRIA
DAMIETTA
CAIRO ●
Nile

ARABS

ARABS

ARABS

© Richard Natkiel, 1986

Right: A Victorian artist's view of the unsuccessful Arab attack on Constantinople in 717-8. At right a ship which has fallen victim to Greek fire burns.
Below right: The Emperor Heraclius enters Constantinople in triumph after his victory over the Persians in 628.

stans II off the coast of Lycia in the 'Battle of the Masts.' Only the death of the Caliph Othman saved the Byzantines from the consequences of this defeat, but they used the time wisely to create a much more powerful navy.

Among the reforms was the adoption of an invention of a Syrian, Callinicus. 'Greek Fire' was an incendiary mixture almost certainly based on naphtha, and it could be hurled at enemy ships in earthenware pots or pumped through tubes, like a modern flame-thrower. What made Greek Fire so successful was that it could not be extinguished by water.

The new weapon was decisive when Moaviah, now Caliph, renewed his attack on Constantinople in 673. When eventually the Arabs abandoned the siege in 677 their fleet ran into a gale on leaving the Dardanelles, and the survivors were destroyed by a Byzantine squadron.

In 698 the Byzantines seized Carthage but were only able to hold it through the following winter, before being expelled by an Arab counter-attack. In the next century the Caliph Suleiman launched another attack on Constantinople, but once again the strength of the city's maritime defenses enabled the Emperor Leo to defeat the invaders. Greek Fire was used with deadly effect, and when the Arab fleet finally withdrew in the summer of 718 it was virtually destroyed in two storms.

The victory at Constantinople confirmed the reputation of the Imperial Navy but it did not destroy the Arabs' naval power. In 827 they attacked Sardinia and Sicily, gaining footholds which enabled them to conquer these strategically vital islands. The fall of Crete followed. Despite attempts to keep Greek Fire secret its composition became known to the Bulgars in 812, and by the beginning of the next century the Arabs were using it, so Byzantium had lost its 'secret weapon.'

During the tenth century the Arabs extended their hold on the southern Mediterranean, but the rise of Venetian naval power checked their advance and helped to preserve the Empire's trade. It was all the more ironic therefore that Venetian jealousy of Byzantine wealth and prestige was ultimately to cause the destruction of the Byzantine Empire.

Left: Greek fire is projected from a blow-pipe at an enemy ship, from a medieval Byzantine manuscript.

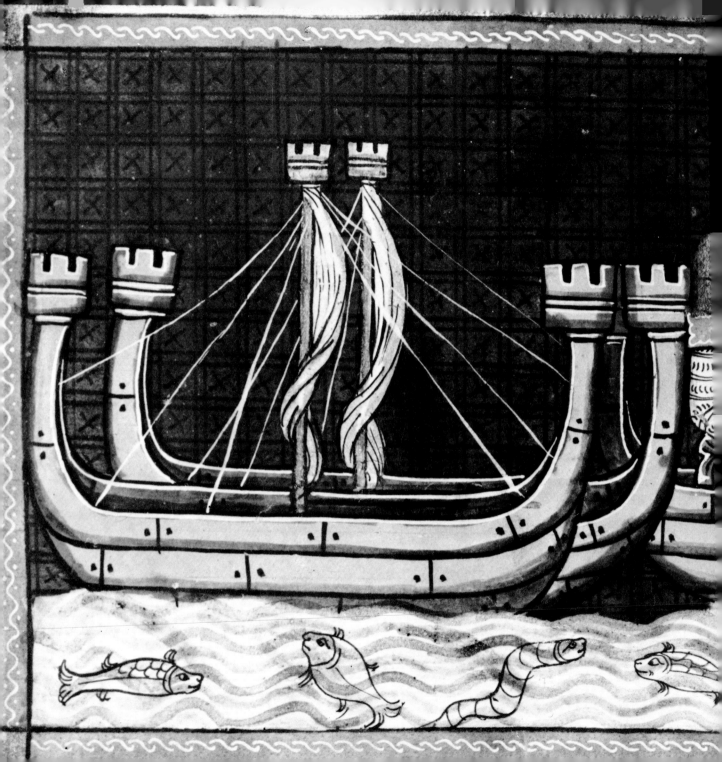

The End of Roman Britain

Roman civilization had been Mediterranean rather than European, but the severing of the link between Rome and Byzantium as the Empire developed and during the subsequent 'barbarian' invasions fractured that Mediterranean framework.

The German peoples had been moving into Western Europe since before the Christian era, but the irruption of the Huns from Asia accelerated the movement. Under this pressure the Romans were forced to draw in the perimeter of their empire, and Britannia was abandoned in 407 AD, after German tribes had crossed the frozen Rhine and ravaged Gaul.

The former Roman province was helpless against waves of Jutes, Angles and Saxons who started to arrive in the middle of the 5th century, and before long the native Britons were driven back. Some were driven to the north of England, others to Wales and Cornwall, from where a considerable number established new settlements in what is still called Brittany.

The Angles established themselves in the north of the country ('Angle-land' or England) and on the east coast (East Anglia), while the Saxons and Jutes established themselves in the southeast and southern part.

Their areas of settlement are still commemorated in the counties of Essex and Sussex (East and South Saxons), although the kingdom of Wessex has long since disappeared.

Although the Saxons destroyed the civilization left by the Romans they were converted to Christianity by missionaries from the Celtic Church of Ireland. By the middle of the 7th century Northumbria, East Anglia and Mercia had been converted, and in the following century Anglo-Saxon missionaries played an important part in re-establishing Christianity in Western Europe.

Although the Romans had appointed a 'Count of the Saxon Shore' with responsibility for putting down piracy, after their departure the sea defenses of Britain fell into decay. This accounted for the rapidity with which the Germanic tribes established themselves, but surprisingly the Saxons themselves never learned that lesson. Lack of any sort of naval opposition made it equally easy for the Vikings to invade. What little evidence has survived suggests that the design of English ships lagged far behind those of the Vikings, and this, along with the fragmented tribal kingdoms left England badly placed to fend off the attacks which were soon to begin.

Previous page: **Damietta in Egypt is besieged by Crusaders during the Fifth Crusade, 1218-19. The illustration is taken from a fourteenth century French manuscript.**
Below left: **A drawing, based on an early manuscript, of typical Saxon ships.**

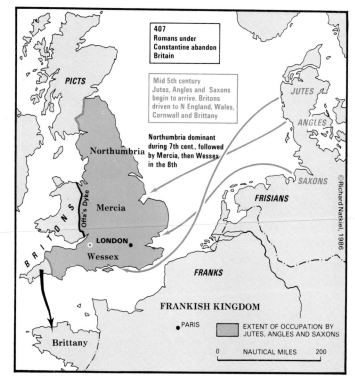

407
Romans under Constantine abandon Britain

Mid 5th century Jutes, Angles and Saxons begin to arrive. Britons driven to N England, Wales, Cornwall and Brittany

Northumbria dominant during 7th cent., followed by Mercia, then Wessex in the 8th

PICTS

JUTES

ANGLES

SAXONS

FRISIANS

Northumbria

Offa's Dyke

Mercia

LONDON

Wessex

B R I T O N S

FRANKS

FRANKISH KINGDOM

PARIS

Brittany

© Richard Natkiel, 1986

EXTENT OF OCCUPATION BY JUTES, ANGLES AND SAXONS

0   NAUTICAL MILES   200

The Viking Explorations

Although the Vikings are perhaps best remembered for the cruelty and rapacity of their attacks on the coasts of northwest Europe, their expeditions in fact ranged much farther afield and seem to have developed from a complex combination of motives.

The earliest Viking raid which can be clearly dated was an attack on the monastery at Lindisfarne in Northumbria in 793, and by that date Norse colonies had already been established in the Shetlands and the Orkneys. Settlements were also established later in the Hebrides off western Scotland, and by 841 Vikings had reached Dublin. From these bases it was even easier to raid towns around the coast of Britain and even the coast of France.

The Danes followed in the footsteps of the Norwegians about a generation later with an attack on Dorestad in 834. By the middle of that century raids by Danes on coastal towns and abbeys in Britain and France were commonplace. So burdensome did these raids become that the English Litany was amended to include the plea, 'From the fury of the Norsemen preserve us, O Lord.' The unfortunate reputation of the Vikings seems to derive in large part from the no doubt somewhat exaggerated accounts of their exploits in the chronicles of their monastic victims. Many seem to have been concerned to settle as farmers or operate as traders rather than simply to pillage. Whatever their motives the Norsemen were soon establishing bases which, whether as part of a deliberate policy of colonization or not, soon transformed sea raiders into settlers and as they put down roots the wild Norsemen became more

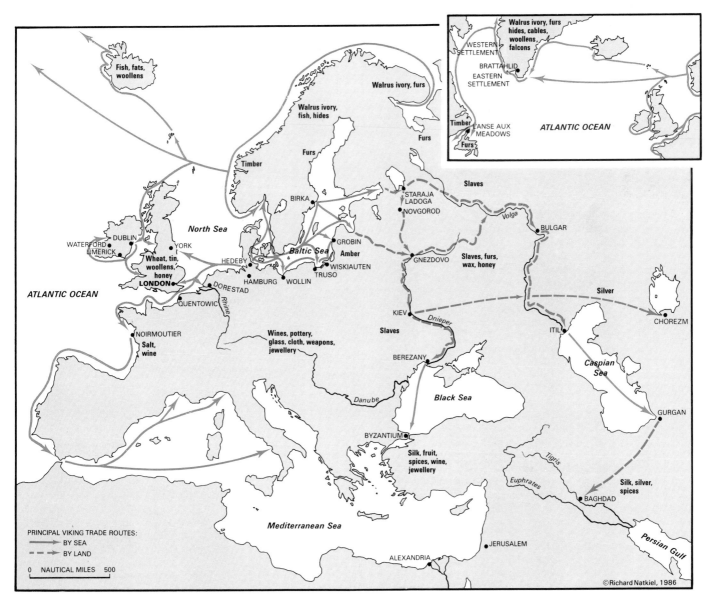

PRINCIPAL VIKING TRADE ROUTES:
BY SEA
BY LAND

0   NAUTICAL MILES   500

©Richard Natkiel, 1986

Above: The figurehead from the bow of a preserved Viking longship.
Right: A Victorian artist's impression of a Viking fleet moving in to land.

amenable to incorporation into local societies. France provides one of the best examples of Vikings settling to become part of the local community. The first Viking settlement in what was to become Normandy (the land of the north men) appears to have been established around 843. Soon the Norse raiders were penetrating inland along the rivers and all across northern France. Paris was besieged by a Norse army in 885-886. Many authorities would describe this as the high point of Viking expansion. The powers of the French king were growing, however, and in 911 the Norse leader Rolf or Rollo made peace with Charles the Simple who in turn created Rollo Duke of Normandy.

From about the seventh century onward traders from Sweden had begun to penetrate into Russia, using the great rivers of the country as their highways. These Varangians as they were known established themselves at centers like Novgorod and Kiev while their trading missions made contact with Byzantium and Persia. A Varangian force even attacked Byzantium in 865. Eventually also the Kievan state was to be the forerunner of what was to become modern Russia.

The Vikings also looked west as well as east and skilful and adventurous sailors reached out into the Atlantic. Their settlement of Iceland began about 870 and within sixty years trade was flourishing to the extent that subsequent emigrants from Scandinavia found no room and were forced to sail farther afield to Greenland. Other adventurers are believed to have gone as far as North America but there is no evidence to suggest that the Markland and Vinland settlements were permanent.

In part this remarkable expansion of Scandinavian influence was caused by a growing demand for the produce of the north. Many of the Scandinavian travellers were primarily merchants and the merchants of Europe were prepared to pay them high prices for such products as furs and walrus tusks and slaves. Other voyages were led by men forced into exile by offenses against local laws and hence compelled to seek fame and fortune abroad. Eric the Red was exiled from Iceland in such a way and led the expedition that founded the colony on Greenland. Eric's father before him had been exiled from Norway for murder while Eric's son Leif Ericsson is believed to have been the first to reach America. Whatever the motives for the great Viking expansion these sailors, soldiers, farmers and traders made their mark all round the European world.

The Vikings in Britain and Ireland

The Viking attack on the monastery at Lindisfarne was one of the first recorded instances of Viking involvement in England and raids on the English, Scottish and Irish coats were soon common. By the middle of the ninth century the Vikings had taken many of the Scottish islands and had made considerable inroads in Ireland, Dublin being captured in 841. By mid-century also the Norsemen had destroyed the former English kingdoms of Northumbria, Mercia and East Anglia and from 870 onward full-scale attacks on the remaining kingdom of Wessex were undertaken. After considerable setbacks King Alfred of Wessex won victories and succeeded in consolidating and extending his kingdom. Among his victories was the capture of London in 885.

One factor in the success of Alfred the Great both before 886 and in his later years was his construction of warships. Patriotic mythology remembers Alfred as the founder of the Royal Navy and although this notion has little connection with reality, there is no doubt that he devoted considerable resources to the construction of a strong fleet. According to some contemporary chroniclers Alfred's ships were 'twice as long' as the Danes' and some had 60 oars. They were also reputed to be swifter and steadier in rough weather. (The Danish drakars or longships are now believed to have carried from 40 to 80 oars and have been manned by crews from 60 to 200 men.)

The limit was reached in 886 of the area under Danish control, the Danelaw, where Danish laws and customs prevailed, and the Anglo-Saxon resistance was stiffening as is shown by a series of English victories culminating in the defeat of Erik Bloodaxe at York in 954. In Ireland too the native population was gaining the upper hand, especially under the leadership of Brian Boru, King of Munster, in the last quarter of the tenth century.

The expanding economy and wealth of England was, however, bound to attract renewed Danish raids. At first they were bought off with financial tribute or Danegeld but as always appeasement was swept aside. In 1013 the country was conquered once more by Cnut (Canute) and ruled as a triple kingdom with Denmark and Norway. The end of Canute's reign in 1042 put an end to his unwieldy kingdom. It also heralded an end to English preoccupation with Northern Europe for Canute's successor, Edward the Confessor, set his country on a course which was to lead to a close alignment with French and Mediterranean culture. It was a turning-point in European history.

In spite of the intermittent fighting and widespread anarchy of the 'Viking Age' maritime trade and exploration continued. Whaling went on in the waters around Greenland and in the Arctic. King Alfred dispatched two Danes, called Wulfstan and Oddr to find the limits of Scandinavia. According to the chronicles they sailed north 'as far as whale hunters ever go, and then north again for three days.' Then the land 'bent east' and the ship sailed along the coast for another four days until it 'bent south.' After five days they came to a great river, up which they dared not sail because it was densely inhabited. Modern scholars agree that this must have been the mouth of the River Dwina on the White Sea.

Not much is known about the type of ship capable of making such a journey but we can deduce that it was big enough to carry the stores for a long voyage, and sturdy enough to withstand the northern gales. The reference to human habitation on the shores of the White Sea suggests a milder climate than today, which also explains the Viking settlements in Iceland and Greenland. Much of what today is bleakly Arctic did not become so until the onset of what has become called a Miniature Ice Age.

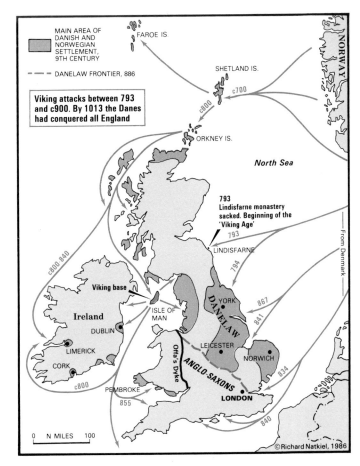

MAIN AREA OF DANISH AND NORWEGIAN SETTLEMENT, 9TH CENTURY

– – – DANELAW FRONTIER, 886

Viking attacks between 793 and c900. By 1013 the Danes had conquered all England

FAROE IS.

NORWAY

SHETLAND IS.
c700
c800

ORKNEY IS.

North Sea

793
Lindisfarne monastery sacked. Beginning of the 'Viking Age'
793
LINDISFARNE
794

Viking base

Ireland

ISLE OF MAN

DUBLIN

LIMERICK

CORK

c800 840

c800

PEMBROKE

855

YORK
DANELAW
867
841
LEICESTER
NORWICH
834
Offa's Dyke
ANGLO-SAXONS
LONDON
840

From Denmark

0   N MILES   100

© Richard Natkiel, 1986

27

The Norman Conquest of England

The death of Edward the Confessor in 1066 brought an end to the tranquillity established for the English kingdom. The venerated Saxon king had succeeded in holding the balance between Danish and Saxon elements in the realm. Edward was also related to the rulers of Normandy and in the early years of his reign had favored Norman advisers. Edward died childless and the problem of his succession was to prove difficult.

The most powerful English lord, Harold Godwinson, claimed he had been designated as successor by Edward before his death and this claim was supported by the customary election by the noble council or *witan*. Duke William of Normandy was also related to the dead king, however, and claimed that he had been promised the throne by Edward and that Harold had sworn to respect this claim. The Bayeux tapestry, a highly important source of information for the period, naturally casts Harold in the role of perjurer and usurper.

The problems for the new King Harold were complicated by the news that King Harald Hardrada of Norway was about to invade England with a force of 300 ships in alliance with Harold's half-brother Tostig. This forced Harold to act vigorously to defend the North.

Had King Harold won his campaign in 1066 it would be remembered as a masterly fight on two fronts, for he retrieved the defeat of Earl Edwin at Fulford on 20 September by a brilliant victory at Stamford Bridge. In the battle both Harald Hardrada and the rebellious Tostig were killed, leaving Harold free to lead his men on what must have been an exhausting forced march back to the south.

As Harold knew, the Duke of Normandy had been preparing to invade England since the spring, and the Norman fleet had finally sailed three days after the Battle of Stamford Bridge. Although he clearly had considerable powers of leadership and a disciplined army Harold had insufficient ships to prevent the

Norman army from crossing the English Channel, and so his brilliant victory in Yorkshire achieved nothing.

The Battle of Hastings on 14 October 1066 was a hard-fought affair but eventually the Norman superiority in mailed knights prevailed against Saxon infantry tactics, and the death of Harold finally decided the issue.

The long-term significance of the Norman Conquest was the severance of English links with northern Europe. In their place there were to be new links with French and Mediterranean culture. A token of this connection was the care Duke William took to receive the Pope's blessing for his claim. With the new alignment came new laws and a radical reconstruction of society. What might have happened if Harold and his Saxons had defeated the Normans is impossible to say, but the Conquest of 1066 was to be the last successful invasion of the British Isles. An adequate navy might not have been able to defeat both the Norwegian and the Norman invasion fleets, but it might at least have prevented one of the landings for long enough to avoid Harold's campaign on two fronts.

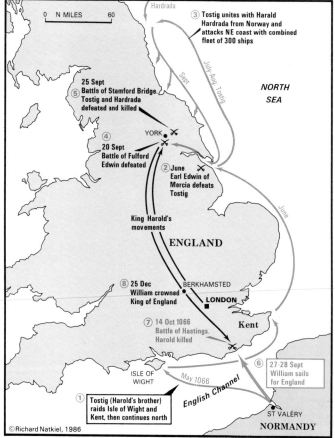

The Normans in Italy

The slow recovery of Europe from the anarchy and dislocation of the Dark Ages was helped by the development of feudal authority. Although rulers were in practice weaker than they might claim to be, they made frequent use of Roman law to uphold their claims. The king claimed his rights as 'liege lord' and in theory permitted all his tenants-in-chief to hold land in his name, in return for protection.

Apart from England, the outstanding example of the new theory of government in action was Sicily, which was also conquered by the Normans. Both countries were acquired by conquest, and so the native aristocracy was not too firmly entrenched to impede the imposition of feudal rule but the Normans were also adept at using and developing the existing framework of laws and royal powers in their new territories.

Norman adventurers had established their first foothold north of Naples in 1027, when they carved out the County of Aversa. The most important Norman leaders were Robert Guiscard and his brothers of the remarkable Hauteville family. The fall of Bari and Palermo in 1071 gave them control of much

of Apulia and Sicily and by 1081 the Normans were challenging the hitherto supreme power of the Byzantine navy. Like the Romans the Normans' prowess on land was little help to them against a well trained navy, but their determination went far to redress the balance. Like the Romans they were also prepared to learn by their mistakes.

The campaign of 1061 was marked by an amphibious crossing of the Straits of Messina, with special horse-transports to carry their vital *destriers* or warhorses across the straits. As they learned to use seapower, doubtless with help from Italians and Greeks their gains increased: Palermo in 1071, Trapani in 1077, Taormina in 1079, Syracuse in 1086, Enna in 1087 and Noto in 1091. The fall of Noto marked the final conquest of the island, less then a century after the first appearance of Norman knights in Italy.

Robert Guiscard had earlier laid siege to Durazzo, and survived a defeat at the hands of the Byzantine Navy to score a decisive victory over the Emperor Alexius Comnenus on land. With a view to overseas conquest Roger I, brother of Robert Guiscard, went on to take Malta in 1090, leaving his son Roger

II to establish a colony on the coast of North Africa between Tunis and Tripoli.

The Norman achievements in Italy were outstanding. Small numbers of knights defeated large numbers of Italians, Greeks and Muslims again and again, by sheer military skill, using the novel shock tactics of charges by armored cavalry armed with the lance. What was equally important was the typically Norman skill in exploiting their military successes by dynastic marriages and sound government.

Below left: **A section of the Bayeux Tapestry showing Harold Godwinson returning to England after supposedly swearing to respect William of Normandy's claim to the English crown. Note the single sail on the ship and the steering oar.**

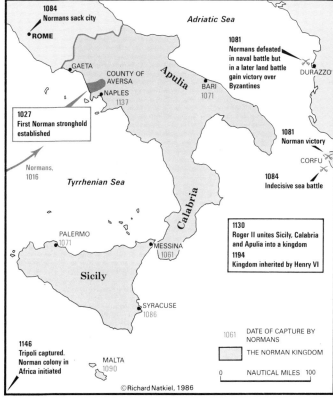

The Crusades

The underlying causes of the Crusades were complex. Religious enthusiasm certainly played a part but other factors also contributed. Famine in Western Europe had made the populace restless, and this unrest went hand in hand with an acute shortage of land. We know, for example, that many of the keenest Crusaders were landless younger sons of the nobility. The Papacy was under threat from warring factions, and to distract the feuding nobles the chance to direct their bellicosity against Islam was understandably appealing.

In such a mixture of secular and religious motives the First Crusade was born. In 1095 at Clermont Pope Urban II preached the need for a Holy War to free the Holy Land from the infidel. Urban had received an appeal for help from the Byzantine Emperor Alexius, and although the schism between the Eastern and Western churches had created a wide rift, there was considerable sympathy for what were still fellow-Christians.

Byzantium had long been the bulwark of Western civilisation against inroads from the east, and while the west struggled to emerge from the Dark Ages the Byzantine Empire preserved much of the best of Greek and Roman civilization. Byzantium's great strength was its professional army and navy, but in 1071 at the Battle of Manzikert the army was totally destroyed by the Seljuk Turks.

The Imperial Army was painstakingly rebuilt but never again would the Empire control the vast revenues or the prime recruiting areas lost after Manzikert. By 1096 when the first Crusaders arrived at Constantinople, the Empire, although still rich and powerful, was a shadow of its former greatness.

The great strength of the Crusaders was their armored cavalry, the Frankish and Norman knights whose mail was virtually impervious to Turkish bows. However their *destriers* or warhorses needed to be transported in considerable numbers, and to achieve this *huissiers* or horse transport were used to move them by sea.

The First Crusade (and the far less successful Second Crusade of 1147-49) showed that

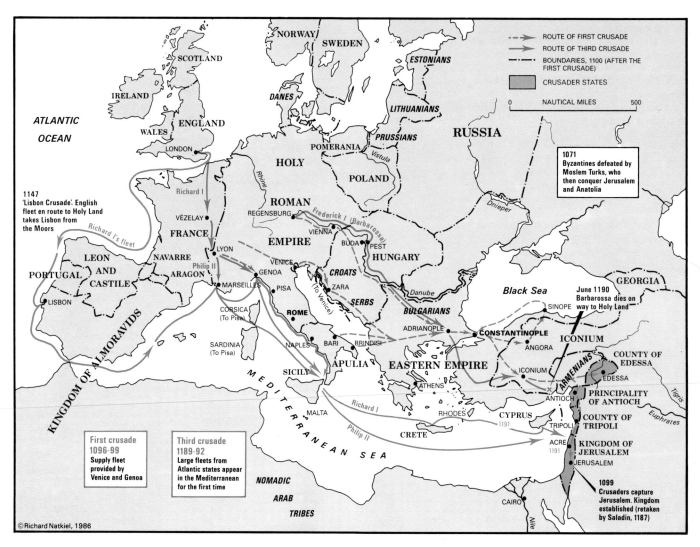

Above: King Richard I, the Lionheart, English leader of the Third Crusade.

the land route to Palestine was all but impossible. A huge host of pilgrims and soldiery trekked through Asia Minor, beating off a Turkish attack at Dorylaeum before reaching Antioch. With the aid of Venetian and Pisan fleets it was possible to keep this army supplied, and after capturing Antioch the Crusaders went on to besiege and capture Jerusalem in 1099.

The Crusaders remained in control of the Holy City until 1187, when a united Islamic army under Saladin destroyed the Christian army at Hattin and captured Jerusalem. In response the Third Crusade was launched

under the joint leadership of the three most important rulers in Europe, Frederick Barbarossa of Germany, Philip Augustus of France and Richard the Lionheart of England. Frederick died on the way to the Holy Land and Philip and Richard effectively frustrated the aims of the campaign by quarrelling but Richard's leadership gained an important land victory at Arsuf. Even more important in the long run was his capture of Cyprus in 1191, which gave the Crusaders a strategic base, without which they could not have supported the operations of their armies in Palestine.

The Fourth Crusade was a hideous fiasco. Backed by Venice, an ill-disciplined Western army landed at Constantinople in 1203 and then proceeded to capture and sack the ancient city in 1204. Quite apart from the treachery and the destruction of irreplaceable treasures, the sack of Constantinople meant the destruction of the inner defenses against the infidel. Nothing else did more to facilitate Turkish incursions into Europe, and the blame for such an act of idiocy by the Crusaders must rest on the shoulders of the cynical Venetians, whose prime concern was to eliminate Byzantium as a trade rival.

The perpetrators of the outrage did not prosper. An attempt to set up a Latin Kingdom of Constantinople failed, and in 1261 with the help of the Genoese, enemies of the Venetians, the Westerners were expelled by the native Greeks.

Right: King Louis IX of France during the Seventh Crusade (1270). Four major crusades were mounted during the thirteenth century but failed to recover lost ground because of the revived Islamic forces.

31

The struggle between Venice and Genoa

The European economy and society had suffered greatly from 'barbarian' incursions by peoples from the east and the Vikings from the north during the long Dark Ages. The repulse of one such group from the east, the Magyars, at the Battle of the Lech in 955 by the German king and later Holy Roman Emperor Otto I is often taken as a convenient date to mark the beginning of the recovery of Europe from the long period of destruction and economic ruin that had gone before. From then until the early fourteenth century the trend was sharply reversed and the European economy made a remarkable recovery.

Venice had clearly emerged as an important trade center during the ninth century, though her trade often suffered from piracy in the Adriatic. By 1000 Pisa and Genoa were also recovering from the Moslem attacks of previous times. The involvement of the Italian cities in the Crusades and the related conflicts with the Byzantine Empire have been discussed earlier, but these were only a small part of the general increase in more peaceful contacts between the Christian and Moslem worlds.

Venice had become established as the leading seapower in the Adriatic but the competition of the maritime republics of Pisa and Genoa was obviously unwelcome. As things turned out it was only Genoa which Venice had to fear for in 1284 Genoa eliminated her weaker rival Pisa at the Battle of Meloria. In any case Pisa's harbor was becoming silted up and her strength was being sapped by internal squabbles which hastened her decline. Both Venice and Genoa were battling for access to the rich markets of the Levant and what remained of the Byzantine Empire.

The first major war between the two maritime republics broke out in 1253. None of the battles proved decisive but the Genoese lost ground and were forced to surrender the Levantine trade to the Venetians. In compensation, however, they gained the Black Sea trade under a special treaty with the Byzantines. In the second war, which began in 1293 the Genoese gained a handsome revenge. Their admiral Lamba Doria beat the Venetian fleet at the Battle of Curzola Island in 1298. The peace treaty signed the following year gave Genoa a virtual monopoly of the Black Sea trade, while leaving Venice to concentrate on the trade with Alexandria.

The rivalry continued on a purely commercial level until 1350, when Genoese attempts to secure their grip on the Levant trade led to another outbreak of hostilities. The Venetians suffered a reverse at the Dardanelles but in 1353 they crushed the Genoese at the Battle of La Loiera, off the coast of Sardinia. However, the Battle of Modon, fought off the southwestern coast of Greece in 1354 gave the Genoese a free hand in the Mediterranean. Under Luciano Doria they attacked the Venetians lying at anchor off the Island of Sapienza, and twelve Genoese galleys worked their way behind the Venetians to attack them from the rear. But in spite of the sweeping victories of their enemies the Venetians struck a good bargain when the peace was signed in 1355.

The fourth and most decisive war broke out in 1378, when both republics laid claim to the island of Tenedos in the Aegean (modern Bozcaada). Venice had received the island, from Byzantium.

The Venetian admiral Vettor Pisani won the first battle in the Tyrrhenian Sea, but the Genoese defeated Pisani the following year at Pola (now Pula in Yugoslavia). In revenge for the death of Luciano Doria the infuriated Genoese butchered many of the 1000 prisoners.

Following up their victory the Genoese under Pietro Doria captured the Island of Chioggia south of Venice. With this strategic foothold they were in a position to strangle Venetian sea trade, and when Venice offered peace terms the Genoese countered by demanding unconditional surrender.

Faced with the threat of extinction Venice reacted vigorously. Vettor Pisani was released from prison, and he immediately blocked the channels leading into the Lagoon, cutting off Chioggia from reinforcement. The Venetians were still too weak to capture Chioggia until their Levant fleet returned. The safe arrival of this fleet forced a Genoese relief expedition to turn back, and left the garrison isolated. As soon as the Venetians had built up their strength they laid siege to the island and eventually its garrison was forced to surrender in June 1380.

Both sides were willing to negotiate now, having been exhausted by the three year war. At the Peace of Turin in 1381 Venice sacrificed some mainland territories but remained strong, whereas Genoa was largely ruined. The defeat at Chioggia marked the start of her decline and by the end of the fourteenth century she had become a vassal of France. Venice was now the leading maritime power in the Mediterranean, a position she did not relinquish until the end of the following century, when confronted by the expansion of the Ottoman Turkish empire.

The Hanseatic League

By the end of the fifteenth century trade in northern Europe was largely under the control of the Hanseatic League or Hansa, an association of German cities which promoted trading agreements and negotiated privileged status in Scandinavia, Russia, the Low Countries, Germany and England.

The main exports of the Hansa were fish, farm produce and timber, but they also traded in minerals. Abroad the cities and traders of the Hansa operated through four great *kontore* or trading posts: the Tyskebrugge in Bergen handled timber and fish, the Peterhof in Novgorod handled furs, the Assemblies in Bruges handled woven cloth and the Steelyard in London handled wool and cloth. Of these the greatest was the Assemblies in Bruges for it linked the northern trading area with the Mediterranean.

Venetian galleys imported spices, silk, wine and fruit across the Mediterranean, and in Flanders these southern products were exchanged for the produce of the North. This rich trade was largely financed by the merchant-financiers of Genoa, who shared the lucrative trade with Venice.

The Hanseatic League was a tightly-knit organisation. Deputies met in Lubeck where they co-ordinated policy and issued trade regulations. The Seal of Lubeck, with its typical Hansa trading ship, the cog, was a universally recognised passport. There were four interlocking 'circles': the Wendish and Pomeranian circle, the Saxony, Thuringia and Brandenburg circle, the Prussia, Livonia and Sweden circle, and the Rhine, Westphalia and Netherlands circle, whose chief cities were respectively Lubeck, Brunswick, Danzig and Cologne.

What distinguished the Hanseatic League from other alliances was that it was purely commercial in purpose. It was dominated neither by craft guilds seeking to promote monopolies, nor by noblemen seeking political power. Only once, when the Treaty of Stralsund (1370) gave the Hansa city-republics control over the Sound and fisheries, and allowed them a voice in the choice of the King of Denmark, did the Hanseatic League seem ready to interfere in Northern European politics. Perhaps fortunately, the moment passed.

The power and influence of the League began to decline during the second half of the fifteenth century. The herring stocks were over-fished, and as a result the English and Scottish fishing fleets took over the market. This shift in the market was by itself insufficient to break the League, but it was simultaneously being overtaken by political changes. The city-state was giving way to the nation-state, and loyalty to the local sovereign was proving more potent than an alliance with a group of mercantile cities. At heart the Hansa towns were trade rivals, not a group of natural allies. Larger entities such as Brandenburg, Burgundy and Sweden were bound to overshadow the cities of the League. By the end of the century the power of the Hanseatic League was over.

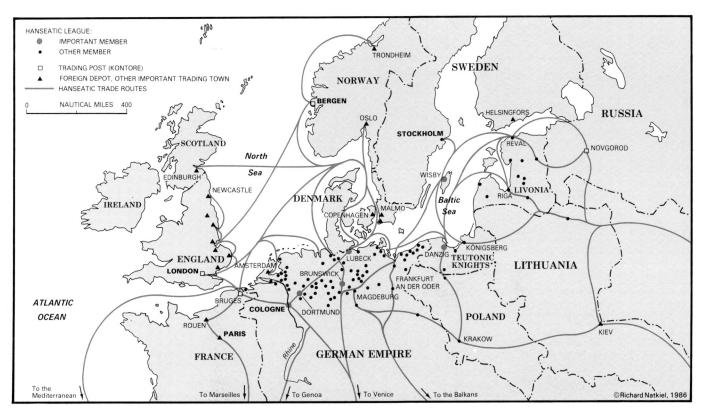

Mediterranean Trade in the late Middle Ages

Trade in the Mediterranean in the fourteenth and fifteenth centuries was dominated by the merchants of the Italian cities and particularly Venice and Genoa. Venice and Genoa waged a long struggle (*see* page 32) for supremacy in the trade but in fact the reasons for their importance and the commodities they traded show many similarities for the two cities.

One key to the success of the great trading cities was that the political leaders in the trading ports were themselves merchants or from merchant families so that the government understood and naturally favored the needs of this class. Clerks and scribes in government service and generals, admirals and diplomats would also have a similar background. Perhaps equally important were the legal and financial mechanisms which existed and were being further developed for the formation and management of corporations and partnerships which could be established for a single trading voyage or a longer period. Share ownership in such companies was similarly flexible and surprisingly widely distributed. Methods of accounting also became increasingly sophisticated; bills of exchange and letters of credit were well-known devices and double-entry bookkeeping was an Italian invention of the fourteenth century. If cash was required the Florentine florin or the Venetian ducat were widely recognised and accepted.

From the beginning of the fourteenth century there were also a number of developments in ship design and equipment which also encouraged trade. Larger ships were built, better able to operate in difficult weather conditions all year round. During the thirteenth century the rudder was invented in northern Europe and eventually came to replace the less effective steerng oar in Mediterranean waters also. Compasses which had long been understood by the Chinese reached the Mediterranean in the twelfth century and so-called portulan charts showing courses from one port to another were introduced probably by Venetians and Genoese around 1300. A token of this technical development were the regular convoys of Venetian and Genoese ships which began to sail to Flanders and England from about 1300 also.

Thus, on the eve of the Spanish and Portuguese disoveries in the New World and the Indian Ocean, the Mediterranean, and Italy in particular, remained the center of wealth and urban development in Europe.

Apart from Paris the only European cities with more than 100,000 inhabitants were to be found in the Mediterranean area: Constantinople, Milan, Naples and Venice.

The Mediterranean held the balance between Northern and Southern Europe and between East and West. Arab caravans brought spices, cottons, silks and even drugs to ports in Egypt and Syria. Other caravans brought African gold and ivory across the Sahara. Venetian and other Italian merchants underwrote the sea trade which was necessary to distribute these commodities throughout the Mediterranean and Europe.

The economic and political setbacks of the fourteenth century including the arrival of plague, the Black Death, meant that by 1400 there was no dominant state in Europe. Both Italy and Germany were fragmented, and the eastern states had also crumbled. Spain and Portugal were in the grip of civil war, and a feud between Armagnacs and Burgundians in France was made even worse when King Henry V of England invaded the country in support of the Burgundians and his own claim to the French throne in 1415.

Above: An illustration of a warship, from a book printed at Verona, Italy, in 1472. Note that the most important weapons shown are handguns and crossbows.

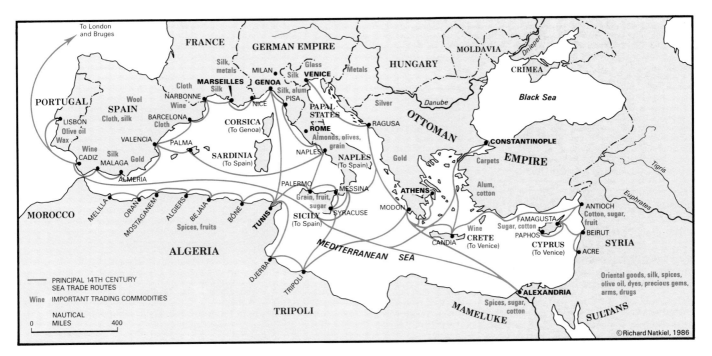

This precarious state of affairs was swept away in the last 50 years of the fifteenth century. The ephemeral empires in Hungary and Poland were destroyed by the Muscovites and Ottoman Turks. In the west Burgundy suffered sudden eclipse after Charles the Bold was killed in battle in 1477, and the English lost all their continental possessions except Calais. In the Iberian Peninsula the warring kingdoms of Aragon and Castile were united in 1479, and 13 years later their combined forces reconquered the last Moorish strongholds. England was indeed to suffer further in the civil strife known as the Wars of the Roses but in 1485 Henry Tudor established a new powerful dynasty.

This new stability implied novel assumptions of royal absolutism, but the inhabitants of most countries were prepared to accept these in return for security and freedom from unending civil war. Stability was particularly welcome to the merchants and traders, who always preferred law and order to chaos.

The new rulers proved just as short of money to prosecute wars, and the mercantile community was, as always, willing to oblige.

But the risks were high, and a wrong choice of client could lose a group of bankers a significant share of the market. Clearly the financing of great states by private banks had outlived its usefulness, and the enormous increase in demand for investment created by the Spanish and Portuguese discoveries was shortly to put that system under even greater strain.

The new united monarchies were organising their administrations in more complex and sophisticated ways, in many cases borrowing the techniques developed by the Italian cities. The result was that while Venice and Genoa and the like continued to be prosperous (Venetian shipping tonnage increased in the sixteenth century), they could no longer compete with the scale of manpower, industry and investment which the new rulers could muster. The focus of maritime affairs was, therefore, shifted from the Mediterranean to the nations of west and northwest Europe.

Left: Venice in 1338, from an early manuscript.
Far left: A Venetian galley probably of the late fifteenth or sixteenth century. The triangular or lateen sails carried and the gun platform mounted over the bows suggest this later date.

Japan against the Mongol Empire

The Great Khan Mongke's death in 1259 sparked off conflict between rival factions in the Mongol Empire, and the direct authority of the Great Khans remained intact only in the Far East. Kublai Khan finally succeeded in eliminating his rivals, and started on a long and bitter struggle against the Chinese Sung Empire. Kublai Khan finally triumphed in this struggle in 1279.

Japan was an independent country, and from the seventh century had been ruled by a centralized monarchy based on Chinese institutions. By the thirteenth century the Hojo Dynasty was in power, and under their rule cultural institutions as well as military skills flourished. Zen Buddhism was in the ascendant, particularly among the new warrior nobility.

Japanese institutions were to be subjected to the most severe of tests. In November 1274 Kublai Khan launched a huge invasion force against the southern island of Kyushu. Using Korean sailors and auxiliary troops to reinforce his 15,000 Mongol soldiers, the Great Khan set sail for Kyushu from Korea. The attackers passed southwest of Ikishima and encountered fierce opposition when they tried to land. Bad weather forced the Mongols to retire at the end of the month, but the Great Khan was determined to achieve victory.

In 1276 the Japanese started a five-year program to fortify Hakata Bay, building stone ramparts to foil another Mongol attempt to land. Kublai Khan took far greater pains for his next attempt, assembling 50,000 Mongol and Korean troops in Korea, with an even larger force of 100,000 troops in southern China. The two invasion forces sailed in June 1281, and the Korean force landed first, on 23 June. Fierce fighting on the shores of Hakata Bay lasted nearly two months, and under the sheer weight of numbers the Japanese began to give ground.

Just when the battle seemed lost a great storm blew up, wrecking the Mongol fleet. The Japanese, convinced that the gods were at last on their side, counter-attacked and inflicted great loss on the invaders. The storm was named *kamikaze* or 'Divine Wind,' and became a major element in Japanese folk-lore. So powerful was its symbolism that the name was revived in 1944 when last-ditch plans were formed to defend the Japanese islands against invasion. The twentieth century *kamikaze* used suicide tactics, mainly by crashing aircraft into ships but also by means of weapons such as midget submarines.

Below: **Kublai Khan, 1216-94, Mongol Emperor of China who ordered the unsuccessful invasions of Japan.**

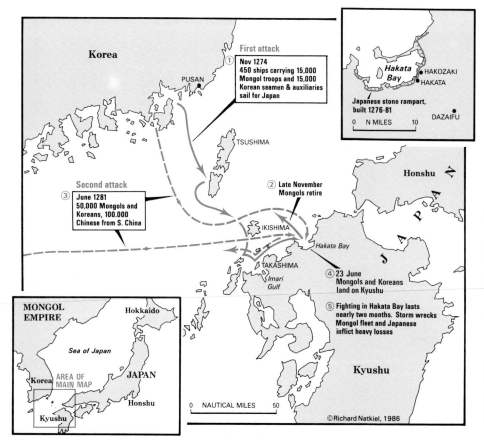

China's Commercial Empire

In the aftermath of the Mongol conquest of China the prosperity of the Sung Empire was largely squandered. Productivity fell and trade declined. Popular unrest generated uprisings against the Mongol or Yuan Emperors and disastrous floods increased distress. Out of these rebellions came a rebel leader, Chu Yuan-Chang, who established the Ming Dynasty in 1368, but the Mongols were not finally defeated for 20 years.

The Ming rulers tried to put the clock back and discouraged foreign trade, but industry gradually developed. As part of their aggressive foreign policy they sponsored a series of large-scale sea expeditions between 1405 and 1433. The admiral Zheng He (also transliterated as Cheng Ho) made seven voyages into the Indian Ocean, returning with exotic goods from Ceylon, East Africa and Java. At their height these expeditions reached a total of 62 ships, manned by 28,000 sailors. Had the Chinese persisted their trade empire could have easily have pre-empted the Portuguese, who were soon to reach the Indian Ocean, but Zheng He's death in 1434 brought the great age of Chinese maritime expansion to an end.

The urge to expand Chinese frontiers was also crippled by disaster in 1449, when an unsuccessful campaign in Mongolia led to the capture of the Emperor. The Ming leaders reverted to a defensive strategy, and during the following century constant pressure from the Mongols and Japanese piracy prevented them from regaining the initiative.

The Japanese constantly raided the coast of China, and after 1550 were able to raid and occupy the coastal districts. They sailed up the Yangtze and even attacked major cities. This disruption continued until 1590, when Japan became more stable.

The external threats were accompanied by a decline in the competence of the Ming rulers. After 1582 the emperors lost interest in court business and refused to see their ministers. Power passed into the hands of eunuchs and private armies of soldiers and police. This resulted in extortionate taxes and wide-scale corruption which officials were powerless to stop. To reduce the vulnerability of coastal shipping to pirate raids it was banned, and all movement of heavy cargoes, mainly tax-payments in grain, were sent via the new Grand Canal.

Although seemingly logical this ban on coastwise shipping was fatal. Instead of building and training a navy capable of putting down piracy, the Chinese merely avoided the problem. The decay of coastal shipping was matched by a corresponding decline of overseas trade, which was already out of favor with the court.

The dissatisfaction broke out into rebellion inevitably and by 1644 the last of the Ming emperors had committed suicide when deposed by the rebel Tzu-Cheng.

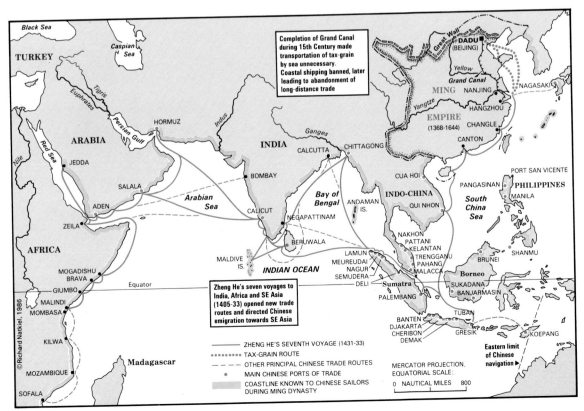

Completion of Grand Canal during 15th Century made transportation of tax-grain by sea unnecessary. Coastal shipping banned, later leading to abandonment of long-distance trade

Zheng He's seven voyages to India, Africa and SE Asia (1405-33) opened new trade routes and directed Chinese emigration towards SE Asia

——— ZHENG HE'S SEVENTH VOYAGE (1431-33)
········ TAX-GRAIN ROUTE
– – – OTHER PRINCIPAL CHINESE TRADE ROUTES
• MAIN CHINESE PORTS OF TRADE
▨ COASTLINE KNOWN TO CHINESE SAILORS DURING MING DYNASTY

MERCATOR PROJECTION, EQUATORIAL SCALE:
0   NAUTICAL MILES   800

Eastern limit of Chinese navigation ▶

©Richard Natkiel, 1986

THE AGE OF EXPLORATION

The Portuguese Explorations and Trade Empire

Portugal was a small and comparatively poor country at the end of the fourteenth century. After the capture of Ceuta in 1415 Portugal had access to gold from West Africa, which gave her an advantage in gold-hungry Europe. With financial aid from Italian banking houses Portugal was able to send expeditions into the Atlantic and south to find the source of African gold. Sugar plantations were established in Madeira in 1419 and these created a demand for slave labor, another incentive to explore West Africa.

As the years passed Portuguese ships passed down the coast of Morocco, past Cape Bojador in 1434 and finally reaching the Gold Coast in the 1460s and the mouth of the Congo in 1482. This was all part of a grand strategy planned by Prince Henry the Navigator (1394-1460), who established the world's first school of navigation at Sagres. Following his lead Bartolomeu Dias sailed around the southern tip of Africa, naming it the Cape of Good Hope, and in 1498 Vasco da Gama found the way to India.

Da Gama was lucky that the enormous Chinese presence in the Indian Ocean virtually vanished by the end of the fifteenth century, and the absence of any opposition left the Portuguese a free hand to establish a mighty empire. They acquired, captured or leased trading posts and fortified settlements from Sofala on the east coast of Africa to Nagasaki in Japan. In 1507 they established a major strategic outpost at Mozambique; in 1511 they established Malacca, in the 'spice islands,' and four years after that they were at Ormuz on the Persian Gulf.

Further east the footholds were more tenuous. Macao, first occupied in 1557, was only maintained through the connivance of local Chinese officials, and the trading post at Nagasaki was only tolerated by the Japanese because the Shogun's edict barred Japanese subjects from trading directly with China and the Portuguese could serve as intermediaries.

The profits from the Far East trade and the gold exported from Sofala helped to finance the purchases of pepper and other eastern spices shipped from Goa back to Lisbon. The Portuguese tried in vain to establish a monopoly of the spice trade, but even after they seized Aden and Zeila on either side of the entrance to the Red Sea they could not prevent Arab, Indian and Persian ships passing through the Red Sea with cargoes bound for Europe. The European end of this Red Sea trade was dominated by Venice and the hope of breaking this monopoly was a major motive for other Italian merchants' investments in the Portuguese explorations. Portuguese ships preyed on this trade in the Indian Ocean and the Red Sea, always trying to channel it into harbors under their control in order to levy tolls and duties. As they had no western rival in these waters it proved an extremely lucrative business.

The unification of Portugal with Spain under one crown in 1580 did not produce any great improvement in the Portuguese overseas empire. In the following century the depredations of the Dutch East India Company and its smaller rival, the English East India Company began to erode the Portuguese share of the eastern trade. The two companies' large and well-armed ships continued to harass Portuguese ships regardless of the state of relations between the respective countries in Europe. The trade in the Red Sea and the Persian Gulf virtually disappeared, while even the main trade with India began to shrink noticeably. Not even the break with the Spanish crown in 1640 could arrest the continuing decline of Portugal's spice empire.

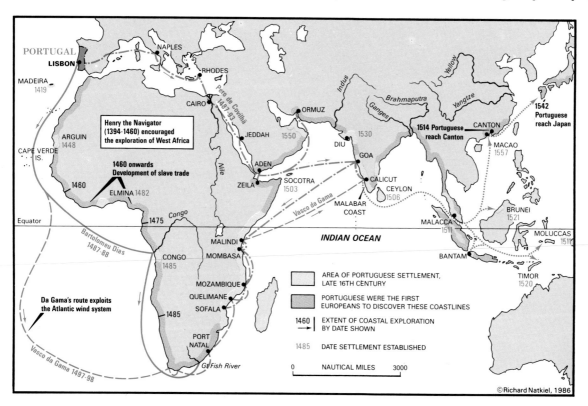

PORTUGAL
LISBON
NAPLES
RHODES
MADEIRA 1419
CAIRO
Pero de Covilha 1487-93
ORMUZ
Indus
Ganges
Brahmaputra
Yellow
Yangtze
1542 Portuguese reach Japan
1514 Portuguese reach Canton
CANTON
MACAO 1557
ARGUIN 1448

Henry the Navigator (1394-1460) encouraged the exploration of West Africa

JEDDAH 1550
DIU 1530
CAPE VERDE IS.
1460 onwards Development of slave trade
ADEN
SOCOTRA 1503
GOA
CALICUT
CEYLON 1506
BRUNEI 1521
1460
ELMINA 1482
ZEILA
Nile
Vasco da Gama
MALABAR COAST
MALACCA 1511
MOLUCCAS 1511
Equator
1475 Congo
INDIAN OCEAN
BANTAM
Bartolomeu Dias 1487-88
MALINDI
MOMBASA
CONGO 1485
TIMOR 1520
MOZAMBIQUE
QUELIMANE
SOFALA
Da Gama's route exploits the Atlantic wind system
1485
PORT NATAL
Gt Fish River
Vasco da Gama 1497-98

AREA OF PORTUGUESE SETTLEMENT, LATE 16TH CENTURY

PORTUGUESE WERE THE FIRST EUROPEANS TO DISCOVER THESE COASTLINES

1460 → EXTENT OF COASTAL EXPLORATION BY DATE SHOWN

1485 DATE SETTLEMENT ESTABLISHED

0 NAUTICAL MILES 3000

©Richard Natkiel, 1986

The Voyages of Columbus

Christopher Columbus (born Cristoforo Colombo and known in Spain as Cristobal Colon) was the son of a Genoese wool-weaver who went to sea as a boy. After a promising career as a professional mariner he moved to Lisbon to promote the idea of an 'Enterprise of the Indies.' Like all educated Europeans Columbus knew that the world was round, and what he proposed was to find a new short route to the Far East, 'the Indies', by sailing westwards. If such a route could be opened up the fabulous riches of the East could be imported at far lower cost, and markets for European produce could be exploited.

For over ten years Columbus tried to get backing for an expedition from Spain or Portugal or England or France. In part antipathy to his ideas was based on scepticism about the distance to be covered: he maintained that Japan was only 2400 miles west of the Canaries, whereas it was actually 10,600 miles. He was also rapacious in his demands for a ten percent commission on all trade, in addition to ennoblement, a viceroyalty and rights of admiralty over any territory discovered. Small wonder that three sovereigns refused to back him, and even King Ferdinand and Queen Isabella of Spain rejected him twice before finally granting his request in 1492.

The voyage started on 3 August 1492 and after many tribulations the three ships, the flagship *Santa Maria* and the *Niña* and *Pinta* made a landfall on 12 October. Columbus named the island San Salvador, and it lies in the group known today as the Bahamas, and because he thought he had reached India he called the native Arawaks Indians.

In a state of puzzlement Columbus proceeded to explore the coast he had discovered. Cuba was so unlike Marco Polo's description of Japan that he concluded that it must be an outlying Chinese promontory, but an 'embassy' failed to find the Emperor. The *Santa Maria* ran aground on a coral reef but the two caravels took the survivors of the expedition back across the Atlantic, arriving off Palos on 15 March 1493.

After a remarkable reception from the Court at Barcelona Columbus was given command of a second expedition to establish a chain of Spanish trading stations in the 'Indies.' A fleet of 17 ships was provided, with some 1200 colonists and ample supplies. The expedition sailed from Cadiz on 25 September 1493 and reached the island known today as Dominica on 3 November. After discovering that the settlement of Navidad established on the first voyage had been wiped out, Columbus established a new settlement at Isabela on the north coast of Haiti. Unfortunately the site chosen was unhealthy and within a week some 300-400 men were ill.

Above: Christopher Columbus as portrayed in a woodcut by Tobias Stimmer. Like several of the other notable explorers of the period Columbus came originally from one of the Italian trading cities, in his case Genoa.

Page 38-39: Henry Hudson, discoverer of Hudson Bay, landing in America.

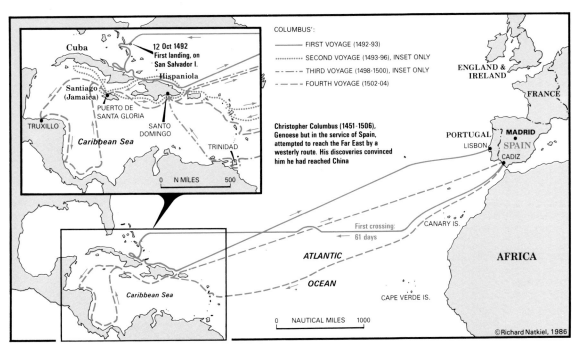

COLUMBUS':
— FIRST VOYAGE (1492-93)
······ SECOND VOYAGE (1493-96), INSET ONLY
—·—· THIRD VOYAGE (1498-1500), INSET ONLY
——— FOURTH VOYAGE (1502-04)

Christopher Columbus (1451-1506), Genoese but in the service of Spain, attempted to reach the Far East by a westerly route. His discoveries convinced him he had reached China

Cuba · 12 Oct 1492 First landing, on San Salvador I. · Hispaniola · Santiago (Jamaica) · PUERTO DE SANTA GLORIA · TRUXILLO · SANTO DOMINGO · *Caribbean Sea* · TRINIDAD · 0 N MILES 500

ENGLAND & IRELAND · FRANCE · PORTUGAL · MADRID · SPAIN · LISBON · CADIZ

First crossing: ← 61 days · CANARY IS.

ATLANTIC OCEAN · AFRICA · CAPE VERDE IS.

Caribbean Sea · 0 NAUTICAL MILES 1000

©Richard Natkiel, 1986

The expedition ended in disaster, mainly caused by the cupidity and cruelty of the Spaniards. The new Governor and his brothers spent most of 1495 subduing a rebellion among the natives, who were being despoiled by gold-hungry settlers. Sadly even Columbus himself could not resist the temptation to enrich himself in the slave trade, and he set a poor example by shipping 500 Indians back to Seville, where the majority soon died. In March 1496 he decided to return to Spain, where he and his brothers faced accusations of arrogance and corruption from the settlers.

In spite of waning enthusiasm for the Indies venture Columbus was given money and ships for a third expedition, which left Spain in May 1498. The first landfall was Trinidad, so called from the three hills, but on 5 August Columbus landed on the coast of what is now Venezuela, marking the first verifiable European landing on the American continent. He still believed that he was in the Far East but conceded that this must be an unidentified land mass off the coast of China.

In his absence Santo Domingo had replaced Isabela as the capital and when the Admiral arrived at the end of August 1498 he found the settlers in revolt. Columbus was forced to make a humiliating peace with the rebel leader Roldan, and when in due course Francisco de Bobadilla was sent out by the Spanish government to restore order he arrested the Columbus brothers rather than the rebels. When they returned to Spain in October 1500 they were released but instead of restoring the Viceroy to his former office the Court appointed a new Governor of the Indies.

By way of compensation for such a humiliation the Court relented and allowed Columbus to fit out a fourth expedition to explore what we know today as the Gulf of Mexico and to find a passage through to the Pacific. The four caravels left Cadiz in May 1502. Although he mapped a remarkable number of discoveries his single trading station was wiped out by Indians and two of his ships succumbed to the teredo and two ran aground in St Ann's Bay, Jamaica. After

a somewhat grudging rescue by the Governor of the Indies Columbus departed for Spain in September 1504.

The teredo or ship-worm is a family of burrowing molluscs particularly prevalent in warmer waters. Teredo worms are capable of eating away sufficient of a wooden ship's timbers that the bottom literally falls out. From the later years of the nineteenth century ships were commonly protected by a covering of copper sheeting underwater. Anti-fouling paints are now generally available.

The last months of Columbus' life were spent in misery. The death of Queen Isabella robbed him of a powerful patron and King Ferdinand showed no gratitude for the gift of vast wealth which the discoveries had bestowed on Spain. When he died in May 1506 he was almost forgotten, and it was to be many years before his ashes were given an honored resting place. His poor record as a colonial administrator should not obscure his skill as a navigator, explorer and seaman. His voyages identified nearly the whole of the Caribbean, a feat unequalled by any other navigator. The discoveries were to transform the European world with the development of trade and empire which soon began.

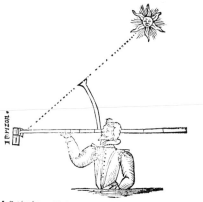

The Seamans Secrets.

How is the use of this Staff?

The use of this staff is altogether contrary to the other, for the center of this staff where the brass plate is fastned, must be turned to that part of the horizon which is from the Sun, and with your back toward the Sun, by the lower edge of the half cross, and through the flit of the plate you must direct your sight only to the Horizon, and then moving the Transuersary as occasion requireth, until the shadow of your upper edge of the Transuersary do fall directly upon the same flit or long hole, and also at the same instant you see the Horizon through the flit, and then the Transuersary sheweth the height desired.

1. Finding by practise the excellency of the cross-staff above all other Instruments, to satisfie the Seamans expectation, & also knowing that those instruments whose degrees are of largest capacity, are instruments of most certainty. I have very carefully labored to search a good and demonstrable mean how a cross-staff might be projected, not only to contain large degrees, but also to auoid the uncertainty of the sight, by diuer-

Spain and Portugal in the New World

The famous Papal award which divided the known world into Portuguese and Spanish spheres of influence was enshrined in a slightly modified form in the Treaty of Tordesillas in 1494. Although its exact demarcation was not easy to determine it effectively excluded Spain from a large part of the eastern part of South America. Despite this the Portuguese did little to exploit Brazil as they did not settle there until the 1530s, and then only to forestall the French.

The administrative capital Bahia was established in 1549 and the first sugar plantations and mills were established shortly afterward using methods perfected in Sao Tome in the Gulf of Guinea. Between the years 1575 and 1600 the sugar industry was expanded to the point where Brazil became the greatest sugar-producer in the western world, and land-hungry settlers began to arrive in large numbers from Portugal and the Azores. The demand for slave-labor for Brazilian plantations enhanced the importance of the older Portuguese trading stations in West Africa, at a time when the gold trade was dwindling as the gold was worked out. Portuguese slave traders began to work further south, as far as Angola, the first 'barracoon' being established at Luanda in 1575.

Slave ships began to ply between Angola and Brazil, where they were exchanged for cheap tobacco grown in Brazil. The surplus slaves were sold for Spanish silver, making the trade extremely lucrative.

Spain's most important new conquest was Peru, which fell to Pizarro between 1531 and 1534. Vasco Nunez de Balboa had been the first European to set eyes on the Pacific, when in 1513 he had struggled across the Isthmus of Panama, although he named the Pacific the Great South Sea. Next came Ferdinand Magellan, who although born Portuguese had quarrelled with the King of Portugal and had taken out Spanish citizenship. As a feat of navigation Magellan's voyage in 1519-1522 has been described as the greatest sea voyage ever made, even though he lost his life in the Moluccas in Indonesia in 1521 and lost four out of five ships. What he had achieved was above all to demonstrate the great extent of the Pacific.

Although Magellan had found a way through to the Pacific around the southernmost tip of South America the opening up of Peru was achieved by Spanish settlers on the Pacific coast of Mexico. The *conquistadores* found the abundant gold, silver and precious stones which they sought. Francisco Pizarro

was appointed in 1529 as viceroy of a country which he had not yet conquered, but his treachery and ruthlessness enabled him to win amazing victories over the hapless Incas. The worst among the many crimes committed by Pizarro in his conquest of Peru was the kidnapping and judicial murder of the Inca ruler Atahualpa in August 1533.

The acquisition of Peru by Spain was a mixed blessing. The fabulous wealth of the Incas undermined the original expansionist energies of the Spaniards and substituted a lust for treasure. Potosi, in Upper Peru was for a century the largest single source of silver in the world. The 'gold and silver fever' inspired many of the settlers to leave the Caribbean and mainland settlements for Peru, depopulating them. Greed led to even greater cruelty against the natives, and corrupted an already unfair system of government.

From the later years of the sixteenth century also, the trans-Pacific trade became a highly important source of revenue. The so-called Manila galleons crossed regularly from the Philippines to Mexico bearing fabulously rich cargoes. Manila itself, which was to be the capital of the Spanish colony in the Philippines, was founded in 1571 and quickly became the center for this trade. Silks, tea and ceramics were obtained from China and paid for with Peruvian silver. Although the trade long continued the growth of the Dutch trading position in the East Indies in the seventeenth century diminished its importance.

As well as the carefully-organised Pacific trade, from 1564 a rigid system of commerce protection was introduced in the Atlantic,

Top: **Ferdinand Magellan who led the first expedition to circumnavigate the world.**
Top, far left: **Columbus lands in America.**
Left: **The great silver mines at Potosi in Peru, heart of the Spanish Empire.**
Second left: **A page from a seventeenth century navigational treatise showing the altitude of the sun being taken with the so-called Davis' quadrant, named after John Davis the English Arctic explorer who invented the device.**

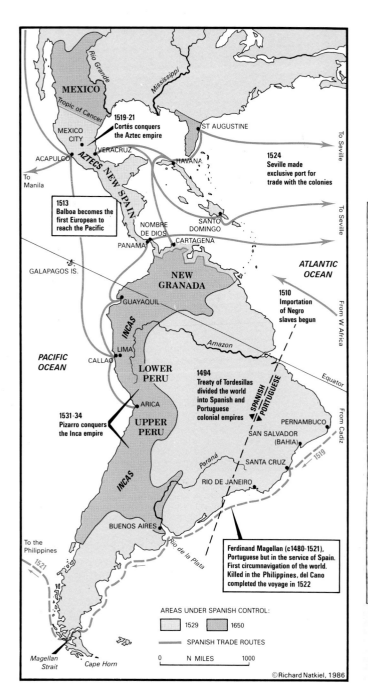

Map labels (left map):

MEXICO

Rio Grande

Mississippi

Tropic of Cancer

1519-21
Cortés conquers the Aztec empire

MEXICO CITY

ST AUGUSTINE

VERACRUZ

ACAPULCO

1524
Seville made exclusive port for trade with the colonies

To Seville

To Manila

AZTECS NEW SPAIN

HAVANA

1513
Balboa becomes the first European to reach the Pacific

To Seville

NOMBRE DE DIOS

SANTO DOMINGO

PANAMA

CARTAGENA

ATLANTIC OCEAN

GALAPAGOS IS.

NEW GRANADA

1510
Importation of Negro slaves begun

From W Africa

GUAYAQUIL

INCAS

Amazon

Equator

PACIFIC OCEAN

LIMA

CALLAO

LOWER PERU

1494
Treaty of Tordesillas divided the world into Spanish and Portuguese colonial empires

SPANISH | PORTUGUESE

From Cadiz

1531-34
Pizarro conquers the Inca empire

ARICA

UPPER PERU

PERNAMBUCO

SAN SALVADOR (BAHIA)

INCAS

Paraná

SANTA CRUZ

1519

RIO DE JANEIRO

BUENOS AIRES

To the Philippines

1521

Rio de la Plata

Ferdinand Magellan (c1480-1521), Portuguese but in the service of Spain. First circumnavigation of the world. Killed in the Philippines, del Cano completed the voyage in 1522

Magellan Strait

Cape Horn

AREAS UNDER SPANISH CONTROL:

1529   1650

SPANISH TRADE ROUTES

0   N MILES   1000

© Richard Natkiel, 1986

AMERICVS VESPVTIVS FLORENTINVS TERRÆ BRESILIANÆ INVENTOR ET SVBACTOR

NIL INTENTATVM

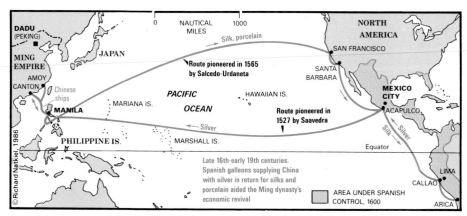

with merchant ships sailing regularly in convoy across the ocean. The annual treasure convoy or *flota* was often a target for foreign raiders and was normally escorted by a large fleet. Strategic harbors such as Cartagena, Vera Cruz, Havana and San Juan del Puerto Rico were soon fortified as bases from which to protect this immensely lucrative trade.

Unlike the subsequent British and Dutch efforts with their companies of merchant adventurers, the Spanish trade empire was based on an inflexible and restrictive system

Above right: Amerigo Vespucci from whose name the word America derives. Although Vespucci seems to have been an experienced seaman, his accounts of his voyages and his claim to have been first to reach mainland America do not stand up well to investigation.

of royal monopolies and licenses which in fact tended to restrict the growth of enterprise and manufactures. In the long run the whole Spanish nation came to confuse money with

wealth, with the result that in the following century Spain suffered a prolonged period of industrial, commercial and, despite income from the New World, financial weakness.

Map labels (lower right map):

DADU (PEKING)

MING EMPIRE

JAPAN

AMOY

CANTON

Chinese ships

MANILA

0   NAUTICAL MILES   1000

Silk, porcelain

Route pioneered in 1565 by Salcedo-Urdaneta

PACIFIC OCEAN

MARIANA IS.

HAWAIIAN IS.

Route pioneered in 1527 by Saavedra

Silver

PHILIPPINE IS.

MARSHALL IS.

NORTH AMERICA

SAN FRANCISCO

SANTA BARBARA

MEXICO CITY

ACAPULCO

Silk

Silver

Equator

LIMA

CALLAO

ARICA

Late 16th-early 19th centuries. Spanish galleons supplying China with silver in return for silks and porcelain aided the Ming dynasty's economic revival

AREA UNDER SPANISH CONTROL, 1600

© Richard Natkiel, 1986

English and French Explorations

Although Spain and Portugal were the chief beneficiaries of the discovery of the New World other European states were determined to share in the spoils. The English in particular showed great initiative after a slow start in finding new routes.

As early as 1497 John Cabot had discovered Cape Breton Island while looking for the route to India. Subsequent English efforts were desultory at first, because Tudor merchants remained unconvinced of the value of new varieties of foreign trade, being content to live off the trade in wool and woollen goods with northern Europe. When the Verazzanos' voyage of 1524, made under French auspices, confirmed the existence of the North American continent it became obvious to some English merchants that new markets in gold, Oriental spices and African slaves could be very profitable, but it took a slump in the cloth trade in 1551 to convince the powerful merchants of the full potential.

When Francis Drake began his three-year voyage around the world in 1577 he had the backing of Queen Elizabeth. There were already a host of companies such as the Turkey Company, the Venice Company, the Muscovy Company and the Levant Company in addition to the older Merchant Adventurers, all ready to promote trading expedi-

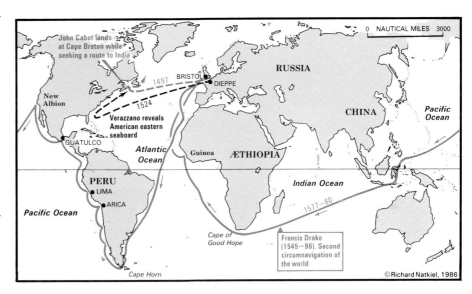

Below: **Drake's *Pelican* in battle with the Spanish ship, *Cacafuego*, captured off Lima in the course of Drake's round-the-world voyage.**

tions to the remote corners of the known world. Cabot had also enjoyed the royal patronage of Henry VII, who demanded 20 percent of any profits, a precedent followed by Elizabeth, who bought shares in Drake's and other speculative ventures and even provided ships.

In addition to profit there was also the strong motivation of religious zeal. Drake's piratical ways were combined with fervent Protestantism and opposition to the Catholic empire of Spain, while Hakluyt, a notable Elizabethan writer on seafaring, talked of the advantage to the Crown of converting pagans to Christianity.

Drake's career as a freebooter-cum-explorer had started in 1566 when he was appointed as lieutenant on a voyage to the West Indies. Thereafter he joined John Hawkins as a captain on a slave-trading voyage to West Africa and the West Indies. His fighting skill was sorely tested on the second voyage, when a Spanish fleet destroyed all but two of the English ships at San Juan de Ulloa; only Drake and Hawkins managed to extricate their ships.

After a brief period of penury he sailed in command of another expedition in 1572, and in this and later freebooting raids he amassed a fortune for himself and his backers. In 1577 a group of investors led by the Queen offered Drake command of a major expedition against Spanish and Portuguese possessions. This resulted in huge profits but also opened a new route to the Pacific around Cape Horn and established a claim to California (New

Albion) in the name of Elizabeth I. Four of his ships turned back at Cape Horn, leaving only the *Pelican* (renamed the *Golden Hind*) to continue.

Despite suffering a serious mutiny among his officers, dealt with by hanging the ringleader, Drake was able to persuade his weary crew to take the *Golden Hind* across the Pacific, around the Cape of Good Hope and back to England. To mark the success, both in terms of profit and national prestige, the Queen knighted him on his own quarterdeck at Deptford in 1580.

Drake's achievements were not unique, and like other Elizabethan 'sea dogs' he was rapacious and brutal, but they expressed very vividly the confidence that the Elizabethans felt about their national destiny. That confidence was to be a vital asset in the major struggle against Spain which started only seven years later.

The Dutch Colonial Empire

The northern Europeans, strengthened by their experience in raiding the Spanish empire in the Caribbean in the sixteenth century, began to establish their own colonies in the Americas. Although individually weaker than Spain, England, France and Holland all had advantages of their own: access to cheaper shipbuilding materials, particularly in the Baltic, and fewer political distractions in Europe.

The people of the seven northern provinces of the Netherlands fought a long and ultimately successful struggle in the so-called Eighty Years War, 1568-1648, to win their independence from Spain. At the start of the war Dutch merchants already had a substantial share of the Baltic trade having overtaken the formerly-dominant Hanseatic towns and in the course of the war greatly extended their participation in this and other European and Mediterranean commerce. Amsterdam, the leading port in the Free Netherlands, also supplanted Antwerp, which remained under Spanish control, as the leading commercial center in northern Europe.

As the seventeenth century progressed the northern Europeans developed better ships, and this was allied to a more commercial attitude and a sophisticated banking and financial system. The mechanism which best illustrates this difference is the chartered joint stock company, developed earlier on a small scale in northern Italy, but never developed in Spain and Portugal. Throughout the century the most formidable trading

force in the East was the Dutch East India Company, which was formally incorporated in 1602 and rapidly became the largest trading corporation in Europe. In 1619 the Company established its eastern headquarters at Batavia, from where the Dutch could dominate Malacca and Goa. After setting up a provisioning station at the Cape of Good Hope in 1652 the Company could send its ships eastwards, running before the wind to the Sunda Straits.

One of the strengths of the Dutch East India Company was its caution and limited ambition. Its directors had no wish to acquire territories, and all bases were acquired for their strategic location, to bring pressure to bear on local rulers and to squeeze other nations out. Even where the Company traded on terms laid down by local potentates, as it did in Japan, the Dutch had no difficulty in holding their own against competition from other European traders.

The counterpart in the Caribbean was the Dutch West India Company, which was established in 1621. It never became as solidly established as its eastern equivalent, but was still a formidable force. In 1630 the Dutch conquered Pernambuco and seized the Portuguese slaving stations in West Africa. This was intolerable to the Portuguese, for it threatened the supply of labor to work the plantations in Brazil, and in the 1640s they succeeded in recovering their slave barracoons (slave shipping depots) in Angola and expelled the Dutch from Brazil.

Frustrated in its attempt to dominate

Brazil the West India Company directed its energies to the West Indies, although many Dutch private merchants continued a lucrative trade in Brazilian sugar.

Dutch, French and English settlements in the West Indies flourished, using African slaves as laborers and selling the sugar crop to Dutch merchants. By the end of the century there was a string of small but expanding colonies among the Caribbean islands and stretching up the coast as far as modern Canada.

The expanding Caribbean trade of the seventeenth century soon attracted the attention of pirates and buccaneers. The buccaneers claimed to carry royal commissions to prey on their kings' enemies but often there was little distinction between their activities and pure piracy. The most famous buccaneer was Henry Morgan who led a successful attack on Panama and Porto Bello in 1671. A number of notable buccaneers also crossed the Isthmus of Panama on land at various times before capturing ships to resume their careers on the Pacific. William Dampier (*see* page 53) is one example. By the early 1700s the day of the buccaneers and pirates was over as the various European navies began to police the trade routes more carefully.

Top right: Sir Henry Morgan, the most famous and successful of the buccaneers who operated in the Caribbean in the later seventeenth century. Morgan eventually died a rich and respectable landowner in Jamaica.
Left: The main trading post of the Dutch East India Company in Bengal in 1665. Both Dutch and local vessels can be seen on the River Hooghly in the background.

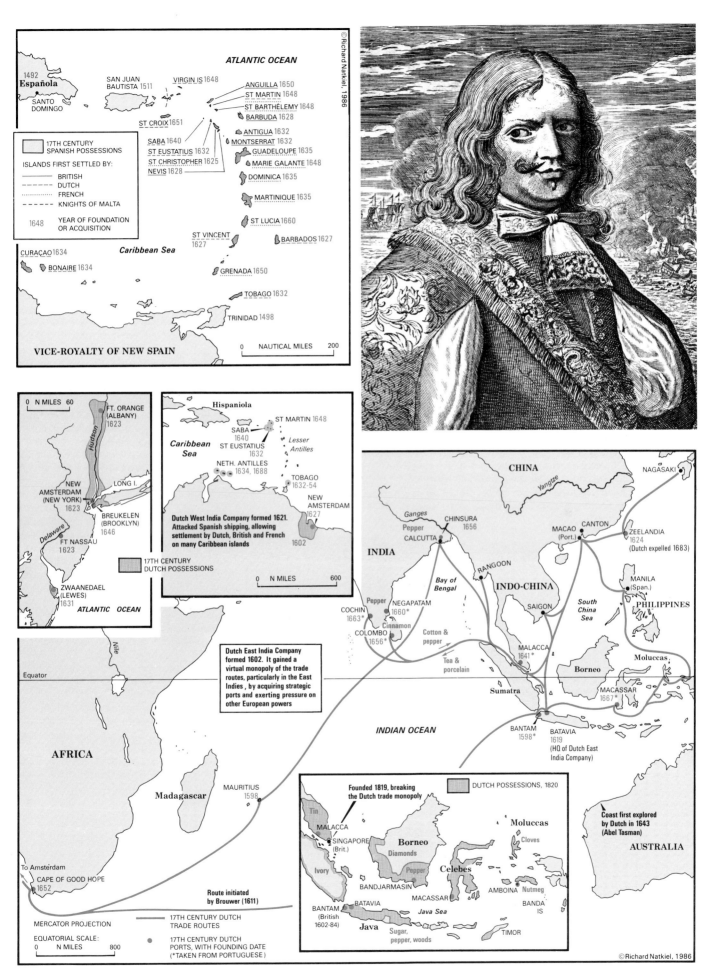

The Battle of Lepanto

The capture of Cyprus by the Turks in 1570-71 was a serious threat to Western control of the Mediterranean, and Pope Pius V promoted the concept of a Holy League between Venice and Spain to stem the tide. A combined Christian fleet was created under the command of Don John of Austria, natural brother of the King of Spain, but local squadrons were under their own admirals. The Turkish forces were commanded by Ali Pasha, with Uluch Ali of Algiers and Chulouk Bey of Alexandria as subordinate commanders. The respective forces were well matched, 208 Christian galleys, six galleasses (powered by both oars and sails) and 62 smaller craft, facing 210 Turkish galleys, 40 galliots and 20 lesser craft. The Christian ships were for the most part, however, more heavily built and carried heavier armament.

The two fleets met in the Gulf of Patras at dawn on 7 October 1571, south of Cape Scropha, and charged headlong at each other in line abreast. It has long been assumed that the ensuing battle was nothing more than a furious and bloody melee, with little or no skill, and that Don John won because his galleys were capable of taking more punishment. Modern research suggests, however, that the Christian commander was far more skilful, using his most powerfully armed galleys as a center force to smash through the Turkish line, while his faster ships formed the wing squadrons where they could dominate the flanks.

Neither side had much room to maneuver, with shoals preventing any major flank movements. This did not prevent the Turkish right wing under Sirocco trying to force its way through, but the Venetians under Barberigo fought hard to prevent their escape, and in the fighting both commanders were killed. When the Spanish right wing under Doria moved to thwart a similar move by Uluch Ali the Turkish commander changed direction rapidly and tried to push through the gap in the Christian line. A potential disaster was averted by the Marquis de Santa Cruz, commanding the reserve. A key element in the Christian tactics was the force of six Venetian galleasses, which were stationed in the van of the center force. With their heavy armament they were able to open a destructive fire on the Turkish ships, sinking several.

The two forces took two hours to close, but by mid-day the range was down to point-blank and a furious close-range battle developed. During the rest of the day the fighting raged. Ali Pasha's flagship was captured and he was killed, and gradually the Christians gained the upper hand. By dusk the Turkish fleet was broken, with 150 ships sunk and an estimated 20-25,000 dead. Only Uluch Ali was able to extricate his force. The price of this magnificent victory was comparatively light, 12 ships and 7000 dead.

Although Lepanto marked a turning point in the defense of the Christian West against the Turkish advance it was not the decisive result sometimes claimed for it. The Turkish fleet could be rebuilt and it was, but the earlier failure in 1565 to take Malta denied the Turks a secure base from which they could dominate the Western Mediterranean. The combination of Lepanto and the survival of Malta freed Spain to co-ordinate the defense of Europe. It also provided a focus for Christian counter-action against the advance of Islam. Had the Christian states not been prepared to fight under one banner it is possible that Spain might have been unable to beat Ali Pasha single-handed. The result of such a strategic failure is incalculable, but it is certain that subsequent European history would have been very different.

It is said that at least one member of each noble house in Italy and Spain was present at Lepanto, but we do know that Sir Richard Grenville and Don Miguel de Cervantes were present, Cervantes losing an arm in the fighting. Lepanto was the last great battle of oared fighting ships, and it is also of note as the first sea battle in which guns played a decisive role.

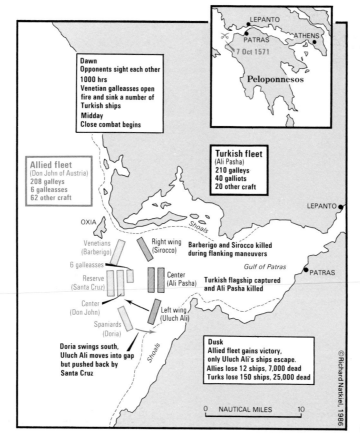

Dawn
Opponents sight each other
1000 hrs
Venetian galleasses open fire and sink a number of Turkish ships
Midday
Close combat begins

LEPANTO
PATRAS
ATHENS
7 Oct 1571
Peloponnesos

Allied fleet
(Don John of Austria)
208 galleys
6 galleasses
62 other craft

Turkish fleet
(Ali Pasha)
210 galleys
40 galliots
20 other craft

OXIA
LEPANTO
Shoals
Venetians (Barberigo)
Right wing (Sirocco)
Barberigo and Sirocco killed during flanking maneuvers
6 galleasses
Gulf of Patras
Reserve (Santa Cruz)
Center (Ali Pasha)
Turkish flagship captured and Ali Pasha killed
PATRAS
Center (Don John)
Left wing (Uluch Ali)
Spaniards (Doria)
Doria swings south, Uluch Ali moves into gap but pushed back by Santa Cruz
Shoals

Dusk
Allied fleet gains victory, only Uluch Ali's ships escape. Allies lose 12 ships, 7,000 dead Turks lose 150 ships, 25,000 dead

© Richard Natkiel, 1986

0 NAUTICAL MILES 10

Top right: Queen Elizabeth I of England as shown in a medal struck in 1602.

The Spanish Armada

By 1588 the commercial rivalry between Protestant England and Catholic Spain had become open war. Spain was the leading maritime power in the Western world and clearly had the money and resources to match any development by small Northern European countries such as the Netherlands and England but in fact Spanish ideas of naval warfare were old-fashioned and outmoded.

Years of reliance on oared ships went with a version of Roman-type tactics, using soldiers to board and capture the enemy. On the other hand English mythology about the Spanish weakness in ship-guns must be discounted; the Spanish ships were better supplied with heavy 'demi-cannon' and 'periers' (the contemporary names for different calibers) than the English. The real difference lay in tactics and the use of gunpower. Whereas the Spaniards always tried to come alongside and board, the English tried to attack downwind, using gunfire to cripple the opponent and cause casualties among her crowded boarding parties. Board-

ing of Spanish ships was expressly forbidden without the Admiral's permission.

To humble the truculent Dutch and English King Philip ordered the Duke pf Medina Sidonia to assemble a *Felicissima Armada* (translated as the 'Invincible' Armada) to destroy the English fleet and then ferry the Duke of Parma's army in the Low Countries across to complete the task by invading England. The First Line comprised 28 ships, the Second Line had 74 more, and there were in addition 27 supply ships in the Fleet Train.

The Armada left Lisbon in May 1588 and the first contact with the English was made on 29 July, south of the Scilly Isles. This brought on the first action off Plymouth two days later. By the time that the English commander, Lord Howard of Effingham and his subordinate Drake could work their ships out of Plymouth it was nightfall, but next morning they engaged the Biscayan squadron flagship under Vice Admiral Juan Martinez de Recalde. The *San Juan de*

Portugal was bombarded for an hour at 'long' range (300 yards) by the *Revenge* (Drake), *Victory* (Hawkins) and *Triumph* (Frobisher). The battered flagship was finally rescued by the ships of her squadron, and the English had to withdraw without having inflicted any serious damage. The Armada's discipline and seamanship remained impeccable, and the English lacked sufficient heavy guns capable of penetrating the heavy timbers of the Spanish galleons. It should be remembered that the rate of fire of warship guns was very low. The system of using the gun's recoil force to run it back inside the ship ready for reloading had not yet been devised and instead muzzle-loading cannon had to be reloaded from outside the main structure of the ship. This was obviously a tricky and time-consuming process and in

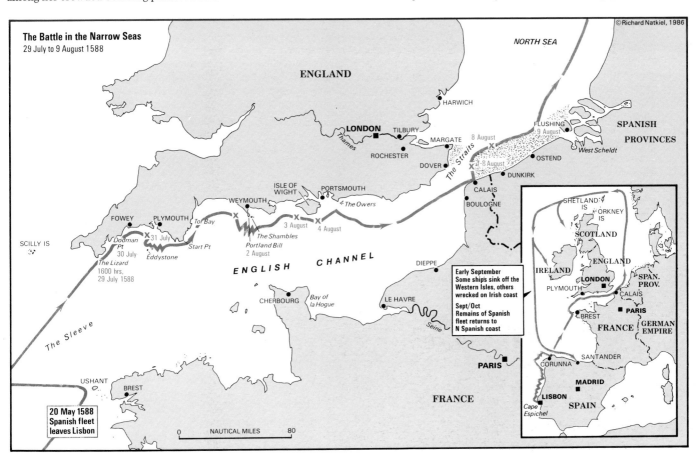

The Battle in the Narrow Seas
29 July to 9 August 1588

© Richard Natkiel, 1986

Early September
Some ships sink off the Western Isles, others wrecked on Irish coast
Sept/Oct
Remains of Spanish fleet returns to N Spanish coast

20 May 1588
Spanish fleet leaves Lisbon

NAUTICAL MILES

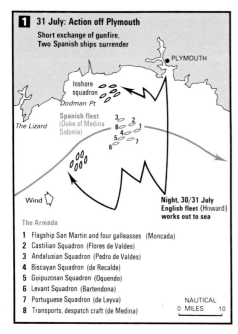

1 31 July: Action off Plymouth

Short exchange of gunfire.
Two Spanish ships surrender

PLYMOUTH

Inshore
squadron
Dodman Pt

Spanish fleet
(Duke of Medina
Sidonia)

The Lizard

3 2
8 1
4
5
6 7

Wind

Night, 30/31 July
English fleet (Howard)
works out to sea

The Armada

1 Flagship San Martin and four galleasses (Moncada)
2 Castilian Squadron (Flores de Valdes)
3 Andalusian Squadron (Pedro de Valdes)
4 Biscayan Squadron (de Recalde)
5 Guipuzcoan Squadron (Oquendo)
6 Levant Squadron (Bartendona)
7 Portuguese Squadron (de Leyva)
8 Transports, despatch craft (de Medina)

NAUTICAL
0 MILES 10

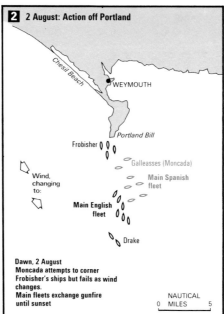

2 2 August: Action off Portland

Chesil Beach

WEYMOUTH

Portland Bill

Frobisher

Galleasses (Moncada)

Main Spanish
fleet

Main English
fleet

Wind,
changing
to:

Drake

Dawn, 2 August
Moncada attempts to corner
Frobisher's ships but fails as wind
changes.
Main fleets exchange gunfire
until sunset

NAUTICAL
0 MILES 5

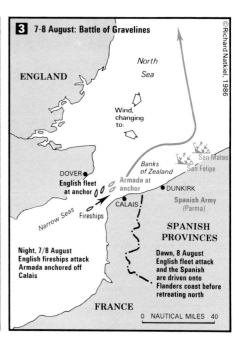

3 7-8 August: Battle of Gravelines

© Richard Natkiel, 1986

*North
Sea*

ENGLAND

Wind,
changing
to:

San Mateo
San Felipe

DOVER
English fleet
at anchor

*Banks
of Zealand*

Armada at
anchor

DUNKIRK

CALAIS

Spanish Army
(Parma)

Narrow Seas

Fireships

SPANISH
PROVINCES

Night, 7/8 August
English fireships attack
Armada anchored off
Calais

Dawn, 8 August
English fleet attack
and the Spanish
are driven onto
Flanders coast before
retreating north

FRANCE

0 NAUTICAL MILES 40

---

fact ships normally had to break an action off temporarily to accomplish reloading.

On 2 August the running fight flared up again as the Armada crept up the Channel in its unusual crescent formation. Once again the English ships stayed clear and used their guns to good effect, while the Spanish captains tried unsuccessfully to grapple and board. But the Duke of Medina Sidonia was achieving his strategic objective, to get through the Channel and unite with the Duke of Parma, and Howard of Effingham could not stop him. By 4 August the Armada was off the Isle of Wight, having lost the *Nuestra Senora del Rosario*, captured after being disabled in a collision, and the *San Salvador* had been badly damaged by an explosion of gunpowder.

When the Armada reached the haven of Calais on the night of 6 August it seemed almost in sight of victory, but the following night the English sent in eight fireships. Fire being the most dreaded weapon against wooden ships the Spanish ships cut their cables and put to sea in confusion. With their cohesion broken it was now possible for the English to pick off individual Spanish ships, and in the ensuing Battle of Gravelines they drove two more ships ashore.

Even after four hours of fierce fighting the decisive result eluded the English, and during the night of 8-9 August a rising gale forced the two fleets apart. As the gale blew his ships northwards the Duke of Medina Sidonia finally gave up any idea of uniting with Parma, and decided to extricate the Armada by making for the northwest coast of Scotland. His crews were being wasted by scurvy and typhus, and with powder and shot nearly exhausted any attempt to get back down the Channel was certain to result in the Armada's destruction.

The return voyage around Scotland turned into a disaster. By 13 August seven First Line ships had been lost, the remainder were badly damaged and a fifth of the men were dead or wounded. Water and food had almost been exhausted, and there were still the hostile shores of Ireland to come.

The first survivors of the Great Enterprise did not get back to the Tagus until the end of September. The full extent of the horror became apparent when only 66 ships limped in, roughly half of the proud fleet which had sailed four months before. The worst losses had been on the west coast of Ireland, where many castaways had been murdered at the behest of English landowners. Storms had achieved what English guns had failed to do.

For England the defeat of the Armada seemed like Divine intervention. Freed from the threat of invasion the country could continue to build up her maritime trade at the expense of Spain. Equally important for the future was the establishment of a 'tradition of victory' which was to be of incalculable value to the Royal Navy during the next four centuries. For Spain it was a bitter rebuff, and although by itself the reverse inflicted no deep harm on Spanish naval strength it foreshadowed the economic decline of the next century.

Left: The fight of the Spanish Armada and the English fleet as shown in a near-contemporary engraving. Two of the Spanish galleasses can be seen in action in the left foreground.

The Search for the North-East and North-West Passages

While the Portuguese and Spanish looked for a southern route around the North and South American continents, others looked for a northern route, the North West Passage. It was also hoped to find a North East Passage to China, north of Scandinavia and Russia.

The search for these two routes became a peculiarly English obsession for nearly 300 years. The original enthusiasm for these ideas was to avoid conflict with the Spaniards and Portuguese, who claimed the rights to all unknown lands in the western hemisphere and were already well established in Africa and South America across the southern route to China.

In 1553 Sir Hugh Willoughby, Richard Chancellor and Stephen Borough rounded the North Cape and reached Archangel. They were foiled by the polar ice but they made contact with Russia, which led to the founding of the Muscovy Company of Merchant Adventurers. In 1574 another Elizabethan, Martin Frobisher reached Baffin Island, but he was prevented from exploring what he took to be a strait when 'gold fever' overtook his men. John Davis explored the west coast of Greenland in 1587 and reached the limit of the icepack at 72 degrees N.

The discovery of Bear Island by the Barents expedition in 1596-97 led to the furthest penetration of the North East Passage; after reaching Spitzbergen the expedition wintered in Novaya Zemlya before returning.

Although the North East Passage was soon recognised as too difficult, the North West Passage continued to attract explorers and traders. In 1610 Henry Hudson sailed through the Strait which bears his name, and

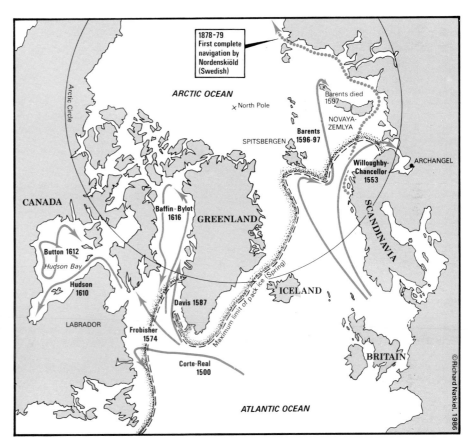

reached the southern extremity of Hudson's Bay, but mistook the vast expanse of water for the Pacific. Two years later the Button expedition explored the west coast of Hudson's Bay and came to the discouraging conclusion that it was landlocked on the western side.

The Bylot-Baffin expedition in 1616 managed to explore the whole coastline of Baffin Bay, but came to the depressing conclusion that no navigable north western channel existed in the area. The western and northern sides of Hudson Bay were further explored by the Dane Jens Munk in 1619-20 and by the Englishman Luke Foxe in 1631-32. Munk had also previously made two unsuccessful attempts on the North East Passage. Foxe's efforts are now remembered in the names of the Foxe Channel and Foxe Basin on the south coast of Baffin Island. English interest in the region was confirmed in 1670 by the establishment of the Hudson's Bay Company which was to play a formative role in the development of northern Canada. For over one hundred years subsequently

there was comparatively little interest in further attempts to find a North West Passage in the light of the difficulties that had become known although the young Nelson did take part in one expedition in 1773. It was not until renewed explorations in the nineteenth century that the passage was made (*see page 105*).

Left: **Willem Barents' ship caught in the ice off Novaya Zemlya in 1596. This was Barents' third arctic expedition and he died in the course of it after being forced to abandon his ship and take to the boats.**

The Discovery of Australia

The most formidable European traders in the East throughout the seventeenth century were the Dutch. The Dutch East India Company was formally incorporated in 1602, and by 1619 it had established its eastern headquarters at Batavia, giving its fleet a fine base and a lasting strategic advantage.

Although not interested in acquiring territory, the East India Company encouraged its employees to look for new strategic trading posts to extend its monopoly throughout the archipelago. Thus in June 1639 Abel Janszoon Tasman, a skilled navigator, was chosen by Antoonij van Diemen, Governor General of the East Indies, to search for 'islands of gold and silver' to the east of Japan.

The first voyage yielded little but in 1642 van Diemen gave Tasman command of a second expedition. This time he was to explore the 'Great South Land,' later christened Australia. Several Dutch navigators had already discovered parts of the northern and western coasts of the continent, but nobody knew whether the land mass was part of a supposed southern continent, *Terra Australis Incognita*.

Tasman's ships the *Heemskerk* and *Zeehaen* made a landfall after sailing east from Mauritius for seven weeks. Not realizing it was an island, he named it Van Diemen's Land (in 1825 it was renamed Tasmania in his honor). Eight days later he sighted high land which he named Staten Landt. According to his calculations this must be the western end of a landmass whose eastern extremity had been

discovered by two earlier East India Company navigators, Shouten and le Maire 27 years earlier. To add to his puzzlement he mistook Cook Strait, separating the North and South Islands of New Zealand, for a deep bay.

Tasman had, however, established one vital truth: by the time his ten-month voyage was over he had circumnavigated Australia and proved it was not part of the mythical southern continent.

The third voyage was designed to discover whether New Guinea was part of the Australian continent or an island. He sailed with three ships in 1644 and sailed along the western coast of New Guinea. He then sheered south into the Gulf of Carpentaria, exploring and charting with considerable accuracy before continuing along the northern coast. He had not achieved what his superiors wanted him to, however, and was not well received on his return to Batavia but to modern eyes his achievements are remarkable.

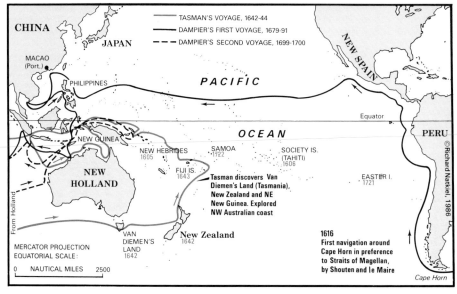

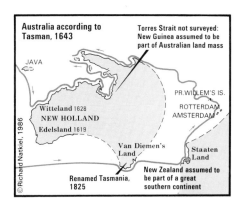

Australia according to Tasman, 1643

JAVA

Torres Strait not surveyed: New Guinea assumed to be part of Australian land mass

PR. WILLEM'S IS.

ROTTERDAM
AMSTERDAM

Witteland 1628
NEW HOLLAND
Edelsland 1619

Van Diemen's Land

Staaten Land

Renamed Tasmania, 1825

New Zealand assumed to be part of a great southern continent

Official displeasure did not last for long, and in 1647 Tasman was put in command of an expedition against the Spanish possessions in the Philippines, and six years later he retired, the greatest of Dutch navigators.

The southern Pacific was now open to navigation from both east and west. The eastern route took longer, and so long as the Dutch held the East Indies, was effectively barred to their competitors. The western route, though shorter, was infinitely more perilous. The Straits of Magellan and the passage around Cape Horn were equally daunting, but attractive because the perils were natural and not man-made. Ultimately the decline of Dutch sea power in Europe weakened the East India Company monopoly in the East Indies, opening the area to other countries' traders and navigators.

The semi-piratical Englishman William Dampier completed a remarkable voyage in 1691, during which he sailed to China, the Spice Islands and New Holland (Australia). This success led the British Admiralty to appoint him as captain of HMS *Roebuck* and to undertake a voyage around Australia.

Dampier had many flaws of character but he made a systematic survey of the west coast of Australia before a lack of fresh water and provisions forced him to head for Timor. From there he attempted a survey of New Guinea, but this was cut short when his harsh treatment of his men sparked off a mutiny.

Dampier's two voyages eliminated much of the mystery about Australia, and his discoveries complemented those of Tasman. Sadly he died in 1711 without reaping the full rewards of a third voyage, which included the rescue of Alexander Selkirk from Juan Fernandez Island, the inspiration for Daniel Defoe's *Robinson Crusoe*.

Above: William Dampier, 1652-1715.
Left: An early European expedition lands on Van Diemen's Land.
Bottom, far left: Abel Tasman, 1603-59.
Below: A page from Tasman's journal.

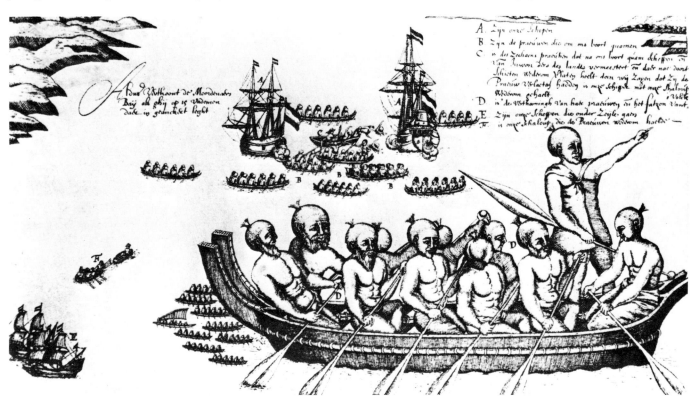

The Slave Trade

In the early years of the sixteenth century the native Indian populations of the new Spanish and Portuguese colonies in the Caribbean and Central and South America were greatly reduced by war and especially by diseases brought by the Europeans and to which they had no immunity. Today the international slave trade is rightly reviled but then it seemed a natural extension of legitimate trade to restock the depleted Indian labor force with African slaves who could also be converted to the Christian faith. The first license or *asiento* to supply slaves to the Spanish territories was granted in 1537 by Charles V. The Portuguese trading stations already established in West Africa quickly joined the trade, buying slaves from African or Arab middlemen, and the demand from Brazil for labor for the sugar plantations resulted in a steady expansion of the business. As the British, Dutch and French began to trade and found settlements in the West Indies they took to slave-worked sugar plantations with equal success. The growing commercial power of these northern Europeans during the seventeenth century was backed by the acquisition of colonies and trading posts throughout the Americas and in Africa and also by a great expansion in their share of the slave trade, although they were in strict legality excluded from trade with the Portuguese and Spanish possessions.

The rationale for slave-labor was the climate, which made hard physical labor exhausting; blacks were regarded as hardier and more resistant to tropical diseases. Initially West Africa was the main source of slaves but as European traders began to operate in the Indian Ocean they made contact with Arab slave traders on the east coast.

The bald statistics of slaves exported from Africa conceal the true horror of the trade. Fast sailing ships were crammed with hundreds of bewildered and terrified men, women and children. Nothing can excuse the brutality and callousness of the slavers, and black states such as Ashanti and Dahomey acquired vast wealth and power through their role as middlemen.

By the middle of the eighteenth century the trade was dominated by the English, who had been allowed to trade with the Spanish lands by the Treaty of Utrecht of 1713. The English share of the trade was probably slightly more than half with the Dutch, French, Portuguese and British North Americans taking most of the remainder. Perhaps as many as 100,000 slaves a year crossed the Atlantic around 1770, being bought at that time for the equivalent of £20 in West Africa and selling in Jamaica, the largest market, for £40. Although the high value of slaves ensured that some minimum effort was made to keep them alive during the notorious 'Middle Passage' it also ensured that the greatest possible number of slaves was packed into each ship. The average death rate on passage is thought to have been one in eight or more and roughly one-third of slaves died within three years of reaching the West Indies, ensuring a continuing high demand.

During the eighteenth century libertarian opinion in Europe, particularly in Britain began to question the morality of slavery. After a long campaign Great Britain passed legislation banning the trade in slaves, in 1807 although slave-owning was not finally abolished until 1833, in deference to politically influential sugar planters in the West Indies. After the Napoleonic Wars the British as the premier maritime power were able to pursue a vigorous international campaign to stamp out slavery, using their trade connections to persuade, cajole or bully other countries into banning it.

The development of slave-worked cotton plantations in the southern states of the United States of America complicated the fight against slavery. Although most states had banned trading in slaves in the last years of the eighteenth century, South Carolina had repealed its ban in 1793 and smuggling was widely practised elsewhere. The importance of the slave-worked cotton plantations can be measured by the fact that cotton

Above: Title page from the official Royal Navy instructions on the slave trade, 1841.

accounted for two-thirds of US exports on the eve of the Civil War. In the early years of the nineteenth century US shipyards also built many fast ships well-suited to the slave trade for American and other owners. The US Government, although coming more and more under the influence of Abolitionist thinking, was deeply suspicious of British motives in asking for 'rights of search' on the high seas. This enabled slave-carrying ships to claim US registry, which had to be countered by allocating US Navy warships to the Anti-Slavery Patrol off West Africa. Ironically these humanitarian measures only worsened the plight of the slaves, for as the blockade grew tighter in the 1840s and 1850s

Below: Slaves being fettered. It was not unknown for the slaves to escape and capture a slave ship from the crew.

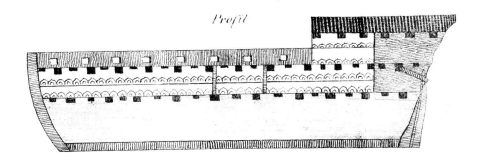

Profil

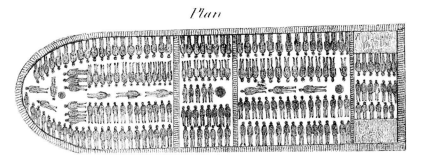

Plan

Left: A late eighteenth century illustration of how slaves would be crammed into a ship for the fearful Middle Passage from Africa to the Americas. Such illustrations, like the engraving reproduced below left, played a part in securing the eventual abolition of the trade.

the ruthlessness of the slave-traders increased. Captains being chased by the Slavery Patrol were known to throw the entire cargo of slaves overboard, weighted with chains, and then escape prosecution for lack of evidence.

France was the last European country to hold out against abolition, but her position was greatly undermined by the defeat of the Confederacy in the American Civil War. The need for slaves on the sugar plantations had declined as well, because European production of sugar beet reduced the reliance on

West Indian sugar. The last major element of the Atlantic trade was with Brazil where in 1825 half the population are reckoned to have been slaves. The trade with Brazil was gradually suppressed during the 1850s and slaves in Brazil were finally emancipated in 1888.

The East African and Persian Gulf trade continued to flourish, and from the late 1860s down to the 1890s the Royal Navy devoted resources to its extermination. There are disturbing signs that the absence of continu-

ous naval patrols in the Red Sea and Arabian Sea is leading to a resurgence of slave trafficking in the 1980s.

The enforced movement of 10 million people from Africa to the Americas over a period of 400 years had profound effects. The extent to which Africa was impoverished by the drain of adult men and women and by the destruction of social order continues to be debated, but the precise effects although undoubtedly great are hard to assess. The effect on the economies of Brazil and the southern United States was profound, and today the descendants of slaves continue to enrich the cultural life of their 'host countries.'

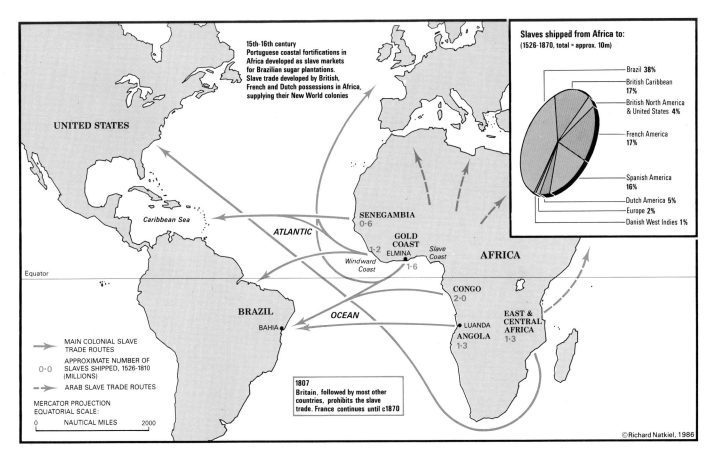

15th-16th century
Portuguese coastal fortifications in Africa developed as slave markets for Brazilian sugar plantations. Slave trade developed by British, French and Dutch possessions in Africa, supplying their New World colonies

UNITED STATES

Caribbean Sea

ATLANTIC

SENEGAMBIA
0·6

GOLD COAST
ELMINA
1·2
Windward Coast
Slave Coast
1·6

AFRICA

Equator

BRAZIL
BAHIA

OCEAN

CONGO
2·0

LUANDA
ANGOLA
1·3

EAST & CENTRAL AFRICA
1·3

→ MAIN COLONIAL SLAVE TRADE ROUTES
0·0 APPROXIMATE NUMBER OF SLAVES SHIPPED, 1526-1810 (MILLIONS)
⇢ ARAB SLAVE TRADE ROUTES

MERCATOR PROJECTION
EQUATORIAL SCALE:
0   NAUTICAL MILES   2000

1807
Britain, followed by most other countries, prohibits the slave trade. France continues until c1870

Slaves shipped from Africa to:
(1526-1870, total = approx. 10m)

Brazil **38%**
British Caribbean **17%**
British North America & United States **4%**
French America **17%**
Spanish America **16%**
Dutch America **5%**
Europe **2%**
Danish West Indies **1%**

© Richard Natkiel, 1986

THE RISE OF
BRITISH SEAPOWER

The Swedish Empire and Baltic Trade

The Baltic covers 16,000 square miles, a large almost land-locked sea which is usually ice-bound in the winter. In early modern times it was vital to the maritime nations of Europe as the Baltic lands provided timber and other supplies essential for shipbuilding, as well as much of Europe's grain.

Denmark controlled the exit to the Baltic and the Sound Tolls levied on shipping gave her enormous wealth, but it was also the cause of bitter rivalry. From 1397 to 1523 Denmark, Norway and Sweden were united under one king in the Union of Kalmar, but early in the sixteenth century Sweden broke away and established her independence.

The new state was surrounded by enemies and economic strangulation remained a constant threat. These tensions led to the Seven Years' War of the North in 1563-70, under the two sons of Gustavas Vasa, Eric XIV and John III. Sweden managed to hold her own, and by 1590 she was the most influential state in the region.

Despite her military prowess Sweden's internal politics were a source of weakness. A major constitutional crisis resulted in the Catholic King Sigismund being deposed in 1599; as he was also King of Poland the two countries became sworn enemies for half a century and the accession of a 17-year old prince seemed bound to perpetuate Sweden's weakness.

Gustavus Adolphus started his reign in 1611 and only two years later suffered a serious setback. At the Peace of Knared Sweden had to pay a heavy price to recover the key fortress of Alvsborg, which guarded the only ice-free outlet to the North Sea. But during the next 19 years until his death Gustavus Adolphus added large tracts of territory, making Sweden a first-class power. In 1643-45 war broke out with Denmark once more, and this time Sweden won Gotland and Osel, and was able to lease Halland for 30 years. Danish attempts at revenge were defeated by Karl Gustav V. Attacking from the south he occupied Jutland and was able to march his troops across the frozen Great Belt to threaten Copenhagen.

Alarmed by her apparently unlimited appetite for expansion, Sweden's enemies at last formed an effective alliance. She was rescued from near disaster in the Scanian War (1676-79) despite naval defeats at Oeland and Kjoge Bay by her ally Louis XIV of France, and during the cautious reign of Charles XI the empire began to shrink. In

1697 Charles XII came to the throne and turned the decline into disaster.

In 1700 the Great Northern War started with a brilliant Swedish victory over the Russians at Narva, when Charles XII defeated an army five times the size of his own. But only four years later Peter the Great recaptured Narva. At the Battle of Poltava in 1709 the Russians annihilated the Swedish army. The war was not brought to an end until 1721, by which time Sweden had lost considerable territory.

The outcome of Sweden's short-lived empire was the start of modern Russia, and Sweden was never again to come near to her ambition to control the Baltic.

Previous page: **Dutch boarding parties in the Medway in June 1667 during the Second Anglo-Dutch War.**

The First Anglo-Dutch War

Although once united in the common fight against Spain in the sixteenth century, the English and Dutch found themselves increasingly in competition as they helped themselves to portions of Spain's sprawling empire. In the years leading up to the English Civil War (1642-51) it is fair to say that only the weakness of successive Stuart governments in Britain prevented war from breaking out. After the Civil War Parliament enacted legislation aimed at excluding the Dutch from domestic trade, and by May 1652 both sides were spoiling for a fight.

The pretext was the appearance of Marten Tromp's squadron in a sheltered anchorage in the English Channel near Dover, on 28 May 1652. English Admiral Blake arrived the next day, demanded a salute from the Dutch and when it was refused, fired a warning shot. This was answered by a broadside from Tromp's flagship the *Brederode*. After five hours of hard fighting the Dutch withdrew, having inflicted severe damage to the *James*, Blake's flagship. Although war had still not been declared Blake was ordered to attack the important Dutch herring fleet and this finally precipitated full hostilities in July.

Blake met Tromp's successor, Witte de With on 8 October off the sandbank known as the Kentish Knock as the Dutch were returning from a cruise in the Channel. This time Blake won convincingly, capturing two Dutch ships, damaging many more and forcing Witte de With to take shelter behind the sandbanks off the Dutch coast. The victory was so convincing that the English Parliament ordered all the major warships to be laid up 'in Ordinary' (reserve) for the winter, but the Dutch, furious at their defeat, kept their entire fleet in commission. As a direct result Blake had only 40 ships against Tromp's 100 when the two fleets next met off Dungeness on 10 December 1652. With Marten Tromp reinstated as commander-in-chief the Dutch had little difficulty in beating the English, and the victory led to the apocryphal story of Tromp having a broom lashed to the masthead of his ship, having 'swept the English from the seas.'

The English Commissioners of the Navy refused to accept Blake's resignation but they instituted several fundamental changes to remedy what they saw as a lack of tactical discipline. Some 1200 soldiers were drafted

Above: **Marten Tromp (1597-1653), one of the most able of the Dutch admirals, already had a substantial reputation from the Dutch-Spanish campaign of 1637 which he added to during the battles of 1652-53.**

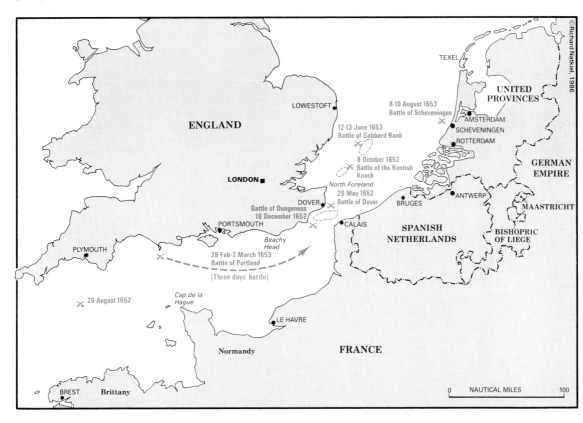

Above: Blake's flagship *Triumph* heavily engaged with the Dutch Fleet during the Battle of Portland (the Three Days' Battle), 1653.
Below: Robert Blake, the leading English admiral of the First Dutch War.

into naval service, the core of what would eventually become the Royal Marines, and new Fighting Instructions were promulgated giving admirals and captains regulations for battle tactics. These Fighting Instructions were to have a profound effect on British naval affairs for the next 150 years, their inflexibility often curbing commanders' initiative.

On 28 February 1653 Blake intercepted Tromp as he tried to shepherd a convoy through the Channel, and in a running fight lasting three days the Dutch ran out of ammunition and lost 19 warships and 57 merchantmen before Tromp could extricate his ships.

The new English Fighting Instructions and the revised code of discipline were tested by the Battle of the Gabbard Bank on 12 June 1653. The new 'General at Sea' George Monk and his subordinate Richard Deane engaged Tromp and the next day Blake arrived with reinforcements. By using their superior gunpower the English ships prevented the Dutch from coming to close quarters, and the Dutch lost some 20 ships and 1300 prisoners, while the English lost no ships and only 126 men.

After the Gabbard victory (also known as the Battle of North Foreland) the Dutch coast was blockaded, forcing the Dutch to sue for peace, but the English terms were so harsh that the Dutch resolved to make one supreme effort to stave off defeat. On 10 August Tromp met Monk in the Battle of Scheveningen (also known as the First Battle of the Texel), a bloody clash of two doughty admirals.

The two fleets, numbering some 100 ships each, actually sighted each other two days earlier on 8 August, but Tromp succeeded in drawing Monk away from the Texel, enabling Witte de With to get out to join him. Apart from a small skirmish late that day the main fleets did not engage, and a fierce gale prevented any fighting on the 9th.

The weather became calmer during the night, and early next morning the two fleets met headlong off Scheveningen. Tromp was killed by a musket ball after four hours of fighting but until about 1300 the Dutch appeared to be holding their own. However, during the afternoon they began to give ground, and by 2000 the entire fleet was withdrawing to the safety of the Texel. Dutch losses were heavy, at least 1000 casualties and ten warships lost, while Monk lost the *Oak* and a fireship and suffered slightly fewer casualties.

Both sides were now feeling the strain of the war and when the English Parliament moderated its demands the United Provinces accepted them. The war was brought to an end by the Treaty of Westminster, on 5 April 1654 and as a result of the Battle of Scheveningen the terms favored the English rather than the Dutch.

The Second Dutch War

At his restoration to the English throne in 1660 King Charles II inherited all the financial and commercial muddle of the last days of the Commonwealth, but he was also bequeathed a powerful navy. It was, therefore, tempting to continue Cromwell's policy of enhancing the country's wealth and prestige, chiefly at the expense of the Dutch. 'Make wars with Dutchmen, Peace with Spain, Then we shall have money and trade again' ran the popular jingle.

With the Dutch equally determined to safeguard their trading interests conflict was inevitable and as was often the case in those days it began 'beyond the line,' far from European waters. Fighting broke out early in 1664 when Captain Robert Holmes recaptured several trading posts in West Africa which had been occupied by the Dutch and then went on to occupy some of the Dutch-owned settlements. In August of the same year a force ejected the Dutch from Nieuw Amsterdam, renaming it New York in honor of James, Duke of York. At the end of the year there was a further attack on a Dutch convoy in the Straits of Gibraltar, and it is only surprising that formal hostilities did not break out until the middle of March the following year. Nonetheless, de Ruyter had already led a Dutch squadron from the Mediterranean to recover the trading posts in Africa.

Although energetically led the newly christened Royal Navy was soon to show the effect of government parsimony when war formally began. In April 1665 a successful cruise off the Dutch coast by the Duke of York had to be cut short because of the shortage of supplies. While trying to follow up this withdrawal the Dutch were drawn into the Battle of Lowestoft on 13 June. Although belittled in England as an indecisive action it achieved the destruction or capture of 31 Dutch ships.

An English attempt to attack a Dutch convoy homeward-bound from the East Indies forced it to take shelter in Bergen in July-August 1665, but a spirited defense by the Dutch and their Danish allies (Norway was under Danish rule at the time) drove off the attackers.

The outbreak of plague in London, coupled with the government's chronic

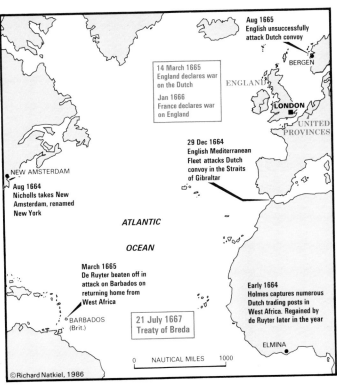

Aug 1665
English unsuccessfully attack Dutch convoy

BERGEN

14 March 1665
England declares war on the Dutch

Jan 1666
France declares war on England

ENGLAND

LONDON

UNITED PROVINCES

29 Dec 1664
English Mediterranean Fleet attacks Dutch convoy in the Straits of Gibraltar

NEW AMSTERDAM

Aug 1664
Nicholls takes New Amsterdam, renamed New York

ATLANTIC

OCEAN

March 1665
De Ruyter beaten off in attack on Barbados on returning home from West Africa

Early 1664
Holmes captures numerous Dutch trading posts in West Africa. Regained by de Ruyter later in the year

BARBADOS
(Brit.)

21 July 1667
Treaty of Breda

ELMINA

0   NAUTICAL MILES   1000

© Richard Natkiel, 1986

Above right: **The Battle of Lowestoft. The engagement was a disordered scramble, the English gaining the upper hand after the Dutch flagship blew up.**

shortage of money, affected the Royal Navy's ability to control the waters around the English coast. In October the new Dutch commander-in-chief, de Ruyter, was able to operate in the Thames estuary unmolested before returning to Holland to lay his ships up for the winter. France declared war on England the following January, but keeping her fleet out of action proved comparatively easy. It did, however, mean that when the Dutch Fleet put to sea at the end of May 1666 the Duke of Albemarle (formerly General George Monk) was badly outnumbered nearly two-to-one by de Ruyter.

The resulting Four Days' Fight, which lasted from 11 to 14 June, was a bloody slogging match. Twenty of Albemarle's ships were sunk to de Ruyter's six, and the English suffered nearly 4000 casualties.

Repairs to Monk's fleet were delayed by shortages of essential stores, and once again de Ruyter's squadron was seen in the Thames. Not until the end of June did Monk get to sea once more, but he was able to

inflict a defeat on de Ruyter at the St James's Day Fight on 4-5 August. Further retribution followed, when Robert Holmes (now Sir Robert) destroyed a newly arrived East Indies convoy in the anchorage known as the Vlie. This action, known as 'Holmes's Bonfire,' resulted in the destruction of 150 merchant ships, a severe blow to Dutch trade.

Despite the victories at sea, by early 1667 the English were heartily tired of the war and 'peace feelers' were put out. When the Dutch seemed willing to come to the conference table the King's ministers decided to economize by not recommissioning the warships which had been laid up 'in Ordinary' during the winter. The Dutch kept talking at Breda but all the while prepared the fleet for a devastating blow against the English.

On 21 June 1667 de Ruyter entered the Medway with his light forces, attacking shipping in the river and landing troops to occupy Sheerness and Chatham. Chatham Dockyard suffered severely, with three ships of the line burned at their moorings and the 90-gun *Royal Charles* towed back to Holland as a prize.

The negotiations at Breda terminated rapidly and on terms much more favorable to the Dutch, exactly as de Ruyter had intended. It had been a bitter and largely unnecessary war, fought for financial gain rather than strategic necessity or national survival. So bitter was the feeling in England that the peace of Breda lasted no more than three years. On the credit side it did hasten the process of reform at the Admiralty. Under the dual direction of Samuel Pepys as Clerk of the Acts to the Navy Board and the Duke of York as Lord High Admiral an entirely new administrative machine was created, out of which grew the Board of Admiralty. This was the body which was to frame and execute British naval policy for another 150 years.

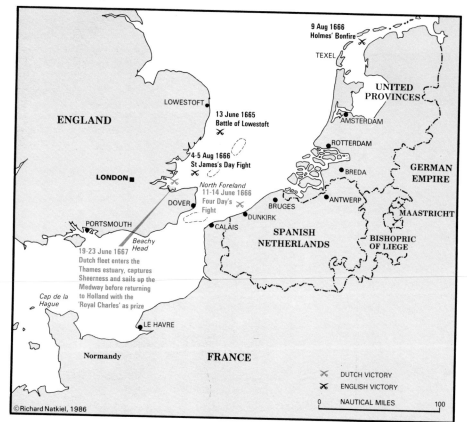

Above left: German illustration of de Ruyter's exploits in the Medway, 1667.
Above right: George Monk, Duke of Albemarle, who conducted a resolute defense against de Ruyter's superior force in the Four Days' Battle, from the portrait by Lely.
Right: During the Four Days' Battle, from a contemporary Dutch print.

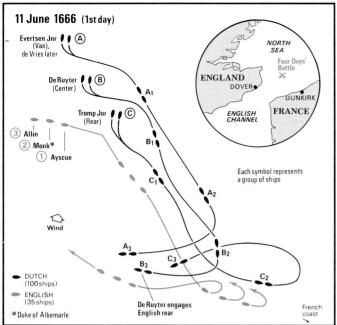

11 June 1666 (1st day)

Evertsen Jnr (Van), de Vries later Ⓐ

De Ruyter (Center) Ⓑ

Tromp Jnr (Rear) Ⓒ

③ Allin
② Monk *
① Ayscue

NORTH SEA

ENGLAND
DOVER

Four Days' Battle ✕

ENGLISH CHANNEL

FRANCE
DUNKIRK

Each symbol represents a group of ships

A₁ B₁ C₁ A₂ A₃ C₃ B₃ B₂ C₂

Wind

● DUTCH (100 ships)
● ENGLISH (35 ships)

* Duke of Albemarle

De Ruyter engages English rear

French coast

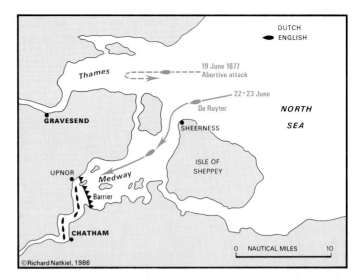

DUTCH ●
ENGLISH ●

Thames

GRAVESEND

19 June 1677 Abortive attack

22-23 June
De Ruyter

NORTH SEA

SHEERNESS

ISLE OF SHEPPEY

UPNOR

Medway

Barrier

CHATHAM

0 NAUTICAL MILES 10

© Richard Natkiel, 1986

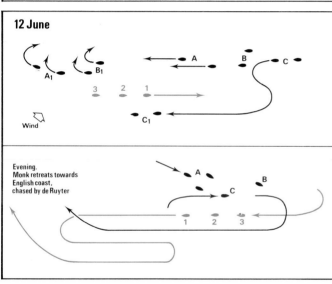

12 June

A₁ B₁ A B C

3 2 1

C₁

Wind

Evening. Monk retreats towards English coast, chased by de Ruyter

A C B

1 2 3

13 June: Monk continues retreat westward followed by de Ruyter. 'Royal Prince' runs aground on Galloper Shoal and is taken by Tromp. Rupert's squadron rejoins English fleet.

14 June

Van Ness with Tromp following gives chase to 3 or 4 English ships

C₁ 1 2 3 4

A₁ 2₁ 3₁ 4₁ A B C

B₁

Two fleets exchange broadsides for two hours

1₁

Wind

C₂ A₂ Tromp returns with Dutch van

English ships receive broadsides from both left and right

3₂ 4₂

A₃ C₃ 2₂

1₃ 1₂

3₃ 2₃

B₂

Monk separated from remainder of fleet

B₃ 4₃

© Richard Natkiel, 1986

The Third Dutch War

The third war between the English and the Dutch was, like its predecessors, bloody and hard-fought. The English were still smarting from the humiliation of de Ruyter's attack on their fleet in the Medway in 1667, so when a Dutch squadron failed to give the traditional salute due to an English man o' war in the Channel the English flagship opened fire. War followed immediately.

The Battle of Sole Bay

On 7 June 1672 a combined Anglo-French squadron (71 ships) weighed anchor and sailed from Sole Bay (modern Southwold) to engage the main Dutch fleet (61 ships) under de Ruyter. The Dutch made great use of fireships to attempt the destruction of the English line but they were foiled when the wind dropped. The 100-gun *Royal James* was burned, however, and the commander-in-

Below: **A Dutch fireship succeeds in setting fire to the English flagship *Royal James*.**

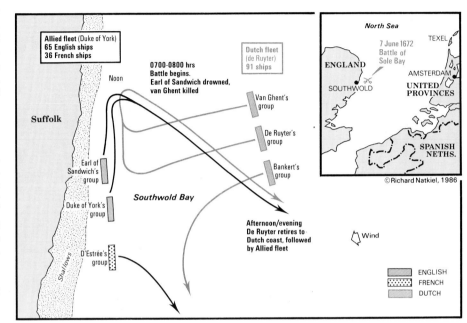

Allied fleet (Duke of York)
65 English ships
36 French ships

Dutch fleet
(de Ruyter)
91 ships

0700-0800 hrs
Battle begins.
Earl of Sandwich drowned,
van Ghent killed

Noon

Suffolk

Van Ghent's group

De Ruyter's group

Earl of Sandwich's group

Bankert's group

Southwold Bay

Duke of York's group

Afternoon/evening
De Ruyter retires to
Dutch coast, followed
by Allied fleet

Wind

Shallows

D'Estrée's group

ENGLISH
FRENCH
DUTCH

North Sea

TEXEL

7 June 1672
Battle of
Sole Bay

ENGLAND

AMSTERDAM

SOUTHWOLD

UNITED
PROVINCES

SPANISH
NETHS.

©Richard Natkiel, 1986

Above: Seal of the Duke of York.
Right: The First Battle of Schooneveldt, 7 June 1673.

chief the Duke of York was forced to shift his flag twice, but the Dutch ships at the rear of the line lost heart and virtually retired out of the action.

Firing died away at about 2100 when de Ruyter retired. Although both sides claimed a victory, the Dutch had had the best of it.

The Battle of the Texel

Following the two Battles of Schooneveldt in June 1673 the next major engagement was the Battle of the Texel on 21 August. As before de Ruyter fought shrewdly, choosing his moment to retire. Once again the French were present under Comte d'Estrées, making 81 ships against 54 Dutch.

As at Sole Bay de Ruyter had no difficulty in distracting the attention of the French, leaving him free to concentrate on the English center under Prince Rupert and the

rear squadron commanded by Admiral Sir Edward Spragge.

On the allies' side there was a particularly disgraceful moment when twelve Dutch ships under Bankert ran through twenty French ships without a shot being fired at them. The conduct of the French squadron throughout suggests that d'Estrées may have had secret orders from King Louis XIV to avoid action with the Dutch. Less easily explained is an extraordinary lapse of fleet discipline on the part of Sir Edward Spragge. To make good a boast to King Charles that he would bring back Cornelis Tromp alive or dead he made the whole of the rearguard squadron stop to enable him to engage Tromp.

The private war was fought as bitterly as the main battle. Spragge was forced to shift his flag twice, and on the second occasion

while moving in a boat to his new flagship he was cut in two by a roundshot. His folly, combined with the timidity or treachery of the French, left Rupert isolated in the center, but de Ruyter lacked sufficient ships to defeat the English, and he withdrew at the end of the day.

Nine days after the battle Holland was offered a tempting alliance by Spain, Lorraine and Germany, an offer which was immediately matched by King Louis. In England the King's alliance with France was immensely unpopular, and the following February he bowed to popular clamor and signed a separate peace. But in spite of de Ruyter's heroic endeavors the Dutch had suffered a strategic defeat. No longer could they dominate the English Channel or the southern half of the North Sea, their main objective throughout the conflict.

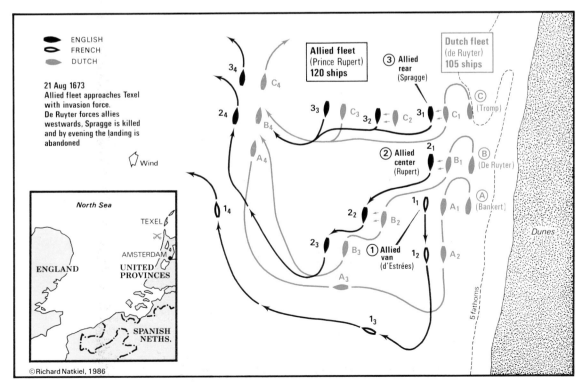

ENGLISH
FRENCH
DUTCH

21 Aug 1673
Allied fleet approaches Texel with invasion force.
De Ruyter forces allies westwards, Spragge is killed and by evening the landing is abandoned

Wind

Allied fleet (Prince Rupert) 120 ships

③ Allied rear (Spragge)

Dutch fleet (de Ruyter) 105 ships

© (Tromp)

② Allied center (Rupert)

® (De Ruyter)

① Allied van (d'Estrées)

④ (Bankert)

North Sea

TEXEL

AMSTERDAM

ENGLAND

UNITED PROVINCES

Dunes

5 fathoms

SPANISH NETHS.

©Richard Natkiel, 1986

65

The Battles of Cape Barfleur and La Hougue

The long struggle between the Catholic King James II of England and his protestant subjects came to a head in 1688, when the King's enemies invited the Stadholder of Holland, William of Orange (married to King James' niece, Mary) to invade the country and take over the throne. When the army and the navy deserted him, James II was forced to flee to France, where Louis XIV was ready with men and money to help James restore the Catholic succession. The resulting War of the English Succession was fought to prevent the return of James.

At first the Jacobites (supporters of King James, from the Latin Jacobus meaning James) achieved considerable success. A landing in Ireland was achieved early in 1689 and a French squadron won a tactical success off Bantry Bay but the Brest Fleet was unable to turn these victories to advantage. The following year the English position improved when William of Orange, now William III, landed with a strong army to protect Ulster. Then in June 1690 Vice Admiral Comte de Tourville met an Anglo-Dutch fleet com-

Below: **James II. The French defeat at La Hougue effectively ended his hopes of regaining the British throne.**

manded by the Earl of Torrington. The resulting Battle of Beachy head was a tactical defeat for the Allies, with eight ships lost against no French losses but Tourville contented himself with sending a small party ashore to burn Teignmouth before returning to Brest.

The English and Dutch responded vigorously by re-equipping their fleets. After his defeat on land at the Battle of the Boyne James was forced to abandon his forces in Ireland and return to France, but Admiral Edward Russell proved unable to bring Tourville to action. Although the remaining Jacobite and French forces had to be evacuated from Ireland late in 1691, the French started to build a large force at Brest to invade England. When the English and Dutch learned of the plans they stationed a force of nearly 100 ships in the Channel to frustrate the plan.

Tourville put to sea with 44 ships on 12

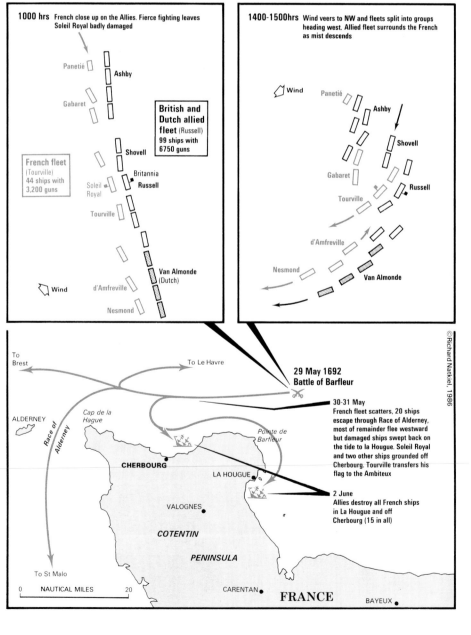

© Richard Natkiel, 1986

A List of the FRENCH Fleet

A List of the English and Dutch Fleet

Blew

Red

Dutch

Tenders and Fire Ships

May, with orders to disperse the Allied fleet as a prelude to the invasion. Unfortunately for him amending orders giving him discretion to avoid action on unfavorable terms failed to reach him before he met Russell's much more powerful force of 99 ships off Cape Barfleur on the morning of 29 May. At first the wind was from the southwest, with both fleets taking a southerly course but at about 1400 the wind shifted to the northwest, and the Dutch seized the opportunity to attempt an encirclement of the French van. The English rear squadron showed the same initiative and pushed its way through a gap whch appeared in the French line. But both attempts were foiled by the stout defense put up by the French. A further attempt by the rear squadron to attack the French center, which was already sorely battered, failed

Below: The boats of the English fleet in action at La Hougue.

when the wind died. The day was coming to an end, and a thick mist blotted out both fleets. The French anchored and this allowed the English ships to drift out of range, bringing the general action to a close.

When the mist cleared about 2000 Russell sent in fireships in an attempt to spread panic among the French but once again the good seamanship of Tourville's captains saved them. At the cost of cutting some cables all the fireships were sunk, and when the mist descended again after two hours the exhausted French were finally allowed some rest.

Having fought off a fleet nearly twice the strength of his own, Tourville now wisely decided to fall back on Brest, but the presence of so many damaged ships made this very difficult. Only five reached Brest, two got to Le Havre, three to Cherbourg, 12 to La Hougue Roads (sometimes rendered La Hogue), and 22 reached St Malo.

Above: Contemporary plan of the Battle of Beachy Head. The superior French fleet failed to make the best of their advantage.

Tourville's proud, disciplined fleet was now in terrible disarray, and worse was in store. The *Soleil Royal*, aground off Cherbourg and the *Admirable* and *Triomphant* inside the anchorage were set on fire and destroyed. Two days later the dozen ships at La Hougue were attacked by Sir George Rooke. Tourville had hoped that the shallowness of the roadstead and its flanking batteries of guns would protect his ships but Rooke sent in his boats.

Despite personal appeals from Tourville and his subordinates Villette-Mursay and Coëtlogon, who all rowed out to their own light forces to encourage them to stand and fight, the French seamen were too exhausted and disheartened to fight off the English. It is said that James II and senior French ministers were watching the debâcle from the shore, with the exiled Stuart king doing little to endear himself to his hosts by exclaiming, 'Who but my brave English tars could do such a thing?'

The disaster was complete: the *Ambiteux, Merveilleux, Foudroyant, Magnifique, Sainte-Philippe, Fier, Fort, Tonnant, Terrible, Gaillard, Bourbon* and *Saint Louis* were set on fire and destroyed. It was ironic that Tourville had fought the main battle at odds of two-to-one and had not lost a single ship, yet the result of the two engagements was the loss of 15 ships.

La Hougue marked the end of French attempts during this war to dominate the Narrow Seas and perhaps invade England. French resources during the next five years of the war were devoted to commerce-raiding, always a popular alternative but one which did little to harm the power of the Royal Navy.

The Triangular Trade in the 18th Century

The origins of the North American slave trade lay in the sugar trade. The hard physical labor of canecutting in a tropical or subtropical climate was judged to be too much for Northern Europeans, so it was necessary to find laborers who were sufficiently hardy to resist the effects of heat and disease. The spread of sugar plantations from Brazil to the Caribbean led to the introduction of slavery in British possessions as well as the old Spanish colonies, and the development of cotton plantations in what eventually became the Southern States of the USA. The economic basis for slavery was greatly assisted by the pattern of trade imposed by geography.

By the middle of the eighteenth century transatlantic trade had developed into a well-established and lucrative business. Fish and furs from Canada flowed to Europe, while the forests yielded timber; the Caribbean exported sugar, molasses, fruit and exotic hardwoods. From Africa came principally slaves but also gold and pepper.

The term 'triangular trade' came to have slightly different meanings for the British and the Americans. For the Americans it meant a voyage from ports like Newport, Boston or Charleston to West Africa carrying rum, iron bars, worn-out or cheaply-made muskets or any of a variety of trade goods to be exchanged at the slave stations or barracoons for the 'black ivory' or other commodities. The notorious 'Middle Passage,' the base of the triangle of trade, took the slaves to the West Indies from where they were transhipped via middlemen to the sugar islands or to North or South America. Sugar and molasses and other Caribbean products like mahogany wood for fine furniture were then taken to the slave ships' home ports to complete the triangular pattern. The British version of the trade differed only in that the

home ports were such as London, Bristol and, in the later days of the slave trade, Liverpool. The advantage of the triangle was the elimination of any need to send empty (and therefore profitless) ships on any leg of the round trip. Naturally not every voyage followed this simple sequence and equally payment or goods might not always be readily available in the West Indies for example. While there were many economic pitfalls for all those engaged in the trade the real losers were the slaves who endured frightful privations on the Middle Passage.

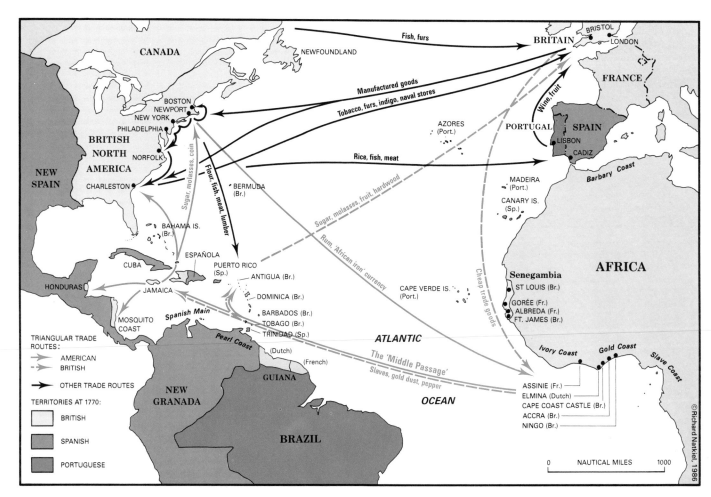

68

Colonial Empires 1756

By the middle of the eighteenth century a clear pattern of European colonial expansion had emerged. The colonies in America, the Caribbean and India were the most important, offering markets for European manufactured goods in return for materials which they could not produce themselves.

In America the original English settlements established during the reign of Queen Elizabeth had been added to during the reign of James I until the whole of the east coast was colonized. Further to the west France had established Louisiana, with New Orleans as its outlet on the Gulf of Mexico. Although thinly populated the American colonies produced furs, tobacco and rice.

The Caribbean settlements had also changed from the days when they were exclusively Spanish. The chain of islands were now partly in the hands of the British and French, while the Dutch retained some footholds. Spain still shipped bullion back from Mexico, but the Caribbean islands also yielded sugar, cocoa and dyes.

India was still made up of a series of unstable native states, and European penetration of the sub-continent was restricted to 'factories' or trading posts around the coast.

The Treaty of Utrecht in 1713 had tried to leave the Spanish Empire intact but the underlying rivalry could not be removed. Illegal trade everywhere sought to evade the restrictions imposed by the trade monopolies, and by 1754 the British and French were at war once again in North America.

Although France gained local military superiority, with a chain of forts established to prevent the British from expanding to the northwest, she could not guarantee lines of

Below: **The seal of the British East India Company. The principal device on the seal shows three fully-rigged merchant ships.**

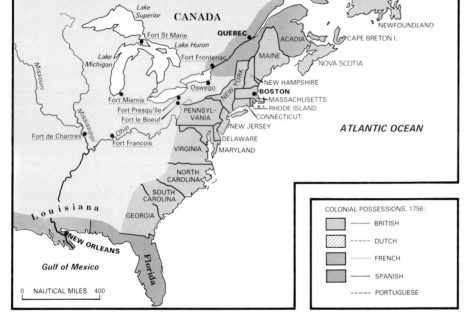

COLONIAL POSSESSIONS, 1756:

- BRITISH
- DUTCH
- FRENCH
- SPANISH
- PORTUGUESE

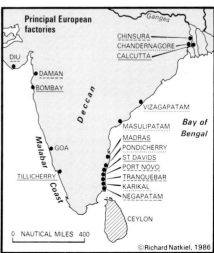

Principal European factories

©Richard Natkiel, 1986

communication with Europe. Once again seapower proved the key to colonial expansion, and the French Navy was unable to equal the achievements of France's armies on land.

The Seven Years' War (1756-63) proved disastrous for the French. Under the able direction of William Pitt the Elder the Royal Navy was used to cut off the French forces in North America. With no hope of reinforcement Louisbourg was the first to fall in 1758, followed by Quebec in 1759, Montreal in 1760 and then the whole of French Canada. Spain fared no better, with Havana lost, and by 1763 all French islands except Santo Domingo (St Domingue) were in British hands. Although the islands were all returned under the Treaty of Paris at the end of the war Britain drove a hard bargain, forcing Spain to cede Florida in return for Havana and keeping all the mainland territory east of the Mississippi.

The struggle for mastery of India was equally fierce. In 1746 Madras fell to the French under Dupleix, and as in North America the French won impressive victories without being able to consolidate them. With their command of the sea the British were able to check Dupleix at Trichinopoly in 1752, putting an end to his plans to conquer the Carnatic.

Clive's victory at Plassey in 1757 proved decisive as it gave the British control of the province of Bengal. Using this as a base for operations the British were able to eliminate French forces in the Carnatic, leaving themselves as the predominant European power in India.

The Seven Years War

Byng's Failure to Relieve Minorca

The island of Minorca, in the Balearic Islands, was an important base for the Royal Navy throughout the eighteenth century. With Gibraltar unprotected against winter Atlantic gales Minorca's magnificent harbor of Port Mahon offered not only shelter but abundant fresh water for Britain's Mediterranean forces. The island had been acquired from Spain under the Treaty of Utrecht at the end of the War of the Spanish Succession and in 1756 was fortified and well garrisoned.

The French, recognizing the value of Minorca to the British, particularly as a base for the blockade of Toulon, landed an attacking force of troops at Ciudadela, at the opposite end of the island, and laid siege to the fortress of St Philip, which guarded the approaches to Port Mahon. Belatedly the government in London dispatched Admiral John Byng with ten ships of the line and a force of troops to raise the siege and strengthen the garrison. Byng was joined by three more ships at Gibraltar and on 20 May 1756, while still 30 miles southeast of Port Mahon he fell in with an equal-sized fleet under the French Admiral the Marquis de la Galissonière.

Byng bore down on the French squadron, but in his attempt to keep his battle line in strict order his ships did not come into action simultaneously. After an indecisive cannonade the French withdrew but Byng did not pursue them, nor did he show any wish to interrupt the supply of the French troops ashore.

A Council of War was held on board the flagship and Byng made clear his wish to return to Gibraltar to await reinforcements and to abandon the British garrison. By 14 June the British ships were back in Gibraltar, and ten days later General Blakeney surrendered the fortress of St Philip, leaving the French in possession of Minorca.

The Admiralty, ignoring the fact that their own dilatoriness, combined with their over-strict Fighting Instructions, had been as much to blame as Byng for the debacle, ordered him to be relieved and put under arrest. On his return to England he was court-martialled for failing to do his utmost

Right: An eighteenth century chart of the magnificent harbor at Port Mahon, Minorca.

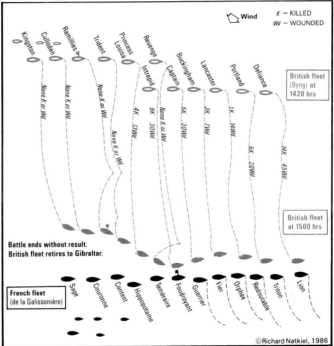

to relieve Minorca. On the available evidence acquittal was virtually impossible, and it carried the death penalty. Byng was actually found guilty of negligence, and acquitted of the major charge of cowardice, but the death penalty had been made mandatory for that offence in 1749.

The travesty of justice might have been reduced if the King had chosen to exercise his prerogative of mercy, but his ministers needed a scapegoat for a whole series of military blunders, and prevented the King from reprieving Byng. The wretched man, son of a very distinguished flag-officer, was executed by firing squad on the quarterdeck of HMS *Monarch* on 14 March 1757. It was this melancholy event which prompted Voltaire's remark in *Candide* about shooting an admiral from time to time *pour encourager les autres* (to encourage the others).

In the long run the Royal Navy did not suffer unduly for the loss of Minorca, and the island was recovered before the end of the war. Its long period under British control did not finish until the end of the Napoleonic Wars, by which time the acquisition of Malta had made it redundant.

The Capture of Louisbourg

Rivalry over American possessions between England and France went back to the early seventeenth century. The English captured Quebec as early as 1629, and the colony of Acadia had changed hands several times by 1700. During the next century every war in Europe generated parallel military operations in North America. The Treaty of Utrecht in 1713 sought to impose a balance of power but by leaving the old Spanish colonial empire intact the treaty perpetuated the causes of conflict.

To compensate herself for the cession of Newfoundland and Nova Scotia to Britain under the terms of the treaty France established a great fortress at Louisbourg. Situated on Cape Breton Island, the fortress guarded the approaches to the St Lawrence, and was in effect the outer bastion of the defenses of French Canada.

In 1745 an expedition of New England settlers led by the Governor of Massachu-

Above left: Execution of Admiral Byng.
Left: General James Wolfe leads his forces ashore at Louisbourg.
Below right: Contemporary chart of the capture of Quebec.

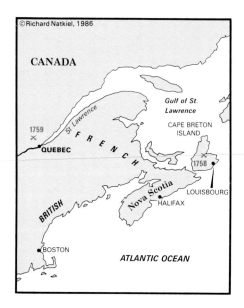

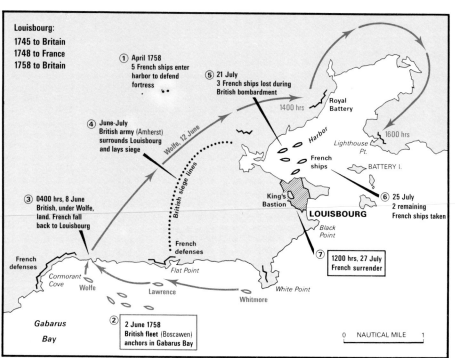

Louisbourg:
1745 to Britain
1748 to France
1758 to Britain

① April 1758
5 French ships enter harbor to defend fortress

⑤ 21 July
3 French ships lost during British bombardment
1400 hrs
Royal Battery

④ June-July
British army (Amherst) surrounds Louisbourg and lays siege

Wolfe, 12 June
1600 hrs
Lighthouse Pt.
BATTERY I.

③ 0400 hrs, 8 June
British, under Wolfe, land. French fall back to Louisbourg

British siege lines

Harbor

French ships

French defenses

King's Bastion

LOUISBOURG

⑥ 25 July
2 remaining French ships taken

French defenses

Cormorant Cove
Wolfe

Flat Point

Lawrence

White Point
Whitmore

Black Point

⑦ 1200 hrs, 27 July
French surrender

Gabarus Bay

② 2 June 1758
British fleet (Boscawen) anchors in Gabarus Bay

0   NAUTICAL MILE   1

© Richard Natkiel, 1986

CANADA

Gulf of St. Lawrence

St Lawrence

1759 ✕
QUEBEC

F R E N C H

CAPE BRETON ISLAND

✕ 1758

Nova Scotia

LOUISBOURG
HALIFAX

BRITISH

• BOSTON

ATLANTIC OCEAN

setts, William Shirley, and assisted by five Royal Navy warships, laid siege to Louisbourg. Remarkably the fortress capitulated after only five weeks but this important strategic gain was thrown away at the Treaty of Aix-la-Chapelle three years later, when Louisbourg was returned to France.

Fighting began again in 1754, but this time the French established local supremacy, winning a series of small actions and building a chain of forts to limit British expansion. Stung by these defeats the British acted vigorously, using their sea power to isolate the French colonies from Europe.

In February 1758 a combined expedition under Admiral Edward Boscawen and Major General Jeffrey Amherst left England for Halifax. After revictualling the entire expedition sailed for Louisbourg on 28 May, a fleet of 157 warships and transports and 14 battalions of troops.

Although the expedition reached its destination on 2 June it could not land for six days, and the landing had to be made under heavy fire from the fortress. Bad weather hampered the siege, and during the next three weeks 100 boats were lost in the heavy surf. On 26 June 200 marines were landed and the following day the ships landed some guns to reinforce the land artillery of the besiegers.

Operations by Major General Wolfe gave the British control of the land approaches to the fortress and enabled the guns to destroy several ships in the harbor. On the night of 25-26 July the boats of the fleet entered the harbor to attack the last two French ships to survive the bombardment; the *Bienfaisant* was captured and the *Prudent* was burnt. This bold stroke showed the French commander, the Chevalier de Drocour that his position was hopeless and next day he surrendered with his 3000-strong garrison.

The fall of Louisbourg was followed by the surrender of Cape Breton Island and St John (to become Prince Edward Island), leaving the St Lawrence defenseless. Amherst wanted to press on to Quebec to bring about the end of French rule in Canada, but Boscawen considered that the obstacles were too great, and the assault on Quebec was deferred to the following year. However the capture of Louisbourg sealed the fate of Quebec, and its fall was only a matter of time while the Royal Navy continued to prevent reinforcements reaching Canada from France.

The Capture of Quebec

One of British Prime Minister William Pitt's main objectives in the Seven Years' War was to attack French possessions in North America, so while a series of 'pinprick' raids on the French coast distracted French attention General Amherst and 12,000 troops were dispatched across the Atlantic in 1758 to attack Louisbourg on Cape Breton Island.

After the fall of Louisbourg a second expedition was sent a year later to attack Canada. This was a much more hazardous enterprise because the upper reaches of the St Lawrence river were commanded by the guns of Quebec.

At first sight the British commanders were an ill-assorted pair. Major General James Wolfe was talented and imaginative but erratic and mercurial in temperament, whereas Admiral Saunders was phlegmatic and prudent. The admiral also had the services of James Cook as fleet navigator, and his meticulous surveys of the river showed that it might be possible to get troops first to bring large warships and transports to Quebec and later farther up the river in boats. Only by navigating through the shallows under cover of darkness would it be possible to get past a line of French guardboats but Cook was able to find a navigable channel.

The French commander, the Marquis de Montcalm, had about 5000 men against some 3000 under Wolfe, and although Quebec's fortifications were considered to be impregnable the French were short of supplies. Montcalm's only hope was for autumn storms and fog in the St Lawrence to drive the British away but the Royal Navy's experience on blockade duty stood it in good stead. On 9 June 1759 Saunders' fleet entered the St Lawrence and just over two weeks later the troops were ashore well upstream.

On the night of 12-13 September Wolfe launched his surprise attack, with his troops in flat-bottomed boats. With oars muffled, the force made its way up the river, creeping past the guardboats and sentries on shore. They landed well upriver of Quebec at a point where a little-known path led to the top of the cliffs. After a long and difficult scramble Wolfe's troops reached the level ground in front of Quebec's landward defenses, known as the Plains of Abraham, and began their march on Quebec.

In the battle which followed Montcalm's troops fought bravely but they were no match for Wolfe's disciplined redcoats. After a first tremendous volley at only 100 yards' range the French never recovered, and the battle ended after little more than fifteen minutes with the French in full retreat. Both Wolfe

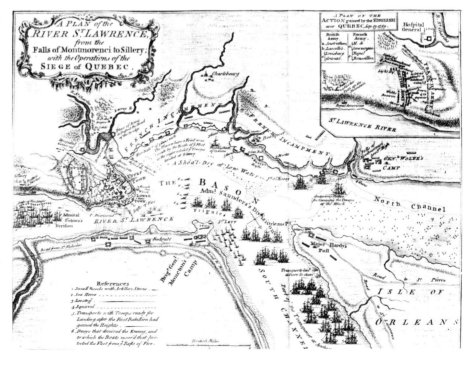

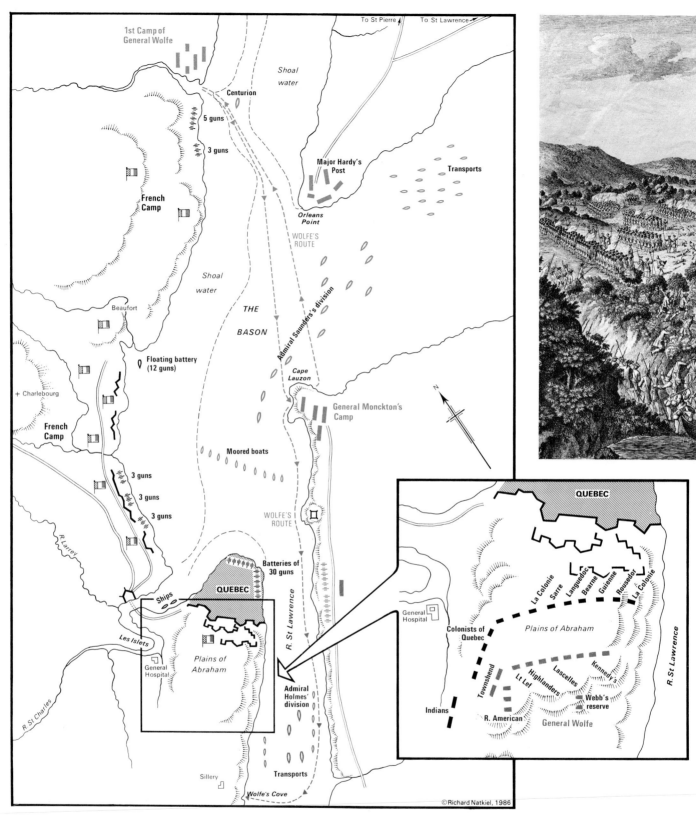

and Montcalm were fatally wounded in the deadly exchanges of musketry but few British victories had been so easily won.

With Quebec in British hands it was only a matter of time before Montreal fell, and with it went French dominion over Canada. With only 82,000 French colonists against some 1,300,000 in British North America the French position in Canada was untenable, a fact which was recognized at the end of the war in 1763 with the cession of Canada to Great Britain.

The conquest of Canada was to have far-reaching consequences. It afforded a useful base during the War of the American Revolution in 1776-83 but its real worth was only realized during the Napoleonic Wars. When Napoleon tried to exclude the British from the Baltic to deny them timber supplies it was the forests of America which filled the gap.

The capture of Quebec was notable for the harmonious relations between the British army and navy. Not only was Saunders able to handle the temperamental Wolfe diplomatically but he also grasped the boldness of Wolfe's plan and gave it his wholehearted support. The Seven Years' War provides the first historical examples of the benefits of Combined Operations which are taken for granted today.

The Battle of Quiberon Bay

After many years of indecisive actions, caused largely by the sterile Permanent Fighting Instructions issued by the Admiralty, a new tactical spirit enthused the Royal Navy in the mid-eighteenth century. It showed to fine advantage in the Seven Years' War when William Pitt the Elder framed a new maritime strategy.

A string of dazzling successes won India and Canada but Pitt was well aware that these gains would be wiped out if France could send reinforcements to recapture her lost colonies. Accordingly Admiral Boscawen

Left: Contemporary impression of the landing to capture Quebec and the subsequent battle.
Below: French warships aground and wrecked during the Battle of Quiberon Bay.

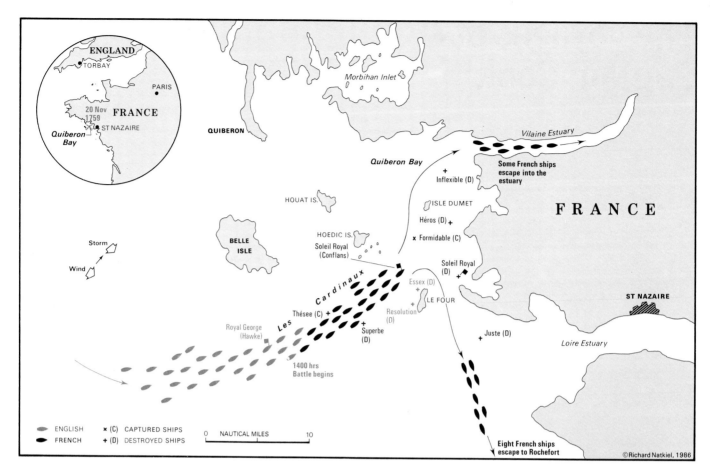

Map labels:

ENGLAND
TORBAY
PARIS
FRANCE
20 Nov 1759
ST NAZAIRE
Quiberon Bay

Morbihan Inlet
Vilaine Estuary
QUIBERON
Quiberon Bay
Inflexible (D)
Some French ships escape into the estuary
HOUAT IS.
ISLE DUMET
FRANCE
Héros (D)
HOEDIC IS.
Soleil Royal (Conflans)
BELLE ISLE
Formidable (C)
Soleil Royal (D)
Storm
Wind
Les Cardinaux
Essex (D)
LE FOUR
ST NAZAIRE
Thésée (C)
Resolution (D)
Royal George (Hawke)
Superbe (D)
Juste (D)
Loire Estuary
1400 hrs Battle begins

Eight French ships escape to Rochefort

ENGLISH   × (C) CAPTURED SHIPS
FRENCH   + (D) DESTROYED SHIPS
0   NAUTICAL MILES   10
©Richard Natkiel, 1986

---

was sent to the Mediterranean to prevent the Toulon Fleet from breaking out and the blockade of the Brest Fleet was reinforced. Both measures paid dividends, Boscawen beating the Toulon Fleet at Lagos in August 1759 and Hawke achieving a similar success against the Brest Fleet.

Sir Edward Hawke's squadron was lying off Brest, watching the main French fleet to prevent it from supporting an invasion of England. Bad weather forced his blockading squadron off station, and while his squadron of 23 ships of the line waited in Torbay for the gales to abate the French Admiral de Conflans escaped from Brest with his 21 ships of the line.

As soon as Hawke learned that the French had sailed he set forth in hot pursuit. De Conflans took his ships into Quiberon Bay, where he hoped he could shelter behind the shoals and tidal rips. Undeterred Hawke took his ships into the shoal water, catching the French at the worst moment, as they entered the bay in tight formation. Without waiting to form a line of battle Hawke engaged the French rearguard, cutting off the 74-gun ship *Formidable* and the *Héros*.

Two of Hawke's ships, the *Essex* and *Resolution* ran aground on the shoals but he pressed on with the attack against the French, who were in complete disarray. When victory was certain the flagship *Royal George* ordered the fleet to anchor for the night, to avoid unnecessary risks, and morning revealed the full extent of the victory. Out of 21 French major ships 11

were sunk or captured. The French losses included the flagship *Soleil Royal* which had been dismasted the night before; she was promptly driven ashore to avoid capture.

What distinguished Quiberon Bay was the completeness of the victory. Apart from a small group of French survivors who had sought refuge in the estuary of the Vilaine and eight more ships which had escaped to Rochefort, the invasion fleet had been destroyed. It was almost the first clear-cut British naval victory since the end of the

Left: **Admiral Sir Edward Hawke who led the British fleet in the Battle of Quiberon Bay. Hawke avoided the delay involved in forming line of battle, as the Permanent Fighting Instructions laid down, by making use of the 'General Chase' signal. Many of the more successful British admirals later in the century were also to employ this device.**

Dutch wars nearly a hundred years earlier. It reaffirmed the importance of the blockade and forced the French to give up any hope of challenging the Royal Navy in open battle in the immediate future.

The Treaty of Paris in February 1763 confirmed the British achievements of the Seven Years' War. France was forced to give up Canada, Nova Scotia and Cape Breton, but kept Guadeloupe and Martinique, while Spain recovered Manila and Havana but lost control of Minorca once again. The shape of the future British Empire was determined, and the campaign is an outstanding example of the value of a sound and coordinated maritime strategy.

The Voyages of Captain Cook

James Cook would have stood head and shoulders above his contemporaries in any age, but in eighteenth century England he was a rare phenomenon. Born the son of a laborer in Yorkshire, he went to sea as an apprentice in 1746. Although he was promoted to mate by 1752 he decided three years later to broaden his experience by enlisting in the Royal Navy as an able seaman. His abilities then took him rapidly through the ranks, and in July 1757 he was appointed Master of HMS *Solebay*.

He distinguished himself for his accurate surveys of the St Lawrence River during the combined Army-Navy operations against Quebec in 1758-59, and it cannot be questioned that his navigational skill played a major role in the conquest of Canada. At the end of the war in 1763 Cook undertook surveys of Newfoundland, and these brought him to the notice of the influential Royal Society. He was chosen as the Society's official observer on an expedition to be sent to Tahiti to observe the Transit of Venus. The scientific purpose of the expedition was linked with an attempt to discover the mythical southern continent, *Terra Australis Incognita*.

Lieutenant Cook left England in a converted coal-ship, the *Endeavour*, in August 1768 and reached Tahiti in April 1769. His attention to the welfare of his men was sufficient to ensure only one death from scurvy, a remarkable feat at the time. The Transit of Venus was observed and recorded on 3 June 1769, leaving Cook free to start the second part of his mission. He not only circumnavigated New Zealand but passed between North and South Island, proving finally that New Zealand was not merely a promontory of a southern continent. While trying to reach Van Diemen's Land he was blown off course and finally made a landfall on the southeast coast of Australia. After a near-disaster when the *Endeavour* ran aground on the Great Barrier Reef Cook headed north and passed through the Torres Strait before returning to England via Batavia.

Although Cook was highly praised for his discoveries on his return in 1771 the existence of *Terra Australis Incognita* had not been disproved, and the following year he left for the South Pacific once more. This time he had two ex-colliers, the *Resolution* and *Adventure*. He also had the benefit of a new accurate timekeeper, Harrison's chronometer, which would greatly assist navigation by making reasonably accurate calculation of longitude possible. It had long been known how to calculate latitude by astronomical observation. To calculate longitude, however, ocean navigators had previously had to rely largely on 'dead reckoning,' simple calculation of course and speed, which could not take accurate account of the effects of currents or the drift of a ship to leeward.

The two barks reached the Cape of Good Hope and then headed southeast to the fringe of Antarctica, searching for evidence of a large landmass. After crossing one-third of the world's circumference Cook decided that he had proved conclusively that the mysterious southern continent did not exist, and as he could get no further south because of the ice, he turned for New Zealand. The *Resolution* (HMS *Adventure* had lost contact and was cruising independently) now headed east, then north to Tahiti, where his weary crew could rest and recuperate. Cook then made two more sweeps to the south, crossing

Left: **Captain James Cook studying a chart.**

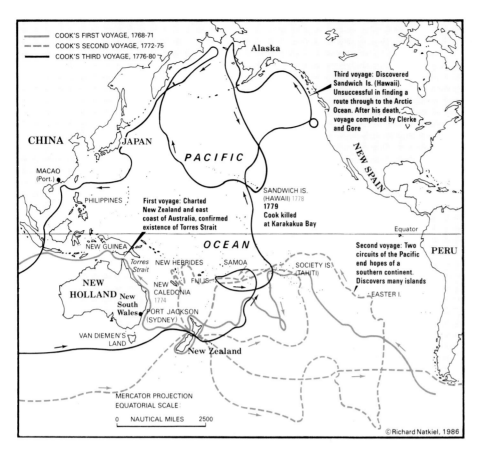

Map labels:
COOK'S FIRST VOYAGE, 1768-71
COOK'S SECOND VOYAGE, 1772-75
COOK'S THIRD VOYAGE, 1776-80

Alaska

CHINA
JAPAN
PACIFIC
MACAO (Port.)
PHILIPPINES

NEW SPAIN

Third voyage: Discovered Sandwich Is. (Hawaii). Unsuccessful in finding a route through to the Arctic Ocean. After his death, voyage completed by Clerke and Gore

SANDWICH IS. (HAWAII) 1778
1779
Cook killed at Karakakua Bay

First voyage: Charted New Zealand and east coast of Australia, confirmed existence of Torres Strait

OCEAN

Equator

Second voyage: Two circuits of the Pacific end hopes of a southern continent. Discovers many islands

PERU

NEW GUINEA
Torres Strait
NEW HEBRIDES
SAMOA
SOCIETY IS. (TAHITI)
NEW CALEDONIA 1774
FIJI IS.
EASTER I.
NEW HOLLAND New South Wales
PORT JACKSON (SYDNEY)
VAN DIEMEN'S LAND
New Zealand

MERCATOR PROJECTION
EQUATORIAL SCALE
0 NAUTICAL MILES 2500

for he brought the mind of a scientist and navigator to the task of exploration. Even today his surveys are remarkable for their accuracy, and his three voyages added enormously to Man's knowledge of the world. His navigational calculations also paved the way for more accurate navigation by enabling longitude to be calculated with precision.

the Antarctic Circle twice to avoid the possibility of missing any evidence of a southern continent.

Although his mission was technically complete Cook felt that his sound ship and healthy crew could achieve more, and he set off on another circuit of the Central Pacific, discovering many more islands. When he finally returned in July 1775 he was immediately promoted to post-captain and elected a Fellow of the Royal Society. Within a year he was sent on another expedition, this time to cross the Indian Ocean and to try to find the North West Passage.

Cook's third voyage seemed blighted from the start. The *Resolution* and *Discovery* were not properly refitted, and both ships suffered from constant defects. In spite of these problems the two ships discovered Hawaii, then named the Sandwich Islands, and reached Nootka Sound on the northwest coast of Canada. A brief survey of the coast of Alaska was made, but ice prevented a passage through the Bering Strait, so Cook sailed back to the Sandwich Islands to refit and repair the ships.

The second visit quickly turned to tragedy. Although Cook was regarded as a Polynesian god, whose return must be marked by plentiful gifts, the very magnanimity of the native priests and chiefs had strained local resources to the limit. When, therefore, HMS *Resolution* sprung her foremast two days after leaving Karakakua Bay and had to put back to repair the damage, her return in such ignominious circumstances was greeted with sullenness. It needed only a series of small thefts to turn the

ill-feeling into open fighting. Although Cook tried to keep the peace he was speared in a skirmish on 14 February 1779.

Despite the death of his leader, Captain Clerke of the *Discovery* continued Cook's work, and reached Petropavlovsk on the Asiatic side of the Bering Strait, but died of tuberculosis a month later. Lieutenant Gore brought the two ships home via Canton and the Cape of Good Hope, reaching London in October 1780.

Cook's achievements are without equal,

Below: **The death of Captain Cook.**

The Battle of Chesma

Although the armies of the Russian Empress Catherine the Great had scored great successes against Turkey in the Russo-Ottoman War, she was determined to use her naval power to drive the Turks out of Europe altogether. In the autumn of 1769 she sent three squadrons, a total of 12 ships of the line under Admiral Orlov from the Baltic to the Mediterranean. Orlov's squadron made a landfall at Navarino in the Morea (Peloponnese), where the Russians were soon able to foment a Greek revolt against the Turks.

Great Britain was sympathetic to the Russian aims and several officers including the Scot Vice Admiral John Elphinston, were serving in the Russian Mediterranean fleet. Elphinston's aim was to take his squadron of four ships of the line and supporting frigates through the Dardanelles to attack the Turkish fleet in the Black Sea. While approaching the straits his superior Orlov encountered the Turks on 6 July at Chesma (also rendered Chesme, Cesme, Tchesme or Tsheshme), a harbor on the Anatolian coast opposite Chios. The main Russian fleet included 9 ships of the line and 11 other vessels, while the Turks under Hassan Bey had 14 ships of the line and several frigates, as well as some 200 transports and storeships lying outside the harbor.

The firing was desultory at first, but after four hours the two flagships *Sviatoy Yevstafy* and *Real Mustapha* caught fire and blew up. The explosion was so enormous that the Turks retired in confusion and withdrew into Chesma. Most of the flagships' crews had been killed, but had the Turks known it, the Russian loss was greater than theirs.

Next morning Elphinston's squadron arrived, and under his energetic direction Lieutenants Dugdale and Mackenzie sailed fireships into Chesma harbor. At first the Turks welcomed them, thinking that they were deserters, but the strangers promptly ran alongside the nearest row of ships lying at their moorings, and lashed themselves alongside with grappling-hooks. Within minutes rockets and inflammable materials were being fired into the packed Turkish ships. An immense blaze soon engulfed the Turkish Fleet, and out of the holocaust only one 64-gun ship and a few galleys escaped.

With the Dardanelles undefended it was the moment to force the straits and even try to capture Constantinople, as Elphinston hoped, but Alexei Orlov was too cautious. While he wasted time besieging Lemnos, Turkey's French allies fortified the straits.

Within a few days Baron de Tott had improvized apparently impregnable defences with 30,000 soldiers to defend them.

For Russia it was to transpire to be the last chance of attacking Constantinople directly, but the victory was an important check to the military power of the Turks. The decline of Turkey continued into the next century, keeping Russian dreams of an outlet to the Mediterranean alive.

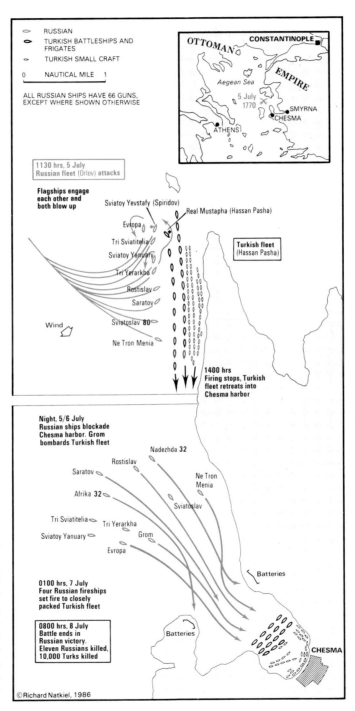

The American Revolution

The Battle of Chesapeake Bay

In 1780 the outcome of the War of American Independence was still in doubt, but early the following year France succeeded in equipping a large fleet of 26 ships of the line under Count de Grasse. This fleet sailed in March 1781 with a large convoy bound for Martinique, and on its arrival de Grasse received a dispatch from General Washington asking for immediate help in the siege of the British garrison of Yorktown.

De Grasse arrived with his fleet off the Chesapeake in August and immediately established a blockade. His aim was twofold: to prevent the Royal Navy from bringing supplies and reinforcements for the Yorktown garrison and to enable the Americans and their French allies to concentrate their land forces around the entrenchments.

As they were bound to, the British attacked as quickly as they could to aid the hard-pressed Yorktown garrison. On 5 September the British Rear Admiral Thomas Graves arrived with 19 ships of the line, bringing supplies for the garrison. At anchor inside Chesapeake Bay was de Grasse with 24 ships of the line, but Graves followed the Permanent Fighting Instructions to the letter and wasted time forming his ships into a line of battle.

The French weighed anchor and started to come out of the bay after mid-day, but it took Graves another four hours to come into action, allowing de Grasse plenty of time to out-maneuver him. Graves' main error appears to have been his angle of approach, which ensured that his rear squadron never came into action at all. In effect de Grasse and his ships were able to deflect the British squadron away from the entrance to Chesapeake Bay, and after desultory firing the action was broken off at 1830.

The French squadron returned to its anchorage six days later but the British were unwilling to renew the engagement. Many of their ships had been damaged and there was a shortage of bread and water. After a Council of War on board the flagship *London* Graves took his ships back to New York to repair the damage and prepare for a second attempt at relieving Yorktown.

It was a fatal miscalculation. In the meantime the French squadron at Newport, Rhode Island sailed for the Chesapeake, bringing the total French force up to 36 ships of the line. With his 19 ships Graves gave up all hope of breaking through, and that decision sealed the fate of Cornwallis and his garrison. Washington's troops were taken by sea to Williamsburg and then marched overland to Yorktown. Under the skilled hand of Washington's Prussian adviser Freiherr von Steuben the stranglehold was tightened until Cornwallis and his weary garrison surrendered on 19 October.

The paradox of the Battle of Chesapeake Bay (also known as the Battle of the Virginia Capes) is that it was such a minor battle, typical of many fought in the earlier years of the century between commanders of a cautious disposition. And yet the fate of British North America hung on the outcome. Although the British still held New York and were still in theory capable of defeating the Americans, the debacle broke the will of the British government to continue the war.

With the end of fighting in America the war was theoretically over but it continued until 1783. It was impossible to stop a worldwide campaign quickly, particularly when all messages had to go by sea. In the Indian Ocean Hughes and Suffren were to fight five fierce battles without either side conceding victory. In the West Indies the British and French continued to spar with one another to protect their sugar islands until Rodney's victory at the Saintes put an end to French naval aspirations.

Below: **Admiral Graves in 1795 after his distinguished service at the Battle of the Glorious First of June.**

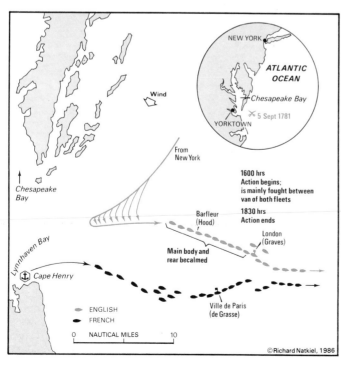

The Battle of the Saintes

The surrender of Yorktown in October 1781 marked the nadir of the Royal Navy's fortunes in the War of American Independence. Fighting the French in the Indian Ocean as well as the Atlantic, and its supplies of cordage, tar and timber threatened by the League of Armed Neutrality in the Baltic, the whole organization was under severe strain. Yet in spite of all its tribulations the Royal Navy rose to the challenge and brought off a brilliant counterstroke.

On 5 April 1782 Admiral Rodney learned that the French Admiral Count de Grasse and a combined Franco-Spanish squadron had sailed from Martinique. Rodney guessed correctly that de Grasse intended to attack Jamaica and determined to intercept the attack. Off the small group of islands known as the Saintes he finally managed to bring de Grasse to action, the French being impeded by the need to tow the damaged Zélé (she had been in collision three days earlier). At first Rodney was content to engage in succession but a sudden shift of wind enabled him to pierce the French line, and the orderly cannonade soon degenerated into a general action. Rodney had 36 ships to 30 French, and by breaking the French line he was able to concentrate overwhelming force against portions of the enemy fleet.

Although Rodney was in poor health his fleet was in first-class fighting condition. Not only were his men comparatively free of scurvy because of the use of anti-scorbutics but Rodney had also begun to adopt the radical reforms of the gunnery expert Captain Charles Douglas, captain of his flagship HMS *Formidable*. Douglas had the satisfaction of seeing the *Formidable*'s broadsides dismast a French ship as she passed through the line. Douglas had stepped up gunnery practice and had changed the guns' equipment to allow a more rapid rate of fire and a wider field of fire. These changes had been widely imitated in the fleet and French accounts of the battle were to stress the superior British gunnery.

The formation of de Grasse's fleet was totally destroyed, and in the confusion five ships of the line and the French admiral were captured. The flagship, the 100-gun *Ville de Paris* was the last to submit, at 1830. She fought with great gallantry, and sustained fire from seven British ships in succession. It is said that toward the end of the day her gun crews ran out of powder cartridges but continued loading the guns with handfuls of gunpowder scooped out of kegs in the magazine.

Rodney's energetic second-in-command, Sir Samuel Hood pleaded with him to allow a vigorous pursuit but the old admiral was content to round up the prizes, saying 'Come, we have done very handsomely.' He was right in a way, for the battle had put an end to French ambitions in the Caribbean. The tentative peace negotiations between Great Britain and the United States had already begun, and in the months after Yorktown it had looked to the British as if they might be forced to relinquish Canada. The news from the West Indies stiffened

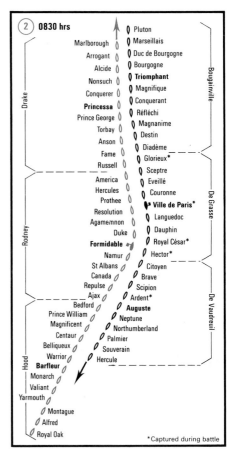

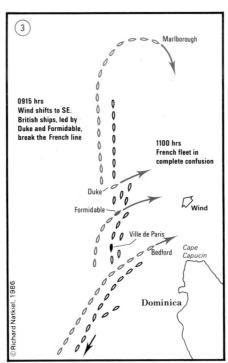

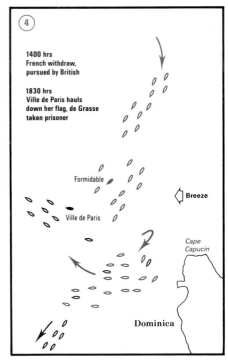

© Richard Natkiel, 1986

their resolve, and although peace did not come finally until 1783 the British were in a much stronger position.

Hood need not have fretted about his failure to capture more ships, for a week later his squadron made four captures, the 64-gun ships *Caton* and *Jason*, and a frigate and a corvette.

Although the War of the American Revolution had been a harrowing experience for the Royal Navy it served to eradicate many weaknesses in tactics and training. Political neglect and a tendency to bask in the glory of the Seven Years' War had reduced the Royal Navy's effectiveness but the frustrations and failures of 1776-82 generated reforms at all levels. Two important innovations were introduced, the carronade and coppering. The former, a short-barrelled but light gun of heavy caliber gave Royal Navy ships an important advantage in short-range fighting, while the technique of covering the bottom planking of ships with copper sheets prevented fouling by marine growths and protected the timber from wood-boring worms. A 'coppered' ship could remain at sea for up to six months without an appreciable loss of speed, and for the Royal Navy this meant an important freedom of action on the far side of the Atlantic.

War in Eastern Seas

At the time that de Grasse took the French Brest Fleet to American waters in 1781 a much smaller squadron was detached to the Indian Ocean via the Cape of Good Hope. The commander, Chevalier-commandeur Pierre-Andre de Suffren St Tropez was an experienced sailor, and during the next eighteen months he was to earn the reputation of being France's finest-ever admiral. Pausing only to take a Royal Navy squadron by surprise at la Praya in the Cape Verde Islands (for which he was promoted to Bailli in the Maltese order of chivalry), Suffren hurried on to India.

The French Indian squadron was in poor shape, but on the death of Admiral Count d'Orves, Suffren was able to impose his standards of leadership. In mid-February he sailed to Madras, offering battle to Admiral Sir Edward Hughes, who offset his 9:12 disadvantage in numbers by keeping under the protection of the shore batteries. But Hughes was Suffren's equal in seizing opportunities for action. As soon as the French squadron moved southward Hughes came out of Madras to try to attack the troop convoy. The Battle of Sadras was the result, on 17 February 1782. Although hard-fought by both sides the French failed to exploit

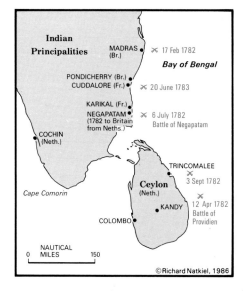

their tactical advantage, and the only positive result was that Suffren landed his troops to capture Cuddalore.

The next fight took place off the small island of Providien, south of Trincomalee on 12 April. Once again Suffren's bold handling of his fleet was frustrated by the timidity and ineptitude of some of his captains. Hughes in contrast kept his fleet in good order, and he emerged the victor by a small margin.

Suffren's biggest problem was the lack of a well equipped base. He had been sent out without spares and only low reserves of food and ammunition. With some help from his Indian ally Hyder Ali and some spars and cordage from the Dutch at Baticaloa he was able to refit his squadron for an attack on Negapatam in July.

When the French arrived off Negapatam on 6 July the British squadron was already putting to sea. As Hughes had the same number of ships he showed no hesitation in offering battle. Once again both sides fought hard, with two hours of fierce cannonading. The French *Brillant* had her mainmast shot away and drifted out of line to leeward with many casualties, and the *Sévère* also found herself between the two battle lines. Each ship was attacked by two British ships, and the *Sévère* struck her colors to HMS *Sultan*, but her officers repudiated their captain's

Left: **The two fleets open fire at the Battle of Negapatam, typical of the five hard-fought battles between Suffren's French and Hughes' British squadron.**

surrender and fought on. Their determination was rewarded by making good their escape.

The French had suffered more than twice as many casualties as the British but Hughes was also aware that his squadron had been badly knocked about. Suffren abandoned his attack on Negapatam and returned to Cuddalore. There he exerted his formidable powers of persuasion to get his battered ships repaired, and by August he was ready to head for Baticaloa, where he could cover the arrival of a fresh convoy from France.

The convoy was carrying troops under the Marquis de Bussy, and once the reinforcements had arrived Suffren was free to launch an attack on the English outpost at Trincomalee. He boldly dashed past the shore batteries and as soon as the troops were landed the enemy garrison surrendered. At last Suffren had gained a safe anchorage for his fleet.

Suffren's failing was impetuosity, and when Hughes appeared to be retiring from Trincomalee the French gave chase. But as Hughes had calculated, the poor French seamanship caused the pursuers to straggle, whereas his own ships remained in good formation, giving him the chance to attack a section in local superiority. Despite repeated signals from Suffren, Hughes was able to form his line of battle without hindrance. The *Heros, Illustre* and *Ajax* suffered more

than three-quarters of the entire French casualties during a fight which lasted nearly three hours.

With only two-fifths of their fleet engaged the French had little to be proud of, and Suffren's anger was not assuaged when *L'Orient* ran aground as she tried to enter Trincomalee. He wrote bitterly to the authorities in France, condemning his captains for incompetence, although his impetuous attack had been as much to blame for the outcome. The intemperate tone of their superior's complaints led at least one of his best officers to resign, a loss which Suffren could not afford.

The onset of the monsoon forced Hughes to withdraw to Bombay, while Suffren wintered at Achin in Sumatra, as Trincomalee was short of food. The French squadron was back in the Indian Ocean before the British. The troop convoy under de Bussy was at last close at hand but these welcome reinforcements were offset by British reinforcements under Rear Admiral Bickerton; Hughes now had 18 ships to Suffren's 15. Nor did things go well on land, once the troops had been put ashore. Hyder Ali had been succeeded by Tippu, who had shown no ability to withstand defeat at the hands of the British. To make matters worse Bussy proved lethargic, and by June the French land forces were once more besieged in Cuddalore.

The fifth and final battle was as hard fought and as indecisive as the rest. Suffren was determined to raise the siege of Cuddalore, and by clever maneuvering managed to slip past Hughes' squadron into the roadstead. After taking on some soldiers and sepoy gunners to make up for his depleted gun crews he stood out to sea once more to give battle. Despite the superior numbers of the enemy Suffren's captains managed to hold their formation and fought so stoutly that the two-and-a-half hour fight only ended with the fall of darkness.

Suffren never won a battle and failed to capture even a single ship of the line, but he deserves great credit for protecting not only French but Dutch possessions in the Far East. When his problems of supply and manning are taken into account his achievements are even more remarkable, and he deserves his reputation as the greatest French admiral of the century.

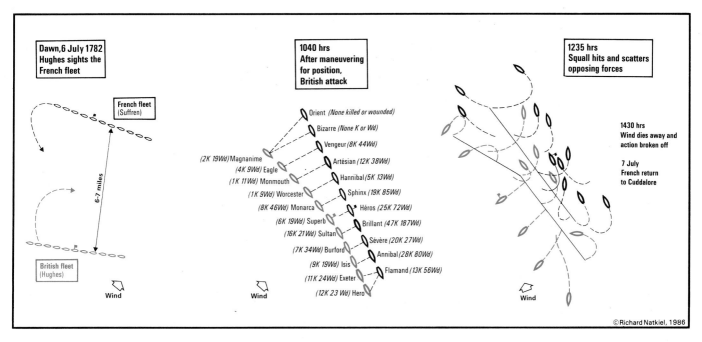

Dawn, 6 July 1782
Hughes sights the French fleet

French fleet (Suffren)

6-7 miles

British fleet (Hughes)

Wind

1040 hrs
After maneuvering for position, British attack

Orient *(None killed or wounded)*
Bizarre *(None K or Wd)*
Vengeur *(8K 44Wd)*
(2K 19Wd) Magnanime
Artésian *(12K 38Wd)*
(4K 9Wd) Eagle
Hannibal *(5K 13Wd)*
(1K 11Wd) Monmouth
Sphinx *(19K 85Wd)*
(1K 9Wd) Worcester
Héros *(25K 72Wd)*
(8K 46Wd) Monarca
Brillant *(47K 187Wd)*
(6K 19Wd) Superb
Sévère *(20K 27Wd)*
(16K 21Wd) Sultan
Annibal *(28K 80Wd)*
(7K 34Wd) Burford
Flamand *(13K 56Wd)*
(9K 19Wd) Isis
(11K 24Wd) Exeter
(12K 23 Wd) Hero

Wind

1235 hrs
Squall hits and scatters opposing forces

1430 hrs
Wind dies away and action broken off

7 July
French return to Cuddalore

Wind

© Richard Natkiel, 1986

HMS *Brunswick* breaks the French line at the Glorious First of June, from the painting by de Loutherbourg.

THE NAPOLEONIC WARS

Sea Power versus Land Power

What has come to be seen as a single 22-year conflict between Great Britain and France was in fact a series of wars, the Revolutionary Wars and the Napoleonic Wars. The Revolutionary Wars were fought by the monarchies of Europe against the Revolution. Fighting began in 1792 and the war became more general after the execution of Louis XVI in 1793. Then the Revolution gave way to the Directory, which was in turn swept away by Napoleon's rise to power. After a brief truce in 1802-03 war was resumed between Great Britain and the French Republic, which in 1804 was to become the Empire when Napoleon had himself crowned at Versailles.

Although the land campaigns against the French Revolution proved largely ineffective the Royal Navy rapidly shook off its peacetime lethargy and established a dominance which was at times shaken but never lost. The French Navy, with many of its aristocratic officers either in exile or guillotined, was in no shape to meet the highly professional Royal Navy on equal terms, and a blockade, applied even more rigorously than

in previous wars, kept the French fleet penned in its harbors except for rare forays which achieved little. Not even the mutinies on British ships at the main home bases at the Nore and Spithead in 1797 could be exploited by the French and their Dutch allies, and that chance never recurred. Shortly after the Nore mutiny was put down Admiral Duncan inflicted a terrible defeat on the Dutch at Camperdown, virtually destroying them as a naval power. Earlier that year France's Spanish allies had been severely defeated at Cape St Vincent, leaving the Royal Navy with no serious challengers to its control of the oceans.

Hemmed in by British sea power, Napoleon sought to project French military power with little success. In 1798 his occupation of Egypt was checkmated by Nelson's brilliant victory at Aboukir Bay. When he turned his attention to Northern Europe Denmark was swiftly knocked out and the Danish fleet was captured by Nelson.

Napoleon reigned supreme over Europe but the incessant blockade could not be offset by internal trade, and all France's nominal

allies and vassals became increasingly uneasy.

To enable resources to be replenished the Emperor negotiated the Peace of Amiens in 1802 but this was never more than a temporary truce and when hostilities reopened he soon put into effect his plan for a Continental System. Under this grandiose scheme British trade would be excluded from the continent of Europe, and heavy punishments would be inflicted on any nation caught trading with Perfidious Albion. It went wrong for two reasons; first, most European nations became increasingly restive under the harsh regulations needed to make the Continental System watertight, and second, the British were opening up new markets in North America, so did not rely exclusively on European trade.

Attempts to coerce his allies to keep to the system led Napoleon to put his brother on the throne of Spain in 1808, which immediately precipitated a Spanish popular uprising. The British were quick to profit by this blunder, and went to the aid of a nation that had once been France's most loyal ally. Britain's trade benefited greatly by contacts with Spain and

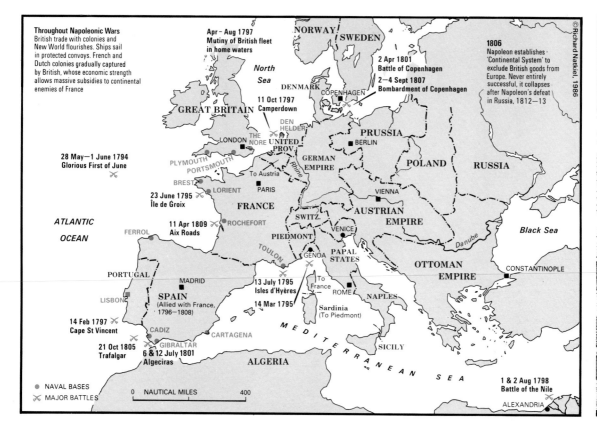

Spanish colonies in South America. Tiring of the long guerrilla war in Spain, Napoleon turned his attention to his Russian allies, and in 1812 began the fatal march on Moscow in a futile attempt to coerce the Tsar to adhere fully to the Continental System.

The war at sea lasted for nearly ten years after the destruction of the French fleet at Trafalgar in 1805, but control of the seas was never again in dispute. Despite the distraction of the 1812 war with the United States the Royal Navy slowly but surely tightened its grip on France. By 1814 the Duke of Wellington's army could cross the Pyrenees and invade France itself.

Against the military background it must also be remembered that Great Britain was reaping the benefits of the Industrial Revolution. Her factories were producing goods wanted by the whole world, making her proof against any continental blockade set up by Napoleon. Even more important, her banking and finances were far more soundly organized than those of the French, so that cash subsidies could be offered to any continental nation which opposed France. Industrial efficiency also ensured that the Royal Navy was maintained to the highest possible standards, with sound weapons and ships.

Top: British naval recruiting poster, 1804. A famous captain like Lord Cochrane could expect to complete his ship's crew without resorting to the press gang.
Above left: Capture of the Cape of Good Hope from the Dutch in 1806 by a squadron commanded by Sir Home Popham who also devised an improved flag signalling system for the Royal Navy.
Left: A satirical view of French invasion plans, referring to a famous reply in parliament by Admiral Lord St Vincent. 'I do not say that the French cannot come, only that they cannot come by sea.'

The Glorious First of June

Although the outbreak of the French Revolution in 1789 worried the British it was not until January 1793 when King Louis XVI went to the guillotine that the British government felt impelled to go to war. But the French National Convention pre-empted any decision by declaring war itself on 1 February.

The Royal Navy was outwardly weak in 1793, having dropped to a strength of only 20,000 sailors and marines since the end of the American War. With most of the 100 or more ships of the line laid up in reserve or in home squadrons it took time to recruit or impress enough seamen to send a squadron to the Mediterranean and to bring the Channel Fleet up to full strength. In fact the Channel Fleet Commander, Lord Howe, did not get his fleet to sea until July, when a blockade of the French Atlantic coast was instituted.

The economy of revolutionary France was in a parlous state, and the arrival of a large grain convoy was expected in the spring of 1794. Howe was cruising off Ushant when he learned that Admiral Villaret Joyeuse had taken the Brest Squadron to sea on 16 May, and immediately set off to find the French ships. After an indecisive action between the 74-gun ship HMS *Audacious* and the 110-gun *Revolutionnaire* on 28 May the two fleets remained close, but fog kept them apart for another two days. Not until 1 June did Howe finally sight the enemy fleet, and when the fog lifted the French were only six miles to leeward.

Howe's fleet formed line ahead and action was joined at 0900. Howe in his flagship *Queen Charlotte* made a determined effort to break the French line but as she passed under the stern of the French flagship, the 120-gun *Montagne*, she lost her foremast and was forced to remain on her opponent's quarter. From there, however, the *Queen Charlotte* directed such a hot fire on the *Montagne* that she was forced to bear away from the French line, and with that movement the French line began to lose cohesion. The rest of Howe's fleet was also hotly engaged. *L'Amerique* was battered to a hulk by the *Leviathan* and the *Marlborough* reduced *L'Impetueux* to sinking condition. The *Brunswick* and *Vengeur* battered each other for nearly three hours, and at the end the French ship sank. Her consort *Achille* had tried to come to her rescue but had been dismasted by a broadside from the *Brunswick* and was forced to strike her colors before the fleets drew apart.

There was considerable criticism of 'Black Dick' Howe when it was learned that the grain convoy had got through, although modern historians tend to be sceptical about the chances of strangling the Revolution in its cradle.

Even without the grain convoy the victory was impressive: the 80-gun ships *Juste* and *Sans Pareil*, and the 74s *Achille, Amerique, Impeteux, Vengeur* and *Northumberland* were either captured or sunk. It should have served as a warning to the hotheads in Paris that, in sea warfare, patriotism and revolutionary fervor were no substitute for basic seafaring skill and experience. It also demonstrated the Royal Navy's ability to make the transition from peacetime neglect and maladministration to wartime efficiency.

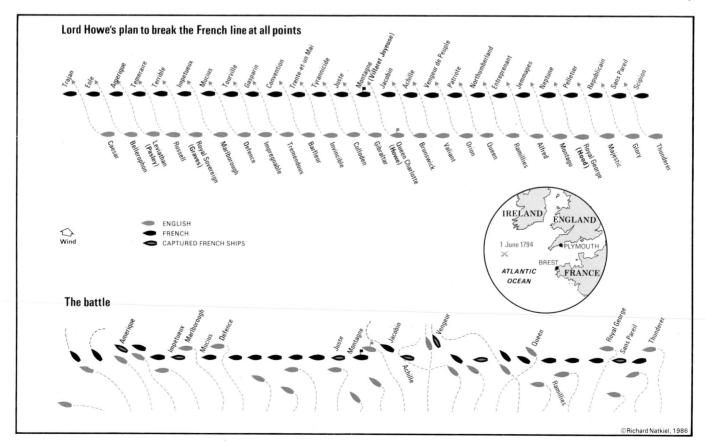

Lord Howe's plan to break the French line at all points

The battle

Wind
ENGLISH
FRENCH
CAPTURED FRENCH SHIPS

IRELAND ENGLAND
1 June 1794
PLYMOUTH
BREST
ATLANTIC OCEAN
FRANCE

© Richard Natkiel, 1986

The Battle of Cape St Vincent

By November 1795 the Jacobin cause seemed close to victory over its enemies, as one by one the enemies of France and the Revolution were defeated or driven to sue for peace. Holland was attacked in 1795, Spain reverted to the French alliance in 1796 and Genoa and Leghorn were persuaded by the French to close their ports to British shipping. Although the fierce ardor of the National Convention had given way to the corrupt government of the Directory the young Corsican general Buonaparte (as he spelled his name at the time) had started to win a series of astounding victories in Northern Italy.

Only Britain seemed prepared to stand firm. Despite prominent Whig 'croakers' who favored a negotiated settlement with France, the Admiralty was ordered to hold the Mediterranean, and to achieve that end the redoubtable Sir John Jervis was sent to take command of the Mediterranean Fleet at the end of 1795. His firm hand was needed, for the ships were worn out by constant patrolling and the men were wasted by disease. Jervis transformed the condition and morale of the fleet. Discipline, training and the supply situation were all overhauled. Long afterwards a French historian was to say that the Royal Navy's 'career of conquest' began on the day that Jervis hoisted his flag in HMS *Victory*.

Following Spain's switch of sides and under threat of an invasion of England, the Admiralty ordered a withdrawal of the Mediterranean Fleet to Gibraltar. Jervis had only 14 ships of the line against a combined Franco-Spanish strength of more than 30 ships, but when Jervis learned that a large fleet had been sighted on 13 February 1797 he did not hesitate to engage next day.

A large Spanish fleet was escorting a convoy carring mercury, essential for refining the silver from the New World. Admiral Don Jose de Cordoba had 27 ships of the line against 15 British ships, but the Spanish were desperately short of trained seamen, with as few as 60-80 per ship, the rest of the crews being made up of pressed landsmen and soldiers.

The British determination to break the Spanish line gave the Spaniards little room to maneuver as the British bore down on them from the north. At little more than six yards' distance HMS *Culloden*'s double-shotted broadside inflicted terrible punishment on a Spanish 1st Rate. An unlucky hit on the foremast of the *Colossus* caused her to swing

across the bows of the flagship *Victory*. Vice Admiral Moreno in the 112-gun *Principe de Asturias* thought he could break the British line but the British flagship refused to give way, and at the last moment as the Spanish ship altered course to avoid a collision she was shattered by more double-shotted broadsides.

A bold attempt by the Spanish Commander-in-Chief to concentrate fire on the British rearguard was frustrated by Admiral Nelson, who took his flagship, the 74-gun *Captain*, out of the line to engage the seven leading enemy ships. Jervis saw the movement and ordered other ships to support Nelson, but until they could get within range the *Captain* was in danger of being sunk by sheer weight of gunfire. Although badly damaged the *Captain* was run alongside the 80-gun *San Nicolas* and Nelson led boarding parties to capture her. They were then able to take the surrender of the *San Josef*, which was lying damaged on the other side of the *San Nicolas*.

When fighting stopped Jervis and his men had captured two three-deckers, the *Salvador del Mundo* and *San Josef* and two two-deckers, the *San Nicolas* and *San Ysidro*. Several other ships had surrendered, but

with so many British ships badly damaged and unable to board the prizes they had subsequently rehoisted their colors and rejoined their flagship.

St Vincent was a sorely needed victory. It prevented the proposed junction of the French and Spanish fleets for the invasion of England, and discouraged the French from taking independent action, even when the Channel and Nore fleets mutinied shortly afterwards.

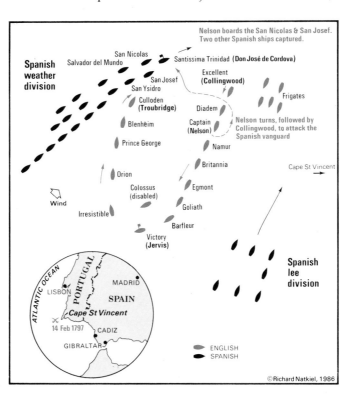

The Battle of the Nile

The first of Nelson's three great victories was in many ways the most interesting. Its strategic impact was more profound than Copenhagen or Trafalgar, for it shattered Napoleon's dreams of an Eastern empire. In the tactical sense it was most unorthodox, using double envelopment against an enemy at anchor, under cover of darkness.

Sir John Jervis, commanding the British fleet blockading the Spanish port of Cadiz, knew that the French were preparing to dispatch a fleet and landing force from Toulon under Napoleon's command. The task of finding out the destination of Napoleon's expedition was entrusted to Nelson, then a young and comparatively inexperienced rear admiral. His first landfall in Egypt found no French ships, but after a short search he found the fleet of Admiral François Brueys sheltering in Aboukir Bay, in what was clearly thought to be a safe anchorage. The French fleet consisted of the 120-gun flagship *L'Orient*; three 80-gun ships, *Franklin*, *Guillaume Tell* and *Tonnant*; nine 74-gun ships and four frigates.

The British, all 74-gun ships except the 50-gun *Leander* and the smaller *Mutine*, crept up both sides of the French line pouring broadside after broadside into the helpless French ships. During the night the French flagship *L'Orient* caught fire, and when the flames reached her magazine she was destroyed in a huge explosion.

When dawn broke the French fleet was in fearful disarray. Only the *Généreux* and *Guillaume Tell* and two frigates had made their escape; all the remaining ships were aground or lay dismasted and helpless.

This was the most decisive victory won by the Royal Navy to date, the sort of 'battle of annihilation' that Nelson dreamed of. Bonaparte abandoned his garrison in Egypt, leaving them to be mopped up later by the British. For Nelson it meant fame and fortune; he was made Baron Nelson of the Nile, Parliament voted him an annual pension of £2000, and the Honourable East India Company voted him an outright gift of £10,000. At the Battle of Cape St Vincent Nelson had shown great bravery but no greater tactical skill than his superior, Sir John Jervis, but the Battle of the Nile demonstrated his brilliance as a tactician and a leader.

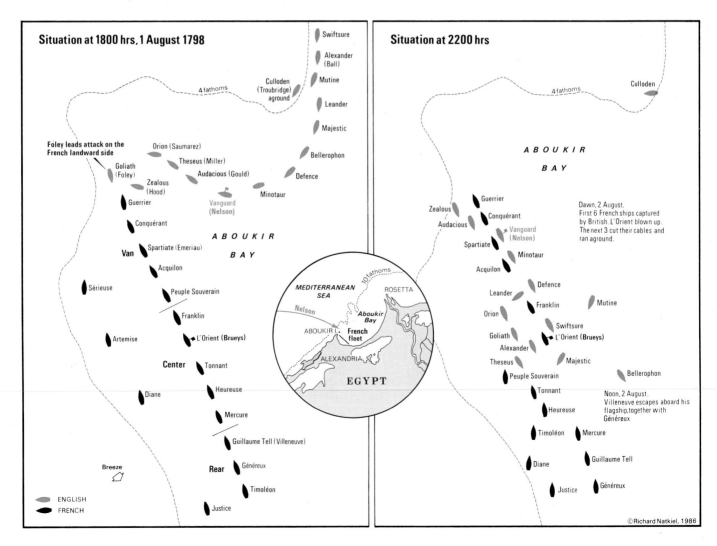

90

The Battle of Copenhagen

Napoleon's antidote to the successes of British seapower was a revival of an Armed coalition of the northern powers, such as had existed during the American Revolutionary War, under the auspices of Tsar Paul I of Russia. Although the mad Tsar Paul was assassinated before the anti-British coalition had any chance of being effective, and his successor Alexander I acted quickly to withdraw Russian support, Great Britain had already set in motion a counterstroke.

Admiral Sir Hyde Parker, with Nelson as his second-in-command was sent to the Baltic with instructions to attack each member of the coalition in turn until it was broken up. On 2 April 1801 Nelson led an attack on Copenhagen, where the Danish Navy lay behind the protection of forts and a line of floating batteries. The Danes had been chosen as the first target because their fleet was vulnerable to a takeover by the French, and it was felt essential to prevent that from happening.

Nelson's plan was audacious; using shallower-draught ships of the line and smaller vessels he would avoid the heavily defended northern end of the channel, putting his fleet behind the city and interposing his ships between the Danes and their allies. The nights of 30-31 March were spent in taking soundings in the channel, but as time was to show the survey was only barely adequate.

After a brief council of war aboard the flagship *Elephant* at 0800 the signal to weigh anchor was hoisted at 0930. The 64-gun ship *Agamemnon* was the first to run aground, and she was followed by the 74s *Bellona* and *Russell*. Despite the temporary loss of three powerful ships Nelson pressed on and by 1130 the battle was at its height. Admiral Parker, watching the fierce fighting, believed that his headstrong subordinate might be suffering unbearable losses and hoisted the recall signal (some authorities claim that he was merely offering Nelson an excuse to withdraw without incurring any accusation of cowardice). Whatever the explanation Nelson's reply was brisk; clapping his telescope to his blind eye, he announced that he could not see the signal, and the battle went on.

By the early afternoon the Danish line had mostly stopped firing and the flagship *Dannebrog* was in flames, but the forts were unharmed, and a number of Danish ships guarding the approach to the city itself were also untouched. Nelson, as good a diplomat as he was a tactician, seized the opportunity

Above: **Nelson turns a blind eye to Parker's recall signal.**

to negotiate with the Danish Crown Prince, offering to spare the city. In fact he used the breathing space to extricate his most badly damaged ships from the shoal water under the guns of the Trekroner battery. Three out of five ran aground, two of them only a mile from the fortress, but Nelson's bluff paid off, and the Danes agreed to an armistice.

Although rightly considered one of Nelson's three great victories the battle did little to reduce Denmark's naval aspirations, and as Nelson warned, the Danes were soon as strong as they had been before the battle. But

the resolute response to the threat posed by the northern coalition had the desired effect, and Napoleon's hopes of freezing British trade out of the Baltic suffered another setback. It was to be another eleven years before France's unwilling allies finally took action to rid themselves of their unwelcome guests, and another bombardment of Copenhagen in 1807 to put the Danish fleet beyond Napoleon's reach. (Map overleaf.)

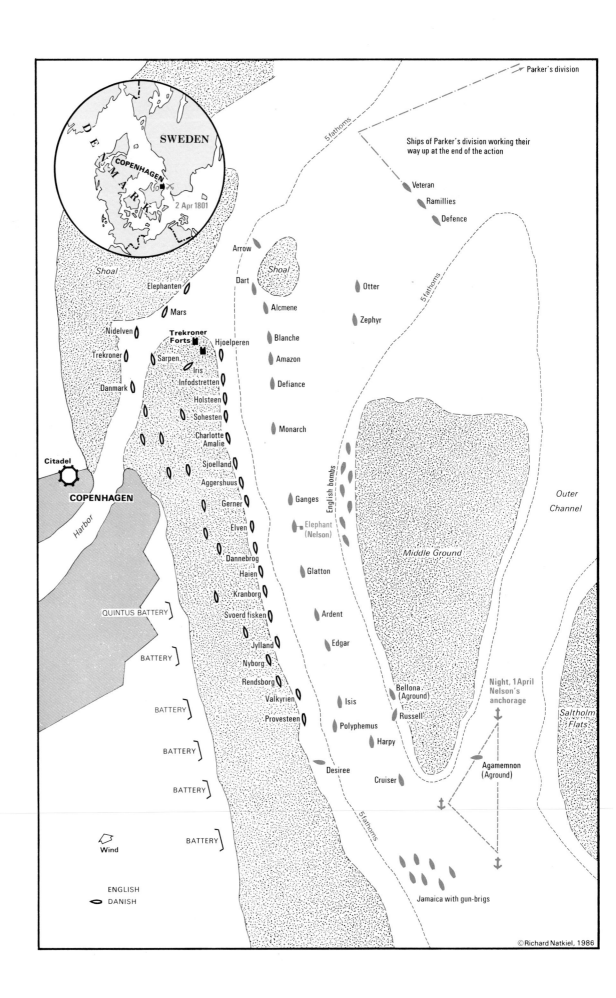

SWEDEN

COPENHAGEN

DENMARK

2 Apr 1801

Parker's division

Ships of Parker's division working their
way up at the end of the action

Veteran
Ramillies
Defence

Shoal

Arrow
Dart

Shoal

Otter

Elephanten

Alcmene

Zephyr

Mars

Nidelven

Blanche

Trekroner
Forts

Hjoelperen

Amazon

Trekroner

Sarpen

Iris

Defiance

Danmark

Infodstretten

Holsteen

Sohesten

Monarch

Charlotte
Amalie

Citadel

Sjoelland

COPENHAGEN

Aggershuus

Gerner

Harbor

Ganges

Elephant
(Nelson)

Elven

English bombs

Outer
Channel

Dannebrog

Glatton

Middle Ground

Haien

QUINTUS BATTERY

Kranborg

Svoerd fisken

Ardent

BATTERY

Jylland

Edgar

Nyborg

Rendsborg

Valkyrien

Bellona
(Aground)

Night, 1 April
Nelson's
anchorage

BATTERY

Isis

Russell

Saltholm
Flats

Provesteen

Polyphemus

Harpy

Agamemnon
(Aground)

BATTERY

Desiree

Cruiser

BATTERY

Wind

BATTERY

ENGLISH
DANISH

Jamaica with gun-brigs

5 fathoms

5 fathoms

5 fathoms

©Richard Natkiel, 1986

The Battle of Trafalgar

Following the brief Peace of Amiens in 1802-03 Napoleon returned to his grand design for the conquest of Europe. After his attempt to revive the Armed Neutrality was thwarted by Nelson's victory over the Danes at Copenhagen in 1801 he had to try other means to outflank British sea power.

Napoleon's new method was to be more sophisticated. An 'Army of England' was assembled in northern France, with a flotilla of flat-bottomed boats to transport it across the Channel. While the army was preparing to cross the Channel it was planned that small detachments of French and Spanish warships would slip out of their harbors and evade the British blockading squadrons. Once clear of the blockade they would head for a secret rendezvous and then swoop back on the Channel while the main strength of the Royal Navy was dispersed to hunt for them.

It was a preposterously complicated scheme, which took no account of weather and tides, nor of what the British might do. In fact the Admiralty ordered what had always been done in times of difficulty since the days of the Armada; its squadrons were ordered to fall back on the Channel, rather than be dispersed. There they were well placed to deny the French Army the clear fortnight it would need to get its 150,000 men across the Channel and could still maintain the blockade of Brest.

Nelson had been put in command of the

Mediterranean Fleet, with strict orders to prevent the French Toulon Fleet under Admiral Villeneuve from uniting with any other force. The French left Toulon in January 1805 and after a wild goose chase through the Mediterranean Nelson learned that Villeneuve had returned to port briefly but had left Toulon a second time, headed this time for the West Indies. In fact Martinique was the secret rendezvous, and Nelson pursued the French right across the Atlantic, so hot on Villeneuve's heels that the French admiral was forced to hurry back across the Atlantic. After a brief action off Cape Finisterre with a British force commanded by Sir Robert Calder Villeneuve abandoned the idea of putting into Ferrol, and slipped into Vigo instead.

Above: **Calder's inconclusive action with Villeneuve off Cape Finisterre.**

Nelson's chase across the Atlantic had dislocated the elaborate French plan. He discovered the secret rendezvous, had frightened Villeneuve into returning to Europe before the other detachments could join him, and had succeeded in getting the news of Villeneuve's return to the Admiralty before the French fleet reached Spain. Armed with that priceless information the First Lord of the Admiralty, Lord Barham,

Below: **Admiral Lord Barham never held a seagoing command after reaching flag rank but his strategic direction played a vital part in Nelson's victory at Trafalgar.**

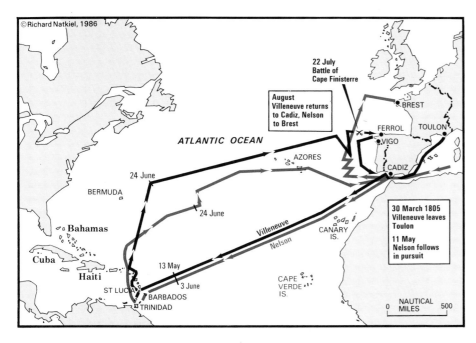

©Richard Natkiel, 1986

22 July
Battle of
Cape Finisterre

August
Villeneuve returns
to Cadiz, Nelson
to Brest

BREST

FERROL   TOULON

VIGO

ATLANTIC OCEAN

AZORES

CADIZ

24 June

BERMUDA

24 June

Villeneuve

CANARY
IS.

30 March 1805
Villeneuve leaves
Toulon

11 May
Nelson follows
in pursuit

Bahamas

Nelson

Cuba

13 May

CAPE
VERDE
IS.

Haiti

3 June

ST LUCIA

BARBADOS

TRINIDAD

0   NAUTICAL   500
     MILES

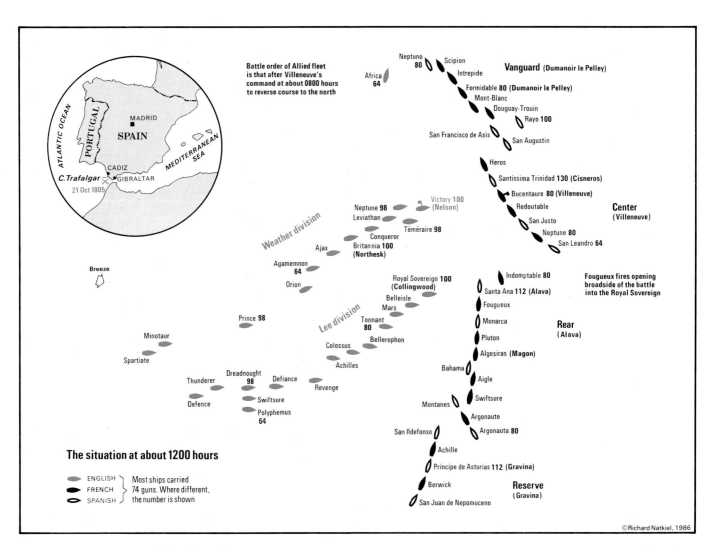

Battle order of Allied fleet is that after Villeneuve's command at about 0800 hours to reverse course to the north

Neptuno **80**
Scipion
Intrepide
Vanguard (Dumanoir le Pelley)
Africa **64**
Formidable **80** (Dumanoir le Pelley)
Mont-Blanc
Douguay-Trouin
Rayo **100**
San Francisco de Asis
San Augustin
Heros
Santissima Trinidad **130** (Cisneros)
Bucentaure **80** (Villeneuve)
Redoutable
Center (Villeneuve)
San Justo
Neptune **80**
San Leandro **64**

Victory **100** (Nelson)
Neptune **98**
Leviathan
Téméraire **98**
Conqueror
Britannia **100** (Northesk)
Ajax
Agamemnon **64**
Orion

Weather division

Royal Sovereign **100** (Collingwood)
Belleisle
Mars
Tonnant **80**
Bellerophon

Lee division

Prince **98**

Colossus
Achilles

Minotaur
Spartiate

Thunderer
Dreadnought **98**
Defiance
Revenge
Defence
Swiftsure
Polyphemus **64**

Indomptable **80**
Santa Ana **112** (Alava)
Fougueux
Monarca
Pluton
Algesiras (Magon)
Aigle
Swiftsure
Argonaute
Argonauta **80**

Fougueux fires opening broadside of the battle into the Royal Sovereign

Rear (Alava)

Bahama
Montanes
San Ildefonso
Achille
Principe de Asturias **112** (Gravina)
Berwick
San Juan de Nepomuceno

Reserve (Gravina)

Breeze

The situation at about 1200 hours

ENGLISH
FRENCH
SPANISH
} Most ships carried 74 guns. Where different, the number is shown

© Richard Natkiel, 1986

Inset map: ATLANTIC OCEAN / PORTUGAL / SPAIN / MADRID / MEDITERRANEAN SEA / CADIZ / GIBRALTAR / C.Trafalgar / 21 Oct 1805

---

was able to act vigorously to bring about the ruin of Napoleon's master plan.

What Barham did was to reduce the blockading force at Brest in order to concentrate a large force off the coast of Spain, where it was most likely to bring Villeneuve to action. The main strategic aim was to prevent the French from slipping back into the Mediterranean, and the British fleet was therefore divided between Ferrol and Brest.

Napoleon knew that his hopes of invading England were over, but to avoid the public humiliation of admitting defeat he continued to bombard the luckless Villeneuve with instructions to unite with Admiral Ganteaume's fleet at Brest. On 13 August 1805 Villeneuve got to sea but was forced to put into Cadiz, where a small Spanish squadron

was being watched by a British force commanded by Collingwood. With the main Franco-Spanish fleet now concentrated in one harbor all that remained for Barham to do was to appoint Nelson to command the fleet off Cadiz.

Villeneuve finally got his Combined Fleet to sea again in October, 18 French and 15 Spanish ships of the line against 27 British, and was sighted on the morning of the 21st. The British formed themselves in two columns as Nelson had planned, the port or Weather Division led by Nelson in the *Victory* and the starboard or Lee Division led

Left: **Admiral Villeneuve had led the only French ships to escape from Nelson at the Nile but was captured at Trafalgar.**

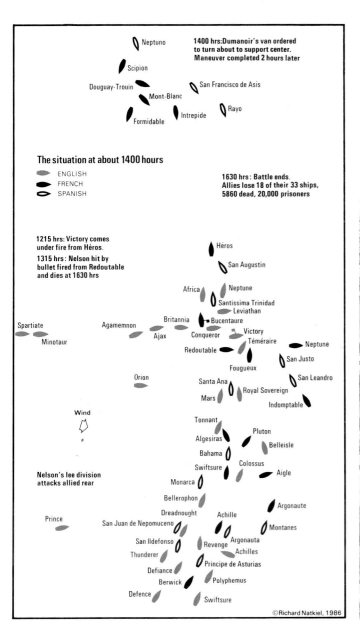

Neptuno

Scipion

Douguay-Trouin   Mont-Blanc   San Francisco de Asis

Formidable   Intrepide   Rayo

1400 hrs: Dumanoir's van ordered to turn about to support center. Maneuver completed 2 hours later

The situation at about 1400 hours

▬ ENGLISH
◣ FRENCH
◜ SPANISH

1630 hrs: Battle ends. Allies lose 18 of their 33 ships, 5860 dead, 20,000 prisoners

1215 hrs: Victory comes under fire from Héros.

1315 hrs: Nelson hit by bullet fired from Redoutable and dies at 1630 hrs

Héros

San Augustin

Africa   Neptune

Santissima Trinidad

Leviathan

Spartiate   Agamemnon   Britannia   Bucentaure

Minotaur   Ajax   Conqueror   Victory

Redoutable   Téméraire   Neptune

Fougueux   San Justo

Orion   Santa Ana   San Leandro

Mars   Royal Sovereign

Indomptable

Wind

Tonnant

Algesiras   Pluton

Bahama   Belleisle

Swiftsure   Colossus

Nelson's lee division attacks allied rear

Monarca   Aigle

Bellerophon

Prince   Dreadnought   Achille   Argonaute

San Juan de Nepomuceno   Montanes

San Ildefonso   Revenge   Argonauta

Thunderer   Achilles

Defiance   Principe de Asturias

Berwick   Polyphemus

Defence   Swiftsure

©Richard Natkiel, 1986

Above: **Nelson falls fatally wounded by a musket shot from a sharpshooter in the rigging of the French ship *Redoutable*. The unorthodox commander of the *Redoutable*, Captain Lucas, had concentrated the fighting training of his crew on small arms marksmanship.**

by Collingwood in the *Royal Sovereign*. In the light breeze the columns moved slowly downwind, while the enemy line lay apparently mesmerized. In theory Nelson's ships should have been annihilated by the enemy gunfire but Nelson knew that the French always fired high at the masts and rigging of enemy ships, and would be unable to destroy his columns before they had closed the range.

The British columns were punished heavily, but they held their fire until within a few hundred yards. The effect of their broadsides was all the more shattering at such close range, and it is said that a double-shotted broadside from the *Victory* killed 400 men aboard Villeneuve's flagship the *Bucentaure*. The Franco-Spanish line was broken in several places, and even though Nelson was mortally wounded by a sharpshooter firing from the rigging of the *Redoutable* at the height of the battle, the issue was beyond doubt. All around the French and Spanish ships were being devastated by disciplined gunfire.

By 1630 when the battle ended 18 French and Spanish ships had struck their colors (one of these had blown up), 11 had escaped to Cadiz and 4 more made off to the south. Several of the prizes were so badly damaged that they were scuttled, and other prizes were later able to make their escape after the small British prize-crews were overpowered. Although only four of the captured ships were brought into a British port, Trafalgar was a clear-cut victory which wiped out French hopes of winning a fleet action ever again.

It meant an end to French invasion plans, and virtually removed a number of other threats such as raids on the West Indies. The war would continue for another ten years but the outcome at sea was never again in dispute. Despairing of beating the British at sea, Napoleon was forced to turn to his Continental System in an attempt to cut them off from European trade. In the long run even that plan misfired, for it aroused the European nations against France, while the British developed other markets outside Europe.

The War of 1812

Washington and Baltimore

The War of 1812 between the United States and Great Britain arose out of a series of minor irritations. The British, in the final throes of their long war against Napoleon, were desperately short of trained seamen and suspected (probably correctly) that many had joined or deserted to American ships and were falsely claiming US citizenship. The Americans, ever watchful against what they perceived as John Bull's wish to recover his lost colonies, were incensed at British attempts to search their ships for deserters. The Royal Navy stuck to its demand for the 'right of search,' and undoubtedly there were some cases in which genuine American citizens were forcibly removed from their ships and impressed into the Royal Navy.

To complicate the issue President Madison was under pressure from 'hawks' in Washington who thought that the time had come to seize territory in Canada, while the British were unable to spare any troops from the continuing struggle with France in Europe. The British repealed the offending Orders-in-Council but it was too late, and war broke out in June 1812.

The initial results were contrary to both belligerents' expectations. The Canadian militia, with the help of only two regular British battalions, defeated the American regulars who invaded Canada, but the small American Navy scored a series of brilliant victories in single-ship actions. But the Royal Navy maintained a strict blockade of the US east coast, and by the end of 1813 American

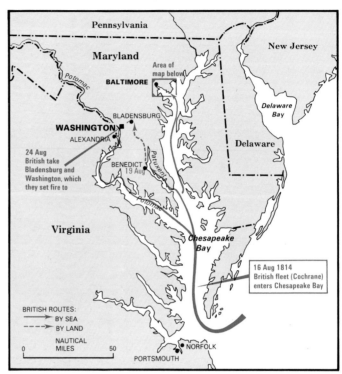

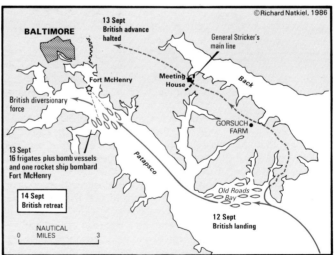

seaborne commerce was at a standstill and the Treasury was empty.

The British were determined to bring this irritating war to a conclusion and during the summer of 1814 as the war in Europe came to an end ships and soldiers could be spared. The new commander-in-chief on the North American station, Vice Admiral Sir Alexander Cochrane and his energetic second-in-command Sir George Cockburn were deter-

mined to strike a heavy blow against Washington, and by 16 August 1814 they had concentrated four battalions of seasoned British infantry and enough ships to threaten several points on the coast.

On 17 August small forces were sent up the Potomac and the Chesapeake, and a day later the main force was carried up the Patuxent to land at Benedict. Only six days later they administered a sharp defeat to the militia

96

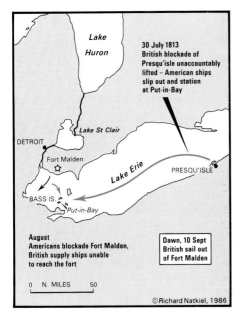

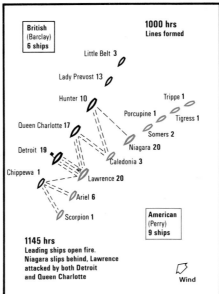

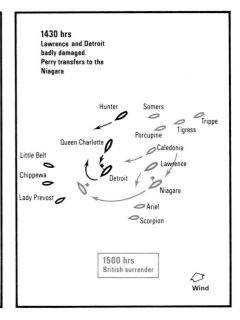

defending Bladensburg, and occupied Washington the same night. As a reprisal for the burning of Fort York (modern Toronto) the year before, Brigadier Robert Ross's troops burned the White House and other public buildings (those which the retreating defenders had not already put to the torch) and withdrew to the ships after only two days. To complete the Americans' discomfiture a force of two frigates and five bomb (mortar) vessels bombarded Fort Washington and took the surrender of Alexandria.

Cochrane wasted no time in mounting a fresh attack on Baltimore. On 11 September he entered the Patapsco River with 50 warships and transports, and next day the troops landed. They drove the defenders back in two skirmishes, but Brigadier Ross was killed by a sniper's bullet, and with his death energetic leadership of the landing forces seemed to vanish.

While the Army waited the Navy was asked to turn the Americans' flank, but Cochrane's bomb vessels could not get within decisive range to subdue Fort McHenry. The troops were deterred by a stolid defense by the Baltimore militia under General Stricker, and when a night attack by seamen was repulsed orders were given to abandon the entire operation. By 14 September the troops were re-embarked and the ships were on the way downriver. It was the bombardment of Fort McHenry with mortar bombs and rockets the night before which inspired Francis Scott Key to write his poem, 'The Star Spangled Banner' and set the words to the tune of a local drinking song.

The Battle of Lake Erie

As in the War of Independence the main British supply-route for an attack on the United States in the War of 1812 was inevitably the Great Lakes. In the first year of the war British General Brock had used his naval superiority on Lakes Huron and Erie to bring about Hull's surrender at Detroit. In contrast the new commander of the British naval forces on the Lakes, Sir James Yeo lacked both energy and tact. His American opponent, Captain Isaac Chauncey appeared to have demonic energy in building up a force of craft to dispute the possession of Lake Ontario, but as a strategist lacked the resolution to select the moment to fight. His only bold move, the sacking of York (now Toronto) merely lulled him into thinking that the British had been destroyed.

In fact both leaders were well matched in timidity, and Yeo and Chauncey remained content to fight skirmishes without risking all in a pitched battle. Both knew that the outcome of the fight for Lake Erie would be decisive.

The British position on Lake Erie was quite precarious, with a small margin of superiority which could be easily overtaken by the Americans. Every single item had to come from Lake Ontario to the east, while at the western end of Lake Erie General Proctor and his Indian allies had to be fed and supplied. The naval rivals were Captain Oliver Hazard Perry and Captain Robert Barclay, but Barclay's lack of adequate supplies and poor support from his land forces exacerbated an already unfavorable position. The worst example of non-cooperation was Proctor's failure to attack the poorly defended American base and shipyard at Presqu'isle at the eastern end of the lake.

Barclay tried to remedy the failure by blockading Presqu'isle from 20 July 1813. Historians still argue about Barclay's chances of stopping Perry by a daring attack on Presqu'isle, but clearly Barclay did not think

any landing could succeed, for on 30 July 1813 he inexplicably sailed away. Perry wasted no time in moving his ships across the bar on the night of 1/2 August. With his entire fleet out of the trap he now commanded the lake and established a new forward base at Put-in Bay in the Bass Islands.

Barclay now had no option but to fight, however unfavorable the circumstances, for Perry had cut his supply-lines. Battle was joined on 10 September 1813. By 1000 both sides had formed line of battle, and a fierce exchange of cannon fire began. Both sides fought with great ferocity. The new American ship *Lawrence* was almost destroyed by the *Queen Charlotte*, losing as many as 80 percent of her crew, but luckily for the Americans Perry remained unhurt, and he was able to transfer his flag to the *Niagara*. Aboard the British flagship *Detroit* Barclay was wounded five times but he was still in command, and by 1430 it looked as if he was the victor.

Barclay was soon disillusioned, however, for as soon as Perry boarded the *Niagara* he set course for the center of the enemy line, raking the bows of the *Detroit* and the *Queen Charlotte* as he crossed. His preponderance in trained seamen was crucial at this moment, and the inexperienced English and Canadian seamen, with most of their officers killed or wounded, could not respond to such a bold move. Resistance collapsed suddenly, with the surrender of the *Detroit*, *Queen Charlotte*, *Lady Prevost*, *Hunter*, *Chippewa* and *Little Belt*.

With the British Lake Erie squadron destroyed the Americans could now wipe out most of the British gains on land. Proctor and his Indian ally Tecumseh were defeated three weeks later and Detroit was recaptured. For the moment there were no British troops on American soil, and the way seemed clear for an assault on Canada. This was not to transpire but the Battle of Lake Erie was clearly a turning point in the war.

The Battle of New Orleans

Despite the British reverse at Baltimore Sir Alexander Cochrane continued to hatch ambitious plans, but without the large numbers of troops required these plans came to nothing. However he had sufficient forces to contemplate an attack on New Orleans, and from his new base in Jamaica he began preparations toward the end of 1814.

Various routes were open to the British, via Barataria, up the Mississippi, through Lake Borgne or via Mobile. Cochrane chose the Lake Borgne route as his ships were already in the sheltered anchorage at Ship Island, and his attack was started before the new army commander, General Sir Edward Pakenham, had joined him.

A small force of five oared gunboats under the command of Lieutenant ap Catesby Jones had to be dealt with before Cochrane's forces could advance on New Orleans. Hiding in the shallows they were able to keep track of the British movements and Cochrane felt obliged to deal with them before committing Pakenham's troops to a voyage in open boat across Lake Borgne. A large force of ships' boats was sent in on 14 December, and after a fierce fight the American flotilla was captured.

Although Catesby Jones had not handled his gunboats with any outstanding brilliance in their final action he had won six vital days for General Andrew Jackson, who used the time well to bolster the flimsy defenses of New Orleans, and to bring in reinforcements. The British build-up was also slower than anticipated, for there were insufficient flat-bottomed boats. The troops had to be ferried across Lake Borgne in successive batches, and not until 22 December were they ready to be ferried the last 30 miles across the bay and up the Bayou Bienvenu.

Pakenham caught up with his command on Christmas Day 1814, the day after peace was signed between Great Britain and the United States at Ghent. Neither of the combatants knew that the battle they were preparing to fight was pointless, for the frigate carrying the good news was still crossing the Atlantic. In ignorance, therefore, both sides continued to jockey for position, Pakenham probing the defenses in a somewhat half-hearted way and Jackson restricting himself to parrying each British move rather than take the offensive.

The one original move by the British was to dig a small canal from the bayou to the river to allow the ships' boats to be dragged along it. Despite this dangerous threat to his flank Jackson did nothing to impede it, but Pakenham decided not to exploit the advantage, and on 8 January 1815 launched his troops in a headlong frontal assault on the defenses of New Orleans. Pakenham's disciplined redcoats advanced in a tight formation on a front only three-quarters of a mile wide, but Jackson's militiamen and regulars backed by artillery, had little difficulty in repulsing the attack. Within half an hour Pakenham was dead and 2000 of his troops had been killed, at a cost of only 20 American casualties.

The reasons for Pakenham's mad attack have never been adequately explained, but friction between him and Cochrane is one of the most likely causes – he was also put in the unenviable position of having to fight on a battlefield virtually chosen for him by Cochrane. The weary British maintained their position before the defenses of New Orleans before deciding to withdraw to the ships. Even at this stage Jackson made no attempt to impede their withdrawal, and by 18 January all but the seriously wounded had got away.

Below: **Jackson's men repulse the rash British frontal attack on the defenses of New Orleans.**

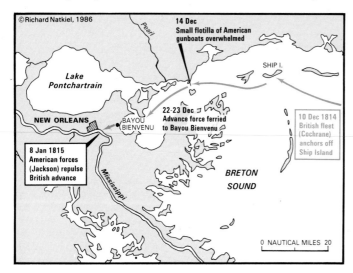

The World After the Napoleonic Wars

The end of the Napoleonic Wars left Great Britain the leading manufacturing country in the world, and with the removal of her great rival France from the scene, the greatest colonial power as well. However the pattern of European overseas possessions had been cast much earlier and remained largely unchanged. Britain kept Australia, Canada and India as her major possessions, but the former Spanish possessions in South America were in the process of casting off the colonial yoke, and would emerge as a series of independent countries. Similarly the Vice-Royalty of Brazil would not remain under Portuguese control for long. The Dutch retained the East Indies and some small possessions, but for the rest, European footholds around the world were no more than that, trading outposts or small settlements.

With her enormous navy Great Britain slipped easily into the role of international policeman. With a large merchant fleet, industrial pre-eminence thanks to the Industrial Revolution and as much overseas territory as she could conveniently administer she had no further territorial ambitions. The role also suited developing British political theories, which held that Free Trade was of universal benefit, and that continuing material progress would lead to the abolition of war. The policy of maintaining a near-mystical Balance of Power, although exemplified by Palmerston in mid-century, was a constant theme of British policy from 1815 until World War I. Although later dignified as 'Splendid Isolation' (the idea that Britain could stand aloof from Europe, needing no allies) it required frequent interventions in Continental quarrels, pledging or withdrawing support for temporary alliances to prevent any single power from controlling Europe.

Preserving the route to India was a cornerstone of British policy, and many possessions were acquired to serve as coaling stations. Another requirement which led to the acquisition of various harbors and bases was the fight against slavery. To provide employment for the large surplus of officers left over after 1815 the anti-slavery patrols off the African coast were stepped up, and they needed anchorages to refit and recuperate. The spread of underwater telegraph cables after the 1850s and the increasing importance of steamships also dictated the acquisition of cable and coaling stations at strategic points such as the Falklands.

In the 1830s France, having recovered from defeat, began to expand in North Africa. Although Algeria was nominally part of the Ottoman Empire it had long been virtually independent, and as related elsewhere, its piratical rulers had long been regarded as a dangerous nuisance by the European powers. However, for the moment the vast bulk of Africa, like China, remained virtually unknown to the rest of the world.

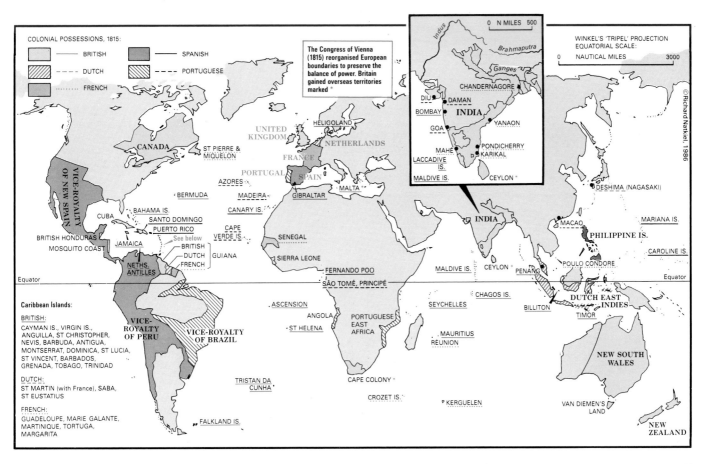

99

The devastation of the Turkish fleet at the
Battle of Navarino in 1827.

PAX BRITANNICA

The Bombardment of Algiers

With the end of the long wars against France the Royal Navy was at last free to turn its attentions to the 'Barbary Corsairs.' For five centuries the North African ports of Algiers, Bone, Salli, Tripoli and Tunis had been bases for Muslim pirates preying on Mediterranean shipping.

The depredations of the 'Algerines' took them far afield. In 1631 they sacked Baltimore in Ireland and sold the population as slaves in Algiers. During the first half of the seventeenth century more than 20,000 Christian slaves are reputed to have been sold in Algiers alone. Piracy declined during the eighteenth century, but it was not eliminated. In 1801-05 in the Tripolitan War and again in 1815 the Americans undertook naval operations against the corsairs, who had understandably tried to take advantage of the war between Great Britain and France, knowing that warships could not be spared to come after them.

The successful commander-in-chief of the British Mediterranean Fleet Sir Edward Pellew was created Lord Exmouth, and in 1816 he was ordered to bring the Barbary Coast under control. Two visits to Tripoli and Tunis were sufficient to persuade the local rulers to release large numbers of Christian slaves as well as to promise to abolish slavery. A similar visit to Algiers obtained the release of a large number of captives but the Dey of Algiers refused to give an undertaking to abolish slavery.

Exmouth's orders gave him no further

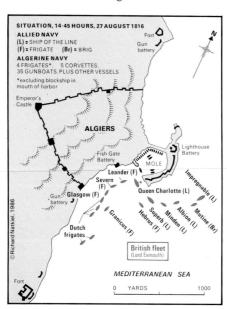

discretion so he returned to England, but shortly after his return it was learned that Turkish troops at Bone had massacred the crews of some Corsican and Sicilian fishing vessels. Coming so soon after Exmouth's mission, this callous act stiffened the resolve of the British government and Exmouth was sent back to the Mediterranean to administer a further lesson to the Dey of Algiers.

The squadron left Plymouth at the end of July 1816: five ships of the line, five frigates and seven smaller warships, with Exmouth flying his flag in the 100-gun *Queen Charlotte* and his second in command, Rear Admiral David Milne flying his flag in HMS *Impregnable* (98 guns).

When the squadron arrived at Gibraltar on 9 August it was joined by a Dutch squadron of six ships under Baron van de Capellan, and five days later the joint force set sail for Algiers, arriving on 27 August after delays caused by head winds. Exmouth sent a demand to the Dey of Algiers, ordering him to release all Christian captives, and comply with previous demands.

No answer was received, presumably because the Dey trusted his fortifications, which boasted some 1000 guns of various calibers. That afternoon Exmouth brought the Anglo-Dutch force into position, close enough to the batteries to ensure accurate shooting. At about 1430 two guns ashore fired, to which the *Queen Charlotte* replied with a full broadside. As the warships opened a heavy fire the Algerian gunners tried to reply but the steady British and Dutch fire caused heavy casualties and numerous guns were dismounted.

A flotilla of Algerian gunboats tried to counterattack but these were all sunk before they could get alongside to board. After some two hours of firing the flagship sent away her barge to board an Algerian frigate, while the rest of the force opened fire on ships moored in the harbor. By 1800 most of the Algerian ships were on fire.

As night fell the firing slackened but Exmouth did not withdraw his fleet until midnight. His ships were intact but several had been hit; in particular the *Impregnable* had been knocked about, largely because Admiral Milne had positioned her badly, suffering numerous dead and wounded. In all the British lost 128 killed and 690 wounded, while the Dutch lost 13 dead and 52 wounded.

The next day the squadron stood in to renew negotiations with the Dey, who with

Above: Admiral Lord Exmouth had led a notable career throughout the Napoleonic Wars having been Commander in Chief of British naval forces in the East Indies, the North Sea and finally in the Mediterranean.

his fortifications in ruins and most of his ships sunk, showed more willingness to comply with Exmouth's demands. In all 1600 captives were released, most of them Sicilian and Neapolitan sailors and an undertaking was given to stop the taking of Christian slaves.

The action was remarkable for its boldness in facing powerful shore batteries, and also for the fact that it succeeded in its ultimate purpose. Never again would piracy on the Barbary coast be a menace to international shipping; in the 1830s the French occupation of Algeria stamped out the last remnants. The bombardment also marks the formal beginning of the *Pax Britannica*, which was to be refined into 'gunboat diplomacy,' with warships of the Royal Navy being sent to potential trouble spots in a policing role or as a peacekeeping instrument to the end of the century.

SITUATION, 14·45 HOURS, 27 AUGUST 1816
ALLIED NAVY
(L) = SHIP OF THE LINE
(F) = FRIGATE (Br) = BRIG
Gun battery
ALGERINE NAVY
4 FRIGATES*, 5 CORVETTES, 35 GUNBOATS, PLUS OTHER VESSELS
*excluding blockship in mouth of harbor

Fort
Emperor's Castle
ALGIERS
Fish Gate Battery
Lighthouse Battery
MOLE
Leander (F)
Severn (F)
Gun battery
Glasgow (F)
Queen Charlotte (L)
Impregnable (L)
Mutine (Br)
Albion (L)
Minden (L)
Superb (L)
Hebrus (F)
Granicus (F)
Dutch frigates
Fort

British fleet (Lord Exmouth)

MEDITERRANEAN SEA

0   YARDS   1000

©Richard Natkiel, 1986

The Battle of Navarino

The first nationalist uprisings in 1821 by the Greeks against their Turkish rulers touched off a wave of sympathy in Britain and France, whose cultural traditions enshrined respect for ancient Hellenic values, and in Russia, through sympathy for fellow-members of the Orthodox Church. For six years a desultory war went on between badly-led Turkish forces and daring but ill-disciplined Greek irregular forces, who were helped by funds and volunteers from Western Europe but not overtly supported by any of the Great Powers.

Only when the Sultan of Turkey called for help from his vassal the ruler of Egypt, Mehemet Ali, did Western and Russian intervention become likely. Mehemet Ali and his stepson Ibrahim Pasha commanded an efficient army and navy, and were likely to crush Greek resistance without difficulty. Although Russia was clearly eager to intervene, the British and French governments were reluctant to initiate any action which could weaken Turkey, which was the traditional buffer keeping Russia out of the Mediterranean.

Against this uncertain background, in the autumn of 1827 three allied squadrons, one British comprising four ships of the line, three frigates and four smaller warships under Admiral Sir Edward Codrington, one French, comprising four ships of the line, a frigate and two smaller ships under Contre-Amiral Comte de Rigny, and a Russian force of four ships of the line and four frigates under Rear Admiral Count de Heyden, were sent to the Eastern Mediterranean. Their mission was the almost impossible task of forcing an armistice on the Greeks and Turks without any fighting.

The Egyptian and Turkish fleets lay in Navarino Bay on the west coast of the Morea, ready to support a land attack on the Greeks at Patras. The combined fleet of seven ships of the line, 15 frigates, 26 corvettes and 17 smaller vessels was moored in a semi-circle in the bay, and after a warning to Ibrahim to stop his army from devastating the Morea, on 20 October Codrington ordered the allied ships to position as to prevent the Egyptian and Turkish ships from getting to sea. The fleet was to enter in two columns, the British leading the French in one, and the Russians forming the second, but the Russians finally formed up astern of the French. In an ominous hush the British 44-gun frigate *Dartmouth* sent a boat to insist that a Turkish fireship should keep its distance. Suddenly a

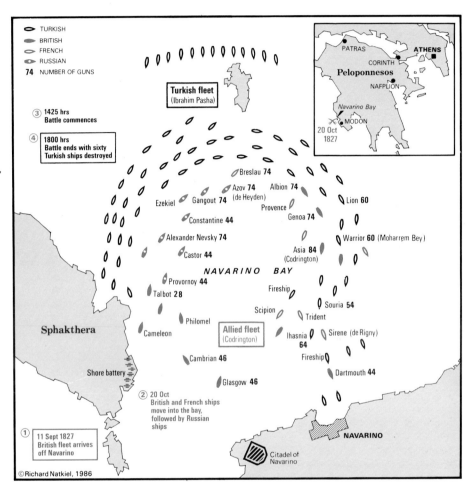

shot was fired at the boat, and then a French boat from the French flagship, the frigate *Sirène*, trying to explain that the allied ships had orders not to fire first, was fired on, killing the messenger.

The waiting British and French gun crews immediately replied with a heavy fire, blanketing the scene with heavy smoke. Although numerically superior the Egyptians and Turks were no match for well trained gunners and seamen, and after some two-and-one-half hours of heavy firing all that remained of Ibrahim Pasha's fleet was a handful of transports and small ships, all of which were destroyed the next day. Apart from a Turkish frigate which struck her colors to the *Armide* the majority of Egyptian and Turkish ships fought until they were sunk or set on fire by their own officers to avoid capture.

The Russians took a long time to come into action, partly because of the thick smoke

obscuring visibility, but also because of their lack of practice in sailing in formation. The British ships bore the brunt of the action and so suffered the most casualties, whereas the French and Russians suffered rather less. Several ships were damaged but not severely.

Navarino was the last of the traditional battles under sail, a slogging match fought at close range with virtually no tactical maneuvering once action was joined. Although embarrassing to the British and French governments, Codrington's victory was so popular that an attempt to censure him for disobeying orders could only be pressed half-heartedly. However far-sighted the statesmen might be in propping up Turkey, the public recognized that the threat to Greek independence had been destroyed, and welcomed it as a decisive victory. Four years later Codrington was appointed to command the Channel Squadron, in belated recognition of his achievement.

Antarctic Exploration

Exploration of Antarctica had to wait until comparatively late. Unlike the Arctic there was no quest for a North-West or North-East Passage, only the fabled 'Terra Australis' to tempt explorers into the barren southern wastes.

Captain Cook's voyage of 1772-75 did much to dispel ignorance about the 'Southern Continent' but serious exploration did not begin until the following century.

In July 1819 the Russian naval officer Thaddeus Fabian von Bellingshausen left the Baltic in command of the sloop *Mirny*, in company with the *Vostok* under Lieutenant Lazarev. His instructions from Tsar Alexander I were to circumnavigate the world, following largely in Cook's wake.

The expedition reached South Georgia in December 1819, where the surveyors completed the survey left unfinished by Cook. Then followed a survey of the South Sandwich Islands, which confirmed that they did not form part of the Antarctic continent. Although the Russians sighted the cliffs of what is now known as Queen Maud Land and penetrated farther south than any previous explorers, nearly reaching Enderby Land, Bellingshausen received virtually no recognition from his contemporaries.

There was now considerable interest in sealing and whaling in Antarctic waters, and the gaps in the charts of Antarctica began to be filled. An additional scientific motive was the need to locate the south magnetic pole, and three national expeditions were dispatched between 1837 and 1843, the French sending Dumont d'Urville, the Americans sent Lieutenant Wilkes and the British followed by sending Captain James Clark Ross in 1839.

Dumont d'Urville failed in his attempt to penetrate the Weddell Sea and again on a second attempt, when he hoped to find the south magnetic pole, but he did make a major discovery, Adelie Land. Wilkes' expedition, which coincided with the French, also failed to get through the Weddell Sea but reached 70 degrees South. The Admiralty expedition succeeded in forcing its way into what is known today as the Ross Sea and discovered Victoria Land and the Ross Ice Shelf. A second expedition by Ross in 1842 failed to penetrate the Weddell Sea as he had hoped but he had found the shortest way to the South Pole.

These late eighteenth century and early nineteenth century expeditions were not to be surpassed for nearly 50 years. Like contemporary Arctic expeditions they were hampered by the lack of knowledge about nutrition and the inescapable need to rely on sailpower. Scurvy was poorly understood, and a severe outbreak could easily cripple an expedition.

The first steam vessel to go to Antarctica was HMS *Challenger* in 1874. Thereafter renewed interest in developing a whaling industry led to a number of commercial expeditions, which in turn led to the so-called 'heroic' period of exploration, which culminated in the discovery of the South Pole by Amundsen in December 1911.

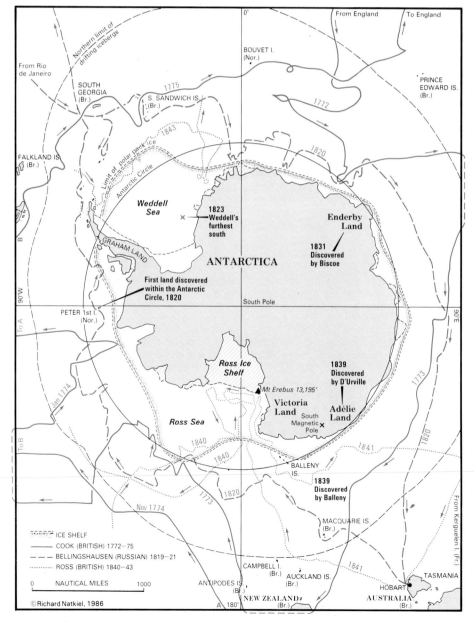

Opening up the Arctic

The first half of the nineteenth century saw a revival of interest in Arctic exploration to equal the attention being given to the Antarctic and reminiscent of the Elizabethan efforts to discover a North West Passage (*see* Chapter 3). Numerous voyages were made as part of the ongoing effort, in which the British Admiralty played a leading part, to survey systematically the whole of the world's oceans and make the resulting charts available to all mariners.

A token of this connection is that Sir William Parry, who led two important Arctic expeditions in 1819-20 and 1821-2, later became Hydrographer to the Navy or head of the British surveying department and while in this post led further, less successful, expeditions in 1823-5 and 1827.

A further notable expedition was led by Sir John Ross in 1829-33 with his nephew, James Clark Ross, later famed for his Antarctic explorations, as second-in-command.

Somerset Island and the Boothia Peninsula were explored and, while the expedition's ship *Victory* was iced in off the Boothia Peninsula, James Ross became the first to locate the North Magnetic Pole.

The most famous of the Arctic expeditions was the Franklin expedition in 1845. Sir John Franklin and his two ships were last seen on 26 July at the head of Baffin Bay.

During the next 14 years no fewer than 39 expeditions were sent to find the Franklin expedition, and finally Leopold McLintock in the steam yacht *Fox* found a logbook in 1859. It confirmed that Franklin's ships had been frozen in the ice near King William Island. After 18 months of deteriorating health through malnutrition the survivors had tried unsuccessfully to march to safety.

It was left to Captain Robert McClure in HMS *Investigator* to find the North West Passage. He sailed through the Prince of Wales and McClure Straits in 1850, but the ship was abandoned in Mercy Bay in 1853, and he and his men suffered badly from scurvy before they were rescued by Captain Kellett in HMS *Resolute*. Captain Richard Collinson had set out with McClure but their ships became separated en route. Collinson spent over three years in the Arctic and he too found a possible route for a North West Passage but McClure had clearly been first.

What defeated the search for the North West and North East passages was the near impossibility of penetrating thick polar ice. The problem was not capable of solution until the third quarter of the twentieth century, when nuclear-powered icebreakers became available. Ironically it is the harder North East passage which is now open, as Russian icebreakers are able to force a passage for shipping between Murmansk and Siberia.

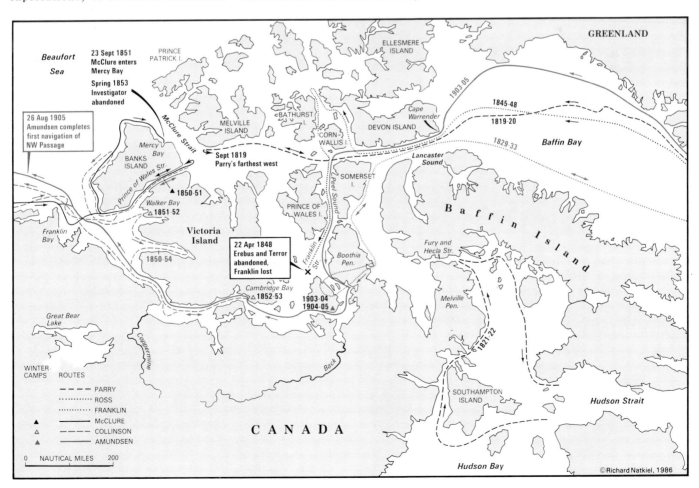

The Bombardment of Acre

Although nominally subordinate to Turkey, Egypt was governed by independent viceroys whose power was virtually independent of the Sultan's. Under Mehemet Ali's rule Egypt's naval and land forces became efficient, due partly to the effect of European officers brought in to raise standards, whereas Turkish military efficiency remained low. Already alarmed by Mehemet Ali's intervention in the struggle for Greek independence, the European powers continued to watch Egypt's growing power with concern.

In June 1839 Mehemet Ali's stepson, Ibrahim Pasha, the commander who had been defeated at Navarino, drove the Turks out of Syria and defeated a counterattack at the battle of Nizib. Shortly afterwards the Turkish fleet at Alexandria fell into Egyptian hands, giving Ibrahim even greater prestige.

Turkey was powerless to intervene, with a 16-year old Sultan newly succeeded to the throne, and in an attempt to redress the balance Britain, Austria, Prussia and Russia stepped in. France, suspicious of the other Powers' motives, refused to join in any action against the Egyptians, but could not stop the intervention. Under Foreign Secretary Palmerston's vigorous leadership France's efforts to support Mehemet Ali were outflanked by the British, with the brusque assurance that France's Egyptian protégé would 'just be chucked in the Nile.'

Under Admiral Stopford a powerful squadron was assembled to expel an Egyptian force from Acre (now Akko in Israel); it included a small number of Turkish and Austrian ships in two divisions. At dawn on 4 November 1840 the British flagship HMS *Princess Charlotte* (104 guns) took the ships of the North Division down the coast off Acre, while the Austrian *Medea* and the South Division moved in from the southwest.

The bombardment began at 1400 and proceeded in desultory fashion until a powder magazine blew up. When the Egyptian defenses of the ancient Crusader fortress appeared to be silenced landing parties were sent ashore, including British sappers to breach the walls. Resistance was not prolonged, and under cover of darkness Ibrahim Pasha's garrison, some 500 men, evacuated the city and made their escape.

The capture of Acre brought to an end nearly two months of naval operations off Syria. The Egyptians eventually evacuated Syria, and the following year Mehemet Ali agreed to return the ex-Turkish ships to the Sultan. In return he was granted independent sovereignty over Egypt with the title of Khedive for himself and his descendants.

This somewhat obscure action was the last for which the Royal Navy's General Service Medal was issued. Despite the limited nature of the bombardment it was an outstanding example of the moral effect of naval intervention; Mehemet Ali remarked that he could do nothing without British friendship, but with it he could achieve anything.

Below left: **Ibrahim Pasha (1789-1848) who was defeated at both Navarino in 1827 and at Acre in 1840.**

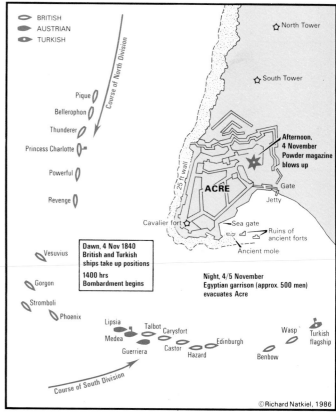

BRITISH
AUSTRIAN
TURKISH

North Tower

South Tower

Course of North Division

Pique
Bellerophon
Thunderer
Princess Charlotte
Powerful
Revenge

Afternoon,
4 November
Powder magazine
blows up

257 wall

ACRE

Gate
Jetty

Cavalier fort
Sea gate
Ruins of ancient forts
Ancient mole

Vesuvius

Dawn, 4 Nov 1840
British and Turkish
ships take up positions

1400 hrs
Bombardment begins

Night, 4/5 November
Egyptian garrison (approx. 500 men)
evacuates Acre

Gorgon
Stromboli
Phoenix

Lipsia
Talbot
Carysfort
Medea
Guerriera
Castor
Hazard
Edinburgh
Benbow
Wasp
Turkish flagship

Course of South Division

©Richard Natkiel, 1986

The Opium Wars and the China Trade

By the beginning of the nineteenth century China was approaching a crisis. Until the seventeenth century she had been in many ways more advanced than the West, and during the next hundred years the new Manchu dynasty's armies achieved even higher levels of prosperity by adding vast tracts of new territory in central Asia. By 1800, however, this prosperity was fading.

What was not changing was the usual Chinese perception of the outer world. The ruling class was nurtured in an unquestioning belief in Chinese supremacy, and an increasingly inward-looking society remained unaware of technological developments in Europe. Thus when European traders appeared in increasing numbers they were belittled as barbarians, and were not recognized as the harbingers of irreversible change which they were. Chinese diplomats were totally unable to comprehend the nature of the challenge from the West and the nation's institutions were therefore not modernized to meet it.

Although external trade was brisk, particularly the export of Chinese tea, it did China a great deal of harm. An acute shortage of silver, previously the only acceptable form of payment, led the Chinese to accept payment in opium, and the British Honourable East India Company astutely planted large quantities of opium poppies in India to cater for the demand for the drug, which soon became insatiable. The authorities in Peking were fully aware of the appalling effects of opium addiction, and tried hard to suppress it, but this brought them into conflict with the sacred rights of Free Trade. This was the era of the fast clipper, carrying opium from Bombay to Canton and tea from Canton to London.

Local friction over opium trafficking led to open warfare at Canton in 1839, and in a desultory campaign lasting three years the British defeated the Chinese decisively. Under the Treaty of Nanking, signed in August 1842 China was forced to cede the island of Hong Kong and to grant trading concessions at five ports, in addition to paying a heavy indemnity.

The defeat weakened Imperial prestige,

Right: Chinese government junks make an unsuccessful attempt to capture a British passenger steamer, *Flying Horse*, in the Canton River in 1856. This was one of a number of such incidents which led to the Second Opium War.

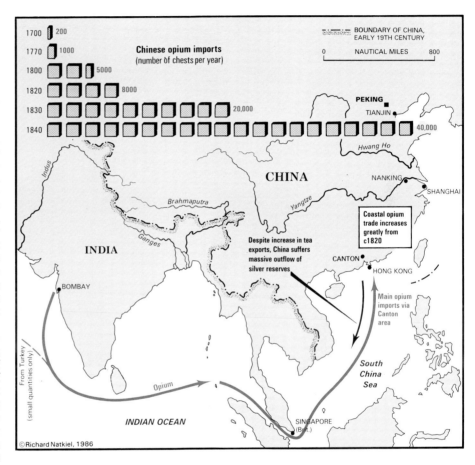

Chinese opium imports
(number of chests per year)

1700	200
1770	1000
1800	5000
1820	8000
1830	20,000
1840	40,000

BOUNDARY OF CHINA, EARLY 19TH CENTURY

0 NAUTICAL MILES 800

PEKING
TIANJIN
Hwang Ho
CHINA
NANKING
SHANGHAI
Brahmaputra
Yangtze
Coastal opium trade increases greatly from c1820
Despite increase in tea exports, China suffers massive outflow of silver reserves
CANTON
HONG KONG
INDIA
Ganges
Indus
BOMBAY
Main opium imports via Canton area
South China Sea
From Turkey (small quantities only)
Opium
INDIAN OCEAN
SINGAPORE (Brt.)

© Richard Natkiel, 1986

107

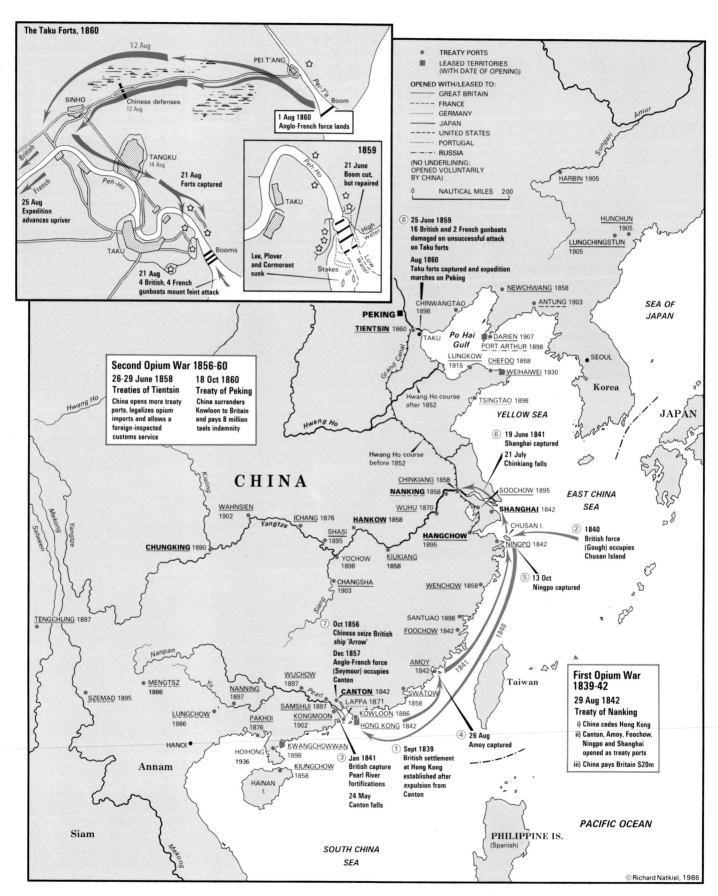

contributing to the general unrest and dissatisfaction with the weak Imperial government, and in the 1850s the first of a series of major rebellions broke out. The worst of these was the Tai'ping T'ien-kuo, or Heavenly Kingdom of Great Peace. Despite its name it caused widespread suffering, and an estimated 12 million Chinese died during a decade of fighting. Although the Court in Peking preferred to devote its energies to restoring traditional values a few far-sighted officials took steps to hire foreign mercenaries capable of training soldiers to put down the rebellions. The most famous of these, a British officer, Major Charles Gordon achieved remarkable results in the 1860s, and with only a handful of European officers succeeded in defeating the Tai'Ping.

Trade relations were still a major problem, and in 1856 another local dispute at Canton led to warfare. This time the British and French conducted joint military operations, and after a reverse at the Peh-Ho River in June 1859, succeeded in forcing their way upriver to Peking the following year. Once again large Chinese armies were dispersed with contemptuous ease by small Anglo-French forces, but when the Manchu leaders proved unwilling to negotiate and tortured some British prisoners the order was given to inflict reprisals. Knowing how much the ruling class revered its glorious past, the British and French leaders ordered the beautiful Summer Palace to be looted and destroyed. This act of gross vandalism so shocked the Chinese that they signed the Treaty of Peking, which in turn ratified the Treaty of Tientsin, signed over two years earlier.

China's relations with the Foreign Powers remained stable for another 30 years, not through acquiescence but because of continuing internal weakness. Rebellion continued in several regions, and in 1877-79 a terrible famine caused at least 10 million to starve. The nations of Europe continued to gnaw at Chinese territory. In 1858 Russia annexed the Amur River region, then two years later occupied the Maritime Provinces. In 1883-85 a disastrous defeat was sustained against the French, who completed their take over of Indo-China, and finally ten years later there was a further disaster when the Japanese defeated Chinese land and sea forces.

Defeat at the hands of the 'backward' Japanese was the last straw, for in theory China should have at least started level in the race to modernize her armed forces. An attempt to introduce sweeping reforms was frustrated by the Dowager Empress, which precipitated a further 'scramble' by the Western nations for more concessions. This inspired the Boxer Rebellion, so-called from the Society of Harmonious Fists which sought to expel all foreigners. Russia seized most of Manchuria, while a multi-national force was sent to relieve the foreign legations at Tientsin and Peking.

The familiar pattern of easy victory over Chinese armies was repeated, and once again China was forced to make humiliating concessions. Not until the revolution of 1911 was China able to shake off the dead hand of Manchu rule, which had been responsible for so much destruction.

Top: How Qua, the leading merchant in Canton responsible for dealings with the Europeans at the time of the First Opium War, from the painting by George Chinnery. Chinnery's paintings provide an important part of the record of the early days of the British settlement at Hong Kong.
Left: Chinese officers haul down the British flag aboard the ship *Arrow*. This 'insult to the flag' was to be the final cause of the Second Opium War.

The Clipper Ships

The introduction of steam made little impact on mercantile sailing ships through the 1830s and 1840s. When steam was used it was more as an auxiliary method of propulsion when winds were contrary or insufficient. Even when steam began to oust sail the longer and more distant trade-routes remained the preserve of sailing ships.

The classic British 'Blackwall frigate,' a style of merchant-ship design with a big carrying capacity but modest speed soon came under challenge from slim, fast American ships known generally as 'clippers' because they 'clipped' time off the regular sailing times. These ships lacked cargo capacity but they were fast, and soon came to dominate the trade in Chinese opium and West African slaves. Variants built in Virginia and Maryland were termed 'Baltimore clippers,' and under that influence what we now know as the true sailing clipper evolved. From 1850 to 1855 American clippers established a virtual monopoly of the English tea-trade with China.

The heyday of the clipper was the California Gold Rush. Until overland communications from the US east coast could be improved everything of any value had to go by sea around Cape Horn, and profits were enormous. British clipper builders and owners came into their own when gold was discovered in Australia. The Black Ball Line founded by James Baines of Liverpool was perhaps the best-known operator of clipper ships.

The Civil War gave British shipowners the chance to displace the Americans from their position as clipper-builders. Adding refinements of their own they were now able to build a series of China tea clippers which were the wonder of the world. Smaller than the American ships, they were not as fast in the best conditions but generally sailed better in a variety of weather conditions. The China tea trade was by 1865 a British monopoly, and the races to get the best price for the fresh tea crop became a legend. The average time of passage was 110-112 days but in 1866 the winners took only 99 days.

The design of clippers reached its peak in 1868-70 with the building of the *Thermopylae* and the *Cutty Sark* but the opening of the Suez Canal in 1869 meant that their decline would be swift. With their much greater reliability steamships could now bring tea cargoes to the London market in half the time taken by the fastest clippers. To survive the clipper owners now turned to the Australian wool trade, taking advantage of the prevailing westerly winds in latitudes around 40 degrees South (the 'Roaring Forites').

The wool trade lasted to the end of the century, but inevitably as coaling stations were extended around the world steamers were able to undercut the sailing ships' rates. Technology continued to improve the sailing ship breed, with wood giving way to composite (teak planking on iron frames) and eventually iron hulls, but nothing could alter the fact that the clipper's elegant hull would only make a profit by carrying a high-value cargo. When those cargoes were lost to steamships the clipper, with her massive spread of sail, large complement and small capacity, was doomed.

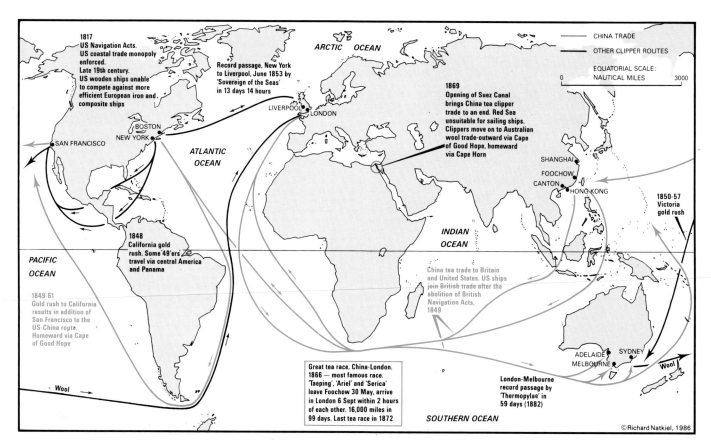

1817
US Navigation Acts. US coastal trade monopoly enforced.
Late 19th century. US wooden ships unable to compete against more efficient European iron and composite ships

Record passage, New York to Liverpool, June 1853 by 'Sovereign of the Seas' in 13 days 14 hours

1869
Opening of Suez Canal brings China tea clipper trade to an end. Red Sea unsuitable for sailing ships. Clippers move on to Australian wool trade-outward via Cape of Good Hope, homeward via Cape Horn

1850-57 Victoria gold rush

1848
California gold rush. Some '49'ers travel via central America and Panama

1849-61
Gold rush to California results in addition of San Francisco to the US-China route. Homeward via Cape of Good Hope

China tea trade to Britain and United States. US ships join British trade after the abolition of British Navigation Acts, 1849

CHINA TRADE
OTHER CLIPPER ROUTES
EQUATORIAL SCALE: NAUTICAL MILES   0   3000

Great tea race, China-London. 1866 — most famous race. 'Taeping', 'Ariel' and 'Serica' leave Foochow 30 May, arrive in London 6 Sept within 2 hours of each other. 16,000 miles in 99 days. Last tea race in 1872

London-Melbourne record passage by 'Thermopylae' in 59 days (1882)

ARCTIC OCEAN
ATLANTIC OCEAN
PACIFIC OCEAN
INDIAN OCEAN
SOUTHERN OCEAN

LIVERPOOL LONDON
BOSTON NEW YORK
SAN FRANCISCO
SHANGHAI FOOCHOW CANTON HONG KONG
ADELAIDE SYDNEY MELBOURNE
Wool
Wool

© Richard Natkiel, 1986

Whaling

Whaling is one of the oldest established forms of large-scale fishery, the first systematic hunters on record being the Basques of northern Spain in the tenth century. During the next two hundred years the Right Whale was the main type being hunted, mainly from small boats. By the sixteenth century the Biscay whaling industry was in decline but the Basques again led the way in establishing new whaling grounds off Newfoundland.

The Arctic whaling grounds were established after Willem Barents discovered Spitsbergen (Svalbard) in 1596, and the first English whaling expedition left for the Arctic in 1610, financed by the Muscovy Company and using Basques to teach the skills. Once again overfishing forced the whalers to move to new grounds, and by the early eighteenth century they were operating as far north as the Davis Strait.

In the British North American colonies whaling also established itself as a major industry, and during the eighteenth century Nantucket and New Bedford in New England and ports farther north in Newfoundland became famous in the whaling trade. Their prey was the Cachalot or Sperm Whale, and they followed it down the American coast as far as Brazil and even into the Pacific. During the following century American whaling ships operated as far afield as Japan, Zanzibar and the Seychelles. This prosperous industry was all but wiped out by Confederate commerce-raiders in the Civil War, and a short-lived recovery was halted in 1871, when virtually the whole North Pacific whaling fleet, by then based on San Francisco, was crushed in the ice.

Modern whaling began with the invention of the harpoon gun by the Norwegian Sven Foyn in the 1860s, and by the 1890s steam-driven whalecatchers were in operation. The final refinement in the 1920s was the whale factory ship, which cruised independently of the licensed shore bases, directing the activities of the whalecatchers and processing their catches aboard. The whale carcasses were winched up a stern ramp and then 'flensed' to strip the blubber so that it could be rendered down to oil, which was stored in huge tanks. By the mid-1930s it was obvious that whale stocks were decreasing fast, and in 1937 the length of the whaling season was regulated and minimum sizes of whale were fixed. In 1947 the International Whaling Commission was set up in a partially effective attempt to regulate the world whaling industry.

Since the 1970s there has been a concerted effort to limit or even abolish whaling, led by environmental groups such as Greenpeace and the Save the Whale Foundation. A ban

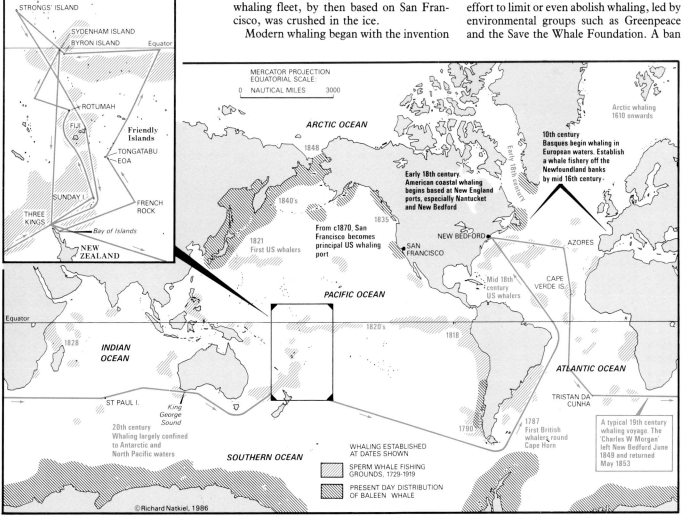

©Richard Natkiel, 1986

on whalemeat imports by the United States and Great Britain has led to a decline in the use of whalemeat as petfood, which promises to rob the trade of much of its profitability. In 1975 the world-wide quota was reduced to 32,450 whales and separate quotas were fixed for the most threatened species. Japan and the USSR are now the principal whaling nations. The probability of more countries banning the import of whalemeat may ultimately save the whale population more than any other measure, for this demand far exceeds all the other uses for whale products.

Top: A sixteenth century illustration of the process of flensing blubber from a whale.
Above: Whaling in the early nineteenth century from a painting by the French artist Garneray.
Left: The waterfront of New Bedford, Massachusetts in the 1890s with whale ships at the quay. By the 1890s the heyday of the New England whalers was past.
Right: The Russian attack on Sinope.

The Crimean War

The Battle of Sinope

A dispute over the right to care for the Holy places in Jerusalem was the nominal cause for hostility between France and Russia in 1853, but in reality it was the ever-present suspicion of France and Britain that Russia wanted to destroy Turkey and gain access to the Mediterranean. Tsar Nicholas had already referred to Turkey as the 'Sick Man of Europe' and had suggested slyly that his death might be hastened to mutual advantage. A Russian demand for a Russian protectorate over all Orthodox Christian subjects of the Sultan was alarming enough, but when Russia occupied Turkish provinces north of the Danube the French and British finally had to act.

On 30 November 1853 a Turkish squadron of seven frigates and three corvettes under the command of Osman Pasha was lying in the harbor of Sinope (Sinop) on the southern coast of the Black Sea. At about mid-day a Russian squadron of six ships of the line and two frigates under the command of Admiral Pavel Nakhimov appeared off the anchorage, trapping the Turks just as they had been trapped at Navarino 26 years before. With clearcut orders to destroy the Turks Nakhimov wasted no time on preliminaries, and his ships opened a deadly fire on the Turks, using shells to set fire to the wooden hulls.

As at Navarino the Turks fought bravely and sustained some 3000 dead, out of a total force of only 4400. It was truly a massacre, and the fact that the Russians were armed largely with guns firing hollow spherical explosive shells made their fire particularly destructive. However, the impression given in numerous accounts that the action lasted only a few minutes is erroneous. Despite his preponderance of numbers Nakhimov's ships took two hours to sink the Turkish ships and a further four hours to complete the destruction of the harbor and fortifications.

The aftermath of Sinope was out of all proportion to the scale of the action. The British and French immediately sent a combined fleet to the Dardanelles as a visible expression of their determination to support Turkey, and took the first steps toward war. Public concern and anger at the highly provocative attack was matched by genuine alarm at the apparent ease with which the Turkish ships had been sunk. Sinope was not the first action in which warships had fired explosive shells, but this time it was reported widely. During the late 1840s there had been growing doubts in naval circles about the value of large wooden three-decker ships of the line, and the speed with which the Turkish ships had caught fire showed how vulnerable wooden warships were to shell-fire. Three-deckers had already been ridiculed as 'eggshells armed with hammers' by their critics, and the outcome of Sinope was seized upon as proof of the argument.

The Crimean War produced little evidence to show that Sinope had many lessons for the future but the long-term implications were that wood had outlived its usefulness, and the age of the wooden sailing warship was all but finished.

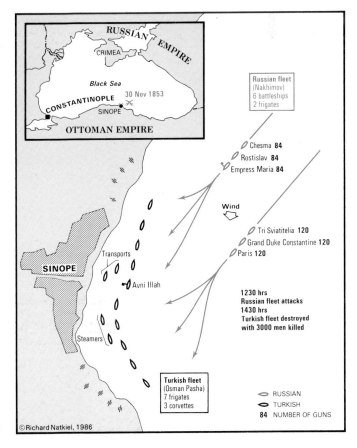

Black Sea Operations

The Turkish had fired the first shots of the Crimean War when they invaded Moldavia after declaring war on 4 October 1853, but the Russian riposte was the brilliant raid by Admiral Nakhimov on Sinope on 30 November. With public opinion inflamed the British Prime Minister Lord Aberdeen was forced to declare support for Turkey, and the French Emperor Napoleon III made common cause with the British. War was declared on 27 March 1854 and an Allied force was sent to Varna on the Black Sea.

The objective was to take the main Russian naval base at Sevastopol, in the Crimean peninsula, with the aim of crippling Russia's naval strength in the Black Sea. The 60,000 Allied troops were landed at Eupatoria in mid-September 1854, with no attempt by the Russian fleet to prevent their passage. As the armies marched to Sevastopol the two navies

Above: The Allied transport fleet and warships photographed in Balaklava harbor in 1855.
Above right: The French ship of the line *Charlemagne* passes Constantinople on her way to the Crimea in August 1854. The *Charlemagne* is shown carrying two flat bottomed lighters to be used in landing operations.

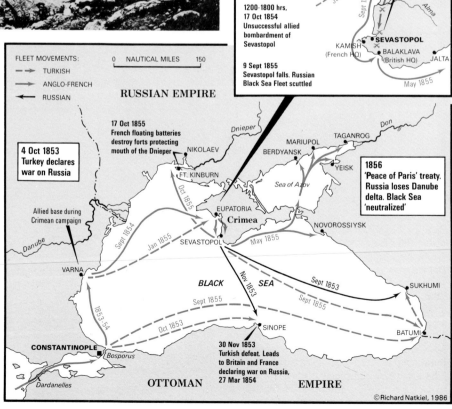

moved their bases south, the British setting up a new base at the little harbor of Balaklava and the French farther up the coast.

A naval bombardment of the fortress of Sevastopol on 17 October 1854 failed to make any impression and one ship of the line, HMS *Albion*, was severely damaged by Russian shells. Although all the other ships which were hit were in action again the next day, this was a further confirmation that the days of the wooden warship were numbered. After the failure of the bombardment there was clearly no alternative to a long and costly siege as the British and French troops lacked the strength to take the fortress by storm.

During an appalling winter the two armies suffered severely from sickness and cold, but the British supply system broke down completely. Despite plentiful supplies landed at Balaklava soldiers and transport horses died of neglect less than 30 miles away. Nor were the conditions at the big base hospital at Scutari (Uskudar) near Constantinople much better, and the plight of the armies in the Crimea brought about the fall of the Aberdeen government.

Several assaults on Sevastopol were repulsed, but in May 1855 the energetic naval leader, Admiral Sir Edmund Lyons was given permission to attack Russian lines of communication in the Sea of Azov. British shallow-draft gunboats and other small warships played havoc with Russian supplies along the shores of the Azov Sea as far as Taganrog at the mouth of the Don, and tied down large numbers of Russian troops.

During the winter of 1854-55 both the British and French navies had taken energetic steps to counter the threat from Russian shellfire. After consultation both navies started a program to build large numbers of small gunboats for inshore work, and a series of armor-plated 'floating batteries,' armored with 4-inch wrought iron plates capable of deflecting or breaking up explosive shells. The first three completed were French, and in October 1855, a month after the fall of Sevastopol, they went into action against the

fortress of Kinburn guarding the mouth of the Dnieper, near Nikolaev.

Despite repeated hits from Russian shells the *Dévastation*, *Lavé* and *Tonnant* proved impervious to all but minor damage, and the engagement marked the start of the new era in technology, a race between armor and the gun. The Black Sea campaign also marked the end of the major sailing warship; the gigantic three-deckers which had been towed into action by steamers in 1854 were all withdrawn and replaced by steam-powered ships of the line in the spring of 1855.

Despite its widespread reputation as a 'comic opera' war the Crimean campaign achieved its object of keeping Russia from gaining control of the Dardanelles. The two Allied navies coped remarkably well with a spate of innovations which were in use for the first time, and the Royal Navy in particular performed heroic exertions to offset the failure of the Army's supply system, using 'floating factories' to repair steam machinery and to bake large quantities of bread.

Under the conditions of the Treaty of Paris, signed in March 1856, Russia made considerable concessions, most of which she

Above: Admiral Lyons, at first second in command but later Commander in Chief of the British Black Sea fleet.

repudiated in 1870. The biggest single beneficiary was Italy, for the wily Count Cavour had sent a division of Sardinian troops to help the Allies in 1855. For their help in winning the Battle of the Tchernaya, the Allies gave their blessing to the cause of Italian reunification.

Below: Royal Navy gun crew in the trenches outside Sevastopol. Navy gun crews served ashore in many British operations in the nineteenth century.

The Baltic Campaign

Although the main Anglo-French effort was directed to the Black Sea theater, the British as the major naval power, turned almost instinctively to the Baltic. Not only was there a need to deter the powerful Russian Baltic Fleet from coming out into the North Sea, but the Baltic was still an important area for the supply of strategic raw materials.

As early as December 1853 (before the declaration of war) it was public knowledge that a joint expedition was planned for the spring of 1854, under the command of Vice Admiral Sir Charles Napier. It proved as difficult to organize as the Black Sea expedition, due largely to the chronic shortage of manpower. Nor did Napier live up to his reputation for audacity, and the Baltic Fleet did not succeed in capturing its first objective until mid-August 1854. The fortress of Bomarsund in the Aland Islands fell to a naval bombardment and was then blown up by a French landing force.

A large force of gunboats was built during the winter of 1854-55 (26 were ordered between June and October 1854, followed by another 130 in 1855) and the first were delivered by June 1855. The British press had been scornful of the Baltic expedition, and claimed that the difference between the Baltic Fleet and the Black Sea Fleet was that, whereas the Black Sea Fleet was expected to do everything but did nothing, the Baltic Fleet was expected to do nothing and did so. But from June 1855 good news began to come in from the Baltic as the shallow-draft ships

began to harass Russian supply-lines. By October the Russian forces guarding strongpoints, telegraph stations and bridges outnumbered the entire strength of the British Army, and the sloops and gunboats had captured 80,000 tons of shipping.

By August 1855 the Allies were ready for a long-planned bombardment of Sveaborg, a large fortress protecting the approaches to Helsinki. For the first time ships had to sweep for mines, and a British sloop was damaged. Vice Admiral Dundas had 16 British gunboats and 16 mortar vessels and the French had 10 gunboats, while the major warships supplied pulling (rowing) boats armed with rockets, and had transferred extra guns to the gunboats.

Fire was opened just after 0700 on 9 August. Although the main inshore force stopped its bombardment at dusk the mortar boats and rocket-armed boats kept up harassing fire during the night. Next day the inshore squadron moved in to 2200 yards and the firing went on well after sunset. The total expenditure was calculated at 100 tons of gunpowder and 1000 tons of shells and mortar bombs. The losses were hard to determine, but the Russians were estimated to have lost 23 ships, sunk at their moorings, and 2000 men, while the Allies lost one man and had 15 wounded.

No further actions took place before ice forced the Allied fleets to withdraw but the Baltic campaign put intolerable pressure on the St Petersburg government. The fall of Sevastopol had been accompanied by cruel losses among the troops marching overland

to the Crimea, and the certainty that St Petersburg itself would come under attack in 1856 combined to force the Tsar and his ministers to discuss peace terms.

The French and British planned to send a much larger fleet into the Baltic in 1856, with up to 50,000 troops for use in Finland and the provinces of Courland, Estonia and Livonia, followed by a large-scale assault on Kronstadt and St Petersburg. The peace signed in Paris meant that the fleet never sailed, and in April 1856 the British contingent was reviewed by Queen Victoria at Spithead.

The chaos and suffering in the Crimea has always distracted attention from the very impressive performance of the Allied navies in the Baltic. As in the Black Sea the early primitive steamships had to be kept running far from their main base, and both admirals and seamen had to grapple with new technology, including explosive shells, rifled guns and even the first effective sea mines. The Russian fleets chose not to fight so the Allied naval activity was humdrum, but it was nonetheless vital to the successful outcome of the war.

Left: The fortress of Bomarsund blows up in the background while French and British ships lie offshore. The largest vessel present is the British HMS *Edinburgh*.

The US Civil War

Strangling the Confederacy

Federal naval strategy against the Confederacy was clear-cut but not easy to implement. Although the pre-war US Navy was officered predominantly by Southerners who joined the Confederate forces, the bulk of merchant shipping and most of the Navy was in Northern hands. Most shipyards were also in the North. King Cotton was vital to the economy of the South, so it was essential to cut the Confederacy off from the sinews of war which could be bought in Europe. That meant a blockade of southern harbors.

The US Navy was in poor shape at the outbreak of war. It had been run down steadily since 1815; out of 90 ships on the Navy List only 41 were in commission, and only half of those were officially regarded as modern. However the US Navy's ordnance side was well served by officers like Captain Robert Parrott and Rear Admiral John A Dahlgren, whose gun-designs were as good as anything available in Europe. More

important was the fact that the bulk of heavy industry was in the North, whereas the South was largely agricultural. Although the bulk of the senior officers chose to join the Confederate States' Navy, a few officers of high caliber such as Farragut remained loyal to the Union and gave the Federal Navy the leadership it needed.

The crisis which led to the fall of Fort Sumter took the government in Washington by surprise and so the Navy could do little to intervene, but when a few days later Confederate President Jefferson Davis urged would-be privateers to take out 'letters of marque' (licenses to attack Federal shipping on the high seas) President Lincoln retaliated by declaring a blockade of the entire Confederacy. The main, if not the only hope of the Confederacy lay in broadening the conflict to embroil Great Britain. As the chief importer of cotton, it was hoped that Britain would side against the North, whose small navy would be powerless.

Of all the miscalculations made by the

Confederacy this was the worst. Patient and assiduous diplomacy prevented Great Britain from being drawn into the war. The need for cotton was balanced by moral sympathy for the Northern anti-slavery movement, and in any case cotton became available from other sources, including Northern states.

The effort to establish privateers had only a brief success. Despite panic the early successes of the privateers brought little profit to the Confederacy. The North quickly established four blockading squadrons, two in the Atlantic and two to close the Gulf of Mexico, and it became difficult for the privateers to carry their prizes back into Charleston and New Orleans. Nor could they sell their prizes abroad, as the State Department ensured that European ports were also closed to the privateers.

The use of 'auxiliary cruisers' was much more successful. Well armed ships like the *Sumter*, *Alabama* and *Shenandoah* preyed on Northern shipping on the high seas and disrupted trade with Europe. The success of

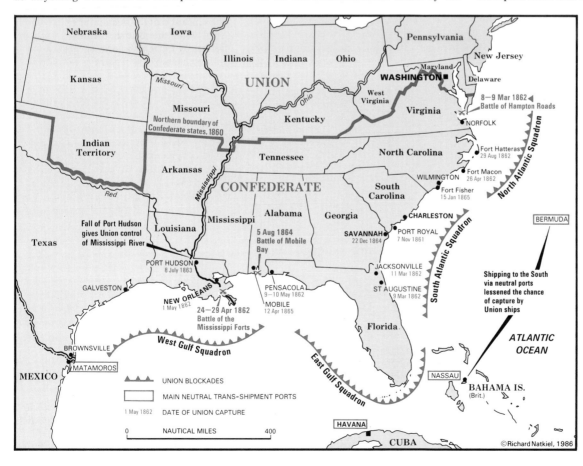

©Richard Natkiel, 1986

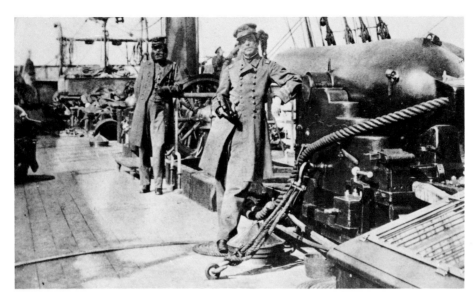

these commerce-raiders lay not so much in the number of captures but the strain which their raiding put on the blockade. The presence of commerce-raiders meant that scarce warships had to be detached from blockade duty. At first only three warships had been available but the Federal Secretary of the Navy, Gideon Welles took energetic steps to fill the gap by purchasing and arming hundreds of merchant ships. This motley collection of paddle- and screw-steamers were badly out-classed by the Confederate ships, but as the Royal Navy had shown against Napoleon 60 years earlier, numbers rather than quality are essential for a successful blockade.

The success of the blockade did much to redress the balance after the Confederacy's string of brilliant early victories on land, and the shortage of vital commodities soon began to tell. In a desperate attempt to beat the blockade the Confederate Navy started building a series of ironclads but this effort was countered by the Federal Navy with its own armored ships. The industrial resources of the North made this an easy task and by the spring of 1862 the first of the new 'monitors,' ironclads and gunboats were beginning to take the offensive.

The hard-won benefits of the blockade were nearly thrown away when the Confederate Army under Lee and Jackson took the offensive in Virginia in June 1862. The failure of that offensive was crucial, for it convinced Great Britain that she should not support the Confederacy. In November that year she vetoed a suggestion by France for an armistice, under which the blockade would have been lifted for six months. A succession of bad harvests in Europe had allowed the United States to increase exports of beef and grain to Europe, and this, combined with serious moral doubts about supporting slavery, prevented the Confederacy from achieving international recognition as an independent belligerent nation.

Although commerce-raiders continued to harry Northern shipping, the blockade was slowly strangling the South and Southern ports were gradually being captured. By the end its patrols had captured or sunk nearly 300 steamships, 44 large sailing ships and 683 schooners. The total value of their cargoes was $24.5 million and a further $7 million was lost when blockade-runners were wrecked. By the surrender all commodities, from uniforms down to necessities of life were almost unobtainable. The blockade did not defeat the Confederacy single-handed, but without it the Union armies could not have succeeded.

Above left: **Captain Semmes of the Confederate raider *Alabama* stands by one of his ship's 110-pounder guns. The *Alabama* was the most famous of the Confederate commerce raiders.**
Below: **Union mortar and gun vessels in action on the Mississippi.**

Battle of Hampton Roads

The outbreak of the Civil War in the United States in January 1861 created an unusual situation. The North retained control over most of the country's ships and industrial assets, but the Confederacy kept the loyalty of many of the ablest officers. The result was a display of considerable ingenuity by the Confederate States' Navy.

In April 1861 Confederate troops captured Norfolk Navy Yard, and found the new steam frigate *Merrimack* lying burned out and scuttled. Salvage proved comparatively easy and when the frigate's machinery was found to be undamaged the new Confederate States' Navy administration decided to convert her into an ironclad, using railroad iron to give her an armored casemate on the cut-down hull. With nothing to fear from Federal artillery she would be able to run the gauntlet and defeat the blockading squadron.

By early spring 1862 she was ready, a cumbersomely slow ship but armed with ten heavy guns firing shells and armor-piercing shot. The Union Navy was well informed about the Confederate plans, and in August 1861 accepted a design for an even more remarkable ironclad, from the Swedish designer John Ericsson. Her name was the USS *Monitor*, 'that she might be a warning to others,' and although armed with only two heavy guns, the revolving turret permitted her to fire on any bearing.

Although built with utmost haste the *Monitor* was nearly too late. The day she was due off Hampton Roads, 8 March 1862 the *Merrimack* (now known as the CSS *Virginia*) put to sea. The ironclad destroyed the wooden Union frigates *Congress* and *Cumberland* with ease, showing just how helpless an unarmored sailing warship could be, especially when caught in restricted waters. The *Cumberland* lost nearly a third of her complement and the *Congress* more than half. Morale in the Union fleet was at a low ebb, and only the *Monitor* could avert a disaster.

Next day the *Merrimack* reappeared, making straight for the big frigate *Minnesota* which had been run aground the previous day. Her lookouts sighted what they first mistook for a water tank, but when the mysterious 'cheesebox on a raft' drew closer and opened fire with her 11-inch guns the *Merrimack* turned on her smaller antagonist. The action continued for some three-and-one-half hours, with the *Monitor* firing every seven or eight minutes, and the *Merrimack*

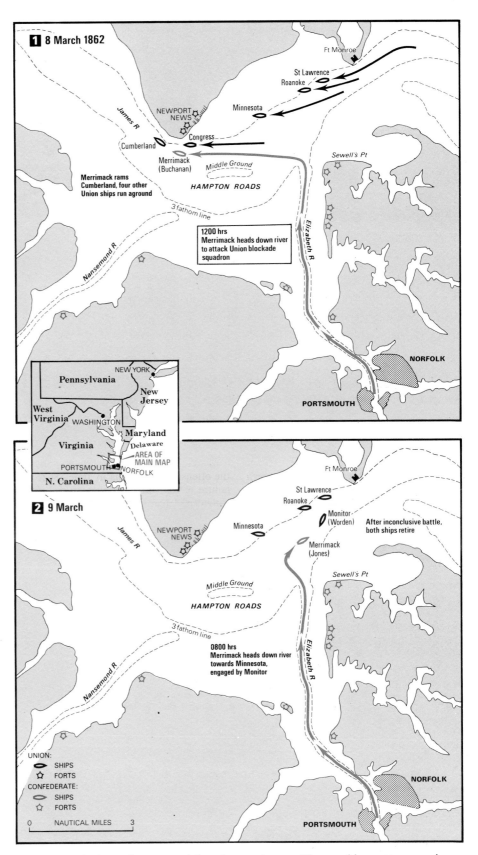

taking up to 15 minutes between each broadside. Neither ship could penetrate the other's armor, and eventually the baffled Confederate ship tried to ram, but the little *Monitor* could turn in one-sixth of the *Merrimack*'s length.

The Battle of Hampton Roads came to an end when the *Merrimack* withdrew to her anchorage. The two ships put to sea again on 11 April but the Union Admiral Goldsborough had strict orders not to allow the *Monitor* to be endangered, and they did not engage. History might have been different if on 9 March the *Monitor*'s gunners had been allowed to use full charges for the 11-inch guns, but as they had not been proof-fired

they were restricted to a light powder charge, and so could not penetrate the *Merrimack*'s armor. Even so, Ericsson's revolving turret and the armored raft hull had proved themselves in battle, and many improved 'monitors' were immediately ordered for the Union Navy.

Although the monitor-style ships were not particularly seaworthy, they were adequate for the inshore and riverine operations which the Union Navy was prosecuting against the Confederacy. Other navies also favored the revolving turret principle but fitted in conventional higher-sided ships rather than with the minimal freeboard of the American monitors. Proof of how limited the monitors' seakeeping qualities were was provided by the fate of the *Monitor* herself, which foundered under tow in a moderate sea later the same year. The *Merrimack* had to be burned by the Confederates in May 1862, after the abandonment of Norfolk to the Union land forces as she drew too much water to go up the James River.

Left: First phase of the Battle of Hampton Roads, the *Merrimack* destroys the *Cumberland*.
Below: The inconclusive engagement between the *Merrimack* and *Monitor*.

The Union Attack on the Mississippi Forts

The naval strategy of the Union had two main objectives, the first to cut the Confederacy off from outside aid, and the second to gain control of the Mississippi and thus cut the Confederacy in two. In accordance with this second aim, in January 1862 the 60-year old Captain David Farragut was given command of a squadron assigned to 'reduce the defenses which guard the approaches to New Orleans' and to 'take possession of it under the guns of [the] squadron,' a daunting task. Farragut began his attack on 17 April, when Commodore Porter began a bombardment of Fort Jackson and Fort St Philip.

The Confederates had scuttled ships in the channel and had thrown a boom across the river, while upriver the incomplete ironclad *Louisiana* was moored as a floating battery. In addition there were a number of gunboats, including the ironclad ram *Manassas*. Although the Union gunboat *Pinola* crept upriver on the night of 20-21 April and succeeded in ramming and cutting the log boom, the bombardment by Porter's 13-inch mortars mounted in small schooners had failed to silence the forts. Six days of

Above: The *Hartford*, Farragut's flagship in the Battle for the Mississippi Forts and at Mobile Bay.

bombardment had caused only 50 casualties and the forts were intact, and Farragut made the momentous decision to ignore his orders. Instead of subduing the forts his ships would try to run past the defenses, and take New Orleans by direct assault.

At 0200 on the morning of 24 April the Union fleet prepared to move upriver, and during the morning began to engage the forts in a fierce gunnery duel. The *Brooklyn* collided with the *Kineo* below the line of sunken hulks, and the *Varuna* was sunk with the loss of 36 men but the three divisions succeeded in forcing their way past the obstructions.

Once past the forts there were still the Confederate ships lying on the east side of the river to be dealt with. The ironclad ram *Manassas* attacked but a fierce fire from the Union ships sank her, and nine smaller gunboats were sunk. Farragut's flagship, the screw corvette *Hartford* was set on fire and ran aground, but was later refloated.

With the forts outflanked New Orleans was now defenseless and the city surrendered to Farragut's forces when they arrived next day. The 4000-strong garrison evacuated its positions without firing a shot. Union troops under General Benjamin Butler besieged Fort Jackson and Fort St Philip, and the Confederate garrisons mutinied on 29 April. Leaving Commodore Porter to take their surrender, Butler marched on to New Orleans to occupy the city.

After so many disappointments, the North took great comfort from the fall of New Orleans. Farragut was plucked from obscurity to become a national hero, and was promoted to Rear Admiral. The subsequent Mississippi campaign took much longer than expected but the first seeds of the Confederacy's defeat had been sown.

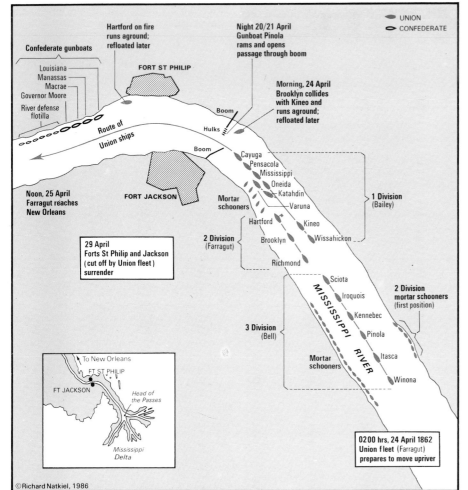

121

The Battle of Mobile Bay

Despite his failure to take Vicksburg in 1862 Farragut retained the confidence of the Union government. After the eventual fall of Vicksburg in 1863, in January 1864 Farragut was given the assignment he had sought for so long, the capture of the Confederate defenses around Mobile, Alabama. The forces available included four of the new monitors, the *Tecumseh, Manhattan, Winnebago* and *Chickasaw* as well as 14 wooden ships, under Farragut's command.

The troops landed on the west side of Dauphin Island in Mobile Bay in late July, and in 20 days methodically advanced to attack Fort Gaines and Fort Powell at the north end of the island. To support these operations it was necessary for the warships to advance into the bay, and there were still formidable obstacles to surmount. The Confederates had sown the approaches with moored mines or 'torpedoes,' as well as sinking old ships and underwater obstructions. Under the Confederate Admiral Franklin Buchanan there were also three wooden gunboats and the big ironclad *Tennessee*.

The Union squadron began to move into Mobile Bay at 0530 on 5 August 1864 led by the four monitors. As the leading ship, the 15-inch gunned *Tecumseh* moved past the barrier of mines opposite Fort Morgan, she was shaken by an underwater explosion, heeled over and sank with most of her crew. As the rest of the line wavered, Farragut, standing in the rigging of his flagship *Hartford* to see over the gunsmoke, issued his famous order, 'Damn the torpedoes, full speed ahead.' His audacity paid off, for although the crews of the surviving ships heard the 'torpedoes' rumbling against their keel plating, none exploded.

Once past the minefields the Union ships closed with the Confederate forces, and surrounded the *Tennessee*. Four ships, the *Hartford, Lackawanna, Monongahela* and *Ossipee* surrounded her, firing at close range and ramming her repeatedly. Crippled and unable to escape, the *Tennessee* finally surrendered at 1000 hours. The gunboat *Selma* withdrew to the northeast but ran aground and surrendered to the sidewheel gunboat *Metacomet*.

The victory was complete, with the capture of all four Confederate ships as well as Admiral Buchanan. General Granger's troops, supported by naval bombardment

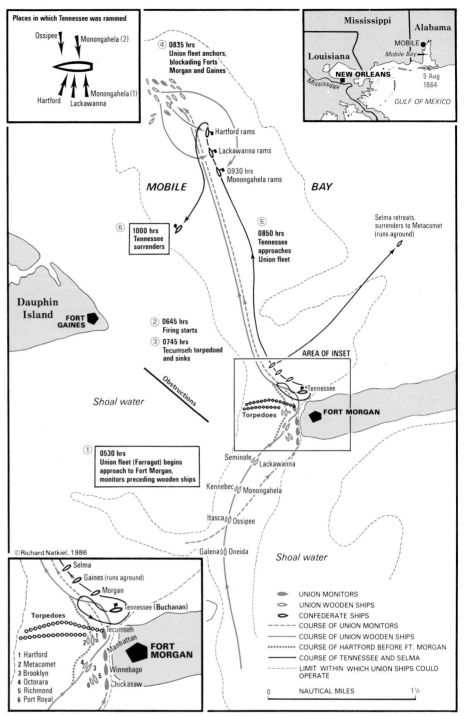

were able to capture Fort Gaines and Fort Powell a few days later, and although Fort Morgan held out longer, it too fell to Union troops at the end of the month.

Despite the fact that Mobile itself did not fall until April 1865 the destruction of its seaward defenses denied a major port to the Confederacy, through which the blockade-runners had been able to bring vital supplies. The *Tennessee* was recommissioned in the US Navy as a prize but did not last long as she was sold for scrapping two years after the war.

Mobile Bay marked the pinnacle of Farragut's meteoric career. The rank of Vice Admiral was specially created for him and a group of wealthy New Yorkers made a presentation of $50,000 in recognition of his victory. Now in declining health he accepted one more assignment to the fleet in the James River, but it was his last active appointment. Although not the genius which his contemporaries thought him to be, his determined and aggressive leadership more than compensated for any lack of tactical finesse. His formula for success is enshrined in his orders before the attack on Port Hudson, 'The best protection against the enemy's fire is well-directed fire from one's own guns.'

The Battle of Lissa

Following the Austrian defeat in 1866 at Sadowa (Koniggratz) at the hands of the Prussian Army the Emperor Franz Josef ceded Venice to Italy, but fighting continued between Austria and Italy. The fighting shifted to the Adriatic, where the Austrian fleet challenged the Italians.

On paper the Italian fleet was more powerful, with 12 armored ships out of a total of 34, against only seven Austrian ironclads in a fleet of 27 ships. But Rear Admiral Wilhelm von Tegetthoff was a bold and imaginative leader whereas Count Carlo Pellion de Persano was irresolute. Tegetthoff knew that with only 74 modern rifled guns against 200 modern guns in the Italian fleet he must either avoid action or try to use superior seamanship and tactics. He chose the latter course, ordering his ships to fight at close range so that his older muzzle-loading guns could penetrate Italian armor. He also ordered his ironclads to ram at every opportunity to throw the Italian squadron into confusion.

The Italian fleet left Ancona on 16 July 1866 to attack the Austrian garrison holding the island of Lissa (now Vis), and four days later they were brought to action by the Austrians from Pola (now Pula). In arrowhead formation Tegetthoff's ships bore down on the Italian line and threw it into confusion. The action quickly degenerated into a melée, with Austrian ships trying ineffectually to ram amid dense clouds of powder-smoke. At first the Italians seemed to do well, and the flagship, the new turret ram *Affondatore* inflicted severe damage on the wooden two-decker *Kaiser*.

Suddenly the tide of battle turned, as through the smoke Tegetthoff's flagship the *Ferdinand Max* sighted the big Italian frigate *Re d'Italia* lying disabled from a hit in the rudder. The Austrian ship bore down and struck her opponent full amidships, tearing an enormous hole with her projecting ram bow. The *Re d'Italia* capsized rapidly, taking over 600 men with her. The Italians had suffered another reverse when the small ironclad *Palestro* caught fire, but the loss of the *Re d'Italia* was too much for Persano. With a show of bravado he hoisted a signal for 'General Chase' but withdrew to Ancona leaving Tegetthoff's fleet the clear victors. Nearly three hours later the blazing *Palestro* blew up. It is generally argued by modern commentators that Persano's poor leadership and lack of drive were the main cause of the Italian defeat.

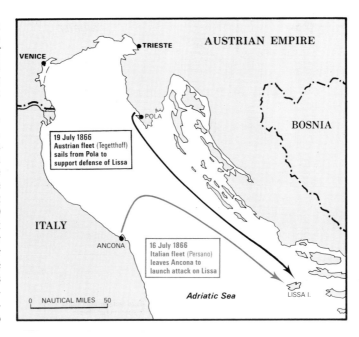

19 July 1866
Austrian fleet (Tegetthoff) sails from Pola to support defense of Lissa

16 July 1866
Italian fleet (Persano) leaves Ancona to launch attack on Lissa

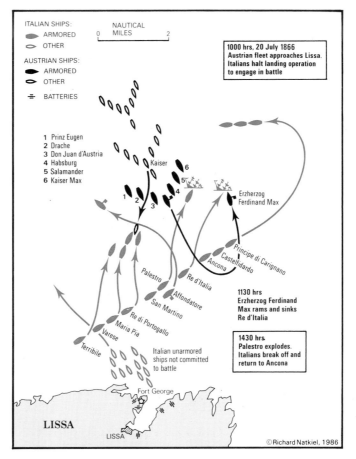

ITALIAN SHIPS:
ARMORED
OTHER

AUSTRIAN SHIPS:
ARMORED
OTHER

BATTERIES

1 Prinz Eugen
2 Drache
3 Don Juan d'Austria
4 Habsburg
5 Salamander
6 Kaiser Max

1000 hrs, 20 July 1866
Austrian fleet approaches Lissa. Italians halt landing operation to engage in battle

1130 hrs
Erzherzog Ferdinand Max rams and sinks Re d'Italia

1430 hrs.
Palestro explodes. Italians break off and return to Ancona

Italian unarmored ships not committed to battle

©Richard Natkiel, 1986

123

Although Lissa was a decisive victory and the fledgling Italian Navy was humiliated Austria gained little. Weakened by the defeat at Sadowa she could not pursue a prolonged war, and could not halt the complete reunification of Italy.

Lissa was the first major action between European fleets since the Napoleonic Wars, and because of its decisive result it had an extraordinary effect on naval opinion. For another 30 years the world's navies built battleships with massive reinforced stems and practiced ramming tactics with great persistence. Yet dispassionate analysis of the battle shows that nearly all Austrian attempts to ram were unsuccessful, and the *Ferdinand Max* only succeeded against an opponent unable to steer. Poor maneuverability and inaccurate gunnery made it very difficult to sink ships by ramming, although consorts were frequently in danger when sailing in close formation.

Once again a wooden ship survived an encounter with an ironclad. The *Kaiser* suffered only 61 casualties in spite of losing her bowsprit, foremast and funnel and catching fire after 14 hits, she lived to fight another day. The light casualties on both sides reflect the general innaccuracy of naval gunnery in the 1860s, a consequence of the many technological innovations being introduced around that time.

Above: The *Re d'Italia* sinks after the successful ramming attack of the *Ferdinand Max.*
Left: Admiral Wilhelm von Teggetthof, victor of Lissa. As well as being influential in the design of future warships with rams, the arrow-head formation used by Teggetthof caused many naval tacticians to look again at the previously standard ideas of fleets operating in line ahead formation in battle. Various schemes for ships to operate in triangular groups of three and other variations were fashionable for a time but eventually the old ideas prevailed.

The Bombardment of Alexandria

The British, ever wary of French efforts to dominate Egypt and the route to India, saved the Khedive of Egypt from bankruptcy by purchasing his shares in the Suez Canal Company. (The canal itself had been completed in 1869). When the Khedive finally went bankrupt Egyptian finances were put under joint Anglo-French control.

The arrangement suited the British and French bondholders but the stringent economies which were enforced bore harshly on Egyptians of all classes, who saw their taxes going out of the country to foreign creditors. By 1882 a powerful nationalist movement had grown up, led by disgruntled army officers. The nationalist movement had felt strong enough to order the new Khedive Tewfik to dismiss his Minister for War in 1881, with the result that *de facto* rule was now in the hands of Arabi Pasha and a group of fellow colonels. The country drifted into anarchy as sporadic violence broke out against all foreigners.

The French proposed joint action to the British but the ruling British Liberal Party was divided, some wishing to support the French and others wishing to avoid any coercion of the Egyptians. As a compromise the British Prime Minister Gladstone agreed to the issue of a Joint Note in January 1882,

intended to bluff Arabi Pasha into submission. It had the opposite effect, and Arabi and the Egyptian Army assumed that foreign intervention was inevitable. They began to fortify Alexandria against a naval landing, and in protest a strong Anglo-French naval force was sent there in May 1882.

The crisis deepened as the Khedive tried to reassert his authority and independence by dismissing Arabi Pasha; public opinion was so antagonized that within five days Arabi and his supporters had been reinstated. The British admiral, Sir Frederick Beauchamp Seymour was ordered to deliver an ultimatum to Arabi, but Seymour exceeded his instructions by demanding the surrender of the forts.

At this point the French squadron was ordered to withdraw, and the British were left to handle the situation on their own. Seymour could do little but carry out his threat to open fire on the forts as the Egyptians had no intention of giving way. Late in the afternoon of 10 July 1882 the ships took up their positions, eight battleships as well as smaller gunboats and gun vessels. Firing began at 0700 next morning and continued for some three hours. When the fire from the forts seemed to slacken Seymour ordered the ships to move in closer,

while the smaller ships sent parties ashore to disable any guns which had been abandoned.

When the British stopped firing at the end of the day they had effectively silenced the forts, but they had won a hollow victory. Rioting broke out all over Egypt, and Arabi Pasha even vowed that he would destroy the Suez Canal if any foreign forces invaded. Reluctantly Gladstone was forced to agree to a military landing to restore law and order and to save the Canal.

An expeditionary force under Sir Garnet Wolseley landed on 16 August, and captured the Canal before it could be blown up by the Egyptians. The disciplined British regulars had no difficulty in defeating Arabi's poorly led troops at Tel-el-Kebir, and by September 1882 Egypt was effectively under their control. But any hopes of making a rapid withdrawal were dashed by the discovery that the British were the only force capable of running the country. What had been intended merely as a police action became the first stage of an informal takeover of Egyptian affairs, conquest in all but name. With that commitment Britain was to take on a whole series of new problems, including the Mahdi's revolt in the Sudan, which would involve her in 13 years of bloodshed and expense.

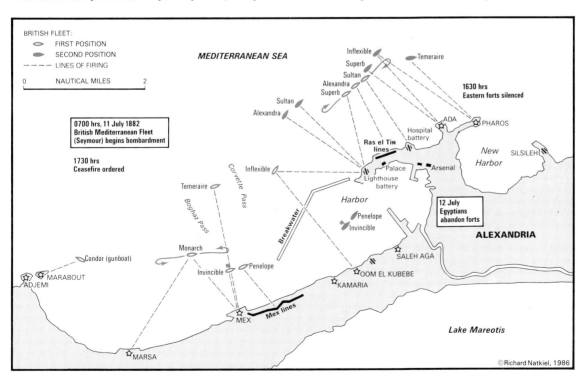

© Richard Natkiel, 1986

The Great Migrations

In the century which followed the defeat of Napoleon in 1815 Europe poured its people forth into the world. The pressures of industrialization would have been sufficient, but improvements in oceanic transport made it comparatively simple for large numbers of Europeans to cross the Atlantic or to go east.

For the British and Western Europeans North America acted like a lodestone. Many migrants were comparatively successful small farmers hoping for a more prosperous life, others were fleeing from the direst poverty, but on more than one occasion reports of gold produced enormous surges of gold-hungry people of all nations and classes. The Californian Gold Rush of 1849 accelerated the process of opening up the American West, and the Victoria Gold Rush two years later provided a much needed boost to Australia's development.

The statistics of the Great Migration are impressive. The United Kingdom alone provided 2,369,000, while Germany provided a further 1,130,000, all before 1850. As industrial pressure continued the numbers increased; in the second half of the century 9,500,000 more Britons and 5,000,000 more Germans crossed the Atlantic, along with

5,000,000 Italians, 1,000,000 Scandinavians and many more from Belgium, Spain, Portugal and the Balkans.

The British went principally to the United States and Canada, while the Germans went in large numbers to Brazil as well as the United States. Not all the migrants went to the Americas; large numbers of French went to Algeria, Italians went to Argentina and Russians settled (voluntarily and involuntarily) in the wilderness of Siberia. Nor were all the movements European; large numbers of Chinese emigrated to Australia, California and British Columbia. Like the Indians who settled in South and East Africa, many of the Chinese were indentured laborers brought to exploit natural resources such as sugar cane (Queensland, Australia and Natal, South Africa, for example), rubber and tin (Malaya) or gold mining (South Africa).

The most significant aspect of the nineteenth century migration was the 'Europeanization' of the world. It is estimated that in 1800 only 22 percent of the world's population was 'white,' and by the first quarter of the next century that figure had risen to 35 percent. The population of Europe rose from 190,000,000 to 423,000,000 during the

nineteenth century, while at the same time the 'European' population of countries overseas rose from some 5,500,000 to more than 200,000,000.

With large numbers of migrants settled in overseas territories the European nations became steadily more involved in colonial expansion. Mines and plantations supplied the manufacturing nations with raw materials for their factories and food for their expanding populations. Inevitably the process increased the political influence of those European countries which possessed overseas colonies. By the end of the century this was reflected in growing friction between the established colonial powers and those who demanded their own 'place in the sun.'

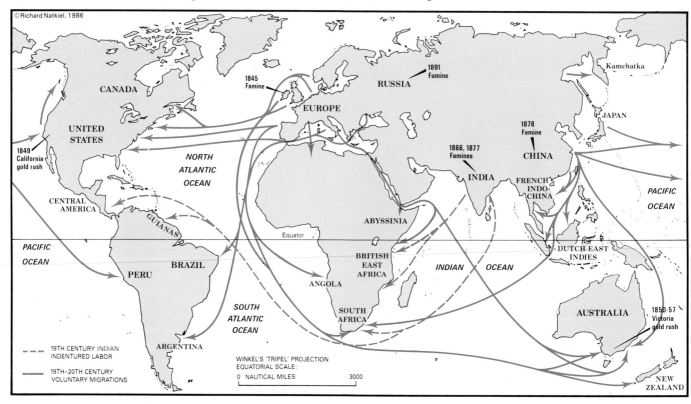

© Richard Natkiel, 1986

- - - - 19TH CENTURY INDIAN INDENTURED LABOR
———— 19TH-20TH CENTURY VOLUNTARY MIGRATIONS

WINKEL'S 'TRIPEL' PROJECTION
EQUATORIAL SCALE:
0   NAUTICAL MILES   3000

Immigration to the United States

Before the Revolution in 1776 American colonists had shown little willingness to settle in the interior, which many denigrated as the 'back country.' By the turn of the century this had begun to change, and as the term 'back country' gave way to 'frontier' the sense of mission and urgency became much more pronounced.

To develop such a vast country called for large numbers of settlers, and the Great Migration provided just what the United States needed. The Frontier offered the immigrants the space and land which they craved and the newcomers were helped enormously by the products of industry. The westward expansion brought the settlers into conflict with the Plains Indians, but three simple examples of 'European' technology gave the settlers victory: the steel plough, the rifle and the six-shooter and the barbed wire fence.

The major turning point was the Civil War. Once that bitter conflict was over the urge to move westward was enhanced by large numbers of discharged soldiers anxious to avoid a return to humdrum civilian life in the comparatively well-populated East. Northwestern Europe remained the principal source of immigrants almost to the end of the century, but thereafter the majority came from Southern Europe, Russia, Italy and the Austro-Hungarian Empire.

The drive to open up the West shaped a unique American character. As in Russia it created in effect a built-in empire which absorbed the boundless energies of the inhabitants. Not until the Spanish-American War of 1898 was there an awakening of any

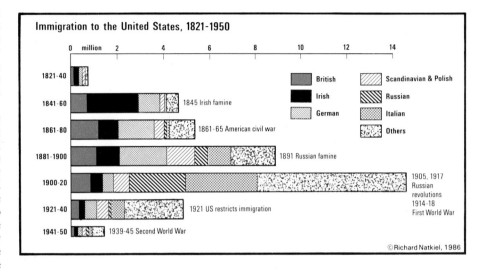

Immigration to the United States, 1821-1950

desire for overseas possessions. Even then the patriotic fervor aroused by the comparatively easy conquest of Cuba and the Philippines marched hand-in-hand with a suspicion of foreign adventures which persisted for many years.

There was boundless scope for internal expansion. Between 1825 and 1910 output grew at an annual average rate of 1.6 percent per capita, during the same period the population doubled every 27 years. The greatest industrial growth was achieved between 1877 and 1892, when US industrial output trebled, pushing the United States to the forefront of world industrial powers. Agricultural output also increased dramatically, allowing the United States to become the world's leading agricultural producer as well.

Because most of the country's energies were directed inwardly there was comparatively little interest in maritime expansion for many years. Much of the American-registered mercantile marine, notably the New England whaling fleet, was destroyed by Confederate commerce-raiders or put out of business by rising costs during the Civil War, and although fast clipper ships enjoyed a brief spell of success before and afterward they were soon eclipsed by the switch to steam. At the same time the switch to iron and steel shipbuilding gave Britain a near-monopoly of world shipbuilding and the beautiful but uneconomic Yankee clipper passed from the scene. Not until 1917 did American shipbuilding revive under the stimulus of the demands of World War I.

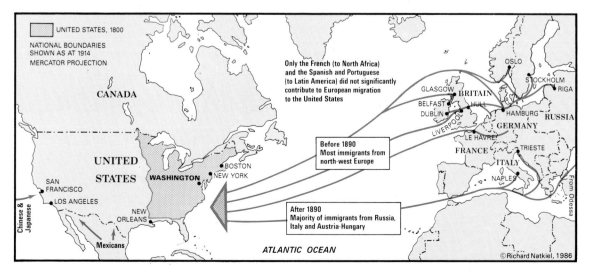

Battle of the Yalu River

The transition of Japan from a medieval society cut off from all foreign influence in the early 1850s to a modern industrial power by the end of the century is one of the most remarkable phenomena of modern times. As soon as Japan's civil war was over in 1868 students were sent to Europe to learn about engineering and shipbuilding and within 20 years the nucleus of a modern navy existed. By 1894 Japan's rulers felt able to use their new-found skills to foster commercial expansion, and inevitably began to copy the European colonial powers in acquiring possessions on the Asian mainland.

Korea, barely 100 miles from the southern Japanese islands and well-placed to command the Yellow Sea and China's northern ports, was chosen as the objective. A series of provocations followed, culminating in landings of troops in the northwest of the country. The Chinese replied by moving troops by sea, and it was this force, covered by a naval squadron, which encountered Japanese warships off the mouth of the Yalu River on 17 September 1894.

The Chinese squadron under Admiral Ting Ju-ch'ang comprised two battleships the *Chen Yuen* and *Ting Yuen*, slow but armed with four 12-inch guns and protected by 14-inch armor, two smaller capital ships armed with two 8.2-inch guns, and six cruisers. The Japanese Admiral Yugo Ito commanded eight cruisers, three with a single 12.6-inch gun. But most important, the latest Japanese ships could make twice the speed of the Chinese ships, and were manned by an ardently professional body of seamen greatly superior in morale and training to their opponents.

Admiral Ting steamed out in line abreast at a speed of only six knots, having given his captains orders to fight in pairs, bows-on wherever possible. Admiral Ito chose the more practical line ahead formation, with his fast ships in the first division. This enabled him to sweep across the Chinese front to attack the weakest ships at a range of 2-3000 yards.

As the two fleets approached across a glassy sea the Chinese opened an ineffectual fire at 5-6000 yards, but the Japanese held their fire for another 15 minutes. As the leading Japanese ships turned to port Admiral Ting in the *Ting Yuen* led her sister out ahead of the formation, trying to close with the Japanese. The Chinese force immediately lost cohesion, turning in pairs to port in a fruitless attempt to follow the Japanese movement and then losing formation as the Japanese fire intensified. The confusion was increased as Ito's flying squadron turned through 180 degrees and started to punish the ships at the rear of the Chinese line. By now the Japanese were circling around the Chinese ships, including Ting's hapless pair of battleships, firing accurately at a range of little more than a mile. Although the *Chen Yuen* succeeded in hitting the cruiser *Matsushima* with a 12-inch shell which decimated her gun crews it could only postpone the result. Four of the Chinese ships had already been destroyed and a fifth had been sunk in collision. After four hours of intense firing, as sunset was approaching Admiral Ting retired with his survivors to Port Arthur, where temporary repairs could be effected, and the squadron then retreated to Wei-hai-Wei.

As the first major fleet engagement since Lissa, the battle was of great interest to contemporary historians and analysts. Despite the tactical success of the Japanese cruisers their quick-firing giuns had not pierced the Chinese battleships' armor, and the big 12.6-inch Canet guns had apparently not scored any hits at all. What was not emphasized was the poor state of Chinese *materiel*: some shells were filled with sand or were simply unfilled, and the ships had virtually no ability to maneuver in unison. Had the Chinese ships been able to shoot accurately the Japanese would have been unable to fight at such short range and with so much freedom of maneuver. As always, a battle between opponents of vastly differing capabilities provided confusing and even incorrect lessons.

After the battle the war was confined to troop movements by sea, bombardments in support of Japanese troops and attacks by torpedo boats on Ting's ships at Wei-hai-Wei. The Chinese defenses were inadequate, with no nets or medium-caliber guns to prevent the Japanese torpedo boats from torpedoing the flagship *Ting Yuen* and another ship.

After the fall of Port Arthur Japanese troops invested Wei-hai-Wei, and when that port fell into their hands they captured the *Chen Yuen*. The negotiated peace which followed gave Japan Korea, Formosa (Taiwan) and the Liaotung peninsula, as well as an indemnity covering half the cost of the war. The European Powers, led by Russia and Germany then forced Japan to give up most of her gains, particularly the Liaotung peninsula and the strategically vital harbor at Port Arthur. It was a humiliation which Japan had to accept but could not forgive. Only a decade later she went to war to expel Russia from the very same area.

Right: **Page from a contemporary magazine showing Japanese ships and uniforms. Top, the *Naniwa*, and bottom, the *Matsushima*.**
Below: **The Chinese ship *Chih Yuen* sinks under the relentless Japanese bombardment at the height of the Yalu River battle.**

Le croiseur japonais « Naniwa-Kan ».

Le comte Saigo, ministre de la marine. London Stereoscopic Cy. — Un lieutenant de vaisseau. Phot. Couturier de Bechard. — Un capitaine de vaisseau. Phot. Pierre Petit. — Un vice-amiral. Phot. Maraki.

Uniformes des officiers de la marine japonaise.

LA MARINE JAPONAISE. — Le croiseur garde-côtes « Matsushima ».

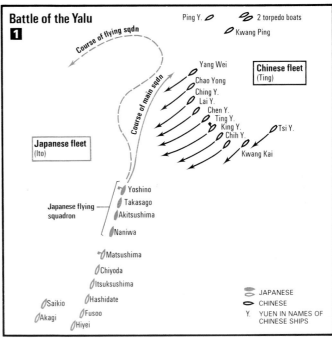

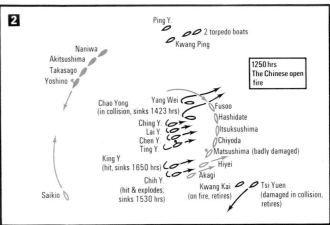

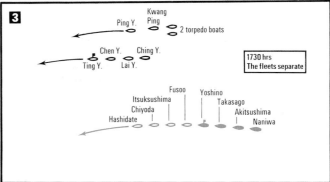

The Spanish-American War

The Battle of Santiago

The United States had long looked for an opportunity to dislodge Spain from her sole remaining footholds in the Caribbean, principally the islands of Cuba and Puerto Rico. The presence of a European power so close to Florida was irksome to public opinion, and the economic wisdom of the day saw colonies as an infallible source of wealth.

When the armored cruiser *Maine* blew up in Havana harbor during a visit there on 15 February 1898, the popular press in the United States chose to regard it as an act of sabotage, although modern opinion inclines toward an internal fire or accidental ammunition explosion as a more likely cause. Since the Cuban rebellion in 1895 popular feeling against Spanish misrule had been running high, and on 19 April Congress approved a resolution which was tantamount to war, and a formal declaration followed six days later.

The US Navy had three battleships on the east coast, the *Iowa*, *Massachusetts* and *Indiana*, as well as the older *Texas* and two armored cruisers, but they were reinforced by the battleship *Oregon*, which made a spectacular 13,000-mile dash around Cape Horn to Key West in Florida. Against this formidable, modern and well-led force Spain could only send Admiral Pascual Cervera with four armored cruisers and a number of smaller vessels. They were all in poor condition and Cervera had no illusions about the outcome.

Rear Admiral William T Sampson was given command of the main force in the Caribbean, with orders to blockade Havana. He proposed a bombardment of the city but the Navy Department opposed it on the grounds that his fleet could not be risked while Cervera's cruisers were at large. The Spanish force had in fact left the Cape Verde Islands on 29 April and was heading for San Juan, Puerto Rico, but to avoid the blockade Cervera slipped into Santiago, on the south side of Cuba.

After much vacillation and muddle Sampson was able to seal the entrance to Santiago with a semicircle of ships by 1 June, with his squadron six miles offshore. On the night of 2 June Lieutenant Richmond P Hobson tried to block the channel with the collier *Merrimac* but failed to sink the ship in the right place.

Troops were then landed to capture the forts guarding the entrance to the harbor, so that the defensive minefields could be swept, but the Army commander, General William

NAVAL OFFICERS THINK THE MAINE WAS DESTROYED BY A SPANISH MINE.

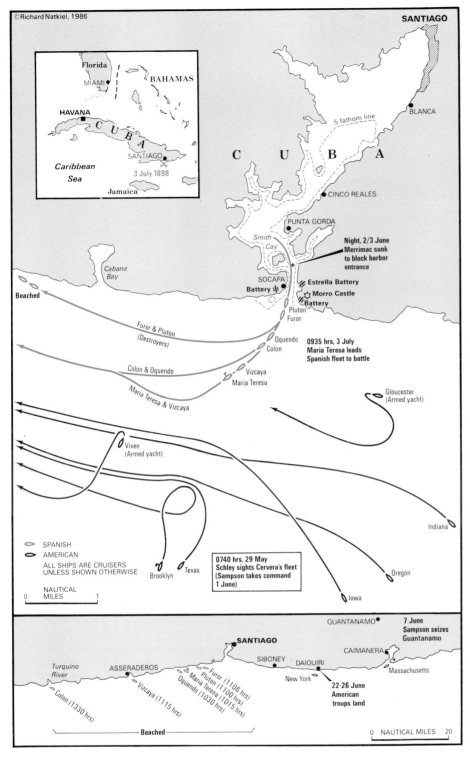

SANTIAGO

Florida

BAHAMAS

MIAMI

HAVANA

CUBA

Caribbean
Sea

SANTIAGO

3 July 1898

Jamaica

CUBA

5 fathom line

BLANCA

CINCO REALES

PUNTA GORDA

Smith
Cay

Night, 2/3 June
Merrimac sunk
to block harbor
entrance

SOCAPA
Battery

Estrella Battery

Morro Castle

Battery

Pluton
Furor

Cabana
Bay

Beached

Furor & Pluton
(Destroyers)

Oquendo
Colon

0935 hrs, 3 July
Maria Teresa leads
Spanish fleet to battle

Colon & Oquendo

Vizcaya
Maria Teresa

Maria Teresa & Vizcaya

Gloucester
(Armed yacht)

Vixen
(Armed yacht)

Indiana

SPANISH

AMERICAN

ALL SHIPS ARE CRUISERS
UNLESS SHOWN OTHERWISE

NAUTICAL
MILES

0   1

Brooklyn   Texas

0740 hrs, 29 May
Schley sights Cervera's fleet
(Sampson takes command
1 June)

Oregon

Iowa

GUANTANAMO

7 June
Sampson seizes
Guantanamo

SANTIAGO

CAIMANERA

SIBONEY   DAIQUIRI

Massachusetts

Turquino
River

ASSERADEROS

Furor (1106 hrs)

Pluton (1100 hrs)

Maria Teresa (1015 hrs)

Oquendo (1030 hrs)

New York

22-26 June
American
troops land

Vizcaya (1115 hrs)

Colon (1330 hrs)

Beached

0   NAUTICAL MILES   20

Above left: Sensational headlines in the popular press succeeded in creating a climate of hostility to Spain which drove America to war.

Left: The wreck of the *Maine* in the harbor at Havana. The force of the explosion which sunk the ship, whatever its cause, can be seen by the buckled plates protruding above the water.

R Shafter mistook his instructions and made an unsuccessful frontal assault on the defenses of Santiago on 1 July. It was now the turn of the Navy to come to the assistance of the Army.

A potential disaster was avoided when on Sunday 3 July lookouts sighted Cervera's squadron steaming out of Santiago, ready to give battle. The Spanish authorities in Havana, convinced that Santiago was about to fall, had ordered Cervera to try to break out. It was a good moment, with Sampson away in the *New York* and the *Massachusetts* sent to Guantanamo to take on coal. Sampson's second-in-command Commodore Winfield Scott Schley had earlier been accused of timidity, but this time he ordered his ships into a headlong charge. The Spanish flagship *Infanta Maria Teresa* headed straight for Schley's flagship, the *Brooklyn* but she was set on fire and was deliberately run aground west of Santiago. The next astern, the *Vizcaya* was also blazing, and ran ashore just before her magazines exploded. Then fire shifted to the *Almirante Oquendo*, which was seen to stagger under repeated hits before she too ran aground. The *Cristobal Colon*, the fastest Spanish ship, managed to outrun her pursuers for a while, but when her speed fell she began to be hit by 13-inch shells from the USS *Oregon*. Eventually she was forced ashore some 70 miles from Santiago. The destroyers *Furor* and *Pluton* were also sunk.

The entire action had lasted no more than three hours, and American casualties amounted to one man killed and one wounded, as against 323 Spanish dead and 151 wounded. The American public was ecstatic at Sampson's somewhat bombastic despatch bestowing a 'Fourth of July Gift,' but the Americans could be thankful that their baptism of fire had been against the weakest possible European adversary. Over 8000 shells had been fired at the Spanish ships, out of which only 120 had hit. Schley and Sampson wrangled for many years over who had won the battle – Schley claiming correctly that Sampson had not been present. It was, however, a 'splendid little war' which enhanced America's prestige and wiped out the last vestige of Spanish influence in Central and Latin America.

The peace settlement forced Spain to grant independence to Cuba and Puerto Rico and the Philippines and Guam were ceded to the United States in return for a payment of $20 million.

131

The Battle of Manila Bay

When the *Maine* sank the Assistant Secretary of the US Navy Theodore Roosevelt immediately assumed that war was inevitable. Indeed he had been preparing for war with Spain ever since his appointment the year before. Ignoring his superior, Secretary John D Long and what he regarded as useless procrastination by the McKinley administration Roosevelt laid plans for the capture of the Philippines as well as of Cuba.

As a first step Roosevelt had appointed Commodore George Dewey to command the Asiatic Squadron, and on 25 February 1898, only ten days after the sinking of the *Maine*, he ordered Dewey to prepare for an attack on the Philippines. His forces included the cruisers *Olympia*, *Baltimore*, *Boston* and *Raleigh*, two gunboats and a revenue cutter, while his opponent, Admiral Patricio Montojo had only one modern cruiser, the *Reina Cristina* and ten very weak ships.

Dewey's ships sailed from the coast of China and arrived early on Sunday 1 May off Manila Bay. Led by the *Olympia*, the squadron slipped through the passage separating Corregidor and El Fraile. Although the revenue cutter *McCulloch* betrayed their presence with sparks from her funnel the coastal artillery failed to hit any of the American ships, and they passed safely into the bay. As dawn broke at about 0500 lookouts sighted the Spanish ships anchored in line off the naval station at Cavite.

The Spanish ships and coastal artillery opened an inaccurate fire at long range as Dewey's squadron drew closer. At 0541 the admiral told Captain Charles V Gridley to open fire at the *Reina Cristina* and the old wooden-hulled *Castilla*, and soon the whole bay was smothered in thick clouds of smoke as the ships approached to a distance of 2000 yards in a series of passes. Despite the short range the Spanish ships showed little sign of being put out of action, and when Dewey was told that his ships were low on ammunition he withdrew.

After a leisurely pause to eat breakfast and allow time for the smoke to clear, the Americans closed with the Spanish once more, but were surprised to find that the Spanish squadron had virtually been annihilated. The *Reina Cristina* and *Castilla* had sunk, and nearly all the other ships had been sunk or set on fire. Fire was resumed at 1116 to finish off the remaining ships, which was achieved within the hour.

The news of Dewey's victory was greeted with nationwide approval, but the US government had no contingency plans for the acquisition of the Philippines. As a result the Asiatic Squadron lay at anchor in Manila Bay for several months until troops could be sent from California to capture Manila and occupy the territory. A major diplomatic incident arose when a German squadron under Vice Admiral von Diederichs arrived, and tried to stake a German claim. Troop landings were carried out, and at one stage the Germans placed their ships in position to open fire on the Americans. A visiting British cruiser shifted her moorings to place herself between the two groups of ships, to signify British support of the American claim, and a dangerous confrontation was averted.

Manila fell on 13 August after token resistance, for the Spanish defenders were more apprehensive of their fate at the hands of Filipino insurgents. The islands were subsequently annexed, providing the United States with the dual cares of a colonial empire, a vast area to administer and a three-year guerrilla war against the insurgents, who had no wish to substitute American domination for Spanish.

It is easy to belittle the victory at Manila Bay as a one-sided affair arising out of an unscrupulous piece of empire-building by Theodore Roosevelt, but the fracas with Von Diederichs' squadron showed that the decaying Spanish Pacific empire was in grave danger of dismemberment. Had the United States not moved in, Germany and Japan would have seized a chance to establish themselves sooner or later. By eliminating Spain's possessions in the Caribbean at the same time the United States secured its flanks, but it was not until the Second World War that the strategic importance of the Philippines became obvious to the American public.

Above: American troops advancing along the shore to attack Manila in August 1898 while supporting units of Dewey's fleet can be seen in the background.
Top right: Commodore George Dewey, seated, hero of the victory in the Battle of Manila Bay.

CHINA
HONG KONG

Formosa

© Richard Natkiel, 1986

Hainan I.

PACIFIC OCEAN

**25 April 1898
Dewey sails**

30 April
Insurgent
leaders
put ashore

Luzon

1 May **MANILA**

**PHILIPPINE
ISLANDS**

South China Sea

MINDORO

SAMAR

PANAY

CEBU LEYTE

PALAWAN

NEGROS

Mindanao

NAUTICAL
MILES
0   200

Borneo

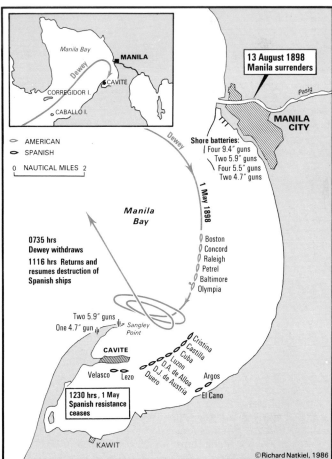

Manila Bay

MANILA

Dewey

CORREGIDOR I.   CAVITE

CABALLO I.

AMERICAN

SPANISH

0   NAUTICAL MILES   2

**13 August 1898
Manila surrenders**

Pasig

**MANILA
CITY**

Dewey

Shore batteries:
Four 9.4″ guns
Two 5.9″ guns
Four 5.5″ guns
Two 4.7″ guns

1 May 1898

*Manila
Bay*

**0735 hrs
Dewey withdraws**

**1116 hrs Returns and
resumes destruction of
Spanish ships**

Boston
Concord
Raleigh
Petrel
Baltimore
Olympia

Two 5.9″ guns
One 4.7″ gun   Sangley
                 Point

CAVITE

Cristina
Castila
Cuba
Luzon
D.A. de Alloa
D.J. de Austria
Duero

Velasco   Lezo

Argos

El Cano

**1230 hrs , 1 May
Spanish resistance
ceases**

KAWIT

© Richard Natkiel, 1986

The Russo-Japanese War

Japan's humiliation at the hands of the Great Powers after the successful war with China in 1894 had been exacerbated by the way in which Russia, with the backing of France and Germany had paid off China's war indemnity in return for a concession to extend the Trans-Siberian Railway through Manchuria to Vladivostok. This strategic link enabled Russia to project its commercial and military power into the heart of the disputed province in a way which had never been possible before. To cap this diplomatic triumph Russia annexed Port Arthur two years later, giving her the base which had been forfeited by the Japanese, and obtained a concession to build a southern spur linking Port Arthur to the Trans-Siberian Railway.

In 1894 Russian territory in the Far East had been surrounded by Japanese possessions, completely at the mercy of a naval blockade. Now these gains had been outflanked, and Japan found herself inexorably driven into the arms of the 'Anglo Saxons.' Both Britain and the United States believed that China should not be dismembered, and were particularly anxious not to see the traditional enemy Russia enrich herself at China's expense.

The British solution was to provide the highest level of technical assistance to the Imperial Japanese Navy, not only selling the most modern designs of warships but also undertaking a massive training program. The Russians, unable to ignore these developments, turned to their French allies for technical assistance, and in 1898 launched a naval expansion program to update their fleet. By the end of 1903 the IJN could muster six battleships which were equal in fighting power to the best in the British Royal Navy, but the Russians had lagged behind, and their eight new battleships were only nearing completion.

Japan's rulers assumed that war with Russia was inevitable, and took the sensible decision to let hostilities start at the most favorable moment. February 1904 had a lot to recommend it: Korean harbors would be ice-free, the new Russian battleships were not yet complete, and the Trans-Siberian Railway was not quite finished.

True to their logic the Japanese decided that the only way to offset the Russian superiority in numbers was to take them by surprise, and on 8 February they attacked without warning, launching a torpedo attack on Port Arthur and sinking the armored cruiser *Varyag* at Chemulpo (Inchon) on the coast of Korea. The attack on Port Arthur was not a great success for even the minimal precautions taken by the Russians were sufficient to limit the damage to two battleships and a cruiser slightly damaged, but the Russians had lost the initiative and refused to undertake any operations until the ships were repaired. This allowed the Japanese to land troops in Korea without opposition, and blockade Port Arthur on the landward side. An attempt to sink blockships in the entrance on the night 23/24 February was unsuccessful, but it further paralyzed the Russian command.

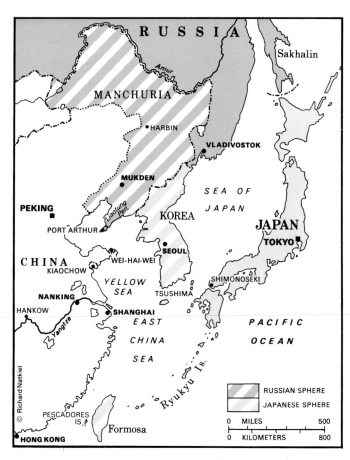

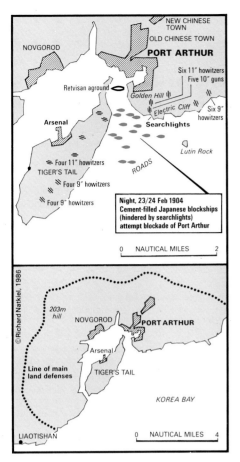

Night, 23/24 Feb 1904
Cement-filled Japanese blockships
(hindered by searchlights)
attempt blockade of Port Arthur

The Imperial Russian Navy tried to repair the damage by appointing Admiral Stefan Makarov to command the Port Arthur fleet. He was a bold innovator and tactician, who could also inspire his officers and men, and under his leadership efficiency improved rapidly. Sadly he lost his life in April 1904, when his flagship *Petropavlovsk* struck a mine during a sortie out of Port Arthur. Offensive mine warfare, laying mines in enemy waters, was a feature of naval warfare for the first time, although mines had pre-

Below left: **Loading a 500-pound shell into one of the Japanese siege guns which pounded the Port Arthur defenses and sunk the Russian ships in the harbor.**
Below: **Contemporary illustration showing the surprise Japanese torpedo attack on the Russian Fleet at Port Arthur, 8 February 1904.**

viously been used defensively. Subsequently the Japanese were caught in a similar trap, when the battleships *Hatsue* and *Yashima* were also lured into a minefield and sunk.

Makarov's successor, Admiral Vitgeft had none of his enterprise, and refused to take advantage of his 6:4 ratio of superiority in battleships. In August he was at last forced to attempt a breakout to Vladivostok but was brought to action by the Japanese Commander-in-Chief Admiral Togo. Both sides opened fire at maximum range without scoring any hits at first. Firing continued through the afternoon of 10 August, with neither side willing to close to more decisive range. After a loss of contact Togo caught up with Vitgeft's force again, and the two lines steamed ahead in parallel, exchanging shots. The Russians were probably doing slightly better than the Japanese up to this point for their long-range gunnery proved remarkably

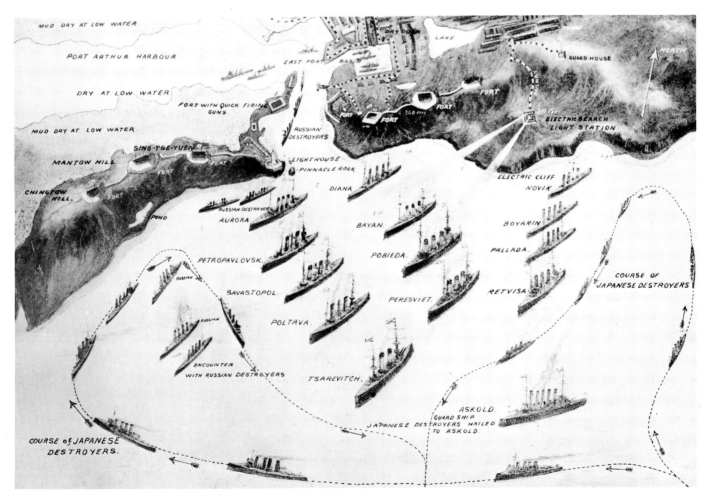

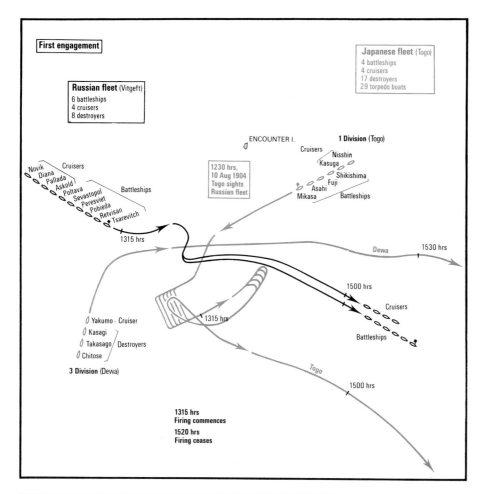

First engagement

Russian fleet (Vitgeft)
6 battleships
4 cruisers
8 destroyers

Japanese fleet (Togo)
4 battleships
4 cruisers
17 destroyers
29 torpedo boats

ENCOUNTER I.

1 Division (Togo)

Cruisers
Nisshin
Kasuga
Shikishima
Fuji
Asahi
Mikasa
Battleships

1230 hrs, 10 Aug 1904 Togo sights Russian fleet

Novik
Diana
Pallada
Askold
Poltava
Sevastopol
Peresviet
Pobieda
Retvisan
Tsarevitch

Cruisers

Battleships

1315 hrs

Dewa
1530 hrs

1500 hrs

Cruisers

1315 hrs

Battleships

Yakumo - Cruiser
Kasagi
Takasago Destroyers
Chitose

3 Division (Dewa)

Togo

1500 hrs

1315 hrs
Firing commences
1520 hrs
Firing ceases

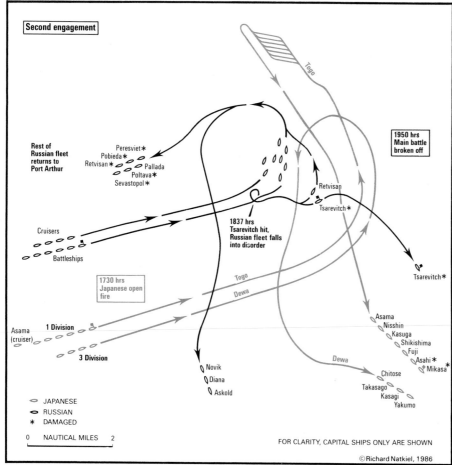

Second engagement

Rest of
Russian fleet
returns to
Port Arthur

Peresviet *
Pobieda *
Retvisan *
Pallada
Poltava *
Sevastopol *

1837 hrs
Tsarevitch hit,
Russian fleet falls
into disorder

Togo

Retvisan

Tsarevitch *

1950 hrs
Main battle
broken off

Cruisers

Battleships

1730 hrs
Japanese open
fire

Togo
Dewa

Asama
(cruiser)

1 Division

3 Division

Novik
Diana
Askold

Dewa

Asama
Nisshin
Kasuga
Shikishima
Fuji
Asahi *
Mikasa *

Tsarevitch *

Dewa

Chitose
Takasago
Kasagi
Yakumo

JAPANESE
RUSSIAN
* DAMAGED
0   NAUTICAL MILES   2

FOR CLARITY, CAPITAL SHIPS ONLY ARE SHOWN

© Richard Natkiel, 1986

accurate, and only chance prevented the Japanese from sustaining severe damage. Then the luck changed dramatically as the *Tsarevitch* was struck by a 12-inch shell which burst in the conning tower, killing Vitgeft and some of his staff and wounding the captain and gunnery officer among others. (Maps left.)

Worse was to follow, as a fault in the steering caused the *Tsarevitch* to turn circles. Her next astern, the *Retvisan* started to follow the flagship round, but when the mistake was discovered she turned in the opposite direction. The ships astern turned in different ways, throwing the whole line into disorder, and Vitgeft's second-in-command seems to have lost his head, and signalled all ships to return to Port Arthur. The Japanese were unable to stop the Russians, despite bringing the range down to 4-5000 yards, but the *Tsarevitch* was cut off from her squadron and eventually escaped to Tsingtao, where the Germans interned her under International Law.

Early in December the Japanese Army after months of heavy losses succeeded in capturing the heights above the harbor, and within a few days their 11-inch howitzers were firing on the anchorage and land defenses. Methodically the Russian ships were sunk at their moorings, apart from one, which was moored in the roadstead, where she was torpedoed.

It had always been assumed that the Russians would send reinforcements as soon as Port Arthur was threatened but the Baltic Fleet did not sail from Kronstadt until late September 1904. It included four of the new *Borodino* class battleships and a motley collection of colliers and auxiliaries, in addition to cruisers and destroyers. The reputation of the Baltic Fleet was not enhanced when on the night of 22 October lookouts mistook British fishing trawlers off the Dogger Bank in the North Sea for Japanese torpedo boats. In 12 minutes of confusion four trawlers were sunk and another was badly damaged, while the cruiser *Aurora* was hit by shells from the battleship *Orel*.

The Dogger Bank Incident infuriated the British, and to add to the troubles of the Russians they were trailed by Royal Navy warships clearly spoiling for a fight. But the British held back and left the Russians to round the Cape of Good Hope and reach Nossi Bé in Madagascar, where they learned of the fall of Port Arthur. After making a rendezvous with reinforcements coming

Above: Togo's fleet opens fire in the early stages of the Battle of the Yellow Sea, 10 August 1904.

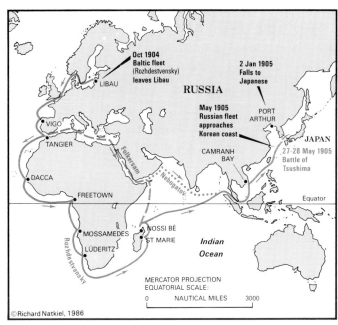

©Richard Natkiel, 1986

through the Suez Canal, the Russian C-in-C Rozhdestvensky set sail for the East Indies early in March 1905.

With fine disregard for the Japanese the Russian commander took the direct route through the China Sea, heading for Vladivostok. Anything more subtle would have been useless anyway, as the fast Japanese cruisers would have kept in touch whichever route he had followed. In fact they detected the Second Pacific Squadron early on 27 May as it approached Tsushima Strait. Little attempt was made to drive off the Japanese scouting forces and so they were able to send Togo a constant stream of radio reports on Rozhdestvensky's strength, formation, course and speed (Map right.)

The Russian line was led by the new battleships *Kniaz Suvorov*, *Imperator Alexander III*, *Borodino* and *Orel*, followed by four more older battleships, then a scratch force of elderly coast defense ships and the cruisers. Togo's four battleships had been reinforced by two powerful armored cruisers to form a first division, and his remaining six large cruisers formed the second division, a more homogeneous force which had the enormous advantage of a margin of six knots' speed. Even more important was the high state of

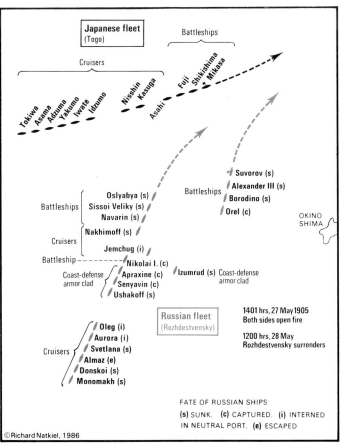

Japanese fleet (Togo)

Cruisers — Battleships

Tokiwa Asama Adzuma Yakumo Iwate Idzumo Nisshin Kasuga Asahi Fuji Shikishima Mikasa

Russian fleet (Rozhdestvensky)

Battleships
Oslyabya (s)
Sissoi Veliky (s)
Navarin (s)

Cruisers
Nakhimoff (s)

Battleship
Jemchug (i)
Nikolai I. (c)

Coast-defense armor clad
Apraxine (c)
Senyavin (c)
Ushakoff (s)

Izumrud (s) Coast-defense armor clad

Battleships
Suvorov (s)
Alexander III (s)
Borodino (s)
Orel (c)

OKINO SHIMA

Cruisers
Oleg (i)
Aurora (i)
Svetlana (s)
Almaz (e)
Donskoi (s)
Monomakh (s)

1401 hrs, 27 May 1905
Both sides open fire

1200 hrs, 28 May
Rozhdestvensky surrenders

FATE OF RUSSIAN SHIPS
(s) SUNK, (c) CAPTURED, (i) INTERNED IN NEUTRAL PORT, (e) ESCAPED

©Richard Natkiel, 1986

137

training and morale in the Japanese ships.

At 1320 Togo saw the leading Russian ships ahead to port, heading on an opposite course, so he turned his ships across the Russian line of advance, then made another turn to bring his fleet onto a course parallel with the Russians, who were now on his starboard bow. As the courses of the two fleets converged slightly the flagship *Mikasa* came within 7000 yards of the Russian flagship *Kniaz Suvorov* and the Russians opened fire. Had they been able to score any hits Togo's bold tactics might have got his ships into a tight corner but although the ships were surrounded by splashes and some secondary shells struck home no major damage was suffered. By 1420 the distance had closed to about 5500 yards and the leading Japanese ships were concentrating their fire on Rozhdestvensky's flagship. She began to take severe punishment from hits in her upperworks, and the admiral and several of his staff were wounded when splinters penetrated the conning tower.

Farther down the line the Japanese cruisers had inflicted severe damage on the battleship *Oslyabya* to the point where she was sinking. They drew ahead and started to engage the Russian leading division. By now the flagship *Kniaz Suvorov* had become detached from the main body and she received terrible punishment as she passed Togo's battleships at a distance of only 1000 yards. Later that day, still burning and steering erratically she was torpedoed by a destroyer but failed to sink. She was finally sunk after sunset. Her dying C-in-C had been taken off by a destroyer but still she fired with the few guns left undamaged. Her long agony was brought to an end with three torpedoes.

The remaining Russian ships had long since lost all formation and were circling aimlessly, trying to cope with fires and fending off attacks by the Japanese, who used their superior speed effortlessly. The battleship *Borodino* tried to shape course for Vladivostock but she and her consorts were soon under attack from Togo's battleships, which cut off their line of escape. The *Imperator Alexander III* staggered out of line, heeled over and sank. Then the *Borodino* blew up when fires reached her magazines. Later the battered *Orel* surrendered to overwhelming force, while Japanese light forces rounded up other survivors.

Tsushima stunned the world by its very decisiveness. A century of inconclusive naval battles had led people to forget Nelson's concept of a battle of annihilation. Togo's tactics had kept the initiative firmly in his hands, leaving the Russians with nothing but dogged heroism to pit against modern guns and training. Even more far-reaching were the consequences of the humiliation of a major European power. The first rumblings of the 1917 Bolshevik Revolution were heard in 1905 when Russia learned that its best ships and men had been destroyed by an upstart oriental nation. Suddenly Japan was a world power, and her statesmen and soldiers had taken the first steps which would lead to Pearl Harbor and Hiroshima.

Remnants of Russian fleet disperse and most are sunk

1900
Alexander III capsizes,
Borodino explodes

1830
1830
1800
1800

Japanese fleet opens fire
1425
1408
1830
1530
1445
Suvorov crippled, sinks later
1425
1408
Russian fleet opens fire
1530
1450
Oslyabya sinks
1345
1320
1700
1500
1345
1320
1800
1500
Japanese fleet (Togo)
1600
1600

Russian fleet
(Rozhdestvensky)

1700

Kamimura
Togo

MANEUVERS DURING 27 MAY
RUSSIAN FLEET (9-10 KNOTS)
JAPANESE FLEET (15-16 KNOTS)

© Richard Natkiel, 1986

138

The United States as a World Empire

The ravages of the Civil War delayed the emergence of the United States as a world power, and in the years immediately after the war the need to reconstruct the country took priority. The need to open up the West and to develop industry also curbed imperial ambitions but a growing perception of the importance of colonies led eventually to the war with Spain in 1898.

That watershed marked the point when the United States entered the stage of world politics permanently. Annexation of new territories had been going on since the acquisition of Alaska in 1867; in the same year Midway Island was annexed, followed by a virtual protectorate over Hawaii in 1875 and a foothold in the Samoan islands, gained in 1878.

The settlement of the Spanish war produced much more significant gains. The Philippines and Guam were ceded, to become stepping-stones toward China, which American businessmen imagined to be a rich field for commercial exploitation. In the Caribbean Puerto Rico was taken, and in 1903 a protectorate was established over Cuba. Potential friction with the British had been averted in 1901 by the signing of the Hay-Pauncefote Treaty, which gave the US a virtual free hand.

Mexico had proved a constant temptation to American expansion. In the Mexican War of 1846-48 Mexico had lost California, New Mexico and Texas. After 1880 American commercial interests exploited Mexican markets steadily, but the 1911 revolution brought this to a halt and provoked serious hostility from Washington.

The French effort to establish the Emperor Maximilian as a puppet ruler of Mexico in 1862-67 came to an end through the efforts of the Mexicans, without overt American intervention, but the attempt by Ferdinand de Lesseps under French auspices to build a canal across the Isthmus of Panama brought a sharper response. In 1879 President Hayes went so far as to claim that any such canal would be regarded as 'part of the coastline of the United States.' As the century progressed their was a growing tendency to treat the whole of Latin America as an exclusive sphere of influence. In 1895 the US Government informed Britain that she was 'practically sovereign on this continent,' but it stirred up resentment in all Latin American countries.

There were many who proclaimed a 'Manifest Destiny' to rule the entire continent, and

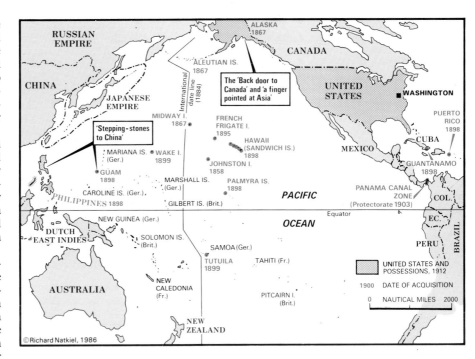

©Richard Natkiel, 1986

the acquisition of Alaska was seen by some expansionists as the first move to encircle Canada. Not surprisingly the Canadians were none too happy, but the pressure acted as a spur toward Confederation in that country in 1867. When the remaining provinces of Manitoba and British Columbia joined the new Dominion of Canada in 1870-71 the American drive on Canada lost some of its impetus. Another area which caused friction was the narrow coastal strip of Alaska. After 40 years of wrangling the American-Canadian border was finally agreed upon in 1903.

The French attempt to build a Panama Canal had been defeated by disease, but the US Government was determined to build a strategic waterway to link the Atlantic to their new Pacific empire. When Colombia failed to oblige with permission to build an Isthmus canal an insurrection ensued, as a result of which Panama was forcibly detached from Colombia. In 1903 the United States signed a treaty with Panama, the terms of which included virtually contradictory clauses, one leasing the ten-mile wide Canal Zone in perpetuity, and another which allows the US to possess the Zone 'as if it were sovereign.'

The building of the Panama Canal was a major engineering achievement, and it transformed the strategic position of the United States. She could now face a threat from either east or west without having her military forces divided. In 1914 the British and the European Powers were still too strong, but their impoverishment in the First World War left the stage clear for the United States to move closer to her constant ambition to be the world's most powerful nation.

Colonial Empires in 1900

Although it is common today to talk of a continuous process of colonial expansion throughout the nineteenth century, nothing could be further from the truth. In the middle of the century most European nations regarded their overseas possessions almost as millstones, although they were reluctant to lose them. Apart from India most British possessions, for example, were impoverished and contributed little to national wealth.

France had been stripped of her conquests in 1815 but she soon set about acquiring a new colonial empire, and by the 1830s had gained control of Algeria. During the next decade various island territories in the Pacific fell into her grasp, followed by Indo-China in the late 1850s. The oldest European colonial powers, in contrast, lost their grip on their empires. The Spanish and Portuguese had lost virtually all their possessions in South and Central America by the 1830s.

The British were impressed by the fact that their greatest volume of trade was with the United States and South America, where they had no political control. They were, however, sensitive to maritime threats to the communications between their territories, notably the route to India. Over the years many strategically useful possessions were acquired as coaling stations or naval bases, and many minor conflicts were fought with unruly local inhabitants, but successive governments refused to sanction the conquest of large tracts of territory.

All this changed toward the end of the century. Most of the European countries were seized by a renewed urge to acquire control of raw materials and markets, in a frenzy of colonial expansion. Inevitably this energy came to be directed to Africa and the Far East, for other areas were dominated by countries which had staked their claims earlier. Thus the Monroe Doctrine proclaimed by the United States and in effect underwritten by British naval power acted as a strong deterrent to European expansion in the Western Hemisphere with its statement that the American continent was not open to further European colonization, forcing the aggressive newcomers Germany and Italy to look elsewhere. The United States wiped out the last Spanish footholds in the Caribbean and the Philippines in 1898 and Russia was able to destroy the last independent khanates in Central Asia, but other countries made only minor gains other than in Africa.

A nationalist revolt in Egypt in 1882 led to a British landing in Egypt to protect the Suez Canal. The direct result was Anglo-French rivalry in Egypt but the longer-term consequence was the 'Scramble for Africa,' during which even the old colonial powers, Portugal and Spain, attempted to reassert their position. Between 1871 and 1914 France acquired some 4 million square miles and nearly 47 million new subjects; Germany acquired about a quarter of that land area and 14 million subjects. Not to be outdone the British Empire was increased by 88 million subjects, and by 1914 covered a fifth of the world's land surface.

There were failures. The Italians conquered Eritrea and Somaliland but suffered a disastrous defeat when trying to conquer Abyssinia. Against all predictions the rump of the Chinese Empire resisted all attempts to partition it, despite numerous concessions in the form of 'treaty ports.'

The turn of the century marked the high tide of colonialism. Thereafter tensions in Europe forced the major powers, Great Britain, France and Germany and to a lesser extent Italy and Austria-Hungary to strengthen their positions in Europe at the expense of their overseas possessions.

Above and above right: A medal presented by the American Chamber of Commerce in Liverpool to commemorate the laying of the Atlantic telegraph cable in 1866.
Right: Admiral Tirpitz, the founding father of the Imperial German Navy which became the second largest in the world in the years before World War I. The arms race with Britain which Tirpitz's expansion program provoked was one of the causes of the war in 1914.
Far right: Insurance underwriters at work at Lloyds of London in the 1880s. The development of facilities for marine insurance and standards of construction and safety for ships were considerably extended in the Victorian era.
Below: The high point of British naval power, the review of the fleet at Spithead in 1897 for Queen Victoria's Jubilee. Britain then maintained a fleet larger than those of any two other nations combined.

Colonial Empires in 1900

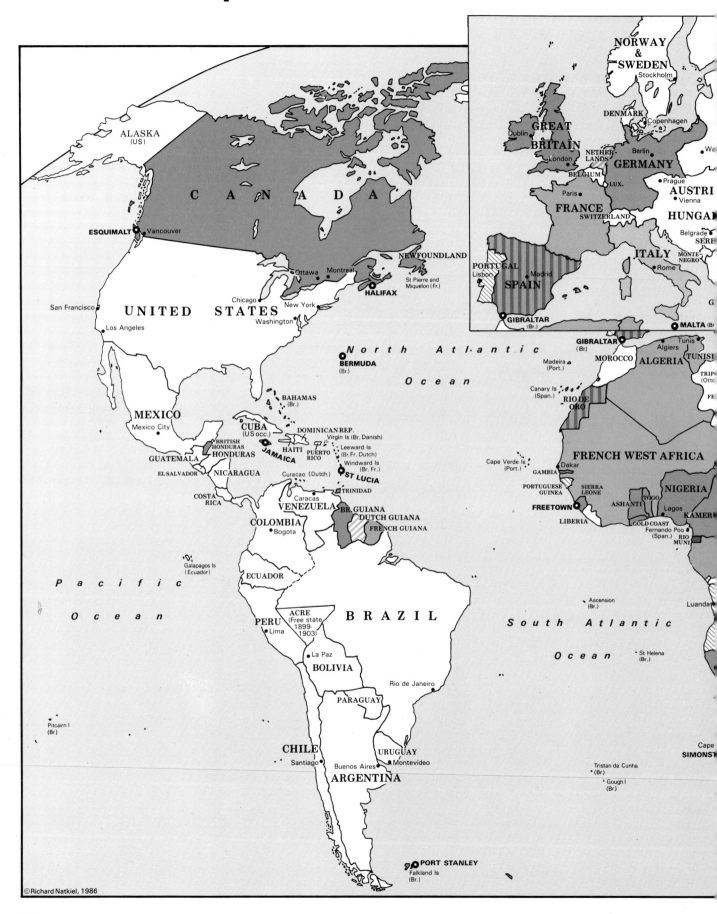

ALASKA (US)

C A N A D A

ESQUIMALT • Vancouver

NEWFOUNDLAND

• Ottawa   Montreal •

St Pierre and Miquelon (Fr.)

Chicago •   New York •

HALIFAX

San Francisco •

UNITED   STATES

Washington •

Los Angeles •

North   Atlantic

Ocean

BERMUDA (Br.)

MEXICO

Mexico City •

BAHAMAS (Br.)

CUBA (US occ.)

DOMINICAN REP.

Virgin Is (Br. Danish)

BRITISH HONDURAS

JAMAICA

HAITI   PUERTO RICO

Leeward Is (Br. Fr. Dutch)

GUATEMALA   HONDURAS

Windward Is (Br. Fr.)

EL SALVADOR   NICARAGUA

Curaçao (Dutch)

ST LUCIA

TRINIDAD

COSTA RICA

Caracas •

VENEZUELA

BR. GUIANA

DUTCH GUIANA

COLOMBIA

FRENCH GUIANA

• Bogota

Galapagos Is (Ecuador)

ECUADOR

Pacific

Ocean

ACRE (Free state 1899-1903)

B R A Z I L

PERU

• Lima

La Paz •

South   Atlantic

Ocean

Ascension (Br.)

Luanda

BOLIVIA

Rio de Janeiro •

St Helena (Br.)

PARAGUAY

Pitcairn I (Br.)

CHILE   URUGUAY

Santiago •   Montevideo •

Buenos Aires •

ARGENTINA

Tristan da Cunha •

Gough I (Br.)

PORT STANLEY

Falkland Is (Br.)

Cape

SIMONST

© Richard Natkiel, 1986

NORWAY & SWEDEN

Stockholm •

DENMARK

Copenhagen •

GREAT BRITAIN

Dublin •

London •

NETHER-LANDS

Berlin •

GERMANY

BELGIUM

LUX.

• Prague

AUSTRI

Paris •

• Vienna

HUNGAR

FRANCE

SWITZERLAND

Belgrade •

SERB

ITALY

MONTE-NEGRO

• Rome

G

PORTUGAL

Lisbon •

SPAIN

• Madrid

GIBRALTAR (Br.)

MALTA (Br

GIBRALTAR (Br.)

Tunis •

Algiers •

MOROCCO

ALGERIA

TUNISI

Madeira • (Port.)

TRIP (Otto

Canary Is (Span.)

RIO DE ORO

FE

Cape Verde Is (Port.)

FRENCH WEST AFRICA

• Dakar

GAMBIA

PORTUGUESE GUINEA

SIERRA LEONE

NIGERIA

TOGO

FREETOWN

ASHANTI

• Lagos

LIBERIA

GOLD COAST

Fernando Poo (Span.)

KAMER

RIO MUNI

142

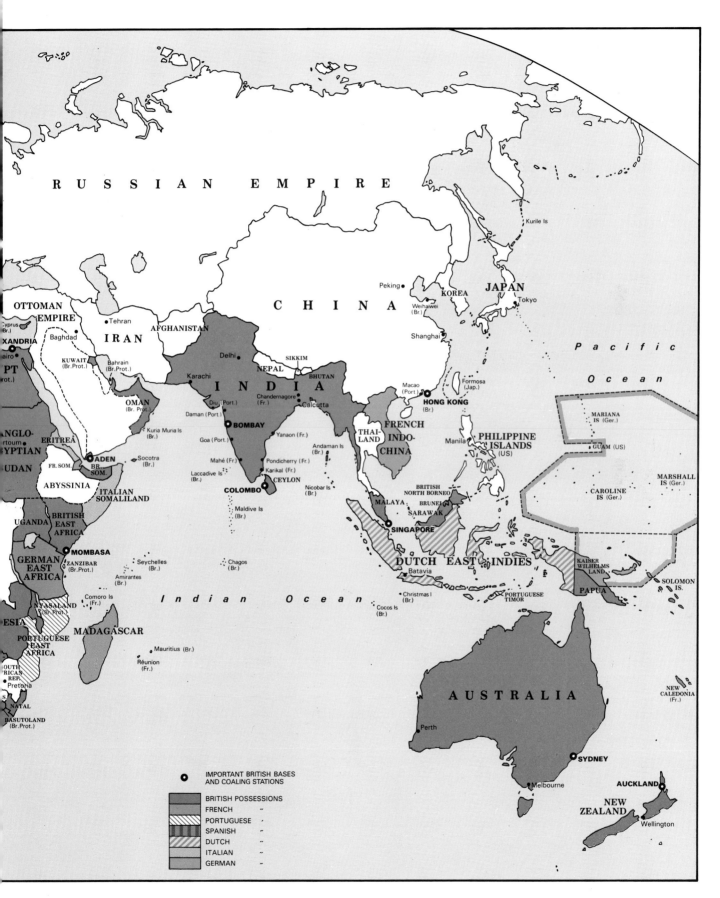

RUSSIAN EMPIRE

CHINA

JAPAN

OTTOMAN
EMPIRE

Cyprus
(Br.)

XANDRIA

PT
rot.)

●Tehran

AFGHANISTAN

Baghdad

IRAN

KUWAIT
(Br.Prot.)

Bahrain
(Br.Prot.)

OMAN
(Br. Prot.)

Delhi

Karachi

INDIA

SIKKIM

NEPAL

BHUTAN

Peking ●

KOREA

Weihaiwei
(Br.)

Shanghai

Tokyo

Kurile Is

Pacific

Ocean

Chandernagore
(Fr.)

Diu (Port.)

Calcutta

Daman (Port.)

Macao
(Port.)

HONG KONG
(Br.)

Formosa
(Jap.)

ANGLO-
YPTIAN

UDAN

ERITREA

FR. SOM.

BR.
SOM.

ADEN

ABYSSINIA

ITALIAN
SOMALILAND

UGANDA

BRITISH
EAST
AFRICA

GERMAN
EAST
AFRICA

●BOMBAY

Kuria Muria Is
(Br.)

Socotra
(Br.)

Goa (Port.)

Mahé (Fr.)

Laccadive Is
(Br.)

COLOMBO

CEYLON

Maldive Is
(Br.)

Yanaon (Fr.)

Pondicherry (Fr.)

Karikal (Fr.)

Andaman Is
(Br.)

Nicobar Is
(Br.)

THAI-
LAND

FRENCH
INDO-
CHINA

Manila

PHILIPPINE
ISLANDS
(US)

MARIANA
IS (Ger.)

GUAM (US)

MARSHALL
IS (Ger.)

CAROLINE
IS (Ger.)

BRITISH
NORTH BORNEO

MALAYA

BRUNEI

SARAWAK

SINGAPORE

DUTCH EAST INDIES

ZANZIBAR
(Br.Prot.)

MOMBASA

Seychelles
(Br.)

Amirantes
(Br.)

Comoro Is
(Fr.)

NYASALAND
(Br.Prot.)

ESIA

PORTUGUESE
EAST
AFRICA

OUTH
RICAN
REP.

Pretoria

NATAL

BASUTOLAND
(Br.Prot.)

Chagos
(Br.)

Indian   Ocean

MADAGASCAR

Mauritius (Br.)

Réunion
(Fr.)

Batavia

Christmas I
(Br.)

Cocos Is
(Br.)

PORTUGUESE
TIMOR

KAISER
WILHELMS
LAND

PAPUA

SOLOMON
IS.

AUSTRALIA

Perth

Melbourne

SYDNEY

NEW
CALEDONIA
(Fr.)

AUCKLAND

NEW
ZEALAND

Wellington

○ IMPORTANT BRITISH BASES
AND COALING STATIONS

BRITISH POSSESSIONS
FRENCH   "
PORTUGUESE   "
SPANISH   "
DUTCH   "
ITALIAN   "
GERMAN   "

Pre-dreadnought battleships of the
German High Seas Fleet on exercise
shortly before the outbreak of World War I.

WORLD WAR I

Causes and Course of the War

The early years of the twentieth century were dominated in naval affairs by an arms race between the British and German navies. Admiral Tirpitz became Germany's Navy Minister in 1897 and soon began a substantial building program. To British eyes it seemed a direct threat to the superiority of the Royal Navy and to Britain's position in the world which was believed to depend principally on the navy. The British, therefore, replied to Tirpitz's Navy Laws with a building program of their own. The most dramatic development in this was the introduction, in 1906, of a new type of battleship, the 'all big gun' dreadnought (named after HMS *Dreadnought*, the first of the type). Another important change which presaged many future developments was the gradual switch from coal to oil fuel for warships which also began. Perhaps most importantly the arms race contributed to an atmosphere of international distrust and hostility which was itself one of the main causes of war in 1914.

Although the British and Germans had by far the largest fleets by 1914, with Britain still some way ahead, the Americans and Japanese among others had also greatly expanded their navies and were to continue to do so during 1914-18. By 1914 also Britain had concentrated the bulk of her fleet in home waters to oppose the Germans and this diminution of the Royal Navy's worldwide presence, combined with the growth in US and Japanese naval power, clearly had many future implications.

After the great arms race the reality of naval warfare came as something of an anticlimax. Instead of the decisive pitched battles between fleets of dreadnoughts which everyone expected, there were only skirmishes of light forces, and a growing insidious threat from mines and submarines.

Great Britain exploited all her geographical advantages to confine the German Navy to the North Sea, and although the blockade was never completely watertight, this strategy ultimately succeeded in winning the war. The German squadrons on overseas stations caused some losses, particularly the commerce-raiding cruiser *Emden* and Admiral Graf Spee's squadron caused considerable damage, but by the end of 1914 they were all sunk or neutralized, having inflicted only trifling losses on the huge British mercantile marine and a few obsolescent warships.

While France concentrated on the Mediterranean, the British faced the Germans in the North Sea. This apparently tidy division of Allied responsibilities was jeopardized by the activities of the German battlecruiser *Goeben* and her escorting light cruiser *Breslau*. Their escape to Turkey triggered off a chapter of disasters culminating in the failure to force the Dardanelles, but once the German ships were safely up the Straits there was no serious threat to Allied seapower in the Mediterranean.

The enormous preponderance of the Allies (who included Italy by the spring of 1915) led the Germans and their Austro-Hungarian allies to make greater use of submarines (U-Boats) as a countermeasure. From timid beginnings the German U-Boats grew bolder, and in 1915 began to inflict enormous losses on Allied merchant shipping. With vast quantities of war material crossing the Atlantic from the United States the U-Boats were able to hamper the Allied war effort, and as casualties in the titanic battles on the Western Front drained Britain and France of money and manpower the U-Boat war became more and more crucial.

The British Grand Fleet had few opportunities to meet the Germans in battle, and when the two fleets met face-to-face at Jutland in May 1916 the expected British victory did not materialize. However the battle left the overall strategic situation unchanged. As a result the German high command gave its blessing to another all-out U-Boat offensive, in the hope that the Allies' Atlantic lifeline could be cut before American public opinion could be mobilized. The gamble failed, and the entry of the United States into the war sealed Germany's fate. New tactics, principally convoy, cut the losses of shipping, and by the summer of 1918 the exhausted Allies were receiving large-scale reinforcements.

As the first 'total' war the conflict was decided by industrial strength, and the British proved that they could not only outbuild the Germans but could also make the innovations needed to counter German successes. The Royal Navy pioneered the aircraft carrier, the magnetic mine and the first underwater sensors, and once their faulty tactics were changed the British proved that they could inflict a savage defeat on the U-Boats.

The Allies suffered from the wide scope of their activities. The British dissipated their strength in small expeditions overseas, of which the Gallipoli landings were the most costly. The naval weaknesses of her Mediterranean allies forced Britain to shoulder the main burden of protecting shipping against the U-Boats, with the result that in 1917-18 the Royal Navy was once again the dominant force in that area, in addition to the main Atlantic routes.

Although the large fleets of dreadnought battleships did not play the decisive role that had been expected of them, their strategic value was important, and as Jutland showed, the Grand Fleet's position at Scapa Flow was almost unassailable. The mine and the submarine's torpedo inhibited the freedom of the battleship but never stopped it from

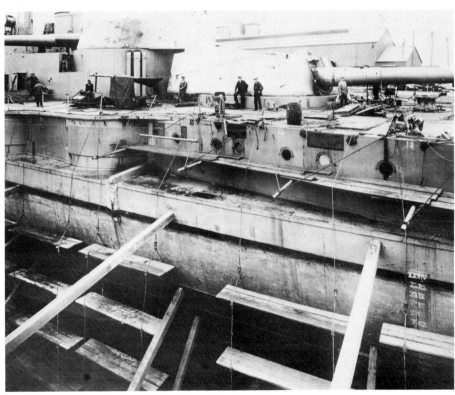

Above: Winston Churchill, First Lord of the Admiralty (Britain's Navy Minister) in the early part of World War I.
Top right: The German light cruiser *Dresden* finally run to earth by the British after the defeat of von Spee' squadron at the Battle of the Falklands.
Above right: The British battleship *Warspite* in dock to have damage repaired after the Battle of Jutland. *Warspite* survived to participate in many important actions in World War II.
Left: HMS *Dreadnought* showing four of the five twin 12-inch turrets which were her principal distinguishing feature from every previous battleship.

functioning, and surprisingly few modern capital ships were sunk at sea: five British, one German, one Italian and one Austro-Hungarian. The rapid advance of technology made the older warships of all types very vulnerable, but in general the modern warships functioned well. The submarine, in spite of its short existence as a practicable weapon of war, proved to be efficient; its period of gestation was already over, unlike the military aircraft, and all the main features were settled by 1914.

Apart from the unexpected impact of submarines, the most radical change in naval power was the adaptation of aircraft to operate from ships. In 1914 the first primitive seaplane carriers could hoist out seaplanes to take off from the water, but by the Armistice in 1918 aircraft carriers were launching and recovering wheeled aircraft. The use of aerial reconnaissance provided early warning of enemy moves and improved long-range gunnery, and by 1918 the first torpedo-bombers were operational.

For the Allied powers the war was always a maritime conflict; for the Central powers it was not so clear, but their downfall in October-November 1918 was just as surely caused by their failure to offset the Allies' maritime power.

The Blockade of the Central Powers

As the world's principal naval power in 1914 Great Britain was able to impose her strategic concepts, as far as maritime affairs were concerned, on her French ally. Broadly it was hoped to repeat the success of the Napoleonic wars by blockading Germany and starving her out.

Geography still favored Great Britain for she dominated the exits to the North Sea, and with France friendly for the first time in 600 years the commitment was in fact smaller than it had been 100 years earlier. In practice, of course, things proved more difficult, and even with the addition of Italy as an ally in 1915 the French Navy was not strong enough to contain the Austro-Hungarian Navy in the Adriatic unaided. Nor could total control of the sea be guaranteed in the face of mines and submarines.

German plans had counted on the Royal Navy trying to maintain a close blockade of their coasts, and it was hoped to use torpedo craft and submarines to inflict serious losses on the British. What was not known was that in 1913 the threat of attrition had been recognized by the Admiralty, and 'close' blockade with ships patrolling near enemy ports had been replaced by a new doctrine of 'distant' blockade to confine the Germans in the North Sea.

The result was that both fleets stayed in harbor much of the time and left their light craft and submarines to probe each other's defenses. The British public was denied a second Battle of Trafalgar in the North Sea but equally the German High Seas Fleet never achieved the position of parity which it had planned for. Although the Royal Navy suffered losses from attack, particularly by mines and torpedoes, its Grand Fleet patrolled regularly from its main base at Scapa Flow, ensuring that only a handful of German commerce-raiders escaped into the Atlantic.

To reduce the demands on major warships a number of liners were armed as Armed Merchant Cruisers (AMCs), and as the Northern Patrol they patrolled the area between Iceland and the Orkneys. A similar patrol line was established in the Western Approaches to the British Isles, and as a result British losses in 1914-15 from commerce raiding were a negligible 2 percent of the total mercantile marine. Conversely the patrols enforced the blockade effectively, preventing contraband (including foodstuffs as well as war materials) from reaching Germany.

The strain of the blockade forced Germany to desperate measures. The first 'unrestricted' U-Boat campaign of 1915 claimed that the harshness of the British blockade justified Germany abandoning the rules of International Law guaranteeing non-naval shipping from being sunk 'at sight.' Allied shipping losses soon rose to alarming levels but the effect on neutral opinion was disastrous and Germany was eventually forced to abandon the campaign under pressure from the United States and other influential neutrals.

Efforts to seal in the U-Boats with minefields were hampered by the lack of an efficient British mine until 1917, by which time the US Navy was able to help in laying the enormous North Sea Barrage. The Dover Barrage was finally made impenetrable to U-Boats in May 1918 but the Otranto Barrage never succeeded in blocking the Adriatic to the same extent.

The disastrous losses in the land battles of 1916, and the ensuing stalemate in 1917 made the German High Command desperate. The German Navy was given authority to start a second unrestricted U-Boat campaign and this time it came close to knocking Great Britain out of the war. When the United States entered the war in April 1917 Admiral Sims (commander of the US naval forces in the European theater) was horrified to learn that the British were losing 25 percent of all ships sailing to UK ports, and food supplies had sunk to only six weeks' reserves.

At the darkest hour defeat was staved off by an apparent miracle. Convoy, the grouping of merchant ships in formations protected by warships, was an old remedy against commerce-raiding but it had been assumed that modern weapons and steam propulsion had made it redundant, or too expensive in escorts. In practice the enormous numbers of Auxiliary Patrol ships wasting their time on fruitless searches were better employed with convoys, and the large number of destroyers attached to the battlefleet could be thinned out with very little risk to the efficacy of the blockade.

Two other measures, less well-known but equally crucial, combined to defeat the U-Boats. A large replacement shipbuilding program was started in 1916, and at about the same time the Admiralty set up a large-scale salvage administration to recover as many damaged merchantmen as possible. It is hard to credit today, but for two years Britain had watched her large merchant fleet dwindle steadily without lifting a finger to reverse the downward trend. These measures amounted to a new drive to conserve shipping, and within a matter of weeks the worst of the crisis was over. Losses fell dramatically and U-Boat losses started to climb.

By 1918 the U-Boats were on the defensive. They had failed to stop the flood of American reinforcements from crossing the Atlantic, and by mid-1918 British offensive minelaying was causing losses even in home waters. Before the Armistice the first magnetic mines had been laid by the British, and although morale in the submarine service remained high the mutiny of the High Seas Fleet brought all resistance to an end.

Below right: **British and French warships in Grand Harbour, Malta.**
Below: **The launch of the British battleship Queen Elizabeth in 1913.**

ALLIED STATES

ALLIED POSSESSIONS

CENTRAL POWERS
AND OCCUPIED TERRITORIES

NEUTRAL STATES

1914 BOUNDARIES

ALLIED BLOCKADES AND
BARRAGES, WITH DATES

0   NAUTICAL MILES   400

Blockade of Denmark Strait (between
Greenland and Iceland)

ICELAND

*Norwegian
Sea*

1915-18

1915-18

North Sea Mine
Barrage: 1918

Inset ①

*North
Sea*

NORWAY

KRISTIANIA
(Oslo, 1924)

SWEDEN

STOCKHOLM

Baltic Sea

COPENHAGEN

ATLANTIC
OCEAN

1914

UNITED KINGDOM

Inset ②

LONDON

THE HAGUE

NETHS.

BERLIN

GERMANY

Vistula

RUSSIA

BRUSSELS

BELG.

Rhine

LUX.

PARIS

FRANCE

Danube

VIENNA

AUSTRIA-HUNGARY

Dnieper

SWITZ.

BERNE

PORTUGAL

LISBON

MADRID

SPAIN

BALEARIC
IS.

CORSICA

ITALY*

*Adriatic
Sea*

BELGRADE

MONTE-
NEGRO

SERBIA

RUMANIA

BUCHAREST

Black Sea

BULGARIA

SOFIA

CONSTANTINOPLE

Tigris

GIBRALTAR
(Brit.)

BRITISH

FRENCH

ROME

SARDINIA

ITALIAN

ALBANIA

GREECE

ATHENS

OTTOMAN EMPIRE

Euphrates

SPANISH
MOROCCO

1915

FEZ

MOROCCO
(French)

ALGIERS

*Mediterranean
Sea*

SICILY

FRENCH

CRETE

CYPRUS
(Brit.)

To Italy

FRENCH

Allied patrol zones
in the Mediterranean,
1914-16

TUNIS

MALTA
(Brit.)

BRITISH

BRITISH

ARABIA

ALGERIA
(French)

TUNISIA
(French)

TRIPOLI

ITALIAN
Gulf of Sirte

LIBYA
(Ital.)

EGYPT
(Brit.)

CAIRO

*Suez
Canal*

Nile

*ITALY NEUTRAL UNTIL DECLARING WAR ON CENTRAL POWERS IN MAY 1915

Inset ①:

SHETLAND IS.

LERWICK

Area C

BERGEN

FAIR ISLE

Area A

NORWAY

ORKNEY
IS.

Area B

Scapa Flow

STAVANGER

Minelaying begun:
B: 3 Mar 1918
A, C: 8 June 1918
Completed in August

0   N MILES   100   ①

Inset ②:

MINE BARRAGES, WITH DATES

EXPLOSIVE NET MINES, 1916

DEEP MINES, 1916-18

SANDBANKS

May 1918
Strait of Dover
abandoned by U-boats

ENGLAND

RAMSGATE

DOVER

1914-15

OSTEND

FOLKESTONE

Strait of Dover

CALAIS

Cap Griz Nez

BELGIUM

1917-18

FRANCE

0   N MILES   25   ②

© Richard Natkiel, 1986

The Pursuit of the *Goeben* and *Breslau*

By August 1914 the main British forces in the Mediterranean included three battlecruisers, four armored cruisers and a number of supporting vessels. Their orders from London were to protect the passage of French troops from North Africa to France against the German battlecruiser *Goeben* and the light cruiser *Breslau* but they were not to engage a 'superior force.'

The German ships bombarded two Algerian ports on 4 August and used their superior speed to escape from two of Admiral Milne's battlecruisers later in the day. The British did not open fire because Britain and Germany were not yet at war. The British then patrolled to the west, thinking of the French troop convoys, while the Germans coaled at Messina and their admiral, Souchon, decided to make for Turkey. The British battlecruisers were not to come as close again to catching the German ships even when they subsequently took on coal at Denusa in the Aegean. The only chance was for the four armored cruisers patrolling off Greece who could have been brought into contact by the clever scouting of the light cruiser *Gloucester*. However, Rear Admiral Troubridge, commanding the cruiser squadron, decided that the Germans were a 'superior force' and turned back.

The Germans carried on to Constantinople (Istanbul) where the ships were 'sold' to the Turkish navy. This was a clever diplomatic move to compensate Turkish pride for two battleships which had been under construction in Britain and had been commandeered by the Royal Navy on the outbreak of war. On 30 October the new Turkish ships, with the connivance of some members of the Turkish government, led a bombardment of Russian Black Sea ports. This brought Turkey into the war on the German side.

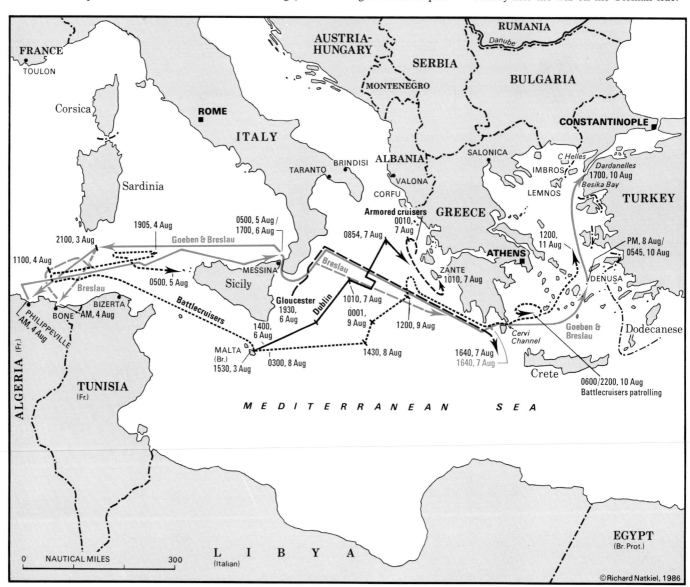

© Richard Natkiel, 1986

150

The Battle of Heligoland Bight

Although the Royal Navy had given up any idea of maintaining a close blockade of Germany, at the outbreak of war in August 1914 both sides still believed that a great sea battle would follow within weeks, if not days. As, however, neither side was prepared to risk its expensive capital ships, what fighting there was fell mainly to the light forces.

The first big operation was a British raid on the German outposts in the Heligoland Bight, to occupy the German High Seas Fleet's attention while the British Expeditionary Force was being transported to France. The plan was ambitious, involving

an outer patrol line of submarines which was to decoy German torpedo boats and destroyers out to sea, where they could be attacked by light cruisers and destroyers.

The forces selected were the Harwich Force of cruisers and destroyers under Commodore Tyrwhitt and submarines under Commodore Keyes, but poor staffwork at the Admiralty resulted in neither commander being told that reinforcements had been sent, in the form of a light cruiser squadron and five battlecruisers from the Grand Fleet, under the command of Vice Admiral Beatty. As well as this potential source of confusion

another error, caused by inexperience, was the uninhibited use of radio signals, which ought to have warned the Germans of the British approach.

In spite of the errors, the Germans were still caught on the wrong foot early on the morning of 28 August, for their heavy units were still at anchor in the Jade River, without steam up and penned behind the bar until high tide. Their first hint of a major action came at 0700 when the destroyer *G.194* came under fire from HMS *Laurel*. During the next hour the light cruisers *Arethusa* and *Fearless* and 32 destroyers engaged the

28 Aug 1914 Battle of Heligoland Bight

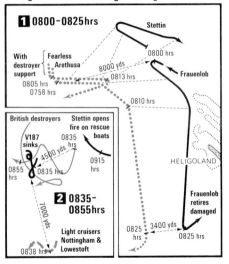

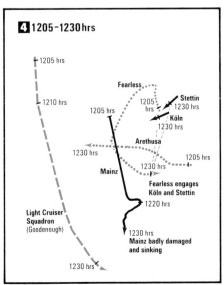

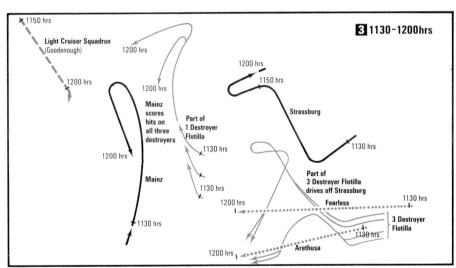

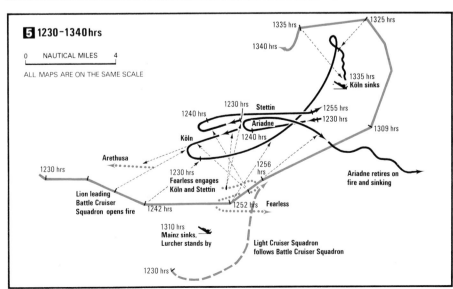

ments sent by the Admiralty. They had arrived in the nick of time, for the *Strassburg* had just appeared out of the midst and had opened fire at long range.

The British force was now intent on extricating itself, for the time allowed for the raid had long passed, and every minute spent in these dangerous waters increased the risk as German ships raised steam in the Jade. The next ship on the scene was the light cruiser *Mainz*, which scored several devastating hits on the British destroyers. For the second time the *Arethusa* prepared to go down fighting, but suddenly the *Mainz* was hit by a destroyer's torpedo. She began to sink slowly, and Goodenough's four light cruisers closed in for the kill.

Commodore Tyrwhitt had already sent a signal asking for reinforcements, and to Vice Admiral Beatty this was ample justification for a bold if risky counterstroke. Disregarding the risk of mines and torpedoes he took his flagship HMS *Lion* and the *Queen Mary*, *Princess Royal*, *Invincible* and *New Zealand* headlong into the fight.

The sight of these enormous ships, thrusting through the seas and firing their heavy guns, marked a disastrous turn for German fortunes. The *Strassburg* prudently fled into the mist, but a salvo of shells caught the *Köln* and inflicted grievous damage. Then the *Ariadne* blundered out of the mist, and it was her turn to be blasted. She took a rapid list to starboard, and with fires glowing lurched away, trying to get to safety.

While the *Arethusa* and her force withdrew under the guns of Goodenough's light cruisers the battlecruisers headed north and then west to find the crippled *Köln*. She was relocated at 1325, and survived this second battering for only ten minutes before sinking

with all hands. The entire British force could now withdraw to the northwest, knowing that the German heavy forces were too late to intervene.

Against the backdrop of World War I the action of 28 August 1914 was no more than an ill-planned skirmish, in which luck had played a big part in saving the British from embarrassing losses. But fortune always favors the bold, and the British had sunk three light cruisers and a destroyer and inflicted heavy casualties. The moral effects, however, far outweighed the matériel losses. The Kaiser reiterated his warnings to his Naval Staff about risking losses in battle, and plans for an offensive policy in the North Sea were hurriedly shelved. The Royal Navy could overlook the slipshod planning of the operation and rejoice at its ability to operate in the enemy's 'back yard' for nearly six hours without suffering more than minor damage to a light cruiser and some destroyers.

German inner patrol line, although the hazy conditions made accurate shooting almost impossible.

The Germans' luck changed dramatically when the light cruisers *Frauenlob* and *Stettin* arrived on the scene at 0800, for they managed to silence the *Arethusa* with 35 hits. Their intervention did little to save the torpedo boats, for the British destroyers continued to engage them fiercely, and eventually *V.187* sank. What was already a confused battle became worse when at 0838 two strange four-funnelled cruisers were sighted approaching. Thinking they were German reinforcements, the battered *Arethusa* and the *Fearless* prepared for a desperate fight, but the arrivals soon identified themselves as HMS *Nottingham* and HMS *Lowestoft*, the first of Commodore Goodenough's four light cruisers, the reinforce-

The Battles of Coronel and the Falklands

Although the Royal Navy outnumbered the German navy by a huge margin in 1914, British strength was concentrated in the North Sea, leaving small isolated detachments on overseas stations to protect shipping and strategic targets such as coaling stations. Although the German Far Eastern Squadron's base at Tsingtao in China was neutralized by Japan's entry into the war on Britain's side, the squadron's cruisers slipped away to inflict whatever damage they could to British commerce. Under their bold and dashing leader, Count Maximilian von Spee, the armored cruisers *Scharnhorst* and *Gneisenau* and the light cruisers *Dresden*, *Leipzig* and *Nürnberg* made a landfall on the coast of Chile in October 1914, where they took on coal at a secret rendezvous with German colliers.

The British soon had wind of Spee's arrival

on the Pacific coast, and Admiral Sir Christopher Cradock, took his South America squadron around Cape Horn to bring the German ships to battle. On paper his squadron was stronger, since in addition to the armored cruisers *Good Hope* and *Monmouth*, the light cruiser *Glasgow* and the armed merchant cruiser *Otranto* he could also count on the battleship *Canopus*. But the battleship was too slow to keep up with his squadron, the two big cruisers were old and weakly armed and the *Otranto* was a vulnerable ocean liner hurriedly armed with eight 4.7-inch guns.

When the two squadrons met on 1 November it was late in the day, and in heavy weather. The British ships were silhouetted against the setting sun, while Spee's ships grew steadily harder to make out against darkness. The British admiral doggedly tried to bring his squadron's firepower to bear but

HMS *Good Hope* and HMS *Monmouth* were raked by accurate enemy gunfire without being able to make an effective reply. As the track chart shows the *Good Hope* sank at 1957, after being completely silenced by an internal explosion. The *Monmouth* turned her stern toward the rising seas in a desperate attempt to stay afloat, but her captain gallantly ordered the light cruiser *Glasgow* to make her escape rather than try to take the *Monmouth* in tow. Having largely escaped the attention of the German cruisers, the *Glasgow* was able to get clear and re-unite with the *Otranto*.

Although small detachments had been overwhelmed before, the Royal Navy had forgotten the taste of defeat in a century of unchallenged supremacy and the sense of humiliation after Coronel was acute. To restore both their own and the Royal Navy's

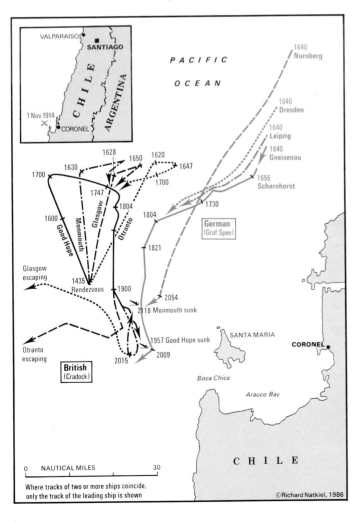

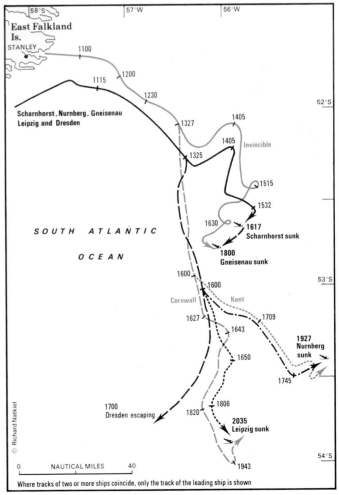

prestige the Board of Admiralty immediately ordered two dreadnought battlecruisers, the *Invincible* and *Inflexible* to head for the South Atlantic, where they were to form the nucleus of a powerful squadron to find and destroy Spee's cruisers.

In a remarkably short time the two 18,000-ton ships were refitted and sailed across the Atlantic to the Falkland Islands, arriving at Port Stanley on 6 December 1914. What was even more remarkable was the total secrecy of the operation; von Spee was planning to attack and destroy the coaling station, with no idea that two very powerful capital ships had arrived.

On the morning of 8 December 1914 the German ships approached Port Stanley without suspecting that anything was wrong. At first it was assumed that the clouds of smoke drifting across Port Stanley's anchorage were from burning coal stocks, and only when it was too late did a lookout report that he could see tripod masts – the trademark of dreadnoughts. The old battleship *Canopus* was the first to open fire, from the mudflats in the harbor, where she had been beached to provide a steady gun-platform.

Although critics were to say later that von Spee might have done better to hold his course and try to damage Vice Admiral Sturdee's battlecruisers as they emerged from the harbor entrance, the German commander headed southeast as fast as he could go, for he must have known that his hours were numbered. The action quickly turned into a long chase, with the British battlecruisers building up to full speed and over-hauling the Germans slowly but surely, and Rear Admiral Stoddart's armored cruisers bringing up the rear. The British had the day in front of them, the weather was cold but clear, and time was on their side.

Gallant to the last, Spee turned his two big ships to face his pursuers while ordering the three light cruisers to make their escape. With their 12-inch guns and superior speed HMS *Invincible* and HMS *Inflexible* were able to wreak a terrible revenge on the *Scharnhorst* and *Gneisenau*, at a range of their own choosing. The flagship *Scharnhorst* sank at 1617 with her ensign still flying, and the *Gneisenau* followed her to the bottom at 1800.

The *Nürnberg* was chased by the armored cruiser *Kent*, which by a quirk of fate was the sister of the *Monmouth*. Any hope that the German ship had that her somewhat elderly opponent might not be able to keep up was dashed, for by heroic exertions the *Kent*'s stokers enabled her to exceed her designed speed. Another sister, HMS *Cornwall* brought the *Leipzig* to bay, sinking her at 2035, just over an hour after the *Nürnberg*.

Although SMS *Dresden* escaped the slaughter, it was the end of the German East Asian Squadron, with the death of von Spee and the large part of his devoted crews. The victorious British cruisers scoured the islands of Tierra del Fuego looking for the *Dresden* for another three months, and finally her old enemies the *Glasgow* and *Kent* trapped her, finding her sheltering in Chilean waters at Mas Afuera. Matching her abuse of Chilean neutrality, they steamed close in and forced her to scuttle to avoid capture.

Top: Graf Maximilian von Spee.
Above: Admiral Sturdee, Spee's opponent.
Above right: The *Canopus* opens fire on Spee.
Right: Pre-war photo of the *Gneisenau*.
Below: German shells fall around Sturdee's flagship.

S.M.S. „Gneisenau" Großer geschützter Kreuzer.

The Battle of the Dogger Bank

The first weeks of the war did not see the decisive battle which both sides expected. Instead both fleets stayed in their defended anchorages, and left skirmishing to light forces. The British Fleet had a submarine scare in October 1914 when it was suspected that a U-Boat had penetrated the defenses of Scapa Flow, but the German High Seas Fleet failed to take the opportunity to intervene in the North Sea while the Grand Fleet was operating from a more distant base.

The Germans had no intention of meeting the full British fleet, and sought instead to isolate and destroy a small detachment. To force the British to divide their forces Admiral Hipper was ordered to make a series of pinprick raids on the east coast of England. A bombardment of Yarmouth in November 1914 was followed by another raid on Hartlepool a month later, and to appease public opinion Vice Admiral Beatty's battlecruisers were ordered to move their base from Scapa Flow to Rosyth in the Firth of Forth, from where they could more easily intercept German raids.

Intelligence sources warned that a similar raid was planned in January 1915, so the Admiralty ordered some of the Grand Fleet battleships to rendezvous with Beatty's force off the Dogger Bank. Before this junction was achieved on 24 January one of Beatty's light cruisers sighted Hipper's battlecruisers, and a high speed chase ensued, with Hipper trying to escape.

Beatty's force included his flagship *Lion*, the *Princess Royal*, *Tiger*, *New Zealand* and *Indomitable*. Hipper had under his command the *Seydlitz*, *Moltke* and *Derfflinger*, as well as the older and slower *Blücher*. The British ships were faster and more heavily armed but the German ships were more heavily armored.

The main weight of the British fire fell on the *Blücher*, which was bringing up the rear of Hipper's First Scouting Group. Only nominally a battlecruiser, this slow armored cruiser fell behind and lost speed after several hits. Beatty wanted his ships to leave the crippled *Blücher* to be finished off by the destroyers, but his orders to follow the main body were garbled, and the British battlecruisers turned back from the pursuit to pour salvoes into the German ship.

The error was compounded by severe damage which the flagship sustained at this point, when a 12-inch shell from the *Derfflinger* caused extensive flooding in the port engine room. As the *Lion* came to a dead

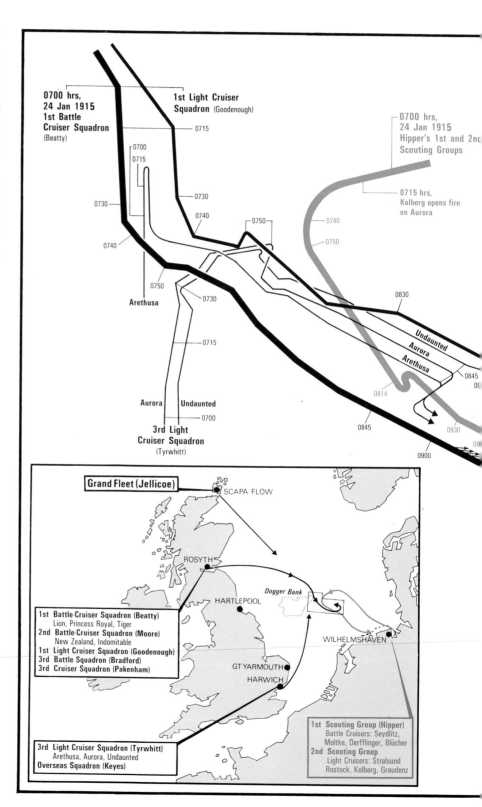

stop Beatty boarded a destroyer to shift his flag to the *Princess Royal*, and by the time he was able to regain personal control of the battle Hipper's ships were drawing comfortably out of range.

As soon as the *Blücher* had been sent to the bottom the *Indomitable* took the crippled flagship in tow to get her back to Rosyth. Beatty was furious at the missed opportunity, but very little was done to improve the system of training which had let Hipper escape. Beatty's signals officer, whose ineptitude had caused the mix-up in the orders, was not superseded (and was to make further errors at Jutland). The battlecruisers' gunnery had been very poor – HMS *Lion* scored only four hits for 243 shells fired, and other battlecruisers had not even done as well. There was no way of knowing that the *Seydlitz* had suffered a serious cordite fire in her after turrets, which had killed 159 sailors and inflicted severe burns on another 33. Investigation of this damage helped the Germans introduce safer procedures for

handling ammunition. Had that knowledge been available to the British they might have avoided the catastrophic explosions which sank three battlecruisers at Jutland 14 months later.

Although indecisive the Battle of the Dogger Bank did have the effect of stopping German raids on the east coast towns for some time. The Admiralty was building up a superb intelligence organization, using decrypted German signals, but the standard of staffwork to interpret, process and distribute such knowledge was still very poor. The Royal Navy had only grudgingly accepted the need for a Naval Staff in 1912, and it is not surprising that an efficient staff was not yet fully functioning in less than three years. It is nevertheless fair to say that the Admiralty had functioned for 300 years without a staff, and many of the organizational problems encountered in 1914-16 were the result of incompetent individuals not being identified and removed rather than the inherent weakness of the system.

Above left: The *Blücher* begins to sink. That the smaller *Blücher* should be serving with the German battlecruiser squadron only underlines the British superiority in numbers.
Above: Commodore Reginald Tyrwhitt of the Harwich Force.

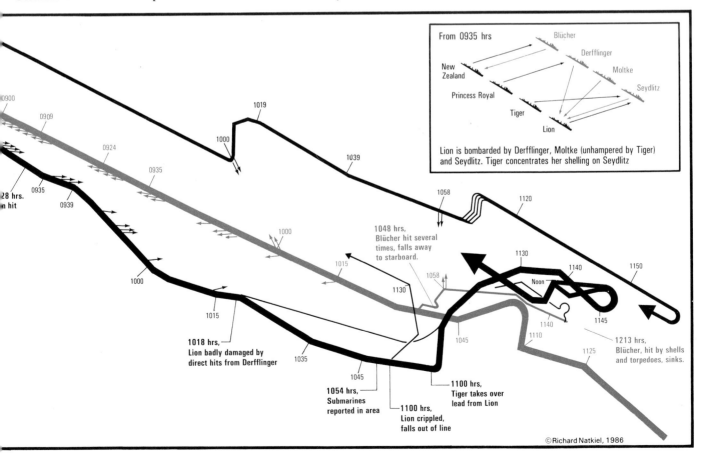

© Richard Natkiel, 1986

Gallipoli

The traditional British policy of using the Army as the 'biggest shot which could be fired by the Navy', or projecting force in subsidiary theaters away from the largest enemy armies, had been replaced by a 'Continental' strategy under French influence before the outbreak of war. But the lack of decisive results in France soon led British strategists to look for ways of attacking the Central Powers at their weakest points. A logical place to mount such an attack was the Dardanelles; Turkey was the newest and least stable ally of Germany, and forcing a way into the Black Sea offered the added advantage of opening a better supply route to the large but poorly-armed Russian armies.

The British and French fleets bombarded the outer forts defending the Gallipoli Peninsula and the approaches to the Dardanelles as early as 3 November 1914, but the decision to mount a full-scale assault was not taken until nearly two months later, giving the Turks time to strengthen the defenses. The British First Lord of the Admiralty (Navy Minister), Winston Churchill, was by now highly frustrated at the failure of the Grand Fleet to bring the German High Seas Fleet to battle in the North Sea, and gave the Dardanelles project his wholehearted support.

The naval forces were, on paper at least, formidable: the modern British battleship *Queen Elizabeth* and the battlecruiser *Inflexible*, two older battleships, the *Agamemnon* and *Lord Nelson*, and five obsolescent pre-dreadnought battleships. The French contingent was made up of four pre-dreadnoughts. This ill-assorted collection carried out an inconclusive bombardment of Cape Helles and Orkanieh on 19 February 1915 and again six days later, followed by three bombardments of the inner forts. The ranges were too great and the amount of ammunition expended too meager for any spectacular success, but in spite of these disappointing results a final 'big push' was planned for 18 March, using additional battleships and supporting ships which had been sent out by the Admiralty.

The day opened in brilliant sunshine, with the Turkish shore batteries replying vigorously to the Allied bombardment. Just after 1300 the line of French battleships wheeled to starboard as planned, in Eren Keui Bay. The leader, the *Suffren* turned successfully but her next astern, the *Bouvet* was suddenly stopped by a huge explosion and almost immediately rolled over and sank, taking

with her 600 men. It was thought at first that her magazine had been detonated by a Turkish shell but later it was learned that a small enemy minelayer, the *Nousret* had laid a field of 20 mines ten days earlier. Two hours later HMS *Inflexible* and HMS *Irresistible* struck mines in the same field. To add to the disaster, the captain of HMS *Ocean* refused to accept the orders of Commodore Keyes to take the stricken *Irresistible* in tow, and fired aimlessly at the shore until his ship too struck a mine and started to sink.

In the face of the unexplained loss of one ship, the crippling of a modern battlecruiser and the imminent sinking of two battleships, Admiral de Robeck had no choice but to withdraw the bombarding force. The rows of mines guarding the Straits could not be swept by minesweepers until the battleships silenced the forts, but the battleships could not get near enough to hit the gun emplacements accurately. It was a stalemate.

The only way forward was to commit the British, French and Australian and New Zealand (ANZAC) troops to an amphibious assault, in the hope that they could capture the high ground on the peninsula, and thereby silence the Turkish guns protecting the Straits. The troops went ashore on 25 April, the British VIII Corps at the tip of Cape Helles in five places, the French in a feint attack on Kum Kale on the Asiatic shore, and the ANZAC Corps at Ari Burnu. After fearful losses the troops established footholds ashore, but were never able to gain the commanding heights. Not even a second landing at Suvla Bay by two divisions of IX Corps on the night of 6-7 August 1915 could overcome the dogged Turkish resistance, while the fierce fighting and disease continued to wear down the Allied strength.

The Gallipoli campaign was regarded as an expensive sideshow by the 'Westerners' in England, who wanted all available manpower and resources concentrated on the Western Front. As the heavy losses continued with no sign of any large-scale gains of territory, and criticism of the conduct of the campaign mounted in Australia and New Zealand the pressure to end the useless sacrifice became unbearable. Lord Kitchener, the War (Army) Minister, went out to see conditions for himself, and the order was finally given to withdraw the troops. Between 10 December 1915 and 9 January 1916 the entire force was evacuated, first from Anzac Cove and Suvla, and then from Cape Helles.

It is a cruel paradox that the skill which

was missing in March and April 1915 was of such a high order in retreat that 83,048 soldiers, 186 guns, 1697 horse-drawn vehicles, 21 motor vehicles and nearly 5000 horses were taken off from Suvla and Anzac at a cost of no more than half a dozen wounded. Even with all chance of surprise gone, nineteen days later it proved possible to get over 37,000 men, 142 guns, 4200 animals, over 1900 vehicles and huge quantities of stores away from Cape Helles under the very noses of the enemy. The hospitals in Egypt had been warned to expect casualties of the order of 30,000 or more.

Historians continue to argue over the value or otherwise of the Dardanelles operations, but modern commentators no longer castigate Churchill for his part. The campaign was a victim of the fatal switch in British strategy which had taken place between 1906 and 1914. The 'Western' school of thought begrudged every soldier, every shell and every ton of supplies diverted to Gallipoli, and so the 'Eastern' enterprise was never given adequate resources. Undivided attention to one or other theater might have been decisive in 1915, but never both. The Royal Navy must also take its share of the blame, for its dismal lack of prewar preparation for amphibious operations. Lack of staffwork had much to do with the absence of any insight into logistics, shore bombardment or any of the myriad aspects of army-navy cooperation.

Against all those criticisms must be set the remarkable effort made by the RN to support the operation once the troops were ashore. The first lessons of amphibious warfare were learned during the Gallipoli campaign, and the German General Staff regarded the evacuation of Cape Helles as a military feat without equal, which would never be surpassed. Much of the success of British and US combined army-navy operations in World War II was owed to the Dardanelles experience.

Opposite, top left: **Admiral John de Robeck who took command of the British forces trying to force the Dardanelles shortly before the main attack on 18 March 1915.** *Opposite, top right:* **The *Queen Elizabeth*, the most modern and most heavily-armed battleship in the Royal Navy, during the Dardanelles operation. Most of the bombardment ships involved were, however, of the obsolescent pre-dreadnought type.**

The Dardanelles : March 18, 1915

⚓ MAJOR TURKISH BATTERIES
⚓ MINEFIELD BATTERIES
⚓ MOBILE HOWITZER BATTERIES
⚓ SEARCHLIGHTS
▬ MINEFIELDS

0 — MILES — 5
0 — KILOMETERS — 8

AEGEAN SEA

Suvla Bay
Tuzlu Golu
Anzac Cove
KILYA •
Nagara Point
Gallipoli Peninsula
The Narrows
KILID BAHR
CHANAK
ACHI BABA •
Kephez Pt
Kephez Bay
FORT DARDANOS
Cape Helles
Sedd-el-Bahr

1615 Irresistible mined
1805 Ocean mined × 1611 Inflexible mined
1345 Bouvet sunk

Line of Allied attack

Kum Kale
Eren Keui Bay
ORKANIEH

T U R K E Y

© Richard Natkiel, 1986

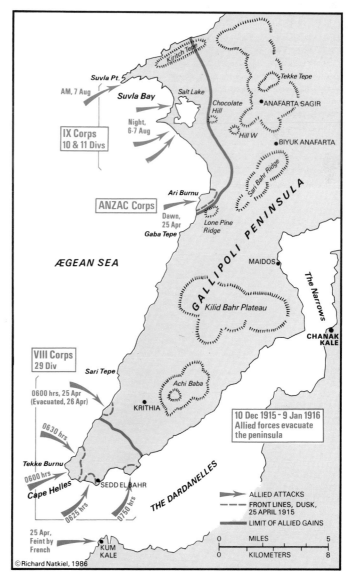

AM, 7 Aug
Suvla Pt.
Kritch Tepe
Tekke Tepe
Suvla Bay
Salt Lake
Chocolate Hill
ANAFARTA SAGIR •
IX Corps 10 & 11 Divs
Night, 6-7 Aug
Hill W
BIYUK ANAFARTA •
ANZAC Corps
Ari Burnu
Sari Bahr Ridge
Dawn, 25 Apr
Gaba Tepe
Lone Pine Ridge

ÆGEAN SEA

G A L L I P O L I   P E N I N S U L A

MAIDOS •
Kilid Bahr Plateau
The Narrows
CHANAK KALE

VIII Corps 29 Div
Sari Tepe
Achi Baba
0600 hrs, 25 Apr (Evacuated, 26 Apr)
06.30 hrs
KRITHIA •
10 Dec 1915 - 9 Jan 1916 Allied forces evacuate the peninsula
Tekke Burnu
0600 hrs
Cape Helles
SEDD EL BAHR
0625 hrs
0750 hrs
THE DARDANELLES

→ ALLIED ATTACKS
- - - FRONT LINES, DUSK, 25 APRIL 1915
▬ LIMIT OF ALLIED GAINS

0 — MILES — 5
0 — KILOMETERS — 8

25 Apr, Feint by French
KUM KALE

© Richard Natkiel, 1986

The Battle of Jutland

Since August 1914 the British Grand Fleet under Admiral Sir John Jellicoe had been trying to bring the German High Seas Fleet to battle. The Germans under their new C-in-C Vice Admiral Reinhard Scheer wished to avoid a pitched battle but hoped to whittle down the British by mining and submarine attack, or to destroy a small detachment of the Grand Fleet in a surface action.

As part of this strategy Scheer's U-Boats mined the exits from the main bases at Rosyth and Scapa Flow, while his surface forces tried to lure the British battlecruisers into a battle with Vice Admiral Hipper's battlecruisers, backed up by the full strength of the High Seas Fleet. The British were fully aware of the general outline of this plan as they had been reading German cipher messages since the end of 1914.

To checkmate the German plan Jellicoe and the Grand Fleet arranged a rendezvous with Vice Admiral Sir David Beatty's battle-cruisers off the Jutland Bank (southwest of the Skagerrak, the name given by the Germans to the battle). The scene was thus set for the first and last battle between large fleets of dreadnoughts.

The first contact was made early in the afternoon of 31 May 1916. Beatty and his six battlecruisers, with four battleships of the 5th Battle Squadron in support, were nearing the end of a sweep off the Jutland Bank and were heading north to meet the Grand Fleet. Two escorting light cruisers, HMS *Galatea* and HMS *Phaeton* were sent off to investigate a nearby merchant vessel, at the same time as Hipper ordered his light cruisers to investigate the same Danish ship. The two groups exchanged fire at 1425 before turning back to report the news to their respective flagships.

The big ships opened fire just before 1548, as Beatty turned south to try to cut Hipper off from his bases, while the German admiral withdrew to the southeast in the hope that Scheer and the High Seas Fleet would help him to destroy Beatty's squadron. Although Beatty's move was strategically sound his ships were at a tactical disadvantage, with the sun low in the west silhouetting his ships, while the German ships were largely hidden by haze and mist.

The action was brisk, with the Germans hitting rapidly and the British ships taking time to find the range. At the rear of the line the *Von der Tann* and HMS *Indefatigable* fought a fierce duel, and at about 1600 the British battlecruiser was hit aft by three shells. She lurched out of line with smoke pouring from her and appeared to be settling by the stern, and then another two hits forward caused a huge explosion as her magazine detonated and destroyed the ship.

The numbers were now even, but worse was to follow. At 1625 HMS *Queen Mary* blew up after being hit by a salvo of 12-inch shells from SMS *Derfflinger*. Only nine men

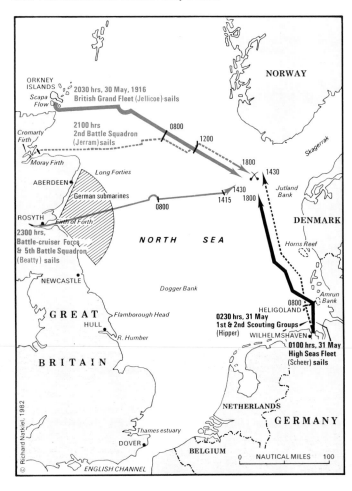

160

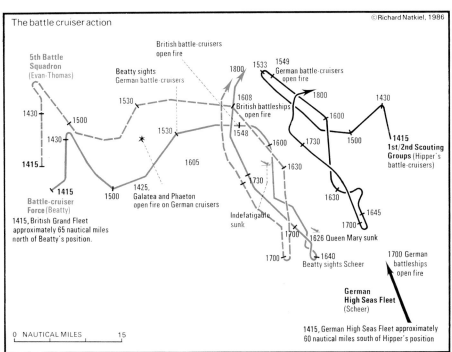

The battle cruiser action

5th Battle
Squadron
(Evan-Thomas)

British battle-cruisers
open fire

Beatty sights
German battle-cruisers

1533
1549
German battle-cruisers
open fire

1800
1800
1430

1608
British battleships
open fire

1430
1530
1600

1500
1530
1600

1430
1415
1st/2nd Scouting
Groups (Hipper's
battle-cruisers)

1548
1730
1500

1415
Battle-cruiser
Force (Beatty)

1605
1600
1630

1415, British Grand Fleet
approximately 65 nautical miles
north of Beatty's position.

1500
1425,
Galatea and Phaeton
open fire on German cruisers

1730
1645

Indefatigable
sunk

1630
1700

1626 Queen Mary sunk

1700
1700

1640
Beatty sights Scheer

1700 German
battleships
open fire

German
High Seas Fleet
(Scheer)

0 NAUTICAL MILES   15

1415, German High Seas Fleet approximately
60 nautical miles south of Hipper's position

Above: Admiral Jellicoe, commander of
the Grand Fleet. Jellicoe's careful
leadership had greatly increased the
efficiency of the ships of his force since the
outbreak of war when he took command but
at Jutland his tendency not to delegate
responsibility to subordinates and their
lack of initiative helped lose the advantage
offered by his astute tactics.
Left: Jellicoe's dashing subordinate,
Admiral Beatty seen later in his career in
the uniform of an Admiral of the Fleet.
Right: The battlecruiser *Queen Mary*
blows up in the first phase of the Jutland
battle.

survived out of her crew of 1285. Beatty was
now in a precarious position, with only four
capital ships; his flagship HMS *Lion* had also
sustained serious damage which had nearly
caused her loss. In his haste to engage
Hipper, and because of a signalling error, his
battlecruisers had outstripped the slower
battleships of the 5th BS, but these had at last
managed to get within range, and HMS
Valiant opened an accurate fire with her 15-
inch guns at nearly 19,000 yards. Then
Beatty's destroyers were sent in to attack
with torpedoes, and one hit the *Seydlitz*,
tearing a large hole in her plating.

As soon as Beatty's light cruisers reported
that they had sighted the High Seas Fleet
(1640) he ordered his ships to turn to the
north. It was now the Germans' turn to be led
into the arms of the Grand Fleet, but once

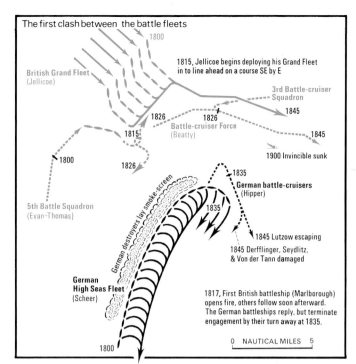

The first clash between the battle fleets

1800

British Grand Fleet
(Jellicoe)

1815, Jellicoe begins deploying his Grand Fleet
in to line ahead on a course SE by E

3rd Battle-cruiser
Squadron

1845

1826   1826

1815   Battle-cruiser Force
(Beatty)

1845

1800   1826

1900 Invincible sunk

1835

German battle-cruisers
(Hipper)

1835

1845 Lutzow escaping

1845 Derfflinger, Seydlitz,
& Von der Tann damaged

5th Battle Squadron
(Evan-Thomas)

German destroyers lay smoke-screen

German
High Seas Fleet
(Scheer)

1817, First British battleship (Marlborough)
opens fire, others follow soon afterward.
The German battleships reply, but terminate
engagement by their turn away at 1835.

1800

0   NAUTICAL MILES   5

again slipshod signalling meant that the change of course was not signalled to the 5th Battle Squadron, which continued on a southerly course for another 20 minutes. During the second phase, the run to the north, the 5th Battle Squadron came under heavy fire and sustained several hits, but they fought back and helped to save Beatty's ships from further punishment.

Aware of Beatty's difficulties, Jellicoe had already sent the three battlecruisers of Rear Admiral Hood's 3rd Battle Cruiser Squadron ahead at top speed, and these ships intervened dramatically as Beatty started to turn his ships across Hipper's bows, forcing him to turn away before he could sight the Grand Fleet. At 1735 the three battlecruisers ap-

peared out of the haze, crippling the *Lützow* with 12-inch salvoes, then damaging the light cruisers *Wiesbaden* and *Pillau*.

From the flag-bridge of the battleship *Iron Duke* Jellicoe could see no further than seven miles, and his deployment had to be based partly on intuition, on messages from the Admiralty and intermittent sighting reports. In spite of these difficulties his deployment of the Grand Fleet from its six-column cruising formation into the 'line ahead' was masterly. It put him between Scheer and his line of retreat, and at the same time permitted him to 'cross Scheer's T,' the ideal position to crush the German line by superior gunpower.

As the huge fleets (252 ships of all sizes)

Above: **Admiral Hipper, commander of the German scouting forces.**
Above right: **The British battleships *Superb* (left, firing) and *Canada* in the line of battle at Jutland.**

wheeled and changed formation amid clouds of coal- and gun-smoke mingled with mist, the British suffered one more disaster. A sudden shift in visibility left Rear Admiral Hood's flagship *Invincible* a perfect target for the *Derfflinger* and *Lützow* at only 10,500 yards. Five hits caused a huge explosion and tore the ship in two, killing Hood and all but three of his crew.

There was, however, only one course left for Scheer, as his fleet was under fire from a line of battleships nine miles long. He ordered the fleet to execute the 'Battle Turnaway,' a simultaneous 180-degree reversal of course which took it at high speed out of the trap.

There was only a short respite before Scheer found himself heading into another trap, and at 1908 he found that Jellicoe had once again 'crossed his T.' To cover his escape he ordered his destroyers and torpedo boats to attack, and sent Hipper's battle-cruisers on a desperate 'death ride' to gain time for another 'Battle Turnaway.' During this phase the High Seas Fleet was at a severe disadvantage and suffered heavy punishment, but Scheer's objective was achieved and the two fleets drew apart.

At this point Jellicoe and Beatty seemed to be on the verge of a clear-cut victory. Twice they had forced Scheer to retreat, and their own ships were firmly placed across his line of retreat back to Germany. But control of events now began to slip from the British C-in-C's grasp. The Admiralty failed to pass on two deciphered messages from Scheer indicating which of several routes home he would use, and a number of British subor-

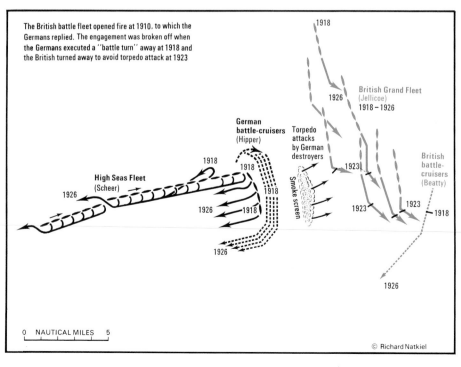

The British battle fleet opened fire at 1910, to which the Germans replied. The engagement was broken off when the Germans executed a "battle turn" away at 1918 and the British turned away to avoid torpedo attack at 1923

1918

1926

British Grand Fleet
(Jellicoe)
1918 – 1926

German
battle-cruisers
(Hipper)

Torpedo
attacks
by German
destroyers

1918

1918

1923

British
battle-
cruisers
(Beatty)

High Seas Fleet
(Scheer)

1918

Smoke screen

1926

1918

1926

1923

1923

1923

1918

1926

1926

0   NAUTICAL MILES   5

© Richard Natkiel

dinate commanders failed to relay sighting reports to the flagship. One of the battle-cruisers imprudently passed the night challenge and reply to a sister-ship by signal lamp, with a German light cruiser within visual distance. Last, and most important of all, Jellicoe's ships were neither trained nor well equipped for night-fighting, and he deliberately declined a night engagement in the hope that he would finish off Scheer in the morning.

Equally Scheer was unable to face the Grand Fleet in daylight, and had already decided on the desperate alternative, a thrust across the rear of the Grand Fleet, where he hoped that there would be only light cruisers and destroyers.

Scheer's gamble worked, and his ships were able to bludgeon their way through the British destroyer flotillas. But the price was heavy; the pre-dreadnought battleship *Pommern* was blown up by a torpedo, the light cruisers *Rostock* and *Frauenlob* were sunk, and the *Elbing* was cut in half when she tried to cross the bows of the battleship *Posen*. The previously damaged battlecruiser *Lützow* finally had to be abandoned and torpedoed by her own side, the second German capital ship to be lost. British losses were also heavy, but the only major unit sunk was the armored cruiser *Black Prince*, which blundered into the German line just after midnight.

The safe return of the High Seas Fleet to its bases enabled the Germans to claim that they had won a victory, especially as they had lost only two capital ships, against three British battlecruisers and three armored cruisers. But the British had won both tactically and strategically, if not by a decisive margin. The lost ships were quickly replaced by newer and better ships, and the Grand Fleet was at sea in possession of the battleground next morning, whereas the High Seas Fleet was heading for home as fast as it could go.

Jutland showed up considerable weaknesses in British matériel and training. Armor-piercing shells tended to break up on impact, and cordite propellant proved unstable, causing fatal magazine explosions. The Royal Navy's tactical training had been over-centralized, and subordinate officers had frequently failed to use their initiative. There would not be another chance to fight the High Seas Fleet, but the shock to British complacency led to far-reaching changes which stood the Royal Navy in good stead 20 years later in another war.

Below left: **Admiral Scheer, commander of the German High Seas Fleet.**

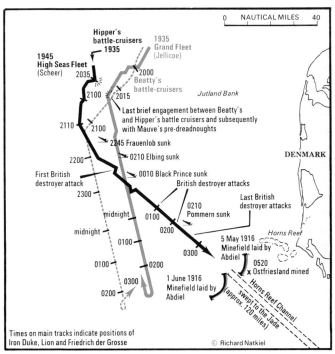

The Crisis of the U-Boat War

Despairing of victory on land, in September 1916 the German High Command authorized a 'restricted' campaign against British and Allied shipping. It ran for four months from 6 October 1916 to the end of January 1917, and in spite of the restrictions placed on the U-Boats they sank nearly 500 ships. In January 1917 the total tonnage sunk reached 368,500 tons in that month alone, and nearly 2000 British merchant ships had been sunk since August 1914. This slaughter had been achieved at a price of roughly 65 ships for each U-Boat sunk.

With such losses it was understandable that the German Naval Staff under Admiral Scheer wanted to switch to 'unrestricted' warfare as soon as possible, that is to adopt a 'sink at sight' policy. Only the fear of offending America held the Germans back. Finally in December 1916 approval was won from the Emperor. The calculations were careful and cold-blooded: if 600,000 tons of Allied shipping could be sunk each month and if 1,200,000 tons of neutral shipping could be 'frightened off' from trading with Britain the Allies' supply system would be wrecked within five months. This in turn would starve Britain into submission and bring about the collapse of her effort on the Western Front where the British armies were now taking the leading role on the Allied side.

At first all went as planned. Losses rose

Below: **British Auxiliary Patrol trawlers move in to assist the crew of a torpedoed merchant ship.**

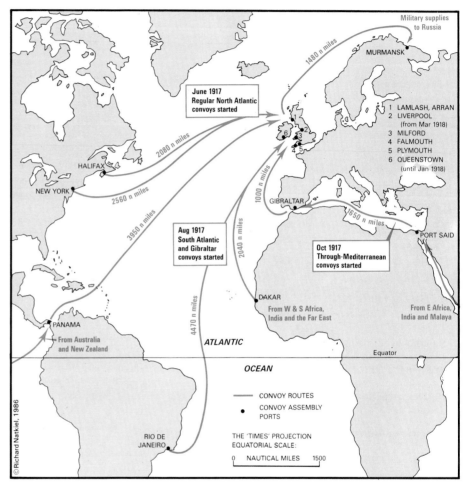

June 1917
Regular North Atlantic convoys started

Military supplies to Russia

MURMANSK

1 LAMLASH, ARRAN
2 LIVERPOOL (from Mar 1918)
3 MILFORD
4 FALMOUTH
5 PLYMOUTH
6 QUEENSTOWN (until Jan 1918)

1480 n miles

2080 n miles

HALIFAX

NEW YORK

2560 n miles

3950 n miles

1000 n miles

GIBRALTAR

1650 n miles

PORT SAID

Aug 1917
South Atlantic and Gibraltar convoys started

2040 n miles

Oct 1917
Through-Mediterranean convoys started

4470 n miles

DAKAR
From W & S Africa, India and the Far East

From E Africa, India and Malaya

PANAMA

From Australia and New Zealand

ATLANTIC

Equator

OCEAN

CONVOY ROUTES
● CONVOY ASSEMBLY PORTS

THE 'TIMES' PROJECTION
EQUATORIAL SCALE:
0   NAUTICAL MILES   1500

RIO DE JANEIRO

© Richard Natkiel, 1986

Above: Otto von Weddigen, commander of the German submarine *U.9*, who sank three British armored cruisers, *Aboukir*, *Cressy* and *Hogue*, in the North Sea on 22 September 1914, largely because of the poor precautions taken against submarine attack.
Below: German submarines meet in the Mediterranean. The larger submarine is *U.35*, the command of the most successful submarine captain ever, von Arnauld de la Perière.

from 368,000 tons in January to 540,000 tons in February, then to 594,000 tons in March, just short of the level required for victory. This was achieved by only 43 U-Boats operating from Germany, 23 each in Flanders and the Mediterranean, and 13 elsewhere.

A typical operating cycle required four U-Boats, one on station, one heading west to relieve her, one returning home and one under repair, but when the boats began to move further west into the Atlantic the cycle was increased to seven boats. This was, however, only a minor inconvenience, and the 'exchange rate' went from 53 merchantmen for each U-boat sunk in February to 74 and then to 174 in April.

It was now a race between Britain's survival (with only six weeks' food supplies left) and American outrage at this slaughter of civilian sailors and passengers on the high seas. One in four ships approaching British waters was bound to be sunk and contemporary accounts describe seas strewn with corpses, mule carcasses and splintered boats.

The countermeasures were totally unavailing. Hundreds of small yachts and other craft had been impressed into the Auxiliary Patrol, disguised 'Q-Ships' tried to trap U-Boats and even the British Army was to attempt the bloody Passchendaele offensive later in 1917 to capture the U-Boat bases in Flanders. Piecemeal improvements in weaponry had been made, the first depth-charges being

165

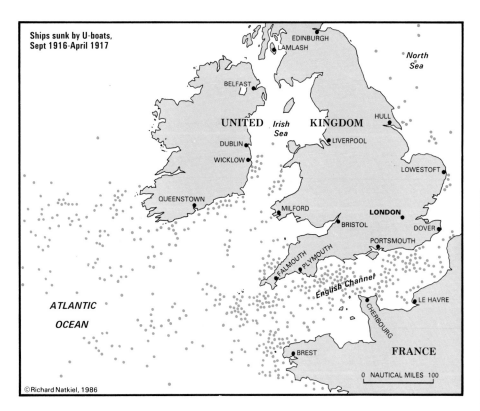

Ships sunk by U-boats,
Sept 1916-April 1917

© Richard Natkiel, 1986

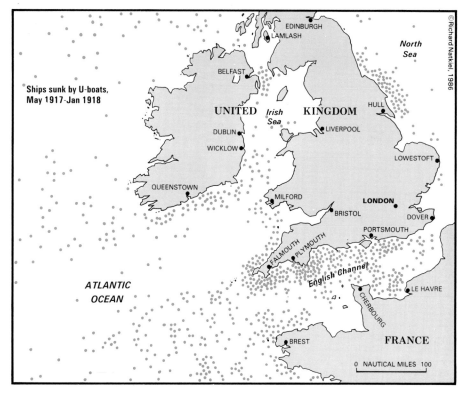

Ships sunk by U-boats,
May 1917-Jan 1918

© Richard Natkiel, 1986

Above: A German submarine engages an armed merchant ship.
Below left: A convoy late in the war is escorted by American destroyers.
Right: The typically cramped control room of a German submarine.

introduced in 1916 and a directional hydrophone in 1917, but apart from minelaying across the exit-routes there seemed little else that could be done. To make matters worse there were no plans to replace shipping and until mid-1916 no salvage organization to recover damaged ships.

Only in May 1917 were the the first fumbling attempts made to introduce a new countermeasure – convoy. This method of protecting merchant shipping had been in use since the fourteenth century but had become discredited during the peaceful years of the nineteenth century. Arguments that there were insufficient escorts were met by redeploying the hundreds of vessels uselessly tied up in patrolling, and the assurance that the intervention of the United States in the war (on 5 April) had made many more escorts available.

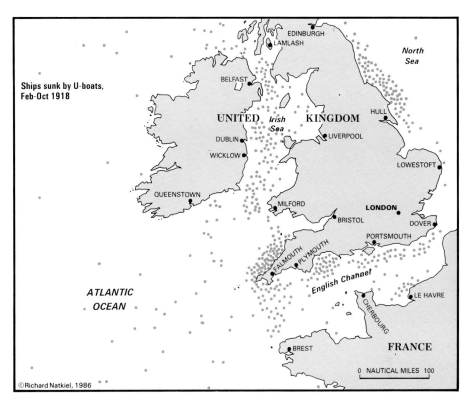

Ships sunk by U-boats,
Feb-Oct 1918

© Richard Natkiel, 1986

The Germans had calculated that America would come into the war eventually, but not so soon. Nor did they allow for the seizure of half a million tons of their own ships, lying interned in American ports, the equivalent of a new building program. At last the Allies tackled the problems of new building and salvage, so that the introduction of convoy was more the final keystone in a policy of conserving shipping than a 'miracle cure.'

A miracle is what it must have seemed like when the sinkings began to fall. On 20 May 1917 the first convoy from Gibraltar arrived

in Britain with no loss, followed by one from Hampton Roads. Even when the U-Boats switched to attacking weakly escorted outward-bound ships they made little impression, and by October only 24 ships out of 1500 had been sunk. Part of the U-Boats' problem was that convoy in effect scoured the sea of targets. Instead of waiting near a focal point where shipping routes converged U-Boats now had to approach a dense mass of shipping surrounded by vigilant warships. At most one target could be fired on before breaking away to avoid counterattack, and

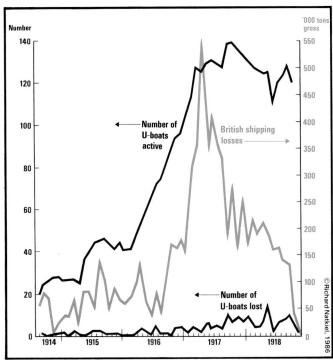

Above: The cruiser *Vindictive* (right) and the destroyer *Warwick*, Admiral Keyes' flagship for the Zeebrugge operation.

even if that target was hit, 19 ships out of the 20 had escaped.

There were other countermeasures too: airships and flying boats flew over the convoys, and destroyers and submarines sowed a new type of mine in the routes from Heligoland and Flanders. Losses of U-Boats began to rise noticeably, putting further strain on the crews.

One of the most important German sub-marine bases in Flanders was at Bruges and on the night of 22/23 April 1918 a dramatic attempt was made to block the entrance to the port at Zeebrugge. Three old British cruisers, *Thetis*, *Intrepid* and *Iphigenia* were to be sunk in the canal entrance while the defenses on the harbor mole were destroyed in a diversionary attack by landing parties from another old cruiser, the *Vindictive*. Despite the bravery with which the attack was carried out it proved a failure because the blockships were not correctly positioned and the port was quickly put back into use.

Despite this failure the Allied navies continued to hold the upper hand. When the Armistice came in November 1918 the U-Boat arm of the Imperial German Navy had lost some 5364 officers and men out of an estimated total of 13,000.

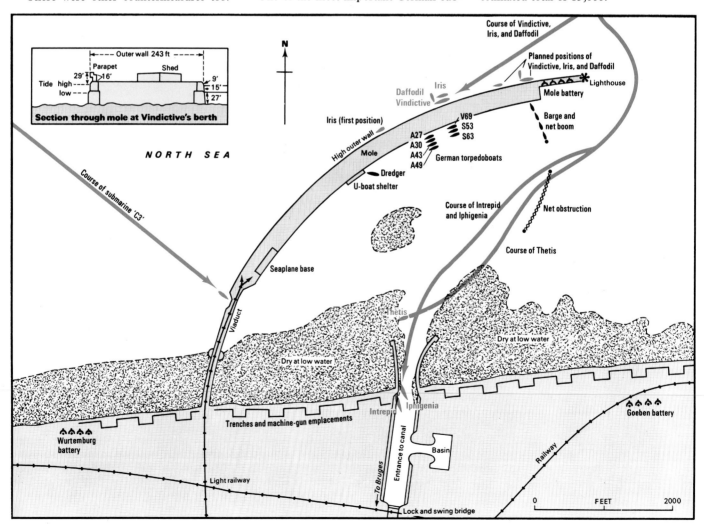

The Scuttling of the German Fleet

Despite German claims to have won the Battle of the Skagerrak the morale of the High Seas Fleet declined. The younger and more intelligent officers and petty officers were posted to U-Boats and torpedo boats, leaving the battleships to make up their complements with conscripts and reservists. Relations between officers and other ranks were not helped by the long periods in harbor and irksome drills ashore, and taunts from the light forces that the battleships were not bearing a fair share of the war.

The first rumblings of mutiny were heard toward the end of 1917, and in 1918 when the sailors heard rumors of a last 'suicide' sortie by the High Seas Fleet they refused to sail. The resulting revolution triggered off the German Army's request for an armistice. Under its harsh terms the High Seas Fleet was to sail across the North Sea to Rosyth, where it would be surrendered to the Allies and interned until its fate was settled at the Peace Conference at Versailles.

The melancholy ceremony took place on 21 November 1918, after which 14 capital ships and their attendant light cruisers and destroyers were escorted to Scapa Flow. There the officers and men were cut off from the outside world, as they received only basic rations and personal letters from Germany. Exaggerated reports in the British press suggesting that the Fleet would be taken over by the Allies and used against Germany to enforce a punitive peace treaty led German officers to plot a mass scuttling to avoid such an eventuality.

The Royal Navy had grown complacent, and on 21 June 1919 the squadron of battleships guarding Scapa Flow went to sea for gunnery exercises. Suddenly it was noticed that some of the interned ships seemed to be sinking. British boarding parties were able to save the battleship *Baden* and a few destroyers, but the rest of the High Seas Fleet went to the bottom.

In retrospect the scuttling was a godsend to the Allies, for it removed one of the knottiest problems from the Versailles negotiations and prevented an unseemly scramble for the spoils. The British patiently raised all the ships and sold them for scrap, although the last of them was not brought to the surface until after the Second World War. The *Baden*, however, was soon put to use in British gunnery trials to test different designs of shell and to look at ways of improving ships' armor protection.

Predictably the surrender and scuttling left a deep scar on the memory of the German Navy, and much of Hitler and Admiral Raeder's subsequent obsession with a battleship fleet can be traced to a desire to wipe out the shame of Scapa Flow.

© Richard Natkiel, 1986

23-27 November 1918 German High Seas Fleet arrives in Scapa Flow
1040 hrs, 21 June 1919 Admiral von Reuter issues signal to scuttle the fleet

(BC) BATTLE CRUISER
(B) BATTLESHIP
(LC) LIGHT CRUISER

0 NAUTICAL MILES 1

Colonial Empires After 1919

The victors were not slow to assert their claims to Germany's colonies and possesions, and at Versailles they were formally taken from her. It was all the more ironic that the treaty which did so much to foster self-determination in Europe merely served as an instrument to further British and French ambitions in Africa and elsewhere.

The pre-1914 colonial boundaries in Africa were little altered, for most of the German colonies merely changed hands. Thus German West Africa became South West Africa and was given to South Africa subsequently under a League of Nations mandate. Most of German East Africa became the Tanganyika Territory, under a British mandate. France took most of Kamerun, renaming the territory the Cameroons, but a small portion was annexed to British Nigeria. A similar settlement gave France most of Togo, while a small portion became part of the British Gold Coast.

Belgium was hardly in a position to demand similar concessions, but in view of her efforts to help defeat the Germans in Central Africa and to compensate her for four years of German occupation it was decided to give her two small parts of former German East Africa. These became the provinces of Ruanda and Urundi.

Strategically not much had changed. The French still had their naval bases and garrisons in Morocco, Algeria and Tunisia, and the British controlled the Suez Canal, the Red Sea and the sea-route around the Cape of Good Hope. The British imperial dream of a Cape to Cairo railway was now feasible, in theory at least, but the old expansionist days were over.

Neither the British nor the French had the financial strength to make large investments in their African colonies, and the world-wide effects of the Depression killed any hopes of economic development on anything more than a shoestring scale. Even the potentially rich, self-governing Dominion of South Africa was hit hard by the Depression, so it is hardly surprising that the colonial territories fared badly. For the British, however, their African possessions were to prove vital in the Second World War, for they allowed British forces virtually undisturbed use as bases for operations against their enemies.

Egypt was the most important, for the British not only controlled the Suez Canal but had the use of Alexandria as a major base for a Mediterranean fleet. The nearest threat came from Italian forces in Libya to the west and in Eritrea, Abyssinia (after the Italian occupation in 1936) and Somaliland. The southern base at Simon's Town was in South Africa, where a minuscule pro-Nazi movement would prove unable to interfere with the war effort, while the colonies in West Africa were flanked by French territory on three sides.

The position in the Pacific was far more complicated. Japan had seized her moment in 1914, and after taking Tsingtao from the Germans had gone on to seize every possible German possession throughout the Pacific. Strenuous efforts to persuade Japan to give up her conquests failed, and it was conceded that German possessions and treaty rights in China would revert to Japan, and the League of Nations put the Marshall, Caroline and Mariana Islands under a Japanese mandate. The only concession made was in 1926, when under strong pressure from the Western powers Japan was forced to withdraw from the Chinese province of Shantung.

The Australians, who had moved during the war to forestall Japanese moves, were confirmed in their occupation of Papua, New Britain and New Ireland, while the island of Nauru was handed over to the British. Similarly New Zealand's wartime occupation of Western Samoa was confirmed by a League of Nations mandate in 1920.

Although the United States still controlled the Philippines, the French were in Indo-China and the British in Malaya, and much seemed unchanged, the Japanese were now the dominant power in the Pacific. Their heavy industries had expanded enormously to meet the Allies' needs for ships and armaments, and the post-war slump threatened their survival as a first-rate power. The vicious competition for world trade in shrinking markets did little to assuage Japanese grievances and suspicions, and perhaps inevitably her leaders went down the familiar road of military expenditure and aggressive nationalism.

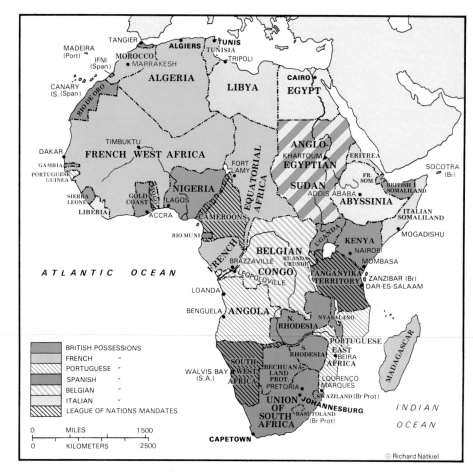

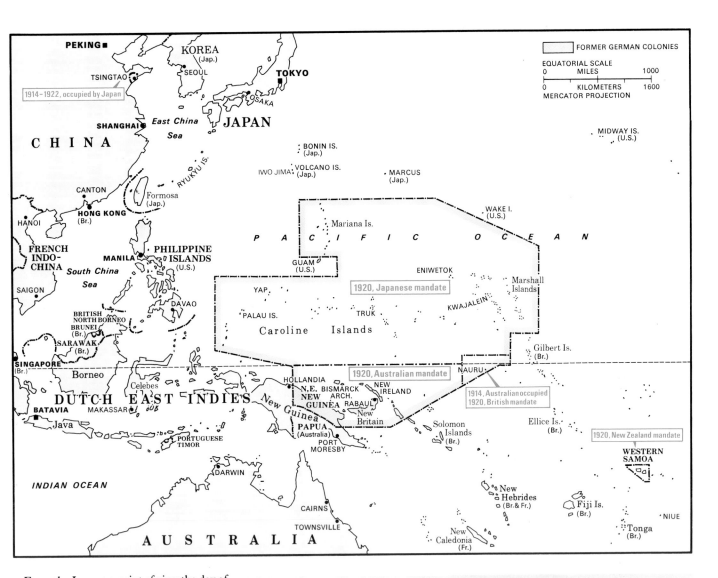

From the Japanese point of view the day of the Western colonial powers had passed, and they believed the Far East should be an exclusively Japanese 'sphere of influence.' American and British protests at the Japanese occupation of Manchuria and the widespread atrocities during the Sino-Japanese War were therefore all the more unwelcome. However, the Japanese economy had underlying weaknesses, not least its lack of certain strategic resources such as oil, and much of Japan's truculence masked uneasiness and uncertainty about the future and Japan's place in the world.

The answer to Japan's problems seemed to be to expand, but the areas richest in oil and other natural resources lay in territory owned or controlled by the Americans, British or Dutch. Out of that conundrum was to emerge the thinking which set Japan on the road to Pearl Harbor.

Right: A phosphorus bomb explodes above the old battleship *Alabama* being used as a target ship during American bombing experiments in 1923. These experiments, the so-called Mitchell tests, while not as conclusive as the participating airmen claimed, presaged the coming dominance of air power in maritime affairs.

Landing ships disgorge their cargoes on the Normandy beaches, June 1944.

WORLD WAR II

The Course of Global Conflict

Although many aspects of World War II seem superficially similar to World War I, many factors had changed by the time World War II broke out in September 1939. The British Empire was still powerful, but a shadow of its former self, while France had also made a slow recovery from the devastation of her industry and manpower. Germany was also weaker than she had been 20 years earlier, with her armed forces limited by the Treaty of Versailles until the advent of Hitler.

The greatest difference was the enigmatic attitude of Russia, now the Soviet Union under the all-powerful leadership of Stalin; in theory the Soviet Union was a close ally of Nazi Germany, so Germany would not have to fight on two fronts, as she had from 1914 to 1917.

As before the British, with the most powerful navy in the world, used their geographical position to enforce a blockade of Germany, to safeguard their own supply-routes from attack and to prevent raw materials from getting through. This time, however, there was no under-estimation of the threat from U-Boats. Although the highly secret ASDIC submarine detection device (now known as Sonar) was not as effective as the Admiralty hoped, the convoy system was introduced immediately to protect shipping.

The British and French hoped to repeat the pattern of 1914-18, using their maritime superiority to weaken Germany while their own land and air power was built up. This strategy was rapidly outflanked in 1940 by the unexpected collapse of France. Suddenly the German armies were on the Channel coast and the British were in danger of invasion. Italy chose this moment to throw in her lot with Germany, to complicate the problems of the British.

Without American help the British could have done little but survive, but with increasing support from the United States it was possible to build up strength and undertake limited operations against the Italians in North and East Africa. President Roosevelt saw clearly that Nazi hegemony over Europe must be destroyed but until isolationism ended with Pearl Harbor any military assistance given to the British was hedged about with restrictions.

In June 1941 Hitler launched a massive attack on the Soviet Union, committing Germany yet again to a war on two fronts. In December the same year the Japanese attack on the US Pacific Fleet at Pearl Harbor brought the United States into the war, and turned what had been a European war into a world-wide conflict.

From the end of 1941 two large-scale naval campaigns were to dominate the naval war, the Battle of the Atlantic and the conquest of the Pacific. The Atlantic battle was one of escorts and convoys against the U-Boats, whereas the Pacific was largely one of aircraft carrier battles and amphibious landings. In both conflicts Allied technology and industrial strength were crucial; shipyards and factories had to produce the ships and aircraft fast enough to ensure the replacement of losses faster than the enemy could replace his losses.

The turning-point of the Pacific War was the Battle of Midway in mid-1942, when the newly won Japanese empire suffered its first setback, but the Atlantic battle reached its climax the following spring, when the U-Boats suffered a severe defeat. Thereafter the Axis powers would continue to score successes, but they would be in retreat.

The Americans and British could do little to help the Soviet Union, apart from shipping war material to Murmansk and preparing a 'Second Front'. Although landings took place in North Africa, then Sicily and the Italian mainland, the long-awaited assault on Europe did not start until June 1944. With the Western Allies and the Soviet armies advancing inexorably from the west and the east there was little Germany could do to stave off defeat, and an unconditional surrender was signed in May 1945.

Despite Midway the Japanese were still very dangerous opponents, and each assault on territory held by them seemed to cost more lives. But the US Navy soon learned to 'leapfrog' strongly defended points, leaving them to be weakened by lack of supplies. The Japanese were slow to realize the threat to their maritime empire from an attack on

shipping, and lost an enormous tonnage to submarines and mines. By August 1945 Japanese shipping was restricted to junks and coasters working inshore, and the losses of tankers had reduced the Navy to impotence.

Japan's precarious industrial base was not equal to the demands of a war of attrition, but the courage of its soldiers, airmen and sailors made the American victory very costly. So heavy had been the losses in the capture of Iwo Jima and Okinawa that the American high command chose to drop nuclear bombs on Hiroshima and Nagasaki to inflict a catastrophic blow to Japanese morale. The two bombs achieved their effect, and Japan surrendered unconditionally a few days later.

Although its tactical and strategic decisions were rarely wise, the Japanese Navy produced remarkable warships, from the biggest battleships ever seen, to super-destroyers and aircraft-carrying submarines. The outstanding tactical innovation was an ultra-heavy oxygen-driven torpedo, which gave them a big advantage in night fighting.

Although traditional sea power seemed severely curtailed by air power a new and more potent form of sea power emerged. The decline of the battleship was more than matched by the rise of the aircraft carrier, which became the new capital ship. Once again maritime power had defeated land power, but unlike World War I, victory was achieved by a judicious blend of land, sea and air power.

Above: An F-6 Hellcat fighter on fire after a crash landing on the American aircraft carrier *Enterprise* in late 1943.
Left: The US destroyer escort *England*, one of the multitude of escort ships built by the Allied navies for anti-submarine work. The *England* set a record by sinking six Japanese submarines in less than two weeks in May 1944.
Right: From right, Admiral Andrew Cunningham, General Dwight Eisenhower and Vice Admiral Willis in 1943. Cunningham was Britain's most distinguished naval commander of the war. This picture was taken in 1943 aboard HMS *Nelson* during the North African campaign.

World Trade in the 1920s

Historians have come to see World War I of 1914-18 as merely the first outbreak of a European Civil War which was not decided until 1945. It is ironic that the enormous efforts made by the European Powers up to 1914 to create a world which they dominated merely resulted in their own eclipse by the Super-powers, first the United States and then the Soviet Union.

In the wake of World War I efforts were made to rebuild the trading patterns. Outwardly the French and British colonial empires remained intact, but both were greatly reduced in vitality. The German Empire had been partitioned among the victors, with the result that even in their decline, the British and French controlled a larger area than before.

It was still a world dominated entirely by maritime trade. The British still possessed the world's largest mercantile fleet and their chain of coaling stations and bases built up in the nineteenth century enabled the Royal Navy to maintain its role of 'world police-man.' A renewed outbreak of naval rivalry had been nipped in the bud by the Washington Naval Disarmament Treaty of 1922,

which limited the relative sizes of the fleets of the United States, Great Britain, France, Italy and Japan.

With the United States firmly isolationist, the British content to rebuild their shattered strength and the French and Italians too weak to do more than threaten each other, the 1920s promised a future of comparative tranquility. But the cloud on the horizon was Japan. With an economy enormously inflated to meet the demands of the British and French for munitions of all kinds, Japan's expectations were hard to fulfil in the depressed post-war world.

By their remarkable efforts the Japanese had turned their country from a feudal backwater in the 1860s to a modern industrial nation by 1900. Their remarkable victory in the Russo-Japanese War had made their military men think of themselves as invincible, and after 1919 there was a seemingly-inevitable slide into militarism as a way of countering the country's bleak economic future. With a large shipbuilding industry created to replace British losses in 1916-17 it seemed to Japan's rulers that she might also create a maritime empire.

Such a strategy might have worked in the nineteenth century but in the first quarter of the twentieth century it could only be achieved by naked aggression against other states. In her confidence Japan failed to see that any major acquisition would bring her into conflict with the Western powers, and it is unlikely that she would have regarded them as a serious threat even if she had known. Japan's only experience of Western soldiers had been the Tsar's ill-trained conscripts in Manchuria in 1904-5 and her military men had but a poor grasp of the industrial might of the United States.

The Soviet Union remained an enigma. Exhausted by the aftermath of the Revolution and the Civil War, her energies were totally absorbed by the gigantic task of modernizing her heavy industry and agriculture. With vast resources of food and raw materials there was little inclination to foster overseas trade, and in any case the Western nations' attempt to 'strangle Bolshevism in its cradle' in 1919-20 by various acts of intervention had widened the ideological rift between the Soviet Union and the rest of the world.

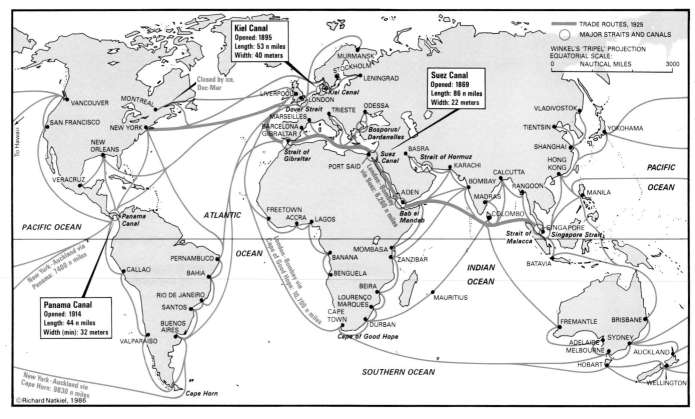

The Battle of the River Plate

At the outbreak of World War II in 1939 the German Navy had no intention of challenging the much larger Royal Navy in open battle, and the major warships built in Germany in the 1930s conformed to a new perception of the old theories of commerce-raiding by surface warships. Well-armed cruisers and capital ships would disrupt the British convoy system, and then the U-Boats would destroy merchant ships piecemeal as they had in 1914-17.

The first manifestation of this policy was the construction of three *panzerschiffe* or armored cruisers, the *Deutschland* (renamed *Lützow* in 1940), *Admiral Scheer* and *Admiral Graf Spee*. On a nominal displacement of 10,000 tons they were armed with six 11-inch guns to conform to the conditions of the Versailles Treaty, which had sought to restrict Germany to nothing more powerful than coast defense ships. The ships were a considerable technical success, and achieved their political purpose, which was to show the British and French that Germany would not tolerate a perpetual state of disarmament. Although their heavy guns helped them become known as 'pocket battleships,' they were in fact little more than an expensive type of cruiser, with similar armor protection to British heavy cruisers but considerably slower.

When war broke out the *Admiral Graf Spee* had already been sent to sea and was heading for the rich hunting grounds of the South Atlantic. She had a few lucky escapes from detection but the disappearance of isolated merchant ships soon alerted the Admiralty to the presence of a commerce-raider. In conjunction with the French Navy eight hunting groups were set up, one of which was Force G, under Commodore Henry Harwood RN, with the heavy cruisers *Cumberland* and *Exeter*. Harwood's force was covering the area off the River Plate, where the concentration of shipping carrying beef from Uruguay and Argentina was likely to attract a German raider.

The Admiralty dispositions were right, and the *Graf Spee* was heading for the River Plate. When, just after 0600 on the morning of 13 December 1939, HMS *Exeter* sent a sighting report, Harwood's command had been reduced by one ship, as the *Cumberland* was carrying out repairs to her machinery at Port Stanley in the Falklands, but she had been replaced by two light cruisers, HMS *Ajax* and her New Zealand-manned sister HMNZS *Achilles*.

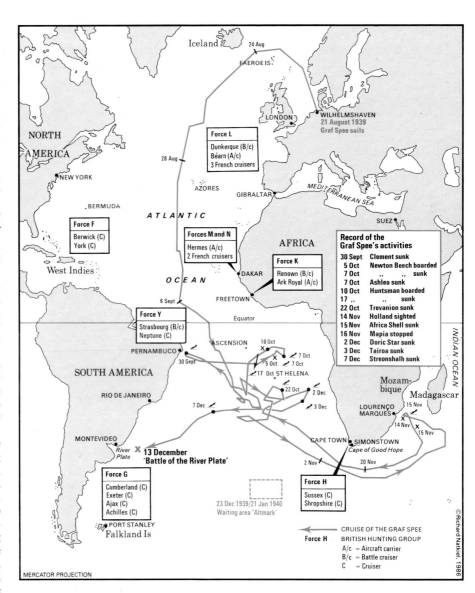

Although on paper Harwood's force was hopelessly outgunned, it would not be a one-sided fight. Harwood's ships had exercised for just such an engagement, and could use their speed to outmaneuver their opponent. By dividing the *Graf Spee*'s fire they would ensure that no single ship would be exposed to the full weight of her 11-inch gunfire, and each British cruiser would be able to spot each other's fall of shot at long range, thereby improving accuracy.

As the most heavily-armed opponent the 8-inch gunned *Exeter* drew the fire of the *Graf Spee*, and soon suffered serious damage and casualties. She was saved from worse damage by the *Ajax* and *Achilles* darting into range and then retreating behind a smoke-screen, tactics which forced the *Graf Spee* to shift target several times. In all the *Graf Spee* suffered three 8-inch and 17 6-inch hits, and eventually she ran for shelter in neutral Uruguayan waters. She had suffered considerable damage, several casualties and had expended more than half of her ammunition.

Under International Law the German ship could stay in Montevideo for 72 hours, long enough for the British to rush reinforcements to the area and to mount a skilful propaganda campaign to convince the Germans that powerful units were already in position. The deception worked, and on the evening of 17 December the waiting *Cumberland* (which had replaced the badly damaged *Exeter*), *Ajax* and *Achilles* saw the *Graf Spee* steam out from Montevideo, but instead of engaging them she slowed down, sent her crew away in boats and then blew up in clouds of flame and smoke as scuttling charges exploded. Her captain, Hans Langsdorff, had told Admiral Raeder, the German Commander-in-Chief, that his position was hopeless and Hitler had concurred in the decision to scuttle, as he could not bear the thought of a major German warship being sunk in battle.

The Battle of the River Plate came at the right moment for Great Britain and her French ally. The 'Phony War' was producing no successes for the Allies, and even a local victory was a boost to morale. The return of the *Graf Spee*'s sister *Deutschland* to her home port in November after sinking only two ships of less than 7000 tons in all brought to an end the first German attempt to strike at British maritime trade.

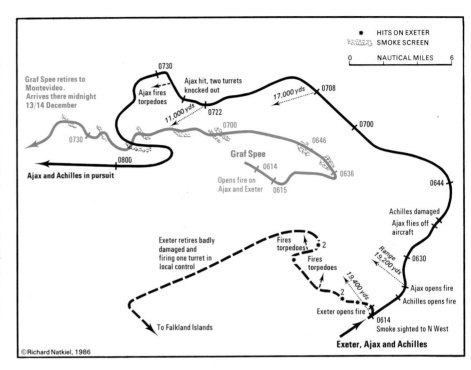

HITS ON EXETER
SMOKE SCREEN

0   NAUTICAL MILES   6

Graf Spee retires to Montevideo. Arrives there midnight 13/14 December

0730
Ajax hit, two turrets knocked out
Ajax fires torpedoes
17,000 yds
0708
0700
11,000 yds
0722
0700
0730
0646
Graf Spee
0800
0614
0636
Ajax and Achilles in pursuit
Opens fire on Ajax and Exeter
0615
0644

Achilles damaged
Ajax flies off aircraft

Range 19,200 yds
0630

Exeter retires badly damaged and firing one turret in local control
Fires torpedoes
2
Fires torpedoes
19,400 yds
Ajax opens fire
Achilles opens fire
2
Exeter opens fire
0614
Smoke sighted to N West

To Falkland Islands

Exeter, Ajax and Achilles

© Richard Natkiel, 1986

Right: The battered *Exeter* arrives home in Plymouth to an enthusiastic welcome after the successful battle with the *Graf Spee*.

The Sinking of HMS *Royal Oak*

At the outbreak of war the British Home Fleet moved to its war station, the same bleak anchorage in the Orkneys that the Grand Fleet had used in 1914-18. But this time Scapa Flow did not prove immune to attack, for on the night of 13-14 October 1939 *U.47* under Kapitänleutnant Günther Prien slipped in undetected and torpedoed the battleship *Royal Oak* with heavy loss of life.

Nothing had been done to update the defenses of the Orkney base since 1918, and twenty years of winter gales had created a narrow passage between the blockships in Kirk Sound. German aerial reconnaissance had detected this gap, and Admiral Dönitz planned a bold operation to get a U-Boat into the enemy's main fleet base. The plan proved workable and under cover of darkness Prien penetrated the defenses and found the *Royal Oak* lying at anchor.

His first salvo of three torpedoes had no apparent effect, and only one detonated partially or struck a mooring chain. After an interval to reload Prien fired again, and this time the salvo detonated under the battleship's keel. She flooded rapidly and sank fifteen minutes later with the loss of 24 officers and 809 men. The court of enquiry came to the conclusion that after only a few weeks at war the ship's company was not yet accustomed to war-routine, and watertight doors and hatches were not all shut, making the ship more vulnerable to flooding.

The loss of a second-line ship which had fought at Jutland did not affect the Royal navy's command of the sea, but the skill and daring of the attack shook confidence in the defenses of Scapa Flow, and the Home Fleet was immediately dispersed to bases on the west coast of Scotland until Scapa's defenses could be strengthened. The German Navy was, however, unable to take advantage of this dispersal of British strength, and the convoys bringing men and raw materials continued to arrive in British ports.

The major improvement to Scapa Flow's defenses was to replace the Kirk Sound and Water Sound blockships with a causeway, the so-called 'Churchill Barriers.' The need to guard the northern exit to the North Sea diminished as the war went on, but the commitment to run convoys to North Russia kept large numbers of ships at Scapa until 1945.

Above right: **Prien is congratulated on his return to Germany after the sinking of the** *Royal Oak.*

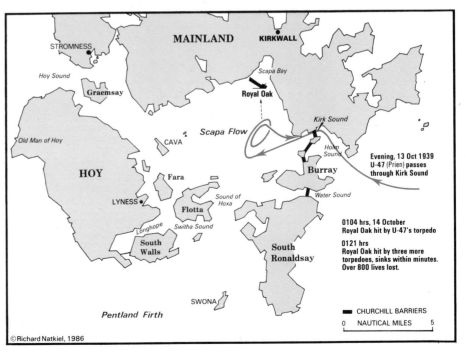

STROMNESS

MAINLAND   KIRKWALL

Hoy Sound

Scapa Bay

Graemsay

Royal Oak

Old Man of Hoy

CAVA   Scapa Flow

Kirk Sound

Holm Sound

**Evening, 13 Oct 1939
U-47 (Prien) passes
through Kirk Sound**

HOY

Fara

Burray

LYNESS   Sound of Hoxa   Water Sound

Flotta

**0104 hrs, 14 October
Royal Oak hit by U-47's torpedo**

Longhope   Switha Sound

South Walls

South Ronaldsay

**0121 hrs
Royal Oak hit by three more
torpedoes, sinks within minutes.
Over 800 lives lost.**

SWONA

CHURCHILL BARRIERS

Pentland Firth

0   NAUTICAL MILES   5

©Richard Natkiel, 1986

The Norwegian Campaign

Sweden was a major supplier of iron ore to Germany and in the winter months when the Baltic was frozen this traffic was routed through Norwegian ports. The British were determined to stop this flow of iron ore from northern Norway to Germany. During the winter of 1939-40, while the Baltic traffic was suspended, an estimated 9 million tons of iron ore reached Germany (roughly 70 percent of her imports) from Narvik through Norwegian territorial waters, the 'Inner Leads,' and the Skagerrak. The interception of the notorious German navy oiler, the *Altmark* during her return to Germany through neutral Norwegian waters in February 1940 lent force to Winston Churchill's demands that the Royal Navy should be allowed to lay minefields to stop the traffic or force the ore ships to use international waters where they could be taken by British warships.

Once the repairs to the defenses of Scapa Flow (shown to be necessary by the sinking of the *Royal Oak*) permitted the Home Fleet to return, the Admiralty was willing to consider such plans, and at the end of March 1940 'Operation Wilfred' was approved. The German High Command was aware of the British sensitivity over Norway, but was less inhibited by considerations of neutral opinion. They wanted nothing less than an occupation of Norway to forestall any British move.

The Germans were lucky but their bold operation deserved to succeed. Both the British and the Norwegians were taken by surprise, in spite of several warnings, and German troops seized Trondheim, Bergen and Narvik virtually unopposed. In Oslofjord a battery manned by elderly reservists sank the heavy cruiser *Blücher* with gunfire and torpedoes. Coastal batteries at Bergen also damaged the light cruiser *Königsberg* on 9 April, and a group of Fleet Air Arm dive-bombers from the Orkneys sank her next day, but these events did nothing to prevent the Germans from gaining control.

The British reacted quickly, reinforcing the ships already at sea to cover 'Operation Wilfred' which had, by chance, been ordered to start just as the Germans were making their move. The battlecruiser *Renown* and

nine destroyers surprised the German battle-cruisers *Scharnhorst* and *Gneisenau* on 9 April off Vestfjord, but the German ships escaped with only light damage in the poor visibility. A small force of British destroyers was sent into Narvik to disrupt the German landing. Despite 2 to 1 odds the First Battle of Narvik accounted for two German destroyers sunk, five damaged and a number of transports damaged, at a cost of two British destroyers lost.

Three days later Admiral Whitworth took the battleship *Warspite* and nine destroyers back to finish off the German force. The Second Battle of Narvik on 13 April resulted in the total destruction of the remaining eight German destroyers, but it did little to influence the outcome of the campaign.

The British and French ground forces sent to Norway subsequently were ill-equipped to do more than fight a series of holding actions against the German forces, and when the main German armies attacked in the Low Countries and France in May the Allies had no choice but to withdraw from an ill-conceived and foolhardy operation. Under a

Above: Admiral Raeder, Commander in Chief of the German Navy and architect of the invasion of Norway.
Left: The forward 11-inch guns of the *Scharnhorst* in action during the sinking of the British aircraft carrier *Glorious*.

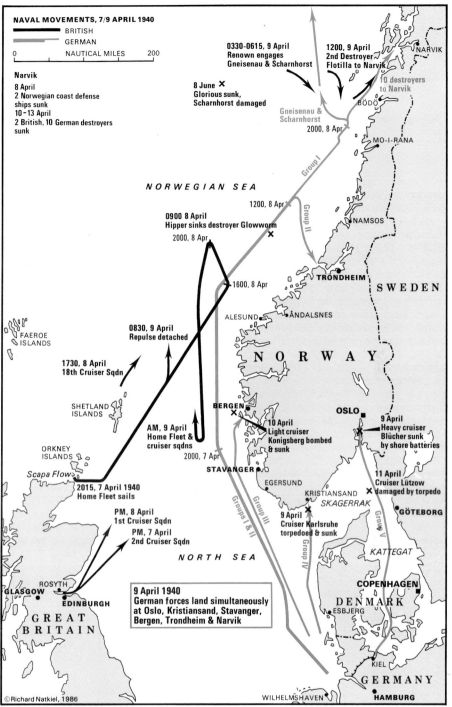

NAVAL MOVEMENTS, 7/9 APRIL 1940
BRITISH
GERMAN
0   NAUTICAL MILES   200

Narvik
8 April
2 Norwegian coast defense ships sunk
10 – 13 April
2 British, 10 German destroyers sunk

0330-0615, 9 April
Renown engages
Gneisenau & Scharnhorst

1200, 9 April
2nd Destroyer
Flotilla to Narvik

NARVIK

10 destroyers
to Narvik

8 June ✕
Glorious sunk,
Scharnhorst damaged

BÖDO

Gneisenau &
Scharnhorst

MO-I-RANA

Group I

2000, 8 Apr

NORWEGIAN SEA

1200, 8 Apr

Group II

NAMSOS

0900 8 April
Hipper sinks destroyer Glowworm

2000, 8 Apr

✕

1600, 8 Apr

TRONDHEIM

SWEDEN

ALESUND

ÅNDALSNES

0830, 9 April
Repulse detached

FAEROE
ISLANDS

1730, 8 April
18th Cruiser Sqdn

N O R W A Y

SHETLAND
ISLANDS

BERGEN
✕

10 April
Light cruiser
Konigsberg bombed
& sunk

OSLO

9 April
Heavy cruiser
Blücher sunk
by shore batteries

AM, 9 April
Home Fleet &
cruiser sqdns

ORKNEY
ISLANDS

2000, 7 Apr

STAVANGER

EGERSUND

11 April
Cruiser Lützow
✕ damaged by torpedo

Scapa Flow

KRISTIANSAND

SKAGERRAK

GÖTEBORG

2015, 7 April 1940
Home Fleet sails

9 April
Cruiser Karlsruhe
torpedoed & sunk

Groups I & II

Group III

Group V

PM, 8 April
1st Cruiser Sqdn

Group IV

KATTEGAT

PM, 7 April
2nd Cruiser Sqdn

NORTH SEA

COPENHAGEN

GLASGOW

ROSYTH

EDINBURGH

9 April 1940
German forces land simultaneously
at Oslo, Kristiansand, Stavanger,
Bergen, Trondheim & Narvik

D E N M A R K

ESBJERG

G R E A T
B R I T A I N

KIEL

G E R M A N Y

© Richard Natkiel, 1986

WILHELMSHAVEN

HAMBURG

growing weight of air attack the various detachments had to be withdrawn, and losses were heavy. In the closing stages the Germans scored a major success when on 8 June the *Scharnhorst* and *Gneisenau* sank the aircraft carrier *Glorious* after she had evacuated Royal Air Force units from northern Norway.

The German Navy seemed to have scored a signal victory but its losses were proportionately heavier. In addition to the two cruisers and ten destroyers already listed, the light cruiser *Karlsruhe* had been torpedoed off Kristiansand, and three heavy units had been damaged. The Norwegian campaign seemed at the time to have been no more than an expensive sideshow, but the lack of warships

was a major factor in the failure of the German plans to invade Britain after Dunkirk. Although the whole question of 'Operation Sealion' turns on doubts about its feasibility, the German Navy's main objection was the scarcity of supporting forces for the invasion fleet. The damaged ships were eventually repaired but the rate of wartime shipbuilding was too slow to make good the losses, and the surface forces of the German Navy never recovered from the Norwegian campaign.

Dunkirk

The speed of the German Army's advance through the Netherlands, Belgium and France in 1940 turned the Allied defeat into catastrophe. In less than a month, France, one of the foremost military powers in the world, was forced into abject surrender and her principal ally's army had been reduced to one effective division.

Fortunately for the British they had foreseen as early as October 1939 a possible need to block Belgian and Dutch ports, and contingency plans existed to reinforce the Nore Command based in the Thames for this purpose. In 1914 the failure to block the Belgian ports of Ostend and Zeebrugge had given Germany's U-Boats a secure base for four years, and this time the Admiralty was determined not to allow this to be repeated. On 10 May four destroyers took demolition parties to Antwerp to destroy the fuel tanks, put the locks out of action and remove all shipping.

The loss of Belgium and Holland was inevitable, but news of a much bigger disaster was received on 20 May, when Vice-Admiral Bertram Ramsay convened a conference at Dover to discuss a possible evacuation of the British Expeditionary Force (BEF) from France. Dunkirk, Calais and Boulogne were designated as the evacuation ports, with a provisional figure of 10,000 men per day through each port.

A trickle of soldiers was taken off by destroyers but the situation was deteriorating fast. By 22 May Boulogne had fallen and the fate of Calais was sealed. The British concentrated their resources on strengthening the Dunkirk defenses, and on Sunday 26 May the order to initiate Operation Dynamo was given, to muster all possible resources to get the defenders of Dunkirk home. The forces available included 35 personnel ships, 40 Dutch *schuyts* and a variety of barges and coasters.

The surrender of Belgium next day forced Ramsay to put more ships into the operation, including all available destroyers. On 28 May it was discovered that the battered piers in the inner Dunkirk harbor were still usable, and this helped to increase the numbers of men being embarked. Apart from the personnel ships, which were mostly commandeered passenger ferries, the destroyers could lift the largest numbers, and their high transit speed improved the 'turn round' time. On 28 May 17,804 soldiers reached England, and Ramsay began to hope that most of the BEF could be evacuated.

All the while the ships were pounded by German dive-bombers and shore artillery. Two of the three navigable channels hugged the coast, and Ramsay's greatest fear was a massed onslaught by German surface forces and blocking of the harbor entrance. But the German Navy's light forces showed very little enterprise and although several ships were sunk in the harbor the fairway was not blocked.

Although the main body of the BEF was finally away by midnight on 2 June there still remained the rearguard, which consisted chiefly of 30,000 French troops. By now the situation ashore was chaotic and the sudden appearance of an estimated 40,000, mostly French, stragglers and deserters from hiding places in the town made it very difficult to get General Barthelemy's rearguard evacuated, but 26,000 men did reach England.

The final total of troops evacuated in Operation Dynamo, not including units evacuated through Western France was 338,000. The cost was heavy in ships sunk and damaged, but Hitler's chance to end the war was missed. However frightening his threats to invade Britain might sound, the British were psychologically undefeated, with their navy largely intact and an army which could be rearmed and retrained. Dunkirk also convinced Britain's friends, principally the United States that she would not be easily defeated.

The British expected Hitler to start an immediate invasion but had no way of knowing how exhausted the German Army was after its drive through the Low Countries.

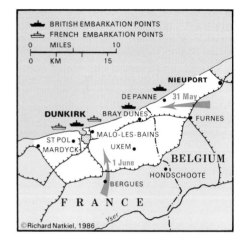

The need to rest and re-equip, combined with the serious naval losses in Norway, made Operation Sealion, as the invasion plan was named, almost impossible to launch before September 1940. Even then the efforts to improvise an amphibious force from Rhine barges and coasters proved too much for the Germans. The Royal Navy had repaired most of its damaged destroyers, and the failure of the Luftwaffe to defeat the Royal Air Force made it clear that the British had not relinquished command of the Channel. Without that command Germany could not hope to launch a successful invasion.

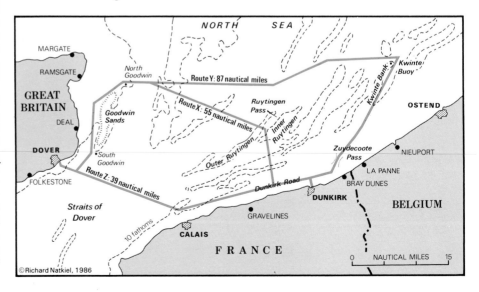

The Battle of the Atlantic

When war broke out in September 1939 the Admiralty immediately set up a system for convoying merchant ships. The essential strategic problem had not changed since 1914, to prevent German warships from getting out into the Atlantic and at the same time to get troops and supplies across the Atlantic from the United States, Canada and the rest of the world.

The sinking of the *Graf Spee* brought the first phase of the sea war to an end, and by the end of December 1939 the distant oceans were firmly under Allied control.

Even though the Norwegian campaign was ended by an undignified scramble to get British and French troops out, the overall situation favored the Allies for their maritime strength was building up rapidly, while Germany's was all but static. The fall of France in June 1940 overturned this almost overnight, and by July 1940 the French were out of the war and the U-Boats were establishing new bases on the Atlantic coast of France.

Up to the end of May 1940 convoys had only been escorted out to 200 miles west of Ireland, but in July–October the limit was extended to 19 degrees West. From that point the merchant ships of the convoy sailed in company for another 24 hours and then dispersed, leaving the escort to take over an incoming convoy. On the other side of the

Below: **Admiral Dönitz. At the beginning of the war Dönitz commanded the German submarine force and became Commander in Chief of the Navy in early 1943.**

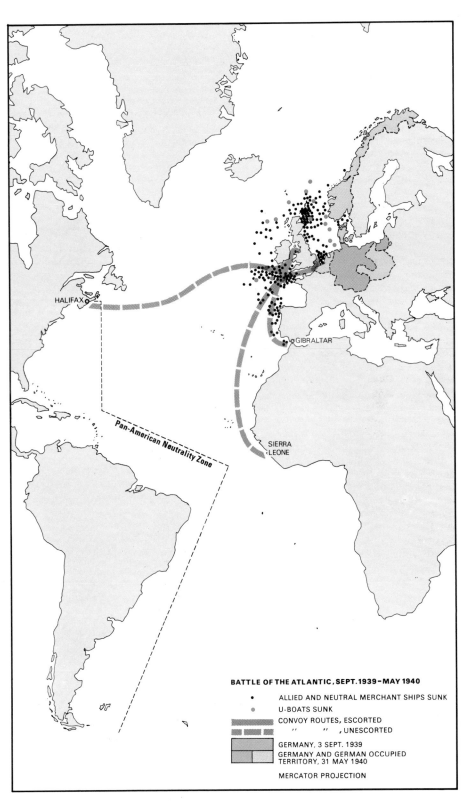

BATTLE OF THE ATLANTIC, SEPT. 1939 – MAY 1940

- •   ALLIED AND NEUTRAL MERCHANT SHIPS SUNK
- •   U-BOATS SUNK
-     CONVOY ROUTES, ESCORTED
-     ″   ″   , UNESCORTED
-     GERMANY, 3 SEPT. 1939
-     GERMANY AND GERMAN OCCUPIED TERRITORY, 31 MAY 1940

MERCATOR PROJECTION

HALIFAX

GIBRALTAR

SIERRA LEONE

Pan-American Neutrality Zone

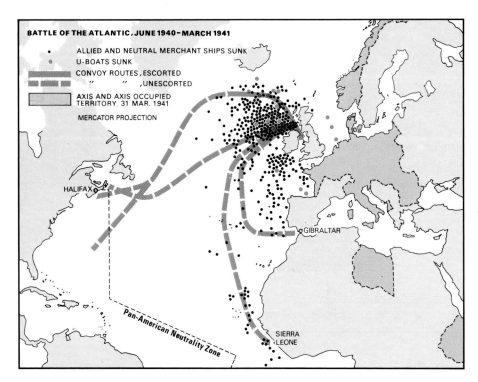

- ALLIED AND NEUTRAL MERCHANT SHIPS SUNK
- U-BOATS SUNK

CONVOY ROUTES, ESCORTED

      "   " ,UNESCORTED

AXIS AND AXIS OCCUPIED TERRITORY, 31 MAR. 1941

MERCATOR PROJECTION

HALIFAX

GIBRALTAR

Pan-American Neutrality Zone

SIERRA LEONE

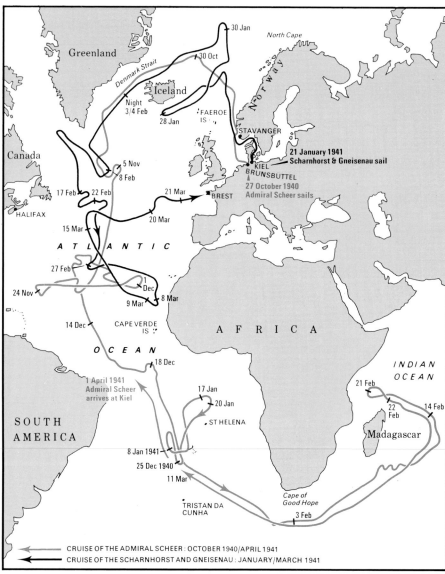

Greenland

30 Jan

North Cape

30 Oct

Denmark Strait

Night 3/4 Feb

Iceland

28 Jan

FAEROE IS

NORWAY

STAVANGER

Canada

5 Nov

8 Feb

21 Mar

**21 January 1941
Scharnhorst & Gneisenau sail**

KIEL
BRUNSBUTTEL

17 Feb   22 Feb

BREST

**27 October 1940
Admiral Scheer sails**

HALIFAX

20 Mar

15 Mar

A T L A N T I C

27 Feb

1 Dec

24 Nov

8 Mar

9 Mar

14 Dec

CAPE VERDE IS

A F R I C A

O C E A N

18 Dec

INDIAN OCEAN

**1 April 1941
Admiral Scheer
arrives at Kiel**

17 Jan

20 Jan

21 Feb

22 Feb

14 Feb

ST HELENA

SOUTH AMERICA

Madagascar

8 Jan 1941

25 Dec 1940

11 Mar

Cape of Good Hope

TRISTAN DA CUNHA

3 Feb

CRUISE OF THE ADMIRAL SCHEER : OCTOBER 1940/APRIL 1941

CRUISE OF THE SCHARNHORST AND GNEISENAU : JANUARY/MARCH 1941

Atlantic the Royal Canadian Navy provided the Halifax Escort Force, but the burden stretched both navies to the limit.

To ease the desperate shortage of destroyers, in September 1940 the British gave the United States a 99-year lease of base rights throughout the Empire, in exchange for the supply of 50 destroyers built in World War I. Matters also improved in the later months of 1940 as the first 'Flower' class corvettes began to appear from British and Canadian shipyards. Unfortunately air co-operation lagged behind. The RAF had devoted few resources to Coastal Command pre-war, and its weapons and tactics took a long time to catch up.

Under the leadership of Admiral Karl Dönitz the U-Boats perfected their tactics and remorselessly exploited any weakness they could find. As early as the summer of 1940 Dönitz made his U-Boats experiment with the first *rüdeltaktik* or 'wolfpack' tactics. The first U-Boat to sight a convoy did not attack but instead sent a signal to HQ, giving convoy course, speed and numbers as well as her own position. This first U-Boat then continued to track the convoy and only when a number of U-Boats had been moved into position did U-Boat HQ give the order to attack under cover of darkness. Many U-Boat commanders played the dangerous game of attacking on the surface, getting in among the ships of the convoy before firing their torpedoes, and then withdrawing. In the confusion there was little risk of being discovered for the escorts' ASDIC sensors (known today as Sonar) could not detect a surfaced submarine, and the escorts were usually looking to seaward for the attackers.

The only answer to such tactics was an efficient surface radar, but the first Type 271 set did not go to sea until May 1941. Another important sensor was a high-frequency radio direction-finder (known from its initials as 'Huff-Duff'), which could pinpoint the source of radio transmissions. These two sensors enabled the escorts to exploit two weaknesses of the wolfpack system. The U-Boats could be detected while they were still shadowing the convoy, and HF/DF gave away the presence of any shadower reporting back to base, and in both cases it was sufficient to force the shadower to submerge to frustrate the planned attack.

Aircraft were particularly useful in forcing U-Boats to submerge, even if they were not always able to sink them. Once underwater the U-Boat was virtually blind, unable to transmit messages and too slow to keep contact with or catch the convoy. But aircraft could not patrol from shore bases all the way across the Atlantic, and in the 'Black Gap' the U-Boats could still hunt convoys on the surface. Even escorts had to husband fuel to get across the Atlantic, and in January 1941 some older destroyers were given extended range by replacing one of their boilers with 80 tons of fuel. The next step was to build a new type of high-endurance escort, the 'River' class frigate but these did not appear until early in 1942.

The first air-to-surface-vessel radar sets had been in service since January 1940 but they were too crude to be effective against U-Boats. The ASV Mk II set was much better but took a long time to get into full production. Late in 1941 Coastal Command started to receive the new Liberator bomber from the United States, and with its fuel-capacity increased the Very Long Range (VLR) Liberator could patrol for three hours 1000 miles out. Aircraft could also be taken with the convoys, to provide local defense, but lack of aircraft and shipping delayed the introduction of small aircraft carriers.

In the autumn of 1940 serious losses to FW-200 Kondor bombers operating against convoys to Gibraltar led the British to fit catapults on the forecastles of a few merchant ships. These Catapult-Armed Merchant Ships or CAMships could catapult off an RAF Hurricane fighter to shoot down the Kondor but each time the Hurricane was 'ditched' and the pilot had to take to his inflatable dinghy. The next step was to provide a mercantile hull with a wooden flight deck, permitting fighters to land as well as take off. The first 'escort carrier' was a captured banana boat rechristened HMS *Audacity*, which went to sea in August 1941. Although she only survived three months her value was so obvious that the US Government was asked to convert more mercantile hulls. As an interim measure the British fitted out a number of grainships and tankers as 'MAC ships' or merchant aircraft carriers, ships which continued to carry cargo under mercantile manning, but could contribute to the defense of the convoy.

The German Navy continued to hope that its surface warships could destroy the convoy system, and in early 1941 the battlecruisers *Scharnhorst* and *Gneisenau* made a sortie but had to take refuge in Brest in March 1941 after sinking only 22 ships between them. Three months later it was hoped to get the

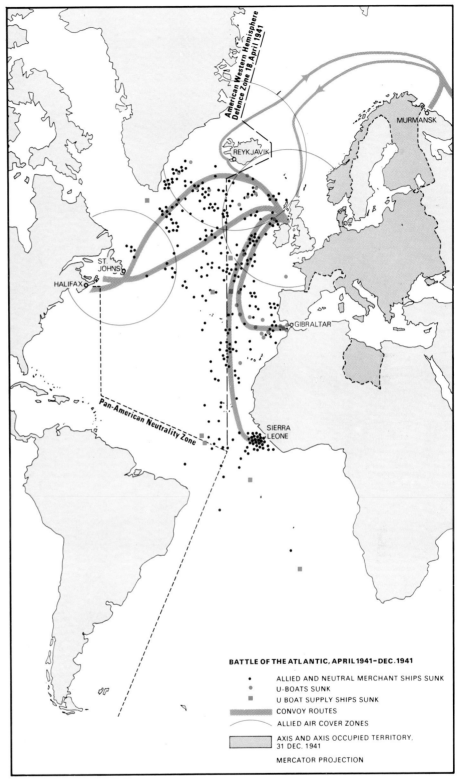

BATTLE OF THE ATLANTIC, APRIL 1941–DEC. 1941

- •   ALLIED AND NEUTRAL MERCHANT SHIPS SUNK
- •   U-BOATS SUNK
- ■   U BOAT SUPPLY SHIPS SUNK
- CONVOY ROUTES
- ALLIED AIR COVER ZONES
- AXIS AND AXIS OCCUPIED TERRITORY, 31 DEC. 1941
- MERCATOR PROJECTION

new battleship *Bismarck* out from the Baltic to join them in a massive onslaught, but this hope came to an end on 27 May 1941 when the *Bismarck* was sunk by the Home Fleet. Thereafter the two battlecruisers, joined in Brest by the *Bismarck*'s consort *Prinz Eugen*, were more and more vulnerable to air attack, and in February 1942 Hitler ordered them home.

The 'Channel Dash,' the brilliantly executed daylight run by these three ships through the English Channel from Brest to German

waters, caused bitter recrimination in Britain, but it was a 'strategic withdrawal' which removed the ships from a position in which they were a constant threat to the Atlantic convoys. The British could take little comfort from the shortcomings revealed by the German escape, but neither the *Scharnhorst* nor the *Gneisenau* was ever such a danger again. (Map overleaf.)

In March 1941 the British escorts also scored a major success by sinking three of the surviving U-Boat 'aces.' By sinking *U.47*,

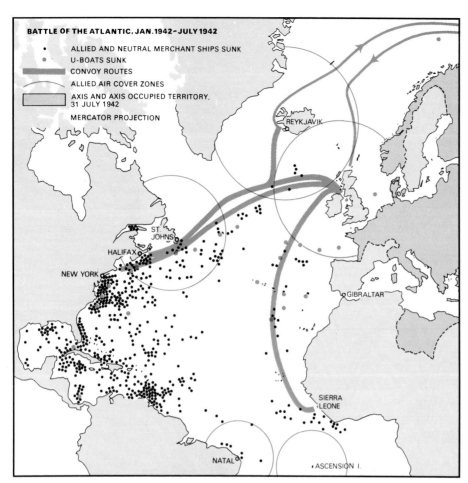

BATTLE OF THE ATLANTIC, JAN.1942–JULY 1942

- ALLIED AND NEUTRAL MERCHANT SHIPS SUNK
- U-BOATS SUNK
- CONVOY ROUTES
- ALLIED AIR COVER ZONES
- AXIS AND AXIS OCCUPIED TERRITORY, 31 JULY 1942

MERCATOR PROJECTION

REYKJAVIK

ST JOHNS
HALIFAX
NEW YORK
GIBRALTAR
SIERRA LEONE
NATAL
ASCENSION I.

U.99 and *U.100* they robbed Dönitz of Prien, Kretschmer and Schepke, three of his most daring and successful captains. Although this loss hastened the adoption of wolfpack tactics, which made fewer demands on the hastily trained wartime commanders, it was a severe blow to the U-Boat Arm.

From 1941 the Royal Navy also began intermittently to enjoy the invisible benefits of the 'Ultra' operation, with the secrets of the U-Boats' Enigma ciphering machine being translated into what by mid 1943 had become a steady stream of information about the U-Boats' dispositions and movements.

Throughout 1940-41 the United States was steadily moving toward overt support of Britain. The original 'bases for destroyers' deal of September 1940 was followed by the Lend-Lease Act in March 1941, which permitted more war material to be transferred to the British. A month later the US extended its Western Hemisphere Defense Zone to 26

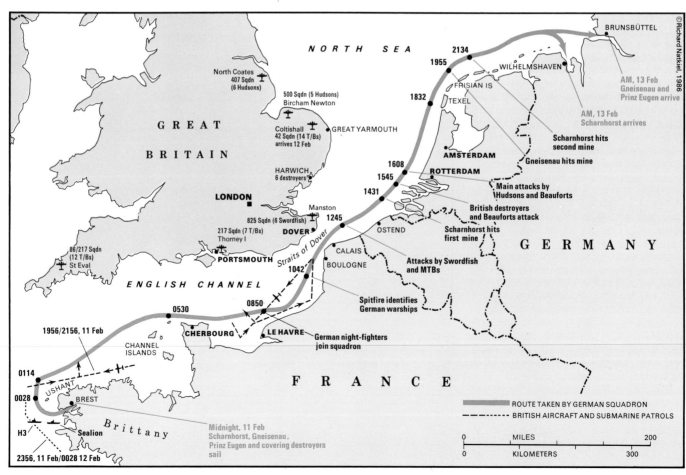

BRUNSBÜTTEL

NORTH SEA

2134
1955
1832
WILHELMSHAVEN

North Coates
407 Sqdn
(6 Hudsons)

500 Sqdn (5 Hudsons)
Bircham Newton

FRISIAN IS
TEXEL

AM, 13 Feb
Gneisenau and
Prinz Eugen arrive

AM, 13 Feb
Scharnhorst arrives

Scharnhorst hits
second mine

GREAT

BRITAIN

Coltishall
42 Sqdn (14 T/Bs)
arrives 12 Feb

GREAT YARMOUTH

HARWICH
6 destroyers

1608
1545
1431

AMSTERDAM

ROTTERDAM

Gneisenau hits mine

Main attacks by
Hudsons and Beauforts

LONDON

Manston

825 Sqdn (6 Swordfish)

217 Sqdn (7 T/Bs)
Thorney I.

DOVER

1245

OSTEND

British destroyers
and Beauforts attack

Scharnhorst hits
first mine

GERMANY

86/217 Sqdn
(12 T/Bs)
St Eval

PORTSMOUTH

Straits of Dover

CALAIS

BOULOGNE

1042

Attacks by Swordfish
and MTBs

ENGLISH CHANNEL

0850

Spitfire identifies
German warships

1956/2156, 11 Feb

0530

CHERBOURG

LE HAVRE

German night-fighters
join squadron

CHANNEL
ISLANDS

0114

USHANT

0028

BREST

Brittany

H3

Sealion

2356, 11 Feb/0028 12 Feb

FRANCE

Midnight, 11 Feb
Scharnhorst, Gneisenau,
Prinz Eugen and covering destroyers
sail

ROUTE TAKEN BY GERMAN SQUADRON
BRITISH AIRCRAFT AND SUBMARINE PATROLS

0   MILES   200
0   KILOMETERS   300

degrees West, which meant in practice that US merchantmen would be escorted by US Navy warships as far as Iceland. In August 1941 a further concession was made, whereby US warships could escort vessels not of US registry, and Canadian warships could escort US merchantmen.

By sharing the escort burden the US Navy was helping the British and Canadians to use their escorts more effectively, but it was only a matter of time before the Germans were provoked into retaliation. The latest USN destroyers looked sufficiently like the British and Canadian 'A-to-I' classes to be mistaken when seen through a periscope, even if the Germans had not been fully aware of what was happening. On 4 September the old destroyer USS *Greer* was missed by a U-Boat torpedo and counter-attacked the submarine with depth-charges. Then on 17 October the USS *Kearny* was badly damaged when hit by a torpedo in the engine room, but she managed to limp to safety in Iceland. Two weeks later the *Reuben James* was not so lucky, and sank with a hundred of her crew after being torpedoed by *U.562*, but isolationism was still too strong to allow President Roosevelt to declare war on Germany.

The isolationists could hardly ignore Pearl Harbor, but any lingering doubts about hostilities with Germany were dispelled when Hitler gratuitously declared war on the United States. If the British expected an immediate slackening of tempo in the Battle of the Atlantic they were disappointed. Despite all the warnings the US Navy had not developed any workable tactics for protecting its own and Allied shipping along the east coast, and losses rose alarmingly. Dönitz had shrewdly prepared a contingency plan, Operation *Paukenschlag* or 'Drumroll,' with U-Boats immediately diverted to the American coast to begin their onslaught on shipping. Only after six months of severe losses was a coastal convoy system brought fully into being, but in the long run the gigantic resources of the United States were able to wipe out these losses and build ships faster than the U-Boats could sink them.

In addition to mass-produced merchant ships the US shipyards turned out enormous numbers of warships, particularly frigates and escort aircraft carriers, many of which were transferred to the RN under Lend-Lease. With these extra ships the RN could now begin to take the offensive, building up Support Groups to go to the support of hard-pressed convoys or to pursue contacts to

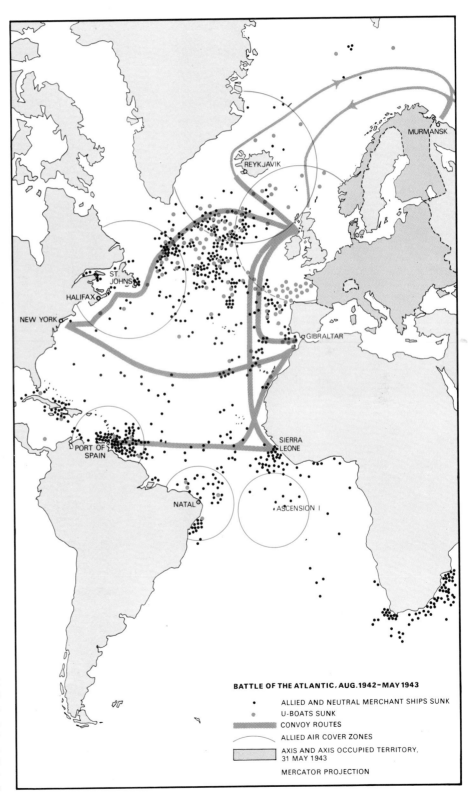

BATTLE OF THE ATLANTIC, AUG. 1942–MAY 1943

- •   ALLIED AND NEUTRAL MERCHANT SHIPS SUNK
- •   U-BOATS SUNK
- ▬ CONVOY ROUTES
- ◯ ALLIED AIR COVER ZONES
- ▬ AXIS AND AXIS OCCUPIED TERRITORY, 31 MAY 1943

MERCATOR PROJECTION

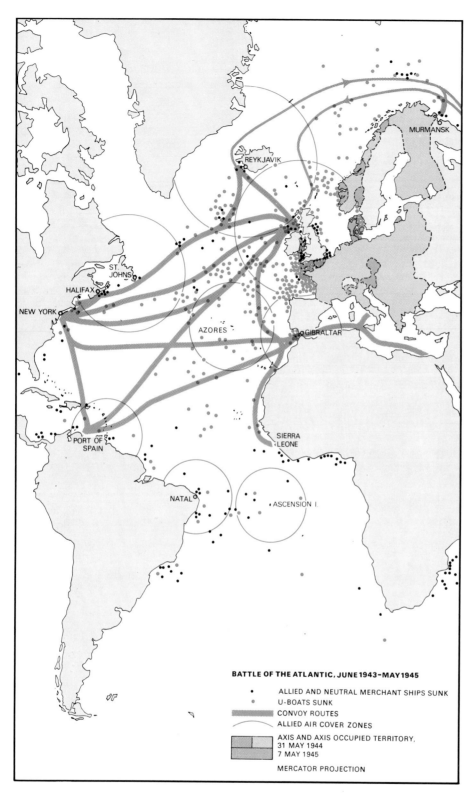

BATTLE OF THE ATLANTIC, JUNE 1943–MAY 1945

- •   ALLIED AND NEUTRAL MERCHANT SHIPS SUNK
- •   U-BOATS SUNK
-      CONVOY ROUTES
-      ALLIED AIR COVER ZONES

AXIS AND AXIS OCCUPIED TERRITORY,
31 MAY 1944
7 MAY 1945

MERCATOR PROJECTION

shipyards had built only 7 million tons in 1942, and losses for that year alone totalled 7.79 million tons. To make matters worse there were now 212 U-Boats in operational service with others being used for training. The implications for the Allies were inescapable: unless shipping losses could be brought under control in 1943 they would be unable to defeat Nazi Germany.

The spring of 1943 was marked by a series of ferocious convoy battles, and at the beginning of March 1943 for the first time the Allies began to contemplate the possibility of defeat. In the first 20 days of the month more than half a million tons of shipping was sunk.

Just in time the reinforcements released from the 'Torch' landings came back into the battle, and a series of scientific aids tipped the scales against the U-boats. Also of vital importance was the breaking of a new U-Boat cipher, and the sum total was a sudden reversal of fortunes. By mid-May Dönitz was preparing to withdraw his U-Boats from operations on the main convoy routes because of the unbearable losses they were suffering. By September 1943 the output of American, British and Canadian shipyards finally made good the tonnage sunk since 1939, and the long-awaited Second Front could go ahead.

Although the U-Boats returned to the battle after a six-month rest to lick their wounds and re-equip with new weapons they were never again to show the determination that they had in March 1943. In spite of the *schnorchel*, which permitted them to stay submerged for longer, and new types of homing torpedoes they were unable to disrupt the convoy system. New U-Boat designs were developed but fortunately for the Allies production was too slow to affect the outcome, and only a handful were ready by the time of Germany's surrender in May 1945.

The Battle of the Atlantic was the single most important campaign of the war. It linked the original European war with the conflict in the Pacific. The United States might have survived without winning the Atlantic battle but she would then have been forced to fight at a disadvantage on two fronts. Without the British Isles as a springboard the liberation of Europe would have been exceptionally difficult if not impossible.

destruction. From September 1942 there were a number of these groups operating in the Western Approaches, carrying the fight to the U-Boats rather than waiting for them to attack.

The western Allies were united in their strategic aim to defeat Germany but differed over the means. There was strong pressure from the Soviet Union to open a 'Second Front' by invading Europe as soon as possible, an idea which was supported by the United States. The British, with the memory of Dunkirk still fresh, counselled a much greater buildup of forces. As a compromise the Allies decided in July 1942 to invade North Africa.

Although the 'Torch' landings in November 1942 were successful the preparations and execution of the operation drew off crucial anti-submarine forces from the Atlantic. The U-Boat Command as always took advantage of any slackening in the opposition, and losses of shipping rose sharply in October and November 1942. The Allied

Sinking the *Bismarck*

The *Bismarck* was one of the two battleships ordered in 1935-36 as the first instalment of what was intended to be a massive program of expansion for the German Navy. Although declared to displace 35,000 tons to conform with internationally-agreed restrictions, she and her sister *Tirpitz* displaced 42,000 tons and were intended as long-distance commerce raiders.

The new battleship was ready for action in April 1941, and with the heavy cruiser *Prinz Eugen* sailed from Bergen on 21 May 1941. The idea was to send the two ships through the Denmark Sraight between Iceland and Greenland, out into the North Atlantic. At the end of the sortie they would return to Brest, where with the *Scharnhorst* and *Gneisenau* which were already in Brest they would paralyze the convoy system.

Two cruisers on patrol in the Denmark Strait, HMS *Norfolk* and HMS *Suffolk* de-tected the *Bismarck* on radar at 1922 on 23 May. Two fast capital ships, the old battle-cruiser *Hood* and the new battleship *Prince of Wales* were sent to intercept and made contact at 0600 next morning. Vice Admiral Holland brought his ships into action on a sharply converging course, hoping to close the range rapidly to reduce the risk of a plunging hit on the *Hood*'s thin deck armor.

Eight minutes after the action started the *Hood* had a fire burning amidships, and when 'straddled' by a salvo from *Bismarck* she blew up. At the time it was believed that her side armor had been pierced, but a more likely explanation is the detonation of her main magazine by the explosion of secondary ammunition nearby.

Fire shifted immediately to the *Prince of Wales*, which had been in commission only two weeks. A hit on her compass platform, the main command post, killed or wounded everyone there except her captain, but in spite of six more hits she fought back. With workmen from the shipyard on board rectify-ing faults as they occurred it was difficult to keep up the rate of fire, but the inexperienced guncrews obtained several 'straddles' on the *Bismarck*. One hit underwater contaminated the German ship's fuel tanks and caused a major leak. Although still prepared to fight, the *Prince of Wales*' captain was ordered to break off the action to avoid the risk of being sunk, while the *Norfolk* and *Suffolk* kept in contact.

While the Admiralty ordered every avail-able unit into the area, the German admiral tried to shake off the pursuit. A night attack by the carrier *Victorious* was unsuccessful, and that night (24-25 May) the *Bismarck* shook off the shadowing cruisers and covered the withdrawal of the cruiser *Prinz Eugen* to Brest. The Atlantic sortie had been cancelled

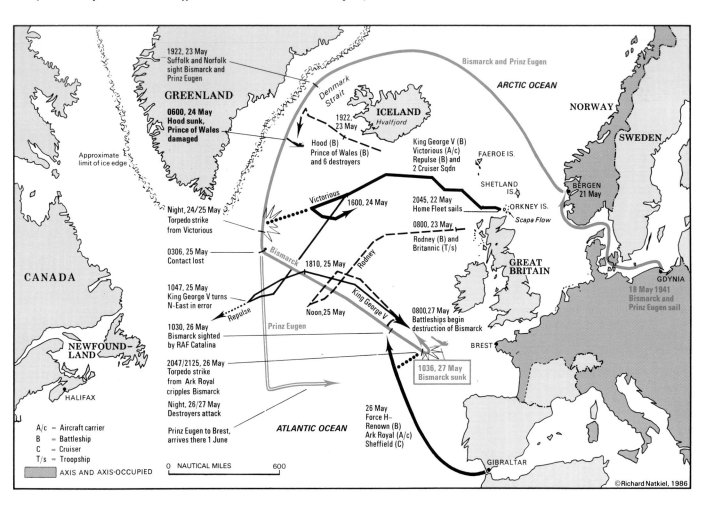

because of a shortage of fuel, and Admiral Lütjens' plan was to get to Brest where he could repair the damage.

A Catalina flying boat relocated the *Bismarck* at 1030 on 26 May and early that afternoon the carrier *Ark Royal* flew off a strike of Swordfish torpedo-bombers. The attack failed because the Swordfish mistakenly attacked the cruiser HMS *Sheffield*, but disaster was averted when all the torpedoes missed. Three hours later a second Swordfish strike found the quarry, and this time a torpedo wrecked the *Bismarck*'s rudders.

The battleship was now doomed, for she could only steer erratically on her engines. During the night she was attacked unsuccessfully by destroyers, and next morning the Home Fleet made contact. The flagship *King George V* and the *Rodney* started a systematic fire which silenced the *Bismark*'s guns after 30 minutes and then started to inflict appalling damage. After two hours of carnage the wreck was still afloat, and the C-in-C Admiral Tovey ordered the cruiser *Dorsetshire* to sink her with torpedoes. Only 110 survivors out of her crew of 2300 were rescued from the icy waters.

The sinking of the *Hood* was ranked as a national calamity, but in the harsh arithmetic of war it was not too heavy a price to pay for eliminating a major threat to the Atlantic convoys. The German Navy's cherished idea of three or four large units roaming at will in the North Atlantic was doomed, and even though the *Tirpitz* proved a hard nut to crack, surviving numerous British attacks and posing a constant threat to convoys to Russia until finally sunk in November 1944, the failure of the *Bismarck* proved that the day for raids on the main convoy routes had passed.

Left: Admiral **Lütjens** inspects the crew of the cruiser *Prinz Eugen*, shortly before Lütjens took command of the *Bismarck* and *Prinz Eugen* for the *Bismarck*'s fatal sortie. *Below:* The *Bismarck* firing her main armament. This photograph is often claimed to show the *Bismarck* in action with the *Hood* but it is more likely that it shows the *Bismarck* in training in the Baltic.

The War in the Mediterranean

At the start of World War II the French Navy was given the main task of watching the Italians, leaving the Royal Navy free to concentrate on the North Sea and Western Approaches. All this changed when French resistance collapsed in May 1940. Italy chose her moment to declare war on France, and the British were faced with the alarming prospect of the French Navy falling into Axis hands.

Although the armistice conditions permitted the French Fleet to remain in North Africa, to the British there seemed little to stop an Italian *coup de main* capturing the powerful French ships. Accordingly Churchill ordered Vice Admiral Sir James Somerville to put the French ships at Mers-el-Kebir (near Oran in Algeria) out of the reach of Germany and Italy, by negotiation if possible but by force if needed. The negotiations broke down and Somerville's ships carried out their distasteful task, sinking the battleship *Bretagne* and damaging the *Dunkerque* and *Provence*.

The Mediterranean Fleet under its brilliant C-in-C Admiral Andrew Cunningham wasted no time in showing the Italians that they would have to fight to control the Central Mediterranean. On 9 July 1940 Cunningham's ships chased the Italian Fleet to within 25 miles of the Italian coast, hitting

the *Giulio Cesare* at 15 miles' range. The Battle of Calabria was indecisive but it established an ascendancy over the Italians which was never lost. Eleven days later the Australian light cruiser *Sydney* sank the Italian *Bartolomeo Colleoni* off Crete.

The Royal Navy's base at Malta was the key to control of the central Mediterranean, and great efforts were made to keep the island supplied. When Malta was active its aircraft, warships and submarines interfered with supply-routes to Rommel's Afrika Korps and the Italian forces in Libya and Tunisia, but when it was neutralized by intense air raids the Italians were able to run fuel and ammunition without interference.

The arrival of a new aircraft carrier HMS *Illustrious* in August 1940 gave Cunningham the opportunity for a daring strike against the Italians' main fleet base at Taranto, in the south of Italy. If the Italian fleet could be neutralized it would be possible to run convoys through the Mediterranean to Alexandria to supply the British forces in Egypt, instead of going around the Cape of Good Hope.

On the night of 11 November 1940 a strike of 21 Swordfish torpedo bombers flown off the *Illustrious* succeeded in surprising the defenses of Taranto. In two hours they sank the modernized battleship *Conte di Cavour*

and severely damaged the new *Littorio* and the *Duilio*, at a cost of only two aircraft. Less spectacular but equally damaging was the destruction of the seaplane base in the inner harbor, which freed the Mediterranean Fleet from the attentions of shadowing aircraft for some months to come. (Map below.)

The British knew that the shallowness of the harbor would make it easy to repair the damaged battleships, but for some months there would be no interference from the Italian main fleet. More important, the Italians had lost the initiative and would never regain it. The British Fleet Air Arm had also shown that no fleet could rest easily in its base, and the same lesson was quickly absorbed by the Japanese Navy.

The British were quick to reap the benefits of Taranto. The carriers *Illustrious* and *Eagle* harassed communications between Italy and North Africa, using their aircraft to sink shipping, lay mines and attack North African harbors at will. On land the Italian armies in Cyrenaica were under strong pressure from British and Empire troops in Egypt, and the

Below: Taranto after the attack. Oil fuel can be seen spreading over the surface of the harbor from the crippled ships.

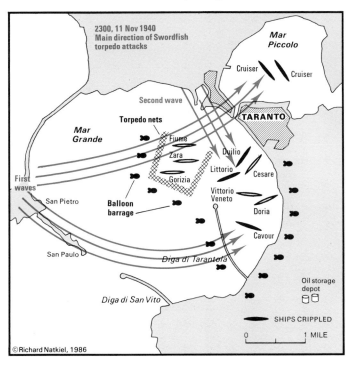

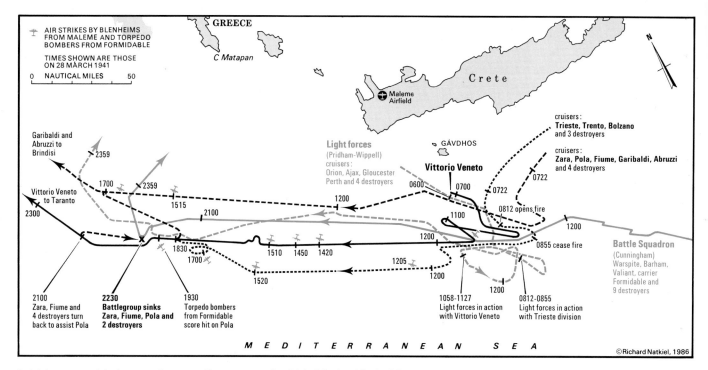

AIR STRIKES BY BLENHEIMS
FROM MALEME AND TORPEDO
BOMBERS FROM FORMIDABLE

TIMES SHOWN ARE THOSE
ON 28 MARCH 1941

0   NAUTICAL MILES   50

GREECE

C Matapan

Crete

Maleme
Airfield

GÁVDHOS

Light forces
(Pridham-Wippell)
cruisers:
Orion, Ajax, Gloucester
Perth and 4 destroyers

Vittorio Veneto

cruisers:
Trieste, Trento, Bolzano
and 3 destroyers

cruisers:
Zara, Pola, Fiume, Garibaldi, Abruzzi
and 4 destroyers

Garibaldi and
Abruzzi to
Brindisi

2359

1700   2359

1515

Vittorio Veneto
to Taranto

2300   2100

0600   0700   0722

0722

0812 opens fire

1100

1200

1200   1200

0855 cease fire

1200

Battle Squadron
(Cunningham)
Warspite, Barham,
Valiant, carrier
Formidable and
9 destroyers

1830   1510   1450   1420
1700

1520   1205   1200

2100
Zara, Fiume and
4 destroyers turn
back to assist Pola

2230
Battlegroup sinks
Zara, Fiume, Pola and
2 destroyers

1930
Torpedo bombers
from Formidable
score hit on Pola

1200

1058-1127
Light forces in action
with Vittorio Veneto

0812-0855
Light forces in action
with Trieste division

M E D I T E R R A N E A N   S E A

©Richard Natkiel, 1986

British were achieving maximum military results for minimum effort.

Success brought its own risks. The string of easy victories over the Italians made the British over-confident, and the decision to send troops to Greece to assist the Greeks in holding off the Germans and Italians was foolhardy. British forces were badly overstretched and were soon unable to prevent large-scale resupply of the Italian forces in North Africa. In January 1941 the Luftwaffe scored a major success when the recently-deployed *Fliegerkorps X* put the carrier *Illustrious* out of action off Malta. Without a modern carrier the British were unable to exercise control over the Central Mediterranean, and the results were obvious: Axis land forces started to threaten Egypt once more and Malta again faced the threat of starvation.

To cover the passage of British and Empire troops to Greece the Mediterranean Fleet had established a forward base at Suda Bay in Crete. It was recognized that the troop convoys would be a tempting target to the Italians, and Admiral Cunningham ordered Vice Admiral Pridham-Wippell to patrol south of Gavdhos (Gaudo) with the light cruisers *Ajax*, *Gloucester*, *Orion* and *Perth*. As soon as he heard on the evening of 27 March that RAF reconnaissance aircraft had sighted Italian heavy units heading for Crete Cunningham ordered his Battle Squadron to sea, the battleships *Warspite* (flagship), *Barham* and *Valiant* and the new carrier *Formidable*. (Map above.)

The reports were confusing for they talked of more than one battleship, whereas there was only one Italian capital ship at sea, the *Vittorio Veneto*. The *Formidable*'s aircraft played a vital role in resolving the uncertainty, and next day at 1510 her Albacore torpedo bombers hit the battleship with one torpedo. At dusk they launched another

attack which failed to hit the *Vittorio Veneto*, but an 18-inch torpedo brought the heavy cruiser *Pola* to a halt at 1930.

Admiral Angelo Iachino, the Italian commander was able to extricate the *Vittorio Veneto* from a very dangerous position, but believing that Cunningham's forces were far to the east, decided to send two heavy cruisers, the *Fiume* and *Zara*, back to try to help the *Pola*. Cunningham's battleships were in fact only 50 miles away and closing. To make matters worse the Italians were ill-equipped for night fighting, whereas the British had exercised constantly for such an eventuality and had surface-warning radar.

When the three British battleships sighted the *Fiume* and *Zara* they were less than 4000 yards away, and the 15-inch guns destroyed them within minutes. Then it was the turn of the *Pola* and two destroyers.

Although Cunningham's main objective, the destruction of the *Vittorio Veneto* had not been achieved, Matapan was a decisive action. Despite the adverse situation of the British (which would continue to worsen in the months ahead) the Italian Navy never regained the initiative which it had lost at Taranto. Even when the efforts to evacuate Greece and Crete exposed the Royal Navy to grievous losses from German air attacks in May 1941, the Italian Navy could not make a decisive move and the British were able to extricate themselves from Crete without interference from the Italian Fleet.

The problem for the British was now the re-supply of Malta, and massive operations were mounted to fight convoys through. The price was heavy, but the beleaguered island held out. The nadir of British fortunes was November-December 1941, when the battleship *Barham* and the aircraft carrier *Ark Royal* were sunk by submarines, and the battleships *Queen Elizabeth* and *Valiant* were immobilized by 'human torpedoes' (midget

submarines) in Alexandria, but still the Italian Fleet did not act, and the moment for winning the Mediterranean passed.

In August 1942 the last and fiercest battle to reinforce Malta was launched. 'Operation Pedestal' epitomizes the problems encountered in 1940-41: long before a convoy from Gibraltar was within reach of Malta it was under surveillance from enemy reconnaissance aircraft stationed in Sardinia, and heavy attacks could be expected for the final two-thirds of the voyage.

The risks had to be faced because of the Allies' planned landings in North Africa. Malta's great value was as a 'platform' for strikes against Axis supply-routes to North

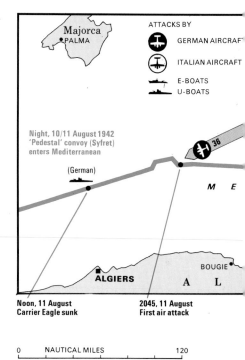

Majorca
PALMA

ATTACKS BY

GERMAN AIRCRAFT

ITALIAN AIRCRAFT

E-BOATS

U-BOATS

Night, 10/11 August 1942
'Pedestal' convoy (Syfret)
enters Mediterranean

(German)

36

M E

ALGIERS

BOUGIE

A L

Noon, 11 August
Carrier Eagle sunk

2045, 11 August
First air attack

0   NAUTICAL MILES   120

Africa, and if the island had fallen in the autumn of 1942 the Germans could more readily have rushed reinforcements into Tunisia and Algeria to defeat the Allied forces. So long as Malta held out the Axis capability to supply its North African forces was severely limited.

The convoy which left Gibraltar on the night of 10-11 August 1942 had the heaviest naval escort yet seen: three aircraft carriers, two battleships, seven cruisers and 24 destroyers, but out of these only four cruisers and 12 destroyers were to go all the way to Malta. The convoy was made up of only 14 fast cargo ships. In addition the old carrier *Furious* was to fly off 38 Spitfire fighters to reinforce Malta's air defense. (Map below.)

At first the operation went well, and the *Furious* flew off her Spitfires when about 550 miles west of Malta, but shortly afterwards the carrier *Eagle* was hit by three torpedoes from *U.73* and sank in eight minutes. At 2045 the first air attacks started, and next morning (12 August) they were renewed. The carrier *Victorious* had a narrow escape when a large bomb broke up on her armored flight deck, but the SS *Deucalion* was damaged at 1215 and had to leave the convoy.

The convoy then passed through a barrier of Italian submarines, dodging numerous torpedoes successfully. At 1835 more air attacks started, and this time the carrier *Indomitable* was put out of action by a bomb hit on the flight deck and the destroyer *Foresight* was sunk by a torpedo hit. At 1900 Admiral Syfret's main covering force withdrew as planned, leaving Admiral Burrough in the cruiser *Nigeria* to take command of the convoy. Only an hour later both the flagship and a second cruiser, HMS *Cairo*, were torpedoed by an Italian submarine; the *Nigeria* limped back to Gibraltar but the *Cairo* had to be sunk. In this attack the tanker SS *Ohio* was also damaged but was able to stay with the convoy.

As dusk fell an air attack caught the convoy at a bad moment, when it was changing formation to pass through the Skerki Channel. The merchantmen *Clan Ferguson* and *Empire Hope* were sunk and the cruiser *Kenya* and the merchantman *Brisbane Star* were both damaged. The main body passed Cape Bon at midnight and soon afterward came under attack from motor torpedo boats (Italian MAS-Boats) from Pantelleria. At 0120 on the morning of 13 August the cruiser *Manchester* was hit by a torpedo at close range, and although she stayed afloat for nearly four hours she had to be abandoned and sunk. Five merchantmen were also hit

and four, the *Almeria Lykes, Glenorchy, Santa Eliza* and *Wairangi* were sunk in the early hours.

Soon after daylight dive bombers appeared, sinking the *Waimarama* and damaging the *Ohio* a second time. Aircraft from Malta could now provide air cover but the *Ohio* was disabled, the *Rochester Castle* was on fire and the *Dorset* was dead in the water. When at 1430 the minesweepers came out from Malta only three ships were left in the convoy, the *Port Chalmers*, the *Melbourne Star* and the damaged *Rochester Castle*. After heroic exertions the damaged *Dorset* and *Ohio* were towed in but the *Dorset* sank and the *Ohio* only reached Grand Harbour when two destroyers lashed themselves alongside to enable her to be steered. The *Brisbane Star* made a brief incursion into French Tunisian waters, but was allowed to proceed and finally reached Grand Harbour shortly before the *Ohio*, bringing the total to five ships, out of the 14 which had set out. And yet their 32,000 tons of cargo and fuel were sufficient to help Malta to survive. Once Malta was secured planning for the Anglo-American landings in North Africa could proceed and once the North African coast was in Allied hands the way was clear for the invasion of Sicily and Italy.

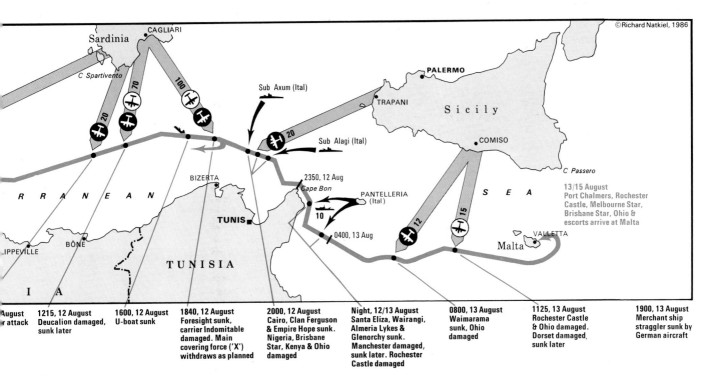

© Richard Natkiel, 1986

| | 1215, 12 August Deucalion damaged, sunk later | 1600, 12 August U-boat sunk | 1840, 12 August Foresight sunk, carrier Indomitable damaged. Main covering force ('X') withdraws as planned | 2000, 12 August Cairo, Clan Ferguson & Empire Hope sunk. Nigeria, Brisbane Star, Kenya & Ohio damaged | Night, 12/13 August Santa Eliza, Wairangi, Almeria Lykes & Glenorchy sunk. Manchester damaged, sunk later. Rochester Castle damaged | 0800, 13 August Waimarama sunk, Ohio damaged | 1125, 13 August Rochester Castle & Ohio damaged. Dorset damaged, sunk later | 1900, 13 August Merchant ship straggler sunk by German aircraft |

193

The Invasion of North Africa

The United States after its entry into the war was anxious to bring its enormous military power to bear in the European theater as early as possible. Balked of a 'Second Front' in Europe, American and British leaders decided to land in North Africa, to cut off German forces in Libya and Cyrenaica.

The plan was to land 70,000 men between Casablanca in Morocco and Oran (subsequently the landing areas were extended to Algiers), and the logistic support provided was lavish. Six advance convoys and four assault convoys, 250 ships, sailed from Great Britain, followed by another four convoys totalling 136 ships direct from the United States. The covering naval forces included six battleships, five aircraft carriers, seven escort carriers, 15 cruisers, 81 destroyers and 38 anti-submarine escorts.

The planners had hoped that the landing would be unopposed but the Allied forces ran into fierce opposition from French troops who did not support the Americans' protégé, General Giraud. Algiers was seized successfully on 8 November 1942, but a similar operation at Oran resulted in the loss of the two ships leading the assault. At Casablanca the opposition was weaker but the battleship USS *Massachusetts* was forced to silence the French *Jean Bart* with her 16-inch guns before resistance collapsed.

Sadly the collapse of French resistance triggered off a much bigger disaster. Since July 1940 the bulk of the French Fleet had been at Toulon, under the control of the 'Vichy' government of Unoccupied France. Despite pleas to break out before the Germans tried to capture the fleet, Admiral de Laborde hesitated, giving the Germans time to launch an assault on the Toulon base. To prevent their capture three capital ships, seven cruisers, 30 destroyers and 16 submarines had to be scuttled. Although most of the former adherents to the Vichy cause in other locations now joined the Allies the bulk of the fine pre-war French Navy no longer existed.

After hard fighting the American and British troops pushed eastward into Tunisia, where the Germans had rushed in reinforcements. Subsidiary landings were made at Bougie and Bone on 11-12 November to forestall German paratroops, but the Germans succeeded in establishing a defense line. Not until May 1943 were the Allies able to link up with the British Eighth Army advancing westward from Libya.

The final act of the North African campaign was an attempted evacuation of the Axis forces, which was doomed to failure in the face of the overwhelming British and American naval forces. Operation 'Retribution' ensured that only a few hundred men of the Afrika Korps and the Italian Army reached Sicily, which would be the next Allied target.

Below: **Landing craft unloading supplies from transport ships on the beach at Oran in the early stages of the Torch operation, 8 November 1942.**

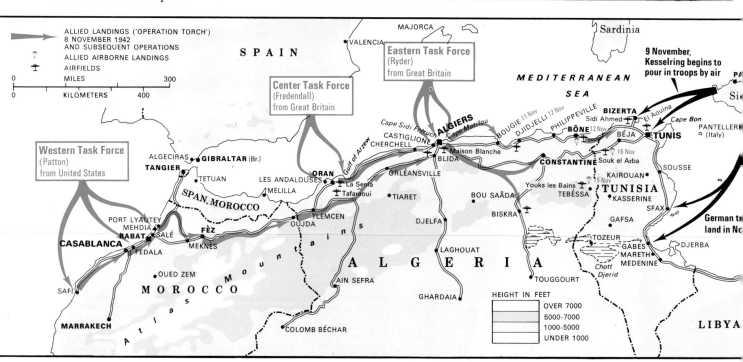

The Invasion of Italy

The temptation to knock Italy out of the war was strong, and after the destruction of Axis forces in North Africa the Americans agreed to British proposals for a two-stage operation against Sicily and the Italian mainland.

The first step was to capture the island fortresses of Pantelleria and Lampedusa in May-June 1943. From here air cover could be provided for the Sicily landings, 'Operation Husky,' on a bigger scale than Malta's already crowded airfields could provide. On 10 July the Allies landed in strength in the southeastern part of Sicily, some 66,000 US and 115,000 British and Empire troops. Massive air cover was provided and over 500 major landing craft, and losses were small.

This time the Germans were more successful in evacuating their troops, and the bulk of the defenders of Sicily escaped: 101,500 troops and nearly 10,000 vehicles.

The second stage, an amphibious assault on the Italian mainland, was to follow as soon as possible, partly to hit the defenders before they had recovered from the 'Messina Straits Regatta' and partly to use the landing craft and warships before they were withdrawn to prepare to take part in the Normandy landings.

The complexity of the operation reflects the growing Allied confidence in the techniques of amphibious warfare. The fleet was to make a feint to suggest an exercise, and then slip into the Tyrrhenian Sea to bombard Reggio Calabria. While the British Eighth Army seized Reggio Calabria the main force landed in the Bay of Salerno to the northwest.

On the eve of the landings the Italian Government indicated to the Allies that it wanted an armistice. But any hopes of an unopposed landing were dashed by the speed with which the Germans moved. They had no hesitation in attacking their erstwhile allies, and a force of Italian battleships heading south to surrender to the British was attacked by Do-217 aircraft armed with FX.1400 glider-bombs. The *Roma* was hit

Above right: **Sherman tanks are landed from an LST at Anzio in May 1944. The LST (Landing Ship, Tank) and other specialised vessels were an essential part of the Allied plans for amphibious operations. The first use of LSTs was in the Sicily landings at the start of the Italian campaign.**
Right: **Fire-fighting aboard the American light cruiser *Savannah* after the ship was hit during the Salerno landings.**

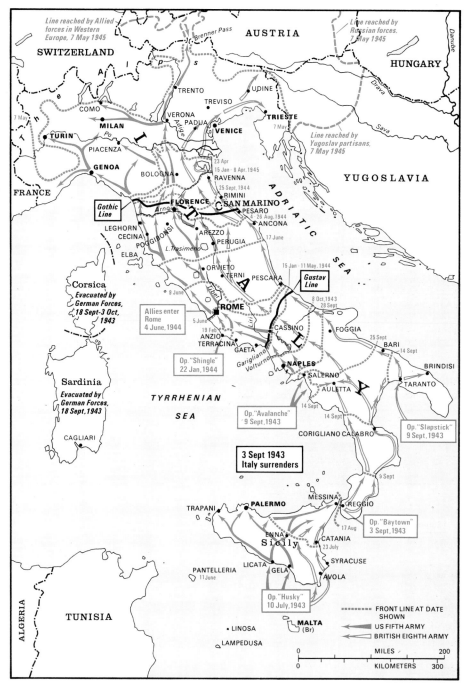

and blew up with heavy loss of life. At Salerno there was bitter fighting, and at times it looked as if the assault troops might be pushed back into the sea. Only massive gunfire support from Allied warships and heavy air support saved the day. By mid-October the beachhead was firmly established and, once Naples had fallen, control over the whole of southern Italy was assured.

Salerno showed that a major amphibious assault could succeed, even when faced by an aggressive and well-prepared enemy. The confusion over the Italian armistice had forced the Allies to suspend their preliminary bombardment, a mistake which proved costly, but the massive gunfire support was available immediately after the landing and helped to keep casualties down.

The Anzio and Nettuno landings, Operation 'Shingle' in January 1944 were inspired by the comparatively slow advance after Salerno. As a bold strategic stroke this landing behind the main German defenses could have shortened the campaign but the swift German reaction coupled with Allied caution after the landings wrecked the Allies' planning. For nearly four months the troops were confined to a narrow beachhead, while a massive logistic effort was mounted to keep them supplied with food and ammunition.

The ships supporting the Anzio landing were attacked from the air by FX.1400 bombs, which sank or seriously damaged several ships. The German Navy also introduced its new 'K-units' or *kleine Kampfmittel* (small battle units), a variety of midget submarines and 'human torpedoes.' Although they added to the problems of maintaining naval support, their influence on the outcome was negligible.

Left: An anti-aircraft cruiser lays a smoke screen to protect the landing forces during the Salerno operation.

Arctic Convoys

Germany's attack on the Soviet Union in June 1941 caused a major shift in British strategy. As the Red Army continued to suffer enormous losses in its attempts to stem the German advance, Stalin appealed to Great Britain for aid. This could only be sent to the Arctic ports of Murmansk or Archangel, through waters dominated by German air, surface and submarine forces based in Norway.

The first North Russian convoys started in August 1941. After the entry of the United States into the war political pressure to maintain the traffic became even more acute. Stalin kept up his pressure for a Second Front, and there was the constant fear that the Red Army might be defeated if it did not receive supplies of tanks, guns and planes.

The first few convoys were not attacked, but in March 1942 PQ-13 was attacked by three large destroyers. During the action the cruiser HMS *Trinidad* was severely damaged

but limped into Murmansk. At the end of April another escorting cruiser, HMS *Edinburgh*, was sunk demonstrating how risky the operations were. Despite misgivings about the long hours of daylight in the summer months the convoys continued to sail, and in July 1942 PQ-17 suffered a terrible fate. Despite the presence of a heavy escort of four American and British cruisers the First Sea Lord chose to interfere directly in the conduct of operations, and on the strength of a premature report that the *Tirpitz* was putting to sea, the convoy was ordered to scatter.

The U-Boats and aircraft took full advantage and hunted down individual merchant ships, sinking 24 out of 37. In all 99,000 tons of supplies and nearly 4000 vehicles, tanks and aircraft were lost. To make matters worse the *Tirpitz* did not sail for another 24 hours, and it became clear that if the convoy had not scattered it would have suffered far fewer losses. (Map page 198.)

To offset the setback of PQ-17, at the end of 1942 a force of eight British escort ships successfully held off an attack by the heavy cruiser *Admiral Hipper* and the *panzerschiff Lützow*.

Under the command of Captain Robert Sherbrooke the destroyers prevented the German heavy units from getting within range of convoy JW-51B. The flotilla leader *Onslow* was badly damaged by 8-inch shells, but in spite of a ghastly wound in the face Sherbrooke and his destroyers won time for the cruisers *Jamaica* and *Sheffield* to come up in support. They drove off the attackers, sinking the destroyer *Friedrich Eckholdt*. Apart from severe damage to the *Onslow* the Royal Navy lost the destroyer *Achates* and the minesweeper *Gleaner* but JW-51B arrived safely at Murmansk. (Map page 199, top.)

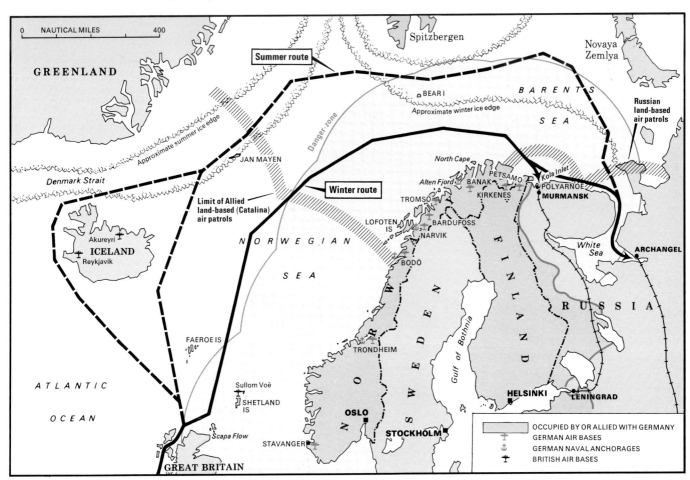

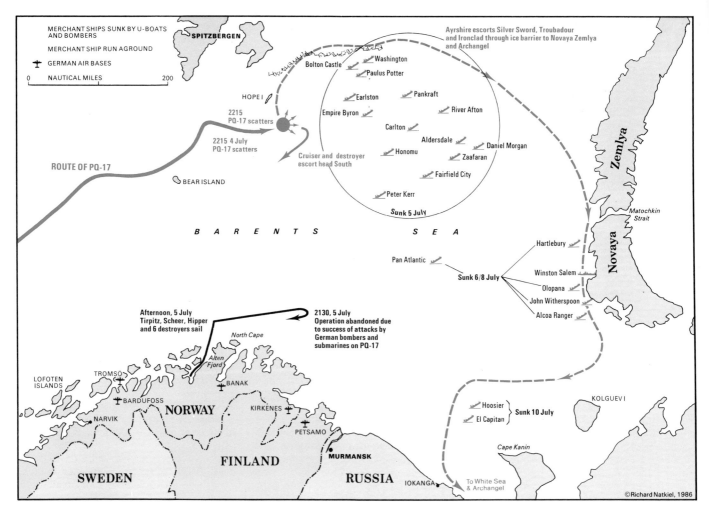

Map labels:
- MERCHANT SHIPS SUNK BY U-BOATS AND BOMBERS
- MERCHANT SHIP RUN AGROUND
- GERMAN AIR BASES
- 0 NAUTICAL MILES 200
- SPITZBERGEN
- Ayrshire escorts Silver Sword, Troubadour and Ironclad through ice barrier to Novaya Zemlya and Archangel
- Bolton Castle
- Washington
- Paulus Potter
- Earlston
- Pankraft
- HOPE I
- Empire Byron
- River Afton
- 2215 PQ-17 scatters
- Carlton
- 2215 4 July PQ-17 scatters
- Aldersdale
- Daniel Morgan
- ROUTE OF PQ-17
- Honomu
- Zaafaran
- Cruiser and destroyer escort head South
- Fairfield City
- BEAR ISLAND
- Peter Kerr
- Sunk 5 July
- B A R E N T S   S E A
- Zemlya
- Matochkin Strait
- Hartlebury
- Pan Atlantic
- Novaya
- Sunk 6/8 July
- Winston Salem
- Olopana
- John Witherspoon
- Alcoa Ranger
- Afternoon, 5 July Tirpitz, Scheer, Hipper and 6 destroyers sail
- North Cape
- 2130, 5 July Operation abandoned due to success of attacks by German bombers and submarines on PQ-17
- Alten Fjord
- TROMSO
- BANAK
- LOFOTEN ISLANDS
- BARDUFOSS
- KIRKENES
- NORWAY
- Hoosier
- KOLGUEVI
- NARVIK
- PETSAMO
- El Capitan
- Sunk 10 July
- SWEDEN
- FINLAND
- MURMANSK
- Cape Kanin
- RUSSIA
- IOKANGA
- To White Sea & Archangel

Although apparently indecisive, the Battle of the Barents Sea touched off a major row in the German High Command. Hitler was so incensed at what he rightly considered a disgraceful performance by the *Kriegsmarine* that he ordered the surface fleet to be disarmed and laid up. This provoked the resignation of Grand-Admiral Raeder as C-in-C in favor of Admiral Dönitz, until then the commander of the U-Boat arm, who naturally favored expansion of the U-Boat force at the expense of the big ships. The hysterical order to scrap the battleships and heavy cruisers was rescinded, but the German Navy had suffered a severe blow to its morale.

The final humiliation for the German Navy was the sinking of the battlecruiser *Scharnhorst* in the Battle of the North Cape on 26 December 1943.

This time there was to be no interference by Hitler, but everything still went wrong. Admiral Erich Bey lost contact with his destroyers, and had no idea that his opponent, Admiral Fraser had reinforced the escort of convoy JW-55B to 14 destroyers. Fraser also had the enormous advantage of Ultra code-breaking information about the

Left: **The British cruiser *Bellona* on Arctic convoy duty. The gun turrets are trained to port to protect the guns from the heavy seas breaking over the bows.**

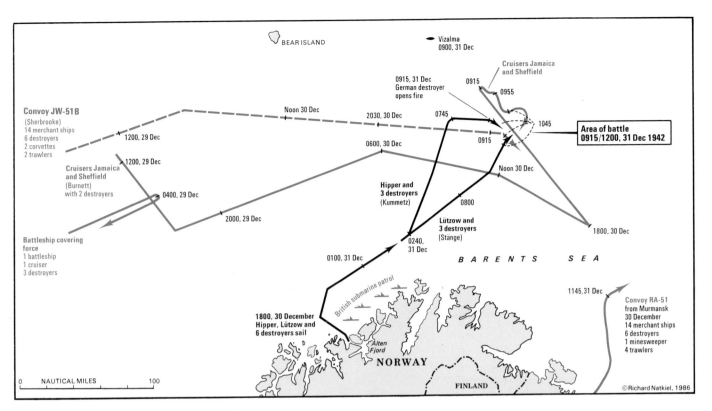

Convoy JW-51B
(Sherbrooke)
14 merchant ships
6 destroyers
2 corvettes
2 trawlers

Cruisers Jamaica
and Sheffield
(Burnett)
with 2 destroyers

Battleship covering
force
1 battleship
1 cruiser
3 destroyers

BEAR ISLAND

Vizalma
0900, 31 Dec

Cruisers Jamaica
and Sheffield

0915, 31 Dec
German destroyer
opens fire

0915

0955

0745

1045

Noon 30 Dec

2030, 30 Dec

1200, 29 Dec

0600, 30 Dec

0915

Area of battle
0915/1200, 31 Dec 1942

1200, 29 Dec

0400, 29 Dec

2000, 29 Dec

Noon 30 Dec

Hipper and
3 destroyers
(Kummetz)

0800

Lützow and
3 destroyers
(Stange)

0240,
31 Dec

B A R E N T S   S E A

1800, 30 Dec

0100, 31 Dec

British submarine patrol

1145, 31 Dec

Convoy RA-51
from Murmansk
30 December
14 merchant ships
6 destroyers
1 minesweeper
4 trawlers

1800, 30 December
Hipper, Lützow and
6 destroyers sail

Alten
Fjord

NORWAY

FINLAND

0   NAUTICAL MILES   100

©Richard Natkiel, 1986

German intentions, but his handling of the battle was nonetheless superb. (Map below.)

The first phase was similar to the Barents Sea action a year earlier, but this time three cruisers, the *Belfast*, *Norfolk* and *Sheffield* held off the *Scharnhorst*. Their spirited action gave time for the C-in-C in the battleship *Duke of York* to close with the convoy. Her 14-inch salvoes quickly hit the *Scharnhorst*, and when the German ship tried to break away destroyers were sent in to torpedo her. The action was the first to be fought entirely on radar, and visibility was so poor that nobody saw the *Scharnhorst* sink at 1945.

The elimination of the *Scharnhorst* marked the end of any serious threat to the North Russian convoys. The *Tirpitz* was out of action following an attack by midget submarines, would be damaged again in April 1944 by carrier aircraft and was finally sunk by the RAF in November 1944.

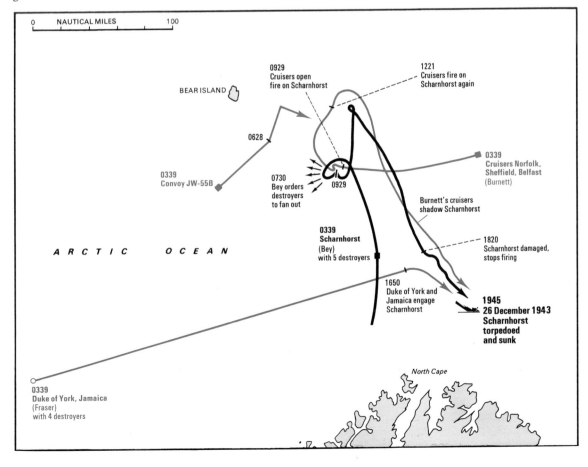

0   NAUTICAL MILES   100

0929
Cruisers open
fire on Scharnhorst

1221
Cruisers fire on
Scharnhorst again

BEAR ISLAND

0628

0339
Convoy JW-55B

0730
Bey orders
destroyers
to fan out

0929

0339
Cruisers Norfolk,
Sheffield, Belfast
(Burnett)

Burnett's cruisers
shadow Scharnhorst

1820
Scharnhorst damaged,
stops firing

0339
Scharnhorst
(Bey)
with 5 destroyers

A R C T I C   O C E A N

1650
Duke of York
and Jamaica engage
Scharnhorst

1945
26 December 1943
Scharnhorst
torpedoed
and sunk

0339
Duke of York, Jamaica
(Fraser)
with 4 destroyers

North Cape

The Liberation of Europe

The Normandy Landings

British and American planning for an amphibious landing in Europe began as early as March 1942, under the codename 'Operation Roundup,' but it remained a paper project for another year, until major problems such as the supply of landing craft and the shipping losses in the Battle of the Atlantic could be solved. In May 1943 a new name was chosen, 'Overlord,' which with its naval component 'Operation Neptune' grew steadily into the greatest amphibious operation in history. The landing area was chosen early, the Normandy coast between the Rivers Orne and Vire, and preparations were made to mislead the Germans into thinking that the Pas de Calais was the real site.

While enormous forces and supplies of fuel, munitions and food were gathered in the south of England the Allied navies set about the task of neutralizing the German naval opposition. In mid-1944 there were 5 torpedo boats, 34 motor torpedo boats (*schnellboote*) and 220 minesweepers and small patrol craft in the Channel area, but on the Atlantic coast the Germans also had 49 U-Boats, six destroyers and large torpedo boats and over 200 minesweepers and patrol vessels. There were in addition 'K-units' similar to those tried out at Anzio.

The strategy was a simple one, to 'cork' both ends of the Channel and prevent the U-Boats from getting at the invasion fleet, and to use massive air cover to prevent surface forces from getting too close. This worked remarkably well, and both U-Boats and surface forces suffered heavy losses.

The actual invasion forces included over 4000 landing craft, many of which were novel types. The planners assumed that neither of the major ports near the landing area, Le Havre and Cherbourg, would be useable for some time after their capture, and two ingenious artificial 'Mulberry' harbors were built to facilitate the rapid transfer of supplies. To fuel the enormous number of vehicles a pipeline was to be laid under the Channel, called 'PLUTO' (PipeLine Under The Ocean).

The Germans were fully aware that a large landing was planned, but their counter-measures were poorly coordinated. The High Command favored the Pas de Calais as the most likely sector, and although enormous resources were thrown into strengthening the 'Atlantic Wall' with guns and beach obstacles the local commanders differed over the best

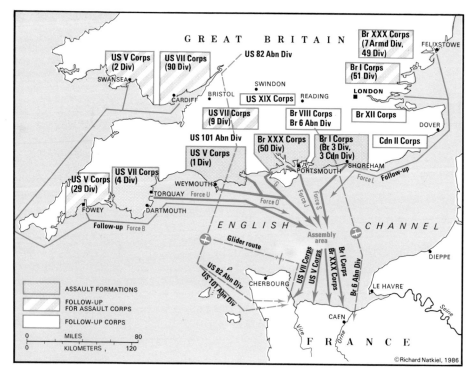

©Richard Natkiel, 1986

tactics. As the Allies had predicted, great efforts were made to demolish Cherbourg and Le Havre, but the creation of the 'Mulberry' harbors enabled the invaders to ignore the two ports.

The Germans also failed to forecast the sheer scale of 'Overlord.' In the first 16 hours of D-Day, 6 June 1944, a total of 132,715 soldiers went ashore, and within a few days over 1 million had been landed. The defenders were lulled into thinking that poor weather would prevent the Allies from mounting the invasion, but General Dwight D Eisenhower and his staff were sufficiently confident of the plan to go ahead.

Bad weather did cause a near-disaster, but not until 19 June. Some 800 landing craft were sunk or disabled in a gale and the American 'Mulberry' at St Laurent was wrecked, but the surviving remnants were used to extend the British 'Mulberry' at Arromanches to get the supplies moving again.

A feature of 'Overlord' was the massive naval support, from seven battleships, two monitors, 23 cruisers and over 100 destroyers. There were in addition numerous support landing craft, some with guns and others with bombardment rockets. With FOOs (Forward Observation Officers)

Below: **British motor torpedo boats on patrol in the Channel. The Allied light forces played a vital part in protecting the thousands of ships in the D-Day convoys from German attacks.**

ashore gunfire support was quick and accurate. The Luftwaffe was also unable to dispute control of the skies, and there was very little interference with the bombarding forces lying off the five landing beaches, Utah and Omaha for the US Army and Gold, Juno and Sword for the British and Canadians.

The beachhead remained constricted for some weeks, but the breakout was not unduly delayed. It was to be nearly another year before Germany surrendered but the Normandy landings opened the long-awaited Second Front, and set in train the liberation of Western Europe.

Left: **The forward 14-inch guns of the battleship USS *Nevada* blast the German positions at Utah beach.**

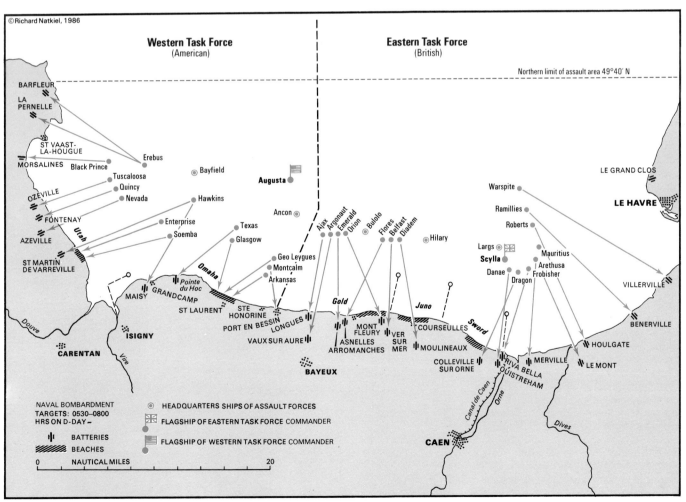

© Richard Natkiel, 1986

Western Task Force (American)

Eastern Task Force (British)

Northern limit of assault area 49°40′ N

BARFLEUR
LA PERNELLE
ST VAAST-LA-HOUGUE
MORSALINES   Black Prince   Erebus
OZEVILLE   Tuscaloosa
Quincy
Nevada
FONTENAY   Enterprise
Hawkins
Bayfield
Augusta
LE GRAND CLOS
LE HAVRE
Warspite
Ramillies
Roberts
AZEVILLE
Soemba
Texas
Glasgow
Ancon
Ajax Argonaut Emerald Orion
Bulolo
Flores Belfast Diadem
Hilary
Largs
Scylla
Mauritius
Arethusa
Frobisher
VILLERVILLE
ST MARTIN DE VARREVILLE
Utah
Geo Leygues
Montcalm
Arkansas
Gold
Juno
Danae
Dragon
BENERVILLE
Douve
Omaha
Pointe du Hoc
GRANDCAMP
MAISY
ST LAURENT
STE HONORINE
PORT EN BESSIN   LONGUES
COURSEULLES
Sword
HOULGATE
ISIGNY
VAUX SUR AURE
MONT FLEURY
ASNELLES
ARROMANCHES
VER SUR MER
MOULINEAUX
MERVILLE
LE MONT
CARENTAN
Vire
BAYEUX
COLLEVILLE SUR ORNE
RIVA BELLA
OUISTREHAM
CAEN
Canal de Caen
Orne
Dives

NAVAL BOMBARDMENT TARGETS: 0530–0800 HRS ON D-DAY –

◎ HEADQUARTERS SHIPS OF ASSAULT FORCES

⊞ FLAGSHIP OF EASTERN TASK FORCE COMMANDER

BATTERIES

BEACHES

⬤ FLAGSHIP OF WESTERN TASK FORCE COMMANDER

0   NAUTICAL MILES   20

The Invasion of Southern France

The amphibious operations against the south of France were the subject of considerable acrimony between the Allies. The Americans were understandably eager to liberate France at the earliest opportunity, and argued that a landing in the south would weaken the Germans in the north. The British argued that the resources were better spent in finishing the Italian campaign, and that the Allied forces in Italy were already tying down German forces in large numbers.

The original plan to mount 'Operation Anvil' (renamed 'Dragoon' in July 1944) simultaneously with 'Overlord' was dropped, but the Combined Chiefs of Staff were anxious to get it under way as soon as possible. The techniques used to such effect at Normandy were repeated, and many ships were allocated to 'Dragoon' after playing their part in 'Overlord.' The beaches were codenamed 'Camel,' 'Delta,' 'Alpha' and 'Sitka.' The bulk of the invading force was American, backed up by French commandos.

The breakout was rapid, and within a month both Marseilles and Toulon had fallen and more than 300,000 men had been landed. Historians continue to argue over the pros and cons of 'Dragoon,' but two points must be remembered. The newly trained French Army in North Africa could only be employed in France, and it could only reach France by using American or British shipping and equipment. Given those criteria landing them in the south of France was the quickest and safest way to bring them into action.

Above right: **The Allied commanders for the D-Day landings and the subsequent operations in France. From left General Bradley, Admiral Ramsay, Air Marshal Tedder, General Eisenhower, General Montgomery, Air Marshal Leigh-Mallory and General Bedell Smith. Admiral Ramsay was the naval commander and had previously been in charge of the Dunkirk evacuation.**
Right: **An invasion convoy en route for Normandy, a picture taken from the USS *Ancon*, headquarters ship for the Omaha beach landing.**

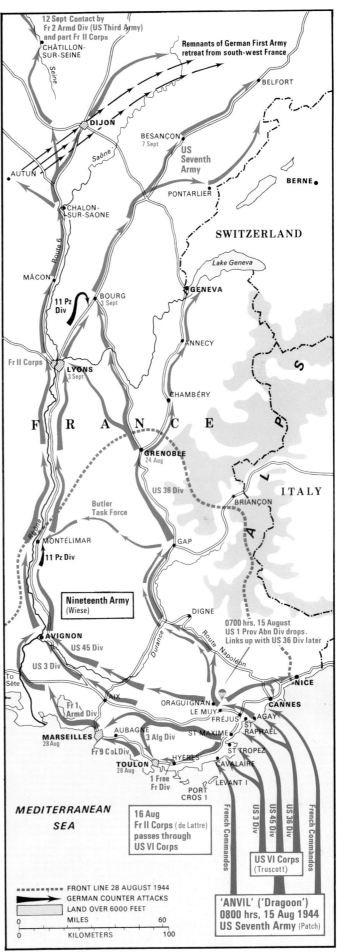

RUSSIA

Kamchatka

ATTU

Sakhalin

Kurile Is

26 Nov 1941
Nagumo's fleet
sails

ETOROFU
Hitokappu B

ULAN BATOR •

MONGOLIA

MANCHURIA
HARBIN •
(MANCHUKUO)

VLADIVOSTOK •

MUKDEN •

Hokkaido

PEKING •

C   H   I   N   A

KOREA
SEOUL •

SEA OF
JAPAN

Honshu

TOKYO •

7 Dec 1941

TSINGTAO •

JAPAN

16 Dec
Part of f
to Wake
support

Hwang Ho

NANKING

NAGASAKI •

Shikoku

Kyushu

DELHI ■

NEPAL

CHUNGKING •

Yangtze kiang

HANKOW •

SHANGHAI

Kagoshima B

BONIN IS

P   A

C

KARACHI •

Ganges

CHANGSHA •
Burma Road

Ryukyu Is

OKINAWA

MARCUS •

O

C

8 Dec
Wake I att
23 Dec
surrendere

INDIA

CALCUTTA •

IMPHAL •

KUNMING •

CANTON •

Formosa
(Taiwan)

IWO JIMA

LASHIO •

BOMBAY •

MANDALAY •

HANOI

HONG KONG

HAIPHONG •

HAINAN

Luzon

BURMA

RANGOON ■

THAI-
LAND

FRENCH
INDO-CHINA

Mariana
Islands

SAIPAN

WAKE

BAY OF BENGAL

BANGKOK ■

SAIGON •

MANILA ■

PHILIPPINE
ISLANDS

GUAM •

MADRAS •

ANDAMAN
IS

LEYTE •

YAP •

ENIWETOK •

KWAJALEIN

TRINCOMALEE •

SOUTH CHINA
SEA

Mindanao

TRUK •

MAJURO •

Ma
Isla

COLOMBO •

NICOBAR
IS

KOTA BHARU •

N BORNEO

DAVAO •

PALAU IS

Caroline   Islands

MA

Ceylon

Maldive
Is

Str of Malacca

MALAYA

SARAWAK

Molucca Passage

TARAWA

Equator

ADDU
ATOLL

SINGAPORE ■

Borneo

HALMAHERA

ADMIRALTY
IS

NAURU •

OCEAN I

Sumatra

Makassar Str

Celebes

NEW
IRELAND

NEW
BRITAIN

RABAUL

NANUM

El

I   N   D   I   A   N

DUTCH   EAST   INDIES

BATAVIA ■

New Guinea

BOUGAINVILLE

Solomon Is

Java

FLORES

PAPUA

NEW
GEORGIA

GUADALCANAL

SANTA CRUZ

TIMOR

ARAFURA SEA

PORT
MORESBY

CORAL SEA

ESPIRITU SA

O   C   E   A   N

COCOS IS

TIMOR SEA

DARWIN •

CAIRNS •

New
Hebrides

EFATE

Northern
Territory

New
Caledonia

NOUMEA

Western

Queensland

ROCKHAMPTON •

Australia

AUSTRALIA

South
Australia

BRISBANE ■

NORFOLK •

PERTH •

New
South Wales

ADELAIDE •

Victoria

SYDNEY ■
CANBERRA

TASMAN
SEA

AUCKLAND •

MELBOURNE ■

WELLINGTO

NEW ZEALAND

Tasmania

CHRISTCHURCH •

JAPANESE EMPIRE, 1933
OCCUPIED BY JAPAN, JULY 1937/DECEMBER 1941
MILITARY BASES ESTABLISHED BY JAPAN, SEPTEMBER 1940

ABDA (American, British, Dutch, and Australian) COMMAND

Mercator projection

Pearl Harbor

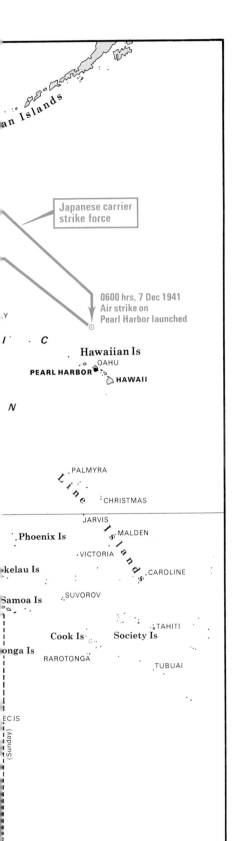

Japanese carrier
strike force

0600 hrs, 7 Dec 1941
Air strike on
Pearl Harbor launched

Hawaiian Is

OAHU

PEARL HARBOR ● ▲ HAWAII

N

PALMYRA

CHRISTMAS

Line Islands

JARVIS

Phoenix Is   MALDEN

VICTORIA

kelau Is   CAROLINE

Samoa Is   SUVOROV

TAHITI

Cook Is   Society Is

onga Is   RAROTONGA

TUBUAI

EC IS

(Sunday)

©Richard Natkiel, 1986

Pearl Harbor is a magnificent natural anchorage on Oahu, biggest of the Hawaiian islands in the central Pacific, and it was a natural choice for the main base of the US Pacific Fleet. With six large air bases, a large garrison, fixed defenses and a large fleet, it was reckoned to be impregnable, but the Japanese showed that it could be taken by surprise.

The surprise attack on Pearl Harbor was only one part of the carefully-coordinated Japanese plan which was to include nearly simultaneous attacks on US positions in the Philippines and the British in Malaya. The Japanese strategy was to cripple the US Pacific Fleet at Pearl Harbor and, with this formidable adversary out of the fight, to seize the oil, rubber, tin and other resource-producing areas in Malaysia and the East Indies. With the benefit of these resources Japan could hope to defend the new acquisitions against any attacks which the supposedly decadent Americans and Europeans could mount. Ironically Admiral Yamamoto, who planned the brilliant surprise attack on Pearl Harbor which was central to the launch of the whole strategy, warned other Japanese leaders that the scheme was fundamentally misguided. He predicted, accurately as it turned out, that Japan could expect a few months of successes but would finally be swamped by the industrial and technological might of the USA.

However, Yamamoto's warnings were not heeded by Japan's leaders and just before 0800 on Sunday 7 December 1941 the first wave of bombers and torpedo-bombers arrived over the naval base and started to attack 'Battleship Row.' At 0810 the battleship *Arizona* was hit by a 1600-pound bomb which detonated her forward magazines. She blew up with heavy loss of life and sank at her moorings. The remaining six battleships lying snugly along the edge of Ford Island, were all hit: the *Oklahoma* capsized and the *California, Maryland, Tennessee* and *West Virginia* were torpedoed. Only the *Nevada* managed to get up steam and try to move out of the trap but she was set on fire by bomb-hits and was eventually ordered to run herself aground rather than sink in the fairway.

The second strike arrived over the island about an hour later, and proceeded to devastate the surrounding airfields and installations to complete the victory. Further damage was caused to the naval base but in

Below: **The US fleet base at Pearl Harbor in October 1941. 'Battleship Row' and the oil storage tanks can be clearly seen.**

spite of sinking two destroyers in the big dry dock the Japanese failed to damage the battleship *Pennsylvania* in the same dock. Although the Japanese losses were small, the second wave suffered casualties from ground AA fire, and the Japanese carrier task force commander, Admiral Nagumo was probably right not to order a third strike.

The Pacific Fleet had been virtually destroyed as a strategic force. The *Arizona* and *Oklahoma* proved to be damaged beyond repair, the *California* and *West Virginia* had sunk at their moorings, and the *Nevada*, *Maryland* and *Tennessee* all needed major repairs. There were, however, compensations. The three carriers *Enterprise*, *Lexington* and *Saratoga* were at sea on exercises well away from the route of the Japanese carriers, and amidst all the damage inflicted the Japanese pilots failed to hit the fuel storage tanks. Had the 4.5 million barrels of oil been destroyed it might have taken years to restore Pearl Harbor to operational efficiency.

The scale of the disaster was almost incomprehensible at the time. United States-Japanese diplomatic relations had been strained almost to breaking point, and in addition US Navy cryptanalysts knew that a major attack on United States forces was planned. Unfortunately many people thought that the Philippines was the target, and nobody in Washington saw fit to warn the local commanders in Hawaii, even when it was learned that the Japanese Ambassador had been ordered to break off diplomatic relations.

There was also a good deal of complacency. Aircraft were neatly parked on the runways (partly to guard against sabotage from an imaginary wave of Japanese saboteurs), AA ammunition was kept locked up, messages about radar warnings and sightings of midget submarines were not passed promptly or taken seriously when received, and above all, it was a peacetime Sunday.

For the Japanese Pearl Harbor proved an illusory victory. Far from cowing the Americans into conceding hegemony of the Far East, the American public abandoned apathy and isolationism in a fierce determination to avenge the defeat. The destruction of the battle fleet also focussed attention on carrier tactics rather than line-of-battle tactics, much to the benefit of the US Navy. In the wider strategic sense the attack on Pearl Harbor broadened what had been a purely European war into a world-wide conflict, for Hitler responded by declaring war on the United States.

Some historians have tried to trace some sinister connection between the destruction of the battleships and the escape of the carriers, suggesting that the withholding of intelligence by Washington was a deliberate (and successful) attempt to provide President Roosevelt with a *casus belli*. The truth is that the pattern of the carriers' movements in and out of Pearl Harbor before the attack was varied and unpredictable. The carriers' training program was related to good flying weather, and they were taken to sea before the attack to give the air groups some extra flying.

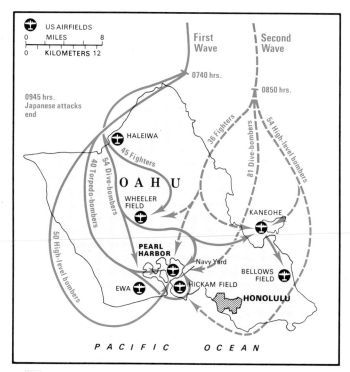

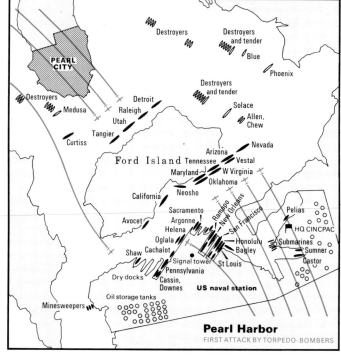

Pearl Harbor
FIRST ATTACK BY TORPEDO-BOMBERS

The Conquest of the Far East

The debacle at Pearl Harbor wrecked any hope of a concerted defense against Japanese attacks. At the eleventh hour the other countries with colonial possessions, Great Britain, Australia and the Netherlands began to work together with the Americans, but it was too little and too late. The British had few forces to spare for the Far East and the Dutch were very weak. In contrast the German attack on the Soviet Union in June 1941 had relieved the Japanese of any need to guard Manchuria against the Russians, and so they could spare troops for the East Indies and elsewhere. By the end of 1941 they were already in Thailand and French Indo-China, and were poised to attack Malaya. The strategic aim of the Japanese was to acquire the tin, rubber and oil of the East Indies, sinews of war which were vital if they were to fight the United States.

The British pinned their hopes on the 'Gibraltar of the Far East,' the fortified base

Right: Zero fighters warm up for take off on a Japanese carrier. After the attack on Pearl Harbor the Japanese carriers moved to support the invasion of the East Indies.

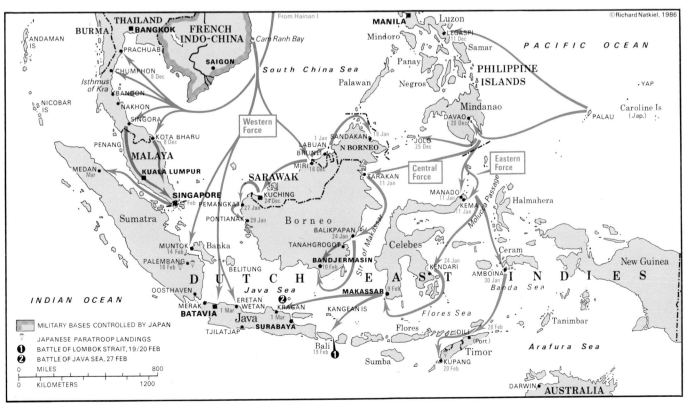

© Richard Natkiel, 1986

MILITARY BASES CONTROLLED BY JAPAN

JAPANESE PARATROOP LANDINGS

❶ BATTLE OF LOMBOK STRAIT, 19/20 FEB
❷ BATTLE OF JAVA SEA, 27 FEB

0   MILES   800
0   KILOMETERS   1200

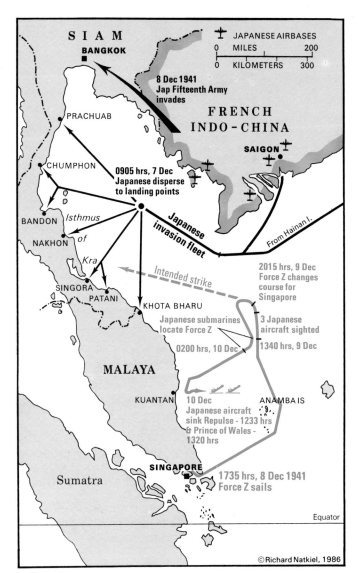

at Singapore. What they had not done was to provide a strong fleet, and there was in addition a dangerous mood of complacency. The Japanese were regarded as inferior troops and the jungle was regarded as an impenetrable barrier to them. The RAF was badly equipped and the morale of most of the defenders was poor, all of which combined to bring about a much bigger debacle than Pearl Harbor. The great base surrendered after only three months, and the defenders greatly outnumbered the attackers.

To reinforce Singapore the British Cabinet decided in October 1941 to dispatch the capital ships *Prince of Wales* and *Repulse* to the Far East. It was hoped that this move would 'overawe' the Japanese, a miscalculation which revealed how poor Allied intelligence had been. On 10 December the two ships were sunk by land-based torpedo-bombers off Kuantan on the east coast of Malaya. Without even the protection of the obsolescent Buffalo fighters of the RAF forces in Malaya the two ships soon fell victim to torpedoes and sank with heavy loss of life.

Before Admiral Phillips went down with the *Prince of Wales* he had discussed a joint plan with Admiral Hart, commanding the US Asiatic Fleet based in the Philippines, and an American-British-Dutch-Australian (ABDA) command was set up late in December. But in the face of simultaneous attacks on Hong Kong, the Philippines, Malaya and the island outposts in the Pacific the Allies could do little. ABDA's first objective was to ensure that reinforcements got through to Singapore, but this soon became irrelevant.

On 24 January 1942 ABDA ships fought Japanese forces off Balikpapan in Borneo but failed to prevent the invasion. Bali and Timor were invaded in February and Japanese carrier aircraft attacked Darwin in Australia. With the Philippines also under attack it was almost impossible for ABDA to organize resistance, and the command was finally destroyed in the desperate Battle of the Java Sea.

Once they had captured Singapore the Japanese wasted no time in overrunning the Dutch East Indies. Using highly integrated air-support they were able to 'leapfrog' from one objective to the next, keeping the defending forces off-balance and bundling them ignominiously out of one position after the other.

Above: **Captain Leach of the *Prince of Wales* pictured shortly before his ship sailed for Singapore.**

Resistance in the Philippines was overrun as easily as the East Indies. No matter how desperately individual units fought, the speed of the Japanese advance overwhelmed the command. The defense of Bataan and of Corregidor were heroically conducted but they inflicted nothing more than a delay on the occupation.

When the Japanese advance ended their new defense perimeter enclosed Wake Island, the Marshall Islands, the Gilbert and Ellice Islands, most of New Guinea and the whole of the East Indies, and most of Burma. The Allies managed to stabilize their own defensive perimeter by May 1942, under a new command formed a month earlier. Under the new arrangements General Douglas MacArthur was Supreme Allied Commander South West Pacific, and Admiral Chester W Nimitz was Commander-in-Chief Pacific. American and Allied fortunes were at their lowest, but the tide of Japanese conquest had reached its highest point.

The Battle of the Java Sea

The hurriedly established ABDA joint command had already fought two minor engagements, off Balikpapan and in the Lombok Strait, when they met the Japanese for the last time in the Battle of the Java Sea. The Dutch Commander-in-Chief, Admiral Karel Doorman took his force of two heavy cruisers HMS *Exeter* and the USS *Houston*, the light cruisers *de Ruyter*, *Perth* and *Java*, and nine destroyers into action against a force of invasion transports heading for Java. The Allied force missed the transports and ran into the covering force of two heavy cruisers, *Haguro* and *Nachi*, the light cruisers *Jintsu* and *Naka* and 14 destroyers, all under the overall command of Admiral Tagaki.

When he sighted the superior Japanese force at 1616 Doorman turned away but at 1708 the *Exeter* was set on fire by an 8-inch shell hit from the *Nachi* and seven minutes later the Dutch destroyer *Kortenaer* was blown up from a torpedo hit. With the *Exeter* still battling to put out her fire the force headed to the southeast. By 1715 the Japanese came into view again, firing at long range with their deadly 'Long Lance' torpedoes as well as 8-inch guns. The *Exeter*'s speed was now down to five knots, and she was sought out by the *Naka* and *Jintsu* and their destroyers. She was saved from their attacks only by the intervention of her destroyers, HMS *Electra* and HMS *Encounter*. The *Electra* was sunk but the *Exeter* was able to limp back to Surabaya.

The rest of the force ran into Takagi's heavy cruisers, and the *Nachi* and *Haguro* hit the flagship *de Ruyter* with torpedoes. She sank with the loss of Admiral Doorman and over 300 men. Minutes later the *Java* was also torpedoed and burst into flames. Doorman's last order to the *Houston* and *Perth* was to escape to Batavia, and not to risk themselves by picking up survivors. His outgunned ships had fought as hard as they could, but the poor communications between the Dutch and their English-speaking allies made tactical coordination very difficult.

The main phase of the Battle of the Java Sea was over, with the destruction of most of the ABDA force. The USS *Houston* and HMAS *Perth* were still at large, having arrived at Batavia, and the damaged *Exeter* and two destroyers were at Surabaya, but powerful Japanese surface forces were already moving in to protect their landings in west Java.

The *Exeter* completed emergency repairs and buried her dead before putting to sea with her destroyers on the night of 28 February. Their mission was only to escape to Ceylon through the Sunda Strait, but even this forlorn hope was doomed when they were spotted next morning by Japanese aircraft. When the three ships were sighted by the Japanese they were about 33,000 yards away to the north east. At 0950 the Japanese heavy cruisers *Nachi* and *Haguro* turned to the northwest, cutting the ABDA ships' line of retreat to Surabaya. The Japanese were reinforced by two more heavy cruisers, the *Ashigara* and *Myoko*, under Admiral Takahashi. The *Exeter* took many torpedo hits and sank at 1130, followed five minutes later by the destroyer *Encounter*. The destroyer USS *Pope* survived a little longer before being sunk as well.

On the same day the *Houston* and *Perth* also came to grief in the Battle of Sunda Strait, when they made a gallant attack on Japanese

Below: **The British cruiser *Exeter* firing at Japanese aircraft while escorting one of the last convoys to reach Singapore before its capture.**

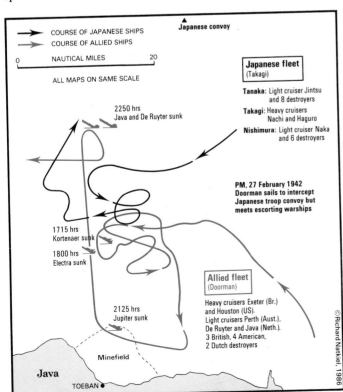

COURSE OF JAPANESE SHIPS
COURSE OF ALLIED SHIPS

0   NAUTICAL MILES   20

ALL MAPS ON SAME SCALE

▲ Japanese convoy

Japanese fleet (Takagi)

Tanaka: Light cruiser Jintsu and 8 destroyers
Takagi: Heavy cruisers Nachi and Haguro
Nishimura: Light cruiser Naka and 6 destroyers

PM, 27 February 1942 Doorman sails to intercept Japanese troop convoy but meets escorting warships

2250 hrs Java and De Ruyter sunk

1715 hrs Kortenaer sunk

1800 hrs Electra sunk

2125 hrs Jupiter sunk

Allied fleet (Doorman)

Heavy cruisers Exeter (Br.) and Houston (US). Light cruisers Perth (Aust.), De Ruyter and Java (Neth.). 3 British, 4 American, 2 Dutch destroyers

Minefield

Java

TOEBAN ●

© Richard Natkiel, 1986

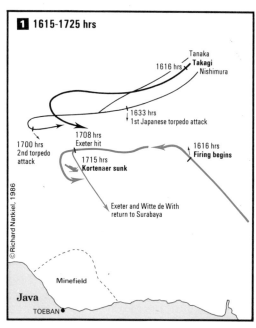

1 1615-1725 hrs

Tanaka
Takagi
1616 hrs
Nishimura
1633 hrs
1st Japanese torpedo attack
1616 hrs
Firing begins
1700 hrs
2nd torpedo attack
1708 hrs
Exeter hit
1715 hrs
Kortenaer sunk
Exeter and Witte de With
return to Surabaya

© Richard Natkiel, 1986

Minefield

Java
TOEBAN

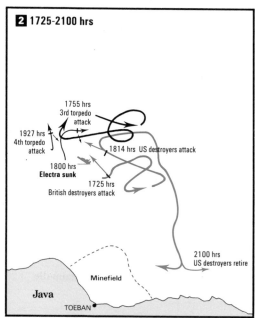

2 1725-2100 hrs

1755 hrs
3rd torpedo
attack
1927 hrs
4th torpedo
attack
1814 hrs US destroyers attack
1800 hrs
Electra sunk
1725 hrs
British destroyers attack

2100 hrs
US destroyers retire

Minefield

Java
TOEBAN

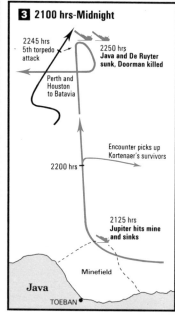

3 2100 hrs-Midnight

2245 hrs
5th torpedo
attack
2250 hrs
**Java and De Ruyter
sunk, Doorman killed**
Perth and
Houston
to Batavia

Encounter picks up
Kortenaer's survivors

2200 hrs

2125 hrs
**Jupiter hits mine
and sinks**

Minefield

Java
TOEBAN

Left: **Last moments of the British cruiser
Exeter at the Battle of the Java Sea.**

transports landing troops in Bantam Bay.
They caused enormous confusion among the
Japanese destroyers, who fired indiscriminately at each other and at the transports. But
the odds of three cruisers and nine destroyers
against two cruisers soon told, and both ships
were torpedoed and sunk. There was nothing
left to oppose the Japanese and the surviving
ABDA ships escaped to Australia and Ceylon
as best they could. There seemed to be nothing to stop a Japanese advance on Australia.

With hindsight it can be seen the ABDA
command had been sacrificed for very little
tactical or strategic gain. The Japanese
advance had been slowed down by 24 hours
at the most, and at trifling loss. Undoubtedly
the ships would have been far more useful if
they had been withdrawn to Ceylon or
Australia, for it took months to rebuild Allied
strength in the Far East. On the other hand
the Allies felt impelled to put up what resistance they could, and if the resources of
the East Indies had been abandoned without
firing a shot there would have been endless
recriminations among the allies. It is only fair
to remember that everyone in the ABDA
command had underestimated the capabilities of the Japanese.

The Battle of the Coral Sea

The strategic plan of the Japanese Commander-in-Chief Admiral Yamamoto had worked well, but its ultimate objective still eluded him. The US Pacific Fleet and the British and Dutch forces in the East Indies had been destroyed, but the US carrier force was still at large. Yamamoto hoped to bring the carriers to battle in the central Pacific, but when the Army asked for support in a drive on Port Moresby, New Guinea, he acquiesced.

'Drunk with conquest' is a phrase often used by historians to describe the Japanese leaders in the early months of 1942, and it

seems a fair conclusion when it is remembered that by April the Japanese had captured all that they aimed for in their war plans, at far less cost than they had expected. Now they decided to neutralize Australia, to prevent it from being used as a base for a counter-offensive against Rabaul. The force chosen to cover the invasion (codenamed Mo) was the Carrier Strike Force, the carriers *Shokaku* and *Zuikaku* under Rear Admiral Takeo Takagi, while the smaller carrier *Shoho* sailed with the invasion transports.

The US Navy was reading the Japanese

ciphers, and with the aid of visual sightings from 'coastwatchers' was able to track the approach of the Japanese. On the morning of 4 May they struck first, with an attack by the carrier *Yorktown*'s air group against the invasion transports in Tulagi harbor. Two days later an Army bomber sighted the *Shoho* and mistook her for one of the Strike Force carriers. At 1135 next day the air groups of the carriers *Lexington* and *Yorktown* sank her with bombs and torpedoes.

The strike had revealed the presence of the American carriers and Admiral Takagi, well

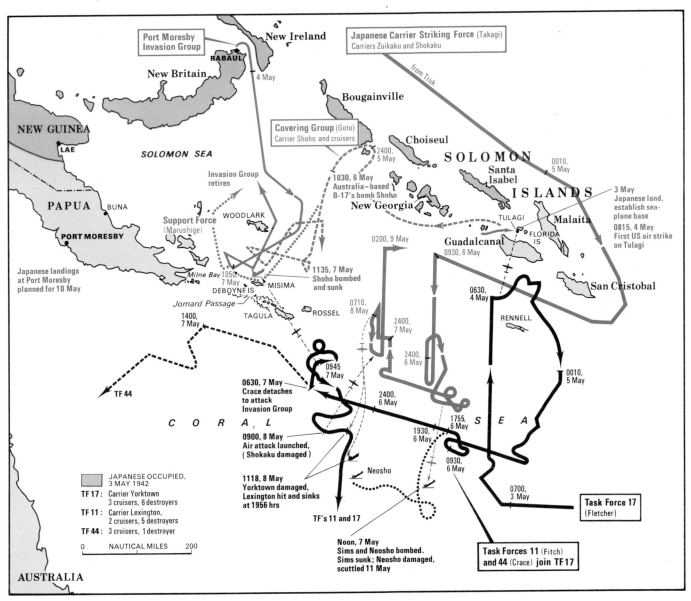

to the west of Task Force 17 under US Admiral Frank Fletcher, immediately ordered his own air groups to fly off a strike. Unfortunately for him faulty reconnaissance had identified the oiler USS *Neosho* as a carrier and her escorting destroyer *Sims* as a cruiser. Both ships put up a spirited defense, and the 51 Japanese bombers and torpedo-bombers took over two hours to put them out of action. The five hours lost in this inept attack cost Takagi the chance to locate TF 17, which was at the time sinking the *Shoho*. A second strike failed to retrieve the situation for the *Yorktown*'s position was wrongly calculated. On their way back the frustrated Japanese were attacked by the *Yorktown*'s combat air patrol, confusing them to such an extent that four Japanese aircraft tried to land on the *Yorktown*. In all they wasted 17 percent of their strength without locating the American carriers.

Both carrier groups were ignorant of the other's exact position until about 0800 on the morning of 8 May, and immediately air strikes were launched, 84 aircraft by the *Lexington* and *Yorktown* and 69 aircraft from the *Shokaku* and *Zuikaku*. The world's first carrier-versus-carrier battle had started.

The American strikes achieved some success, three bomb hits on the *Shokaku*, at a cost of five aircraft. The Japanese attack began at 1118, and in spite of being detected at 70 miles on radar, succeeded in outwitting the defending combat air patrol. The *Yorktown* succeeded in dodging the torpedoes but a 250-kg bomb hit inboard of the 'island' superstructure and burst three decks down. The *Lexington* was not so lucky and was hit by two torpedoes, and then by two 60-kg bombs. At first she seemed to withstand the damage well. Three fires were tackled by the fire-parties, but gasoline vapor from her refueling system had begun to permeate compartments deep in the hull. About an hour after the attack a chance spark set off a major internal explosion.

Even this did not prevent the giant carrier from recovering 39 aircraft and launching a combat air patrol but at 1445 another big explosion shook her. She was abandoned after 1700 and three hours later a destroyer sank her with torpedoes.

The *Yorktown* was luckier as her fires were brought under control, and she was able to continue operating aircraft. The Japanese were certain that she would sink, a mistake that was to prove crucial at Midway. The *Shokaku* by comparison was badly damaged

and was not ready for action for three months. Her sister *Zuikaku* also suffered damage, and so the two best Japanese carriers were out of action on the eve of Midway.

Coral Sea was an indecisive battle. The Americans had won an important strategic victory by frustrating the invasion of Port Moresby, despite the sinking of the *Lexington*, in exchange for the weaker *Shoho*. But the high-water mark of Japanese expansion had been reached, even if their opponents did not recognize the fact.

Above: Attack aircraft being marshalled ready for take off on the flight deck of a US carrier during the Battle of the Coral Sea.
Top: An American torpedo strikes home on the Japanese carrier *Shoho* on 7 May during the Coral Sea battle.

The Battle of Midway

Following what he regarded as a sideshow in the Coral Sea, Admiral Yamamoto, the Japanese C-in-C, was more determined than ever to bring the US carriers to battle, and pressed ahead with his plans to force a decision by attacking Midway Island. This little atoll comprising two islands of just over 1100 acres was an important listening post. In American hands reconnaissance aircraft could watch the Central Pacific, but in Japanese hands it would be a wedge driven into the Pacific Fleet's defenses. Yamamoto knew that any attack on Midway must draw the US Pacific Fleet out to defend it.

Yamamoto's plan was basically sound but complex. Four of his fast carriers would attack Midway's airfields, backed up by a strong surface force. A second force, comprising two light carriers, was to occupy the Aleutian Islands as a diversion and a third covering force of three battleships and a light carrier was to be stationed 1150 miles northwest of the main carrier force. The plan was to occupy Midway as fast as possible to set up reconnaissance facilities. It was expected that the Americans would take a

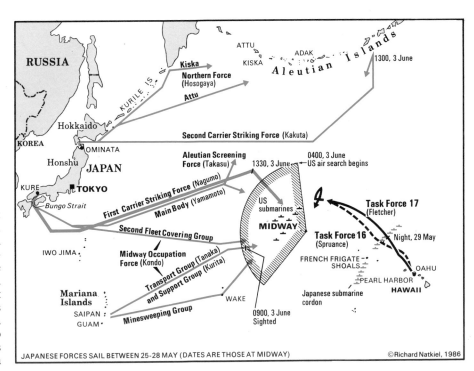

JAPANESE FORCES SAIL BETWEEN 25-28 MAY (DATES ARE THOSE AT MIDWAY) ©Richard Natkiel, 1986

Left: A destroyer comes to the aid of the badly-damaged *Yorktown* shortly before the carrier sank at Midway.

day to react to the initial attacks, leaving another two days for occupation of Midway and preparation for the decisive battle which would follow.

The two snags to this plan were, first, a total reliance on surprise, and second, an assumption that the numbers and location of the US carriers were known. The first requirement could not be met because cryptanalysis had given Admiral Nimitz forewarning of the operation, and the second suffered a series of setbacks, some of them bad luck but others caused by Japanese complacency. A submarine sent to refuel a Japanese reconnaissance seaplane off French Frigate Shoals was counter-attacked by two destroyers, and the reconnaissance of Pearl Harbor had to be cancelled.

The patrol line of 13 submarines was only put into position *after* the carriers of TF 16 and TF 17 passed from Pearl Harbor to Midway. Last, and most serious, the Japanese had convinced themselves that the *Yorktown* had been sunk or at least badly damaged in the Coral Sea battle. She had been seriously damaged, but the navy yard at Pearl Harbor had put 1400 men on to the job

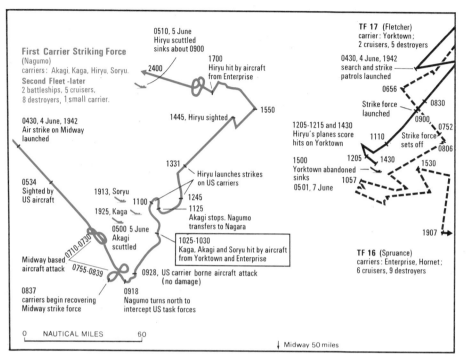

First Carrier Striking Force
(Nagumo)
carriers: Akagi, Kaga, Hiryu, Soryu.
Second Fleet -later
2 battleships, 5 cruisers,
8 destroyers, 1 small carrier.

0430, 4 June, 1942
Air strike on Midway
launched

0534
Sighted by
US aircraft

0710-0730

Midway based
aircraft attack   0755-0839

0837
carriers begin recovering
Midway strike force

1913, Soryu
1100
1925, Kaga

0500 5 June
Akagi
scuttled

0918
Nagumo turns north to
intercept US task forces

0928, US carrier borne aircraft attack
(no damage)

1245
1125
Akagi stops. Nagumo
transfers to Nagara

1025-1030
Kaga, Akagi and Soryu hit by aircraft
from Yorktown and Enterprise

1331
Hiryu launches strikes
on US carriers

0510, 5 June
Hiryu scuttled
sinks about 0900

2400

1700
Hiryu hit by aircraft
from Enterprise

1445, Hiryu sighted

1550

0 NAUTICAL MILES 60

↓ Midway 50 miles

TF 17 (Fletcher)
carrier: Yorktown;
2 cruisers, 5 destroyers

0430, 4 June, 1942
search and strike
patrols launched

0656

Strike force
launched

0830
0900
0752

1205-1215 and 1430
Hiryu's planes score
hits on Yorktown

1110   Strike force   0806
         sets off
1205   1430
1500   1530
Yorktown abandoned
sinks   1057
0501, 7 June

1907

TF 16 (Spruance)
carriers: Enterprise, Hornet;
6 cruisers, 9 destroyers

wave lost 10 out of 13. Another 35 bombers and 11 fighters lost their way and ran out of fuel; only 11 bombers returned.

All might have been lost but for a further group of Devastator divebombers from the USS *Enterprise*, which had missed the Japanese carriers and were heading back to their ship. The sight of a lone destroyer led the air group commander, Lt Commander McClusky to guess that she would lead him to the carriers. At about 1025 the four carriers were seen, in a diamond formation with the *Hiryu* leading. In a brilliantly executed attack the *Kaga* was hit with four 1000-pound bombs, the *Akagi* with one 1000-pounder and a 500-pounder, and the *Soryu* with three 1000-pounders. These hits inflicted terrible carnage as they started uncontrollable fires which gutted the ships. Even at this desperate stage Nagumo kept his head, and as soon as he had transferred his flag to the undamaged *Hiryu* he ordered a strike against the American carriers.

The strike succeeded in setting the *Yorktown* on fire, and about an hour later a second strike hit her with two torpedoes. The gap in Japanese intelligence now became crucial, for the returning pilots reported in each case that they had sunk a carrier, and as there were supposed to be only two available, the conclusion was that TF 16 and TF 17 had no carriers left. The *Hiryu* was thus caught unawares when at 1700 a last strike from the *Enterprise* hit her with four bombs. As before fires and explosions wrecked the ship, although she remained afloat until 0900 next morning.

Admiral Yamamoto was stunned by the news of the loss of all four carriers and tried to concentrate his scattered forces for a second attempt to bring the Americans to battle on his own terms, but it could not be done in the time available and he finally conceded defeat early on 5 June. Although seen at first as a check to the apparently invincible Japanese, Midway was later seen to be a turning point in the war. The pilots lost could be replaced, and so could the carriers and the aircraft, if given time, but the Japanese Army continued to make heavy demands on the Navy, as if Midway had not happened. What was left of the magnificent air groups which had started the war was frittered away in useless attrition in the southwest Pacific. When most of the experienced pilots had been killed it proved impossible to train a new generation, and the Japanese carriers never again posed the threat that they had in June 1942.

of repairing her, and she was ready in only three days.

Before the battle began TF 16 and TF 17 were in position 400 miles northeast of Midway, close enough to cover the island. On 3 June a Catalina flying boat sighted Admiral Kondo's invasion force some 800 miles west of Midway, and it came under a series of largely ineffectual attacks by bombers from Midway. By nightfall the opposing carrier forces were approaching the island, neither of them aware of the other's position, and by dawn on 4 June they were only 428 miles apart, with the Americans to the east of the Japanese. The Americans had at least the certainty that they were looking for the Japanese carriers, whereas the Japanese were by no means sure that any US carriers were in the area.

Admiral Nagumo launched his first strike of 108 aircraft against Midway Island itself at 0430, but held back the carrier *Kaga*'s 90-strong air group in case any US ships were sighted. When Admiral Fletcher learned of the whereabouts of the Japanese carriers he ordered Admiral Spruance in command of TF 16 to launch an attack, and Spruance decided to attack immediately in the hope of catching the Japanese carriers in the middle of recovering and refueling the aircraft returning from Midway.

At this point Nagumo made a fatal decision. Under the impression that Midway's defenses needed further softening up he ordered the aircraft held back to be rearmed for ground attack. This involved sending the torpedo-bombers down to the hangars to allow torpedoes to be replaced by bombs. At 0728, just 14 minutes later, he learned from a floatplane that TF 16 had been sighted. As the report did not mention the two carriers or the fact that they were flying off a strike, Nagumo remained undecided and ordered the remaining B5N torpedo-bombers to stop their rearming.

Three attacks from Midway pushed the Japanese further off balance. The first two attacks achieved nothing, but the third coincided with the return of the first Japanese planes from Midway, and the hostile presence delayed the recovery until 0837. In fact the last aircraft was not recovered until 0917, nearly an hour after the sighting of the enemy task force. Notwithstanding Nagumo turned to get his carriers into position for an attack. Not even the arrival of a first wave of attackers at 0928 deterred the Japanese from finishing the operation for the uncoordinated attacks were easily dealt with by the defending combat air patrol. The first wave of 15 aircraft were shot down, then the second wave lost 10 out of 14 aircraft, and the third

The Battles for Guadalcanal

Although the Japanese plans to take control of the Solomon Island chain and New Guinea had received a setback at the Battle of the Coral Sea, they continued to plan to extend their presence on the islands of Tulagi and Guadalcanal in the Solomons. The US Joint Chiefs of Staff were aware through crypt-analysis that the Japanese were building an airfield on Guadalcanal and quickly formulated 'Operation Watchtower' to forestall this move and as the first stage of a counter-offensive aimed eventually to reach the Philippines.

'Watchtower' began with an assault by US Marines on Guadalcanal and Tulagi on 7 August 1942. While the Marines battled to establish themselves ashore and to protect the single airstrip taken from the Japanese the US Navy and its allies battled to stop the Japanese from reinforcing the defenders. The Japanese reaction was rapid; on the night of 8-9 August Vice-Admiral Mikawa surprised a force of cruisers lying off Savo Island. The Japanese skill at night-fighting enabled them to administer a sharp defeat to their opponents, and the heavy cruisers *Astoria*, *Quincy* and *Vincennes* and HMAS *Canberra* were sunk with comparative ease. However Mikawa failed to achieve his main objective, the destruction of the large fleet of amphibious transports, as he withdrew prematurely. The only comfort the Allies could draw from this action was the torpedoing of the heavy cruiser *Kako* on her way back to Rabaul. (Map below left.)

Although American air power enabled the Allies to dominate the waters around Guadalcanal by day, the Japanese ruled at night, when ships from Rabaul ran fresh troops, ammunition and food into Guadalcanal and bombarded the airfield, renamed Henderson Field. Known as the 'Tokyo Express' these fast convoys were conducted with great audacity by Rear Admiral Raizo Tanaka.

On 23 August the American Task Force 61, including the carriers *Enterprise*, *Saratoga* and *Wasp* under the command of Vice Admiral Frank Fletcher, intercepted an attempt to run supplies to Guadalcanal in daylight. The Japanese transports were supported by a Striking Force under Admiral Nagumo, with the carriers *Shokaku* and *Zuikaku* and a diversionary group based on the small carrier *Ryujo* (below right).

The first American strike on 23 August was avoided by a reversal of course but next day search aircraft found the *Ryujo* and a strike was launched. An attempt to divert the strike to the bigger carriers which were located after the aircraft took off was frus-trated by communications problems, and only a few aircraft from the *Enterprise* were able to attack the *Shokaku*, but the *Ryujo* was sunk at 1550. Nearly an hour later the main Japanese carrier air group retaliated by inflicting severe damage on the *Enterprise*, and both carrier task forces retired to lick their wounds, leaving Rear Admiral Tanaka's Transport Group to continue on its way.

Tanaka's force was badly mauled next day by shore-based aircraft, and as a result the Tokyo Express was forced to resume night operations. Daylight operations were impossible in the face of American air superiority.

On the night of 11-12 October 1942 the Americans tried their own version of the Tokyo Express, with a supply convoy to Guadalcanal, and a night action ensued off Cape Esperance. The US covering force, Task Force 64 under Rear Admiral Norman Scott, ran into a similar force under Rear Admiral Goto, but a sighting by the light cruiser *Helena* was not passed to Scott, who assumed he had missed the enemy. While the Americans were reversing course, the Japanese were detected by the destroyer *Duncan*, which opened fire independently, but the US cruisers did not join in the firing until 2346. In the confused fighting which followed the

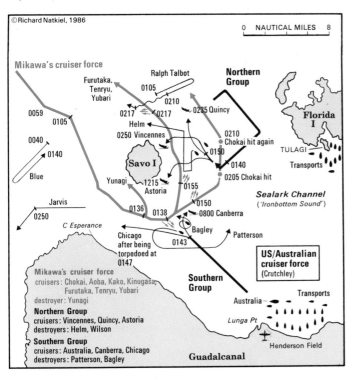

© Richard Natkiel, 1986

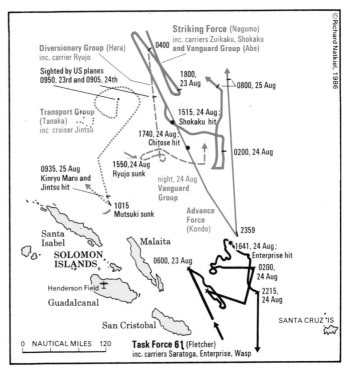

© Richard Natkiel, 1986

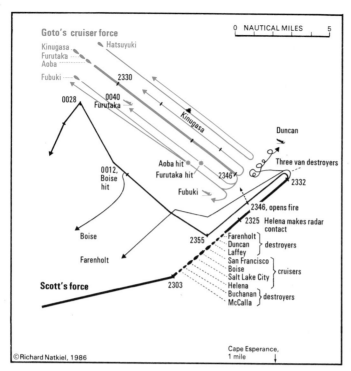

Goto's cruiser force

0 NAUTICAL MILES 5

Kinugasa
Furutaka
Aoba
Hatsuyuki
Fubuki
2330
0028
0040 Furutaka
Kinugasa
Duncan
0012, Boise hit
Aoba hit
Furutaka hit
Three van destroyers
2346
2332
Fubuki
2346, opens fire
2325 Helena makes radar contact
Boise
2355
Farenholt
Duncan } destroyers
Laffey
San Francisco
Boise
Salt Lake City } cruisers
Helena
Buchanan } destroyers
McCalla
Farenholt
Scott's force
2303
©Richard Natkiel, 1986
Cape Esperance, 1 mile

Above right: The carrier *Wasp* sinking after being torpedoed by the Japanese submarine *I-19* on 14 September 1942 during operations in the Solomons.
Right: The transport ship *President Jackson* under attack off Guadalcanal on 12 November 1942.

heavy cruiser *Furutaka* and the destroyer *Fubuki* were sunk, in return for only one destroyer, the USS *Duncan*. Unfortunately for the Americans they had no idea how lucky they had been, and they believed that they had mastered the Japanese in the art of nightfighting. (Map above.)

The Japanese command planned a new land offensive on Guadalcanal and this began on 21 October. Substantial naval forces were sent to support the attack with the four carriers being ordered to send their aircraft to Henderson Field once it had been captured from the defending US Marines. In the event the Marines' defense proved too strong for the Japanese land forces and at sea a major naval battle, the Battle of Santa Cruz, developed. Although the Japanese had four carriers with 212 planes to the Americans' two carriers and 171 planes the result was by no means a clear victory. Although the *Hornet* was sunk and the *Enterprise* badly damaged in return for two Japanese carriers hit, Japanese losses in aircrew left their surviving ships crippled and they, like the Americans, had to withdraw. (Map right.)

Fighting was renewed in November in the so-called Battle of Guadalcanal. On the first night, 12/13 November, a force of five cruisers under Rear Admiral Daniel J Callaghan encountered a Japanese force, including the battleships *Hiei* and *Kirishima* and a heavy and a light cruiser under Admiral Abe. Once again it was the light cruiser *Helena* which detected the enemy on her radar, but

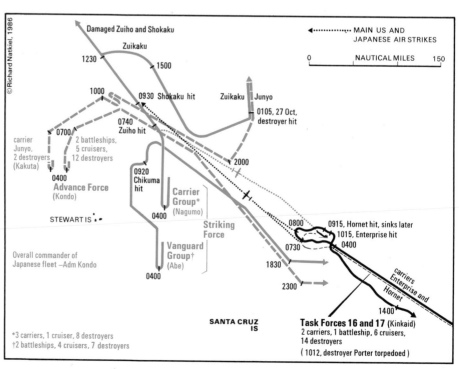

©Richard Natkiel, 1986

Damaged Zuiho and Shokaku
Zuikaku
1230
1500
1000
0930 Shokaku hit
Zuikaku Junyo
0105, 27 Oct, destroyer hit
0700
0740 Zuiho hit
2000
carrier Junyo, 2 destroyers (Kakuta)
2 battleships, 5 cruisers, 12 destroyers
0400
Advance Force (Kondo)
0920 Chikuma hit
0800
0915, Hornet hit, sinks later
1015, Enterprise hit
STEWART IS
0400
Carrier Group* (Nagumo)
Striking Force
0730
0400
Vanguard Group† (Abe)
1830
carriers Enterprise and Hornet
0400
2300
Overall commander of Japanese fleet –Adm Kondo
1400
MAIN US AND JAPANESE AIR STRIKES
0 NAUTICAL MILES 150
SANTA CRUZ IS
Task Forces 16 and 17 (Kinkaid)
2 carriers, 1 battleship, 6 cruisers, 14 destroyers
(1012, destroyer Porter torpedoed)
*3 carriers, 1 cruiser, 8 destroyers
†2 battleships, 4 cruisers, 7 destroyers

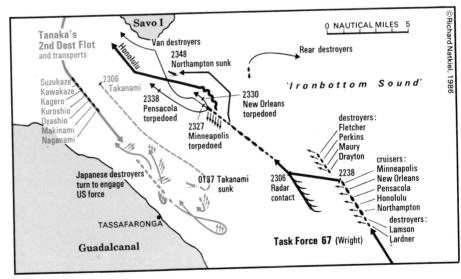

Map 1 (top):

Abe's force (inc 14 destroyers)

PM, 13 Nov
Hiei torpedoed by US aircraft, scuttled later

0 NAUTICAL MILES 6

Savo I

Kirishima and Nagara retire

Aaron Ward damaged

0124

Barton sunk

battleships Kirishima and Hiei

Cushing sunk

Laffey sunk

Ironbottom Sound

Monssen sunk

cruiser Nagara

0140

Callaghan's force

Akatsuki sunk

Yudachi on fire and abandoned

destroyers:
Cushing, Laffey, Sterett and O'Bannon

Juneau sunk; Portland damaged; Atlanta damaged, sunk later

0141 Cushing makes visual contact

cruisers:
Atlanta, San Francisco, Portland, Helena and Juneau

Guadalcanal

0124 Helena's radar locates Abe's force

destroyers:
Aaron Ward, Barton, Monssen, Fletcher

© Richard Natkiel, 1986

Map 2 (center):

0 NAUTICAL MILES 10

Kondo's force

Hashimoto's force

2210 Lee's force sighted

0035

battleship Kirishima cruisers Atago, Takao & 2 destroyers

cruiser Nagara & 4 destroyers

cruiser Sendai & destroyer shadow TF 64

0035

2330

destroyers Ayanami & Uranami

2355 Kirishima

2330

Task Force 64 (Lee)

0020

Savo I

2330

battleships
South Dakota
Washington

2359 Washington fires on Kirishima

Ayanami

2317

Washington

South Dakota damaged

2330

Gwin
Preston
Benham
Walke } destroyers

South Dakota

Walke

Preston

2322 Destroyers open fire

2316 Battleships open fire

2300 Washington's radar locates Sendai

Gwin and Benham retire damaged

Guadalcanal

© Richard Natkiel, 1986

Map 3 (bottom):

Savo I

0 NAUTICAL MILES 5

Tanaka's 2nd Dest Flot and transports

Van destroyers

Honolulu

2348 Northampton sunk

Rear destroyers

Suzukaze
Kawakaze
Kagero
Kuroshio
Oyashio
Makinami
Naganami

2306 Takanami

2338 Pensacola torpedoed

2330 New Orleans torpedoed

2327 Minneapolis torpedoed

Ironbottom Sound

destroyers:
Fletcher
Perkins
Maury
Drayton

0137 Takanami sunk

2306 Radar contact

2238

cruisers:
Minneapolis
New Orleans
Pensacola
Honolulu
Northampton

Japanese destroyers turn to engage US force

TASSAFARONGA

Guadalcanal

destroyers:
Lamson
Lardner

Task Force 67 (Wright)

© Richard Natkiel, 1986

---

poor radio discipline prevented Callaghan from interpreting the reports correctly. What he could not know was that his ships had blundered into the middle of the Japanese force, and the first intimation was a blast of 14-inch gunfire and torpedoes. Callaghan and his staff were killed aboard the heavy cruiser *San Francisco*, as Admiral Scott had been aboard the anti-aircraft cruiser *Atlanta* shortly before. Nor was the Japanese admiral in control of this savage close-range battle, in which ships fired at whatever target appeared. (Map top right.)

When the firing died away at 0200 the Japanese battleship *Hiei* was crippled and on fire, and the destroyers *Akatsuki* and *Yudachi* were sinking, while the Americans had lost the destroyers *Barton*, *Cushing*, *Laffey* and *Monssen* and the anti-aircraft cruiser *Juneau*. Next day the Japanese battleship *Hiei* was sunk off Savo Island by attacks from carrier- and land-based aircraft.

On the following evening two battleships, the USS *South Dakota* and USS *Washington*, engaged a force under Admiral Kondo, comprising the *Kirishima* and four cruisers. Once again radar gave the Americans the benefit of surprise, but this time a technical failure caused a near-disaster aboard the *South Dakota*. Blast from a 5-inch gun firing starshell to illuminate the Japanese ships put the ship's principal electrical system out of action, robbing the ship of all power except her main engines. With no radars and key personnel thrown into confusion she blundered to within 5000 yards of the Japanese line, drawing heavy fire from the *Kirishima*. Fortunately the *Washington* kept her searchlights switched off and kept clear of her consort. When she opened fire at 2353 her 16-inch broadsides crippled the *Kirishima* and left her in a sinking condition. The battle was marginally a victory for the Americans, in spite of the sinking of two destroyers, but it revealed more grave defects in the night-fighting organization (center right).

The Battle of Tassafaronga on the night of 30 November-1 December was another bungled attempt to derail the Tokyo Express, in which Tanaka's destroyers torpedoed the heavy cruisers *Minneapolis*, *New Orleans*, *Northampton* and *Pensacola*. Rear Admiral Carleton H Wright missed an opportunity to take the Japanese by surprise, and his force was then overwhelmed by the accuracy of their Long Lance oxygen-driven torpedoes. Good damage control procedures saved three of the cruisers but the *Northamp-ton* had to be abandoned. (Map above.)

What all these battles showed to greater or lesser degree was that radar by itself could not offset Japanese training and their highly effective torpedoes. Only toward the end of 1943 did the answer emerge, radar-controlled barrage fire from cruisers' 6-inch and 8-inch guns. Long before that the Japanese High Command was driven to admit that the unceasing heroism of its forces could not hope to save Guadalcanal. On 1 February 1943 the Tokyo Express went into reverse, lifting 12,000 troops from the island in one week at the cost of only one destroyer sunk. The US counter-offensive could now get fully under way.

The American Counter-offensive

The defeat of the Japanese at Midway was a turning point, at which the counter-stroke became feasible. Up to that point Admiral Yamamoto's planning had worked perfectly; the Americans, British and Dutch had been expelled from their possessions and the 'island chain' of forward bases had established a defensive perimeter around the new Japanese conquests.

After Midway, however, the question for the Americans was not when to attack, but where? The Army under General MacArthur wanted to concentrate on aiming for the Philippines while the Navy under Nimitz wanted to strike directly at Japan across the Central Pacific. However, proponents of both strategies agreed that the first priority must be the Solomons, to secure New Guinea and Australia. It was the right decision for the Japanese were drawing up their own plans to seize the Solomons.

The first stage in the battle for the Solomons, the struggle for Guadalcanal, raged from August 1942 to January 1943, with the US Marines locked in a deadly struggle and the supporting forces at sea fighting to stop the Japanese from reinforcing their garrisons. In a series of night battles the Americans and their allies fought to dominate the 'Slot' between the northeastern and south-western islands, triumphing eventually only because of radar. Only after heavy losses did the Japanese admit defeat and evacuate their troops. This hard-won Allied victory cleared the way for the counter-offensive.

Although MacArthur's plan for a drive on the Philippines was not dropped it was not given priority over the Central Pacific campaign, which had the virtue of being econo-

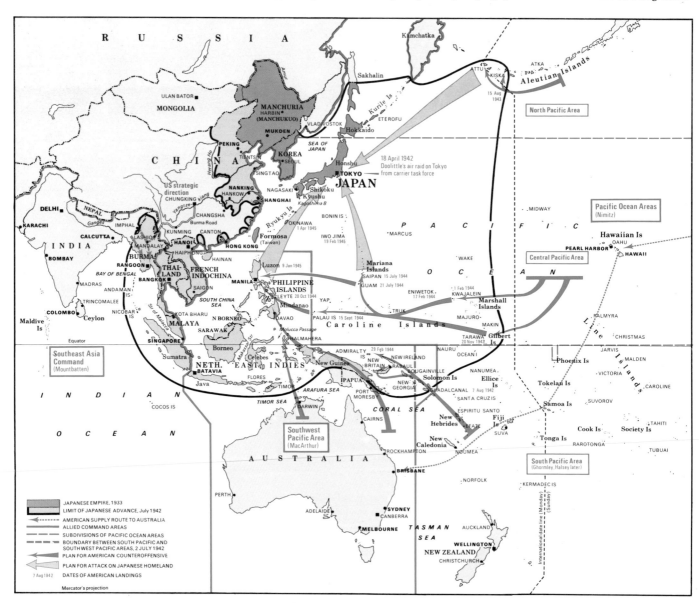

mical in manpower and ships. In brief the US Navy proposed to bypass the most strongly defended outposts and so outflank the Japanese defensive chain.

By mid-1943, with well-trained forces now available the Americans hoped to break through the 'Bismarck Barrier' of bases in the Bismarck Archipelago. Admiral Koga's Combined Fleet had been withdrawn from Truk in June 1943 to regroup but when it returned a month later there was still a crucial shortage of trained carrier pilots, whose numbers had been frittered away in the fighting in the Solomons. The Japanese were thus ill-prepared for the Allied offensive against the northwestern coast of New Guinea and the attacks on New Georgia and New Britain.

The first example of what came to be known as 'island hopping' was in the Solomons in August 1943, when Admiral William Halsey decided to attack Vella Lavella instead of Kolombangara. The former was closer to Rabaul, and once it was in American hands it made an attack on the heavily-defended Kolombangara unnecessary. In the next offensive, against Bougain-

ville, Halsey chose to hit the weakly defended garrison at Empress Augusta Bay.

The strike against the Marshall Islands was foreshadowed by an attack on the Gilberts, and although costly the assaults on Tarawa and Makin made the conquest of the Marshalls much easier. The scale of this achievement is hard to comprehend, even when looking at the map. The US Pacific Fleet's main base at Pearl Harbor was over 2000 miles from the West Coast of the United States, and the Gilberts and Marshalls were another 2000 miles from Pearl Harbor. The Solomons were 3000 miles from bases in Australia, and 9000 miles from the United States. To keep large numbers of troops fed, clothed and armed required a vast logistic effort, an effort which only the vast resources of the United States could sustain.

In the absence of properly equipped naval bases ships had to be maintained and repaired by a brilliantly extemporized series of forward bases. Floating docks were towed to quiet Pacific lagoons such as Ulithi (a very important base from September 1944), where the US Navy's Seabees (Construction Batallions) had built temporary base facilities

Above: Left to right, the heavy cruisers *Salt Lake City, Pensacola* and *New Orleans* at Pearl Harbor in October 1943.

ashore. All but the most serious battle damage could be repaired at these forward bases, and very few damaged ships proved unable to make the long voyage back to the West Coast.

After Pearl Harbor the only element of the Pacific Fleet which could immediately take the offensive had been the submarine force. Despite problems with torpedoes in the early months the US submarines began what was ultimately a highly successful campaign against the Japanese maritime empire. They attacked supply-lines, laid mines and conducted clandestine missions on a growing scale. Even more important was their role in reconnaissance; by reporting Japanese ship-movements time and time again submarines gave warning of major operations.

The tonnages sunk by US submarines never approached those of the German U-Boats in the Atlantic but their version of 'wolf pack' tactics proved deadly. By the end of hostilities the Japanese mercantile marine had been virtually wiped out, and trade was reduced to junks operating well inshore. Aerial minelaying on a colossal scale completed the work of the submarines by making many harbors unusable.

The Japanese decided late in 1943 to retrench by drawing in their defensive perimeter, running from the Mariana Islands down through Truk and Rabaul to Northern New Guinea and Timor. From behind this new line they hoped to deliver counterattacks on the American carrier task forces, but however admirable in theory, the new plan was too late to check the Allied advance.

The assault on the Marshalls at the end of January 1944 showed the new 'island-hopping' strategy to perfection. Kwajalein and Majuro were taken with light losses, and bomber bases were set up immediately, but the larger islands were left in Japanese hands until the end of the war, by which time their garrisons were starving and wasted by disease. Not all garrisons could be bypassed so easily but whenever possible they were left to 'wither on the vine.'

The next decision was to bypass Truk and attack the Mariana island chain in the Central Pacific. In a three-day air battle the carrier pilots of Mitscher's Fast Carrier Task Force destroyed the defenders of Saipan, Tinian, Rota and Guam, and defeated the Japanese Fleet in the Battle of the Philippine Sea. Four

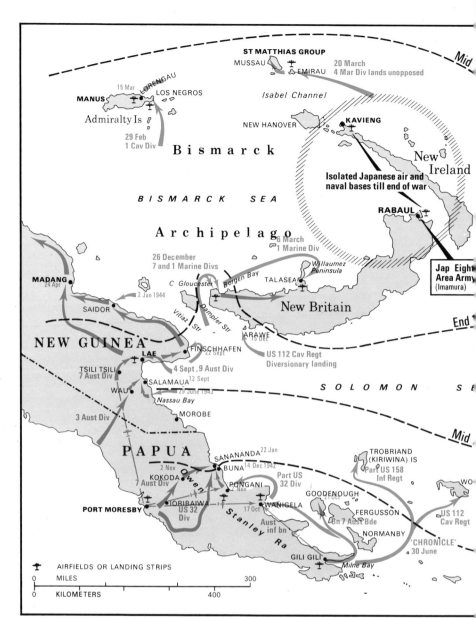

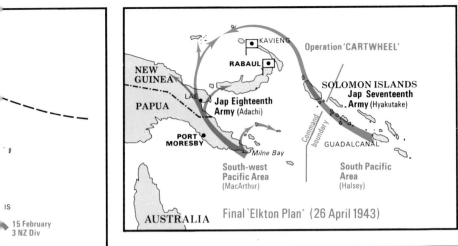

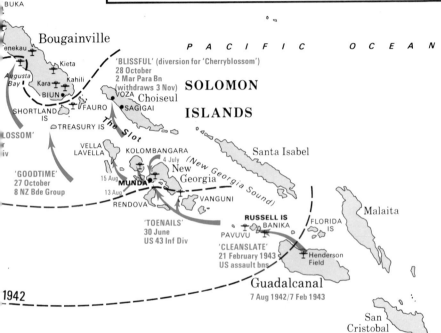

months later, in October 1944 MacArthur began the liberation of the Philippines. This provoked the Japanese into launching their final attempt to stave off defeat. The great Battle of Leyte Gulf saw the last unified operation by the Imperial Japanese Navy as it attempted to destroy the Leyte landing forces, but in a series of large-scale actions the Japanese fleets were destroyed without achieving their objective.

As the final phase approached island hopping became less feasible. Okinawa was only 800 miles from the Japanese mainland, and although the smaller island Iwo Jima was atacked first its capture could not avoid the need to land on Okinawa. The ferocity of the fighting on both islands led the Americans to the conclusion that an invasion of the Japanese home islands would be enormously costly, and confirmed the decision to use the atom bomb first. The Philippines and Okinawa landings were also noted for the appearance of *kamikaze* tactics, crashing aircraft into Allied ships as a deliberate form of attack.

The fall of Okinawa on 21 June 1945 brought the island campaign to an end. By that time B-29 bombers could fly round-the-clock missions against Japanese cities and the fast carrier task forces and the submarine fleet could maintain a close blockade. Without fuel to send their ships to sea or launch aircraft the Japanese were now helpless, and with or without the attacks on Hiroshima and Nagasaki the end was inevitable.

Left: General Douglas MacArthur makes his triumphant return to the Philippines in 1944.
Far left: The USS *Tinosa* returning to Pearl Harbor from a war patrol in 1944. The part played by the American submarine force in the Japanese defeat is sometimes forgotten but was central to the Allied victory.

The Battle of the Philippine Sea

After the fierce fighting in the Eastern Solomons the American carrier task forces went from strength to strength. All the vast industrial might of the United States was now harnessed to the production of new carriers and thousands of aircraft. Equally important, training of aircrew was expanded to keep pace, and by mid-1944 the US Navy's carrier air groups were much better trained and equipped than they had been in 1942.

The Japanese still hankered after a decisive battle, even though they were now forced to adopt a new inner defensive chain of islands. It was hoped to bring the American carriers to battle west of Saipan, where the shortage of carrier aircraft could be made up by land-based aircraft flying from Guam, Rota and Yap. Vice Admiral Ozawa's 'A-Go' plan was to use the extra range of Japanese naval aircraft (because of their light construction and lack of armor protection) to launch an attack outside the range of US carrier planes, after the enemy's numbers had been reduced by attacks from the land-based planes in the

Mariana Islands. It was also Ozawa's intention to fly his aircraft on to Guam for refueling and rearming for a second strike against TF 58 on the way back.

In charge of the US Fifth Fleet, of which TF 58 formed part, was Admiral Raymond Spruance, the wily tactician who had triumphed at Midway. He interpreted his main duty as providing cover for the Saipan invasion force, and his four carrier Task Groups (TGs) were disposed to prevent Ozawa from slipping past to the north or the

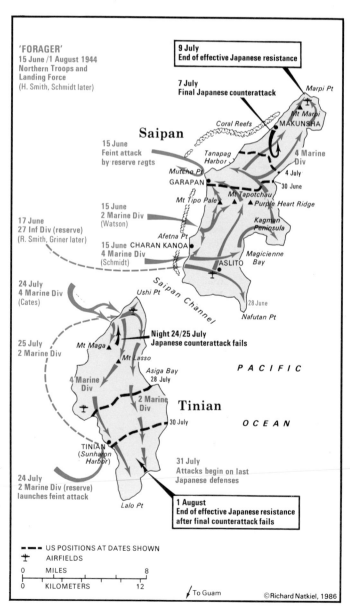

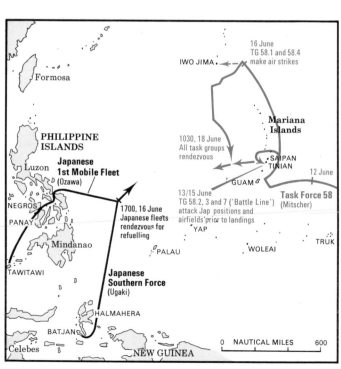

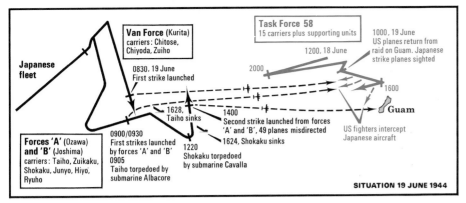

Van Force (Kurita) carriers: Chitose, Chiyoda, Zuiho

Task Force 58 15 carriers plus supporting units

1000, 19 June
US planes return from raid on Guam. Japanese strike planes sighted

1200, 18 June

2000

Japanese fleet

0830, 19 June
First strike launched

1628, Taiho sinks

1400
Second strike launched from forces 'A' and 'B', 49 planes misdirected

1600

Guam

Forces 'A' (Ozawa) **and 'B'** (Joshima) carriers: Taiho, Zuikaku, Shokaku, Junyo, Hiyo, Ryuho

0900/0930
First strikes launched by forces 'A' and 'B'

0905
Taiho torpedoed by submarine Albacore

1220
Shokaku torpedoed by submarine Cavalla

1624, Shokaku sinks

US fighters intercept Japanese aircraft

SITUATION 19 JUNE 1944

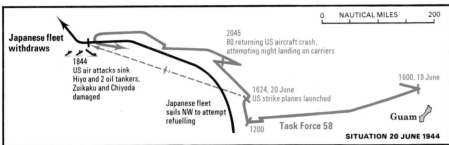

0   NAUTICAL MILES   200

Japanese fleet withdraws

2045
80 returning US aircraft crash, attempting night landing on carriers

1844
US air attacks sink Hiyo and 2 oil tankers, Zuikaku and Chiyoda damaged

1624, 20 June
US strike planes launched

1600, 19 June

Japanese fleet sails NW to attempt refuelling

1200   **Task Force 58**

Guam

SITUATION 20 JUNE 1944

Left: **A burning Japanese bomber plunges toward the sea beyond an American aircraft carrier during the Battle of the Philippine Sea. The American air defense system was so effective that few Japanese aircraft succeeded in reaching the American carriers.**

south. To protect his carriers he devised a new tactic, putting all the battleships in a 'battle line' capable of putting up an ultra-heavy barrage of AA fire. This would thin out the incoming waves of attackers, breaking up their formation before they reached the carriers' defending fighters.

Ozawa's 1st Mobile Fleet left Tawitawi on 14 June 1944, and was spotted by two US submarines next day. To forestall attacks from Japanese land-planes TF 58 began a series of devastating raids on airfields on Iwo Jima, Chichi Jima, Guam and Rota, putting Ozawa's 'staging post' airfields out of action. For reasons never explained, the commander of the land air forces, Vice Admiral Kakuta concealed the bad news from Ozawa, who steamed on thinking that Spruance's air groups had suffered heavy losses. As late as the night of 18-19 June Kakuta continued to conceal the truth, telling Ozawa that Guam was secure and well-supplied with aircraft, whereas he had only managed to fly in 50 out of the 500 planned.

Not realizing that he faced a virtually unharmed adversary, Ozawa drew up his battle formation on the morning of 18 June. His Van Force under Vice Admiral Kurita had the light carriers *Chiyoda*, *Zuiho* and *Chitose* in line abreast, 100 miles ahead of his Main Force. The main force was divided into Force 'A,' the large carriers *Shokaku*, *Taiho* and *Zuikaku*, and Force 'B,' the smaller *Hiyo*, *Junyo* and *Ryuho*. The first strikes were launched between 0830 and 0930 next day,

but at 0905 the US submarine *Albacore* hit the flagship *Taiho* with a single torpedo. She stayed afloat for several hours, and could well have survived, but at 1530 an accidental spark ignited gasoline vapor. The luckless carrier was torn apart by a series of deep explosions, and over 1600 crewmen died.

The first two strikes were destroyed by TF 58's Battle Line and the defending fighters; out of a total of 179 aircraft only 68 survived, and their only achievement was a near-miss against the carrier USS *Wasp*. The partly trained Japanese pilots were no match for the US Navy and Marine Corps pilots and gunners, who dubbed the one-sided battle the 'Great Marianas Turkey Shoot.'

Just after mid-day Ozawa suffered another disaster when his new flagship the carrier *Shokaku* was hit by four torpedoes from the submarine *Cavalla*. She caught fire quickly and the admiral shifted his flag to the *Zuikaku*. The stricken carrier sank about four hours later, but in spite of this loss Ozawa believed that his remaining 102 aircraft could still cripple TF 58. From Kakuta's optimistic reports he understood that several US carriers had been knocked out, and that land-planes were about to inflict further losses.

The two fleets drew apart overnight, and did not sight one another until the afternoon of 20 June. For Spruance the problem was acute: if he attacked at over 300 miles distance so late in the day, his aircrews would not return until after dark and they would be very low on fuel. However the chance to inflict a decisive defeat on the Japanese carrier force was not to be missed, and at 1624 a massive strike of 85 fighters, 77 dive-bombers and 54 torpedo-bombers was ordered.

The Japanese were still launching their own strike when the American aircraft

arrived at 1844. The *Hiyo* was sunk with two torpedoes and the *Junyo*, *Chiyoda* and *Zuikaku* were damaged. With the appalling losses already inflicted, 400 carrier aircraft and over 100 land-based aircraft, it was the end of the Japanese Navy's Air Arm as an effective force.

It was almost the end of TF 58 as a fighting force as well, for the American pilots did not get back to their carriers until late that night, exhausted and out of fuel. In the darkness aircraft collided and began to 'ditch' in the sea. In a desperate attempt to save lives Admiral Mitscher ordered the landing lights to be turned on, in spite off the risk of torpedo attacks by Japanese submarines. More and more ships turned on their lights or fired starshell to help the pilots find their carriers, but the losses mounted up. Nearly half of the 216 aircraft launched that day were lost, although many of the aircrew were rescued. Only 20 of the 100 aircraft lost had been shot down in combat.

The Philippine Sea was the last and in many ways the greatest of the carrier battles, for it succeeded in wiping out what was left of the magnificent Japanese carrier air groups. Spruance was criticized by some of his hotheaded subordinates for not sinking more of Ozawa's carriers, but the criticisms are hardly justified. At all times he remained aware of his prime objective, protection of the Saipan invasion fleet. He was also aware that the aircrews were physically and mentally exhausted, and could hardly have mounted another strike. Four months later at Leyte Spruance's chief critic, Halsey, showed what could go wrong when a pursuit was pressed too recklessly.

The Battle of Leyte

Leyte's claim to be the greatest naval battle in history, in terms of numbers of ships, total tonnage and numbers of people can be disputed for it was really a series of battles fought over an enormous area. Like Jutland it involved every category of warship, all functioning perhaps for the last time in their designed roles. Battleships fought battleships, destroyers attacked with torpedoes and submarines attacked surface fleets.

Once again a powerful American amphibious landing triggered off a Japanese counterstroke, but this time the Leyte Gulf landings of 20 October 1944 forced the Japanese to make a last desperate bid to stave off defeat. Virtually the entire navy was mustered for a strike against the US Navy. Admiral Ozawa was to command the Mobile Force, Kurita was given Forces 'A' and 'B,' the First Striking Force, Nishimura was given command of Force 'C' and Shima was given the Second Striking Force. The Mobile Force, identified by the Americans as the 'Northern Force' was to use its four carriers to lure the fast carriers of Admiral Halsey's TF 38 away from the invasion area. Kurita's Forces 'A' and 'B,' known in the American reports as the 'Center Force' would then destroy the invasion fleet, in conjunction with Force 'C' (the 'Van of the Southern Force') and the Second Striking Force (the 'Rear of the Southern Force'). (Map right.)

Like previous Japanese plans it was complex, and would have needed a lot of luck to work. There could be no question of using the carriers to strike at the enemy for there were now too few trained pilots and fuel. Everything would depend on the surface fleet. As things turned out the Japanese had very little luck, but their enemies made some surprising mistakes which nearly turned the tables.

Two US submarines sighted part of Kurita's force as they moved through the Palawan Passage. Two heavy cruisers were sunk, the flagship *Atago* and the *Maya*, and the *Takao* was damaged, and the sighting was relayed rapidly to Admiral Kinkaid to warn him that hostile forces were heading for the invasion area.

US carrier aircraft located the Center Force in the Sibuyan Sea later that day and began a series of attacks, concentrating on the 64,000-ton giant battleships *Yamato* and *Musashi*. Eventually the *Musashi* succumbed to an estimated 20 torpedoes and 40 bomb hits, and damage to other ships forced Kurita to make a temporary withdrawal. Under the

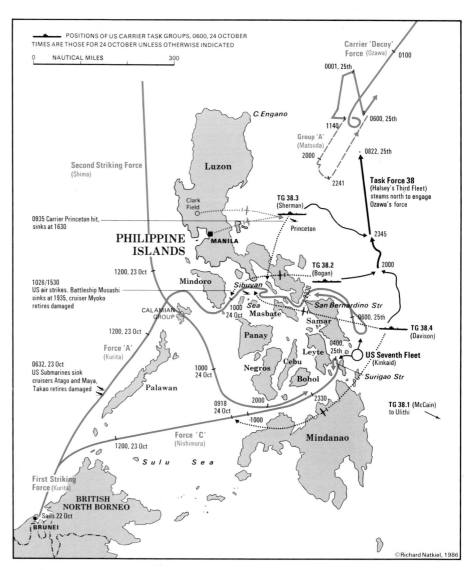

POSITIONS OF US CARRIER TASK GROUPS, 0600, 24 OCTOBER
TIMES ARE THOSE FOR 24 OCTOBER UNLESS OTHERWISE INDICATED

0   NAUTICAL MILES   300

© Richard Natkiel, 1986

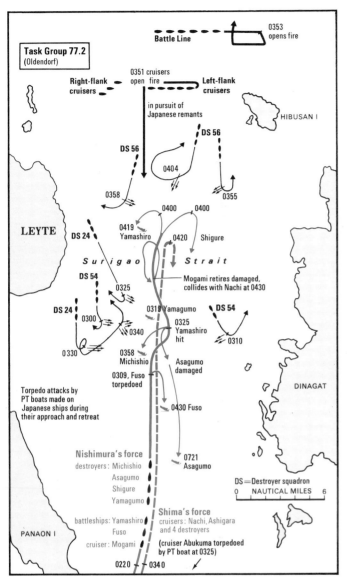

Task Group 77.2
(Oldendorf)

0353
opens fire
Battle Line

0351 cruisers
open fire
Right-flank
cruisers
Left-flank
cruisers

in pursuit of
Japanese remants

HIBUSAN I

DS 56

DS 56

0404

0358

0355

LEYTE

DS 24

0419
Yamashiro

0400

0400

0420   Shigure

Surigao   Strait

Mogami retires damaged,
collides with Nachi at 0430

DS 54

0325

0318 Yamagumo   DS 54

DS 24

0300

0325
Yamashiro
hit

0340

0310

0330

0358
Michishio

Asagumo
damaged

DINAGAT

0309, Fuso
torpedoed

Torpedo attacks by
PT boats made on
Japanese ships during
their approach and retreat

0430 Fuso

0721
Asagumo

Nishimura's force

destroyers: Michishio
Asagumo
Shigure
Yamagumo

DS = Destroyer squadron
0   6
NAUTICAL MILES

battleships: Yamashiro
Fuso
cruiser: Mogami

Shima's force

cruisers: Nachi, Ashigara
and 4 destroyers

(cruiser Abukuma torpedoed
by PT boat at 0325)

PANAON I

0220 — 0340

Above right: Admiral Nimitz, commander
of the US Pacific Fleet, gives a briefing to
President Roosevelt and the president's
Chief of Staff, Admiral Leahy.
Right: Heavily-laden landing ships move in
to unload their cargoes on the beaches at
Leyte.
Below left: The 8-inch guns of the heavy
cruiser *Portland* fire in support of the Leyte
landings.

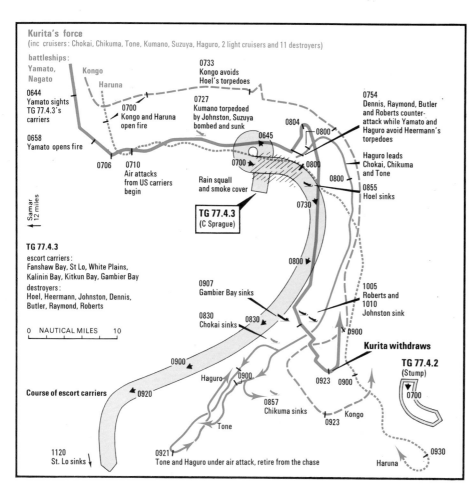

Kurita's force
(inc cruisers : Chokai, Chikuma, Tone, Kumano, Suzuya, Haguro, 2 light cruisers and 11 destroyers)

battleships:
Yamato,
Nagato

Kongo

Haruna

0733
Kongo avoids
Hoel's torpedoes

0644
Yamato sights
TG 77.4.3's
carriers

0700
Kongo and Haruna
open fire

0727
Kumano torpedoed
by Johnston, Suzuya
bombed and sunk

0754
Dennis, Raymond, Butler
and Roberts counter-
attack while Yamato and
Haguro avoid Heermann's
torpedoes

0658
Yamato opens fire

0804

0800

0645

0706

0710
Air attacks
from US carriers
begin

0700

0800

Haguro leads
Chokai, Chikuma
and Tone

Samar
12 miles

Rain squall
and smoke cover

0800

0855
Hoel sinks

TG 77.4.3
(C Sprague)

0730

TG 77.4.3
escort carriers:
Fanshaw Bay, St Lo, White Plains,
Kalinin Bay, Kitkun Bay, Gambier Bay
destroyers:
Hoel, Heermann, Johnston, Dennis,
Butler, Raymond, Roberts

0800

0907
Gambier Bay sinks

1005
Roberts and
1010
Johnston sink

0   NAUTICAL MILES   10

0830
Chokai sinks

0830

Kurita withdraws

TG 77.4.2
(Stump)

0700

0900

Course of escort carriers

0900

0920

Haguro

0900

0923   0900

0857
Chikuma sinks

0923   Kongo

1120
St. Lo sinks

0921
Tone and Haguro under air attack, retire from the chase

Tone

Haruna

0930

impression that the Japanese striking force was too badly knocked about to play any further role, and believing that Ozawa's Northern Force was the main enemy fleet, Admiral Halsey ordered the entire TF 38 in pursuit.

With Admiral Kinkaid believing that part of TF 38 was guarding the vital San Bernardino Strait the scene was now set for a major Japanese victory. The southern route through Surigao Strait was also vulnerable, but Kinkaid was able to order Admiral Jesse Oldendorf's bombarding squadron of six old battleships to guard it. Despite having their shell rooms filled with high explosive shells for shore bombardment rather than armor-piercing for ship-to-ship use, these veteran ships were able to destroy Nishimura's Southern Force. The battleships *Fuso* and *Yamashiro* were overwhelmed by gunfire and torpedoes from the waiting ships, and only a heavy cruiser and a destroyer escaped. This

action, the Battle of Surigao Strait, was the last time in history that battleships fought battleships. (Map page 225.)

In contrast Kurita's force was able to get through the San Bernardino Strait unde-tected, after a series of signalling errors and delays. As a result the US escort carriers and their light escorts off Samar came under fire from battleships and heavy cruisers at a range of 17 miles on the morning of 25 October. Three out of seven destroyers were sunk, while aircraft without bombs made 'dummy runs' against the Japanese ships in desperate attempts to stop them from getting through to the defenseless invasion fleet. These tactics worked well enough to ensure that Kurita's ships took three hours to sink the small escort carrier *Gambier Bay*, and when reinforcements arrived from the big carriers and sank three heavy cruisers Kurita ordered a withdrawal. This brought an end to the Battle of Samar, second of the major battles

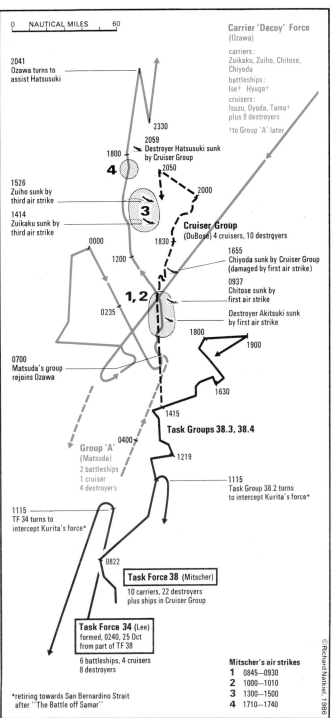

Carrier 'Decoy' Force
(Ozawa)

carriers:
Zuikaku, Zuiho, Chitose,
Chiyoda
battleships:
Ise† Hyuga†
cruisers:
Isuzu, Oyoda, Tama†
plus 9 destroyers

†to Group 'A' later

0 NAUTICAL MILES 60

2041
Ozawa turns to
assist Hatsusuki

2330

2059
Destroyer Hatsusuki sunk
by Cruiser Group

1800

4

2050

2000

1526
Zuiho sunk by
third air strike

3

1830

Cruiser Group
(DuBose) 4 cruisers, 10 destroyers

1414
Zuikaku sunk by
third air strike

1655
Chiyoda sunk by Cruiser Group
(damaged by first air strike)

0000

1200

0937
Chitose sunk by
first air strike

1,2

Destroyer Akitsuki
sunk
by first air strike

0235

0700
Matsuda's group
rejoins Ozawa

1800

1900

1630

1415

Task Groups 38.3, 38.4

0400

Group 'A'
(Matsuda)
2 battleships
1 cruiser
4 destroyers

1219

1115
Task Group 38.2 turns
to intercept Kurita's force*

1115
TF 34 turns to
intercept Kurita's force*

0822

Task Force 38 (Mitscher)

10 carriers, 22 destroyers
plus ships in Cruiser Group

Task Force 34 (Lee)
formed, 0240, 25 Oct
from part of TF 38

6 battleships, 4 cruisers
8 destroyers

*retiring towards San Bernardino Strait
after "The Battle off Samar"

© Richard Natkiel, 1986

Mitscher's air strikes
1 0845—0930
2 1000—1010
3 1300—1500
4 1710—1740

Above: The crew of *PT.131* prepare to take part in the Surigao Strait phase of the Leyte Gulf battle.
Left: The escort carrier *St Lo* and her consorts make smoke to try to give some protection against the attacks of Admiral Kurita's battleships and cruisers.

around Leyte, although the escort carriers suffered further losses from *kamikaze* attacks from Luzon. (Map above left.)

Ozawa's carrier decoy force now suffered the full weight of Halsey's wrath. The carriers *Zuiho* and *Zuikaku* were sunk quickly, followed by the *Chitose* and *Chiyoda*. It was an easy victory, for Ozawa's two carrier divisions had only 108 aircraft, of which only 13 fighters were still on board by the morning of 25 October, flown by partially trained pilots. The Battle of Cape Engaño destroyed the remnants of Japan's carrier forces. (Map above right.)

The final phase of the battle was an attempt to stop Japanese stragglers from escaping. In spite of an enormous number of sorties being flown comparatively little damage was done, and the survivors escaped to Brunei or to home waters. It was, however, the last time that Japanese warships sailed as a fleet, for shortages of fuel and ammunition were acute. All that was left was a resort to suicide tactics, and a fanatical determination to fight to the bitter end.

The Capture of Iwo Jima and Okinawa

The capture of Saipan and Tinian in mid-1944 enabled B-29 Superfortress bombers to mount heavy attacks on the Japanese home islands, but the great distance led to heavy losses of crippled aircraft. The US Chiefs of Staff decided to occupy island bases in the Ryukyu Islands, only 800 miles from Japan, to provide fighter support and to act as a forward base for the final assault on the home islands.

Initially it was planned to seize Iwo Jima in the Bonin Islands on the same day as Okinawa, in the Ryukyu chain, but subsequently it was decided to take Iwo Jima first, beginning on 19 February 1945.

Despite the customary heavy air and sea bombardment most of the 22,000-strong garrison survived in a honeycomb of caves and deep bunkers. The defenders held their fire until the Marines hit the beaches, but then caused heavy casualties. The Americans had to fight literally yard by yard, sustaining 17,000 wounded and 4000 dead. But with 30,000 troops landed in the first 24 hours the result was not in doubt, and when the fighting ended all the defenders were dead or wounded.

By comparison the landing on Okinawa on 1 April suffered fewer casualties initially, but the naval forces suffered very heavily for the first time. Five days after the first landings a massed air attack was made by 700 aircraft, of which half were from the newly-formed *kamikaze* units. The response was to set up a 'picket line' of destroyers and destroyer escorts equipped with radar and fighter-direction gear to allow them to direct defending fighters to the correct sectors. Being up to 70 miles from the main fleet, however, the picket-line ships were vulnerable and suffered heavy casualties.

On 6 April carrier aircraft sighted the battleship *Yamato* steaming toward Okinawa, escorted by a light cruiser and eight

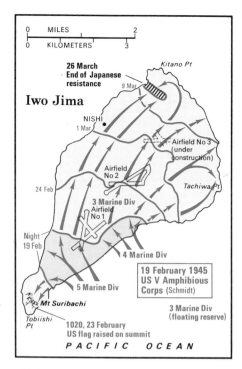

Right: The battleship *Idaho* moving in to join the pre-landing bombardment of Iwo Jima. Mount Suribachi in the background.
Below right: Rocket-launching landing craft add their firepower to the Okinawa bombardment.
Below: Damage control aboard the carrier *Saratoga* after a kamikaze hit off Okinawa.

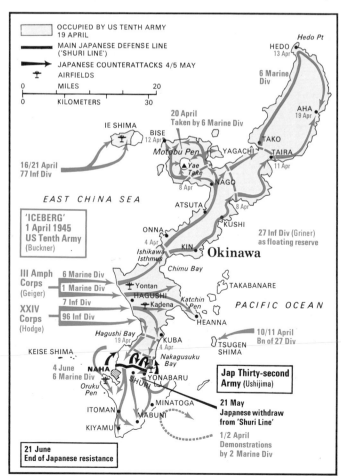

destroyers. The blockade of Japan had reduced oil stocks to the point where the giant ship could be given only sufficient fuel for a one-way trip, and her orders were to beach herself and use her 18-inch guns to destroy the invasion fleet.

Admiral Marc Mitscher 'scrambled' 380 planes from the carriers, and just after midday they found their target. For two hours they pounded the *Yamato*, and finally she capsized after taking 20 torpedoes and 17 bombs. Most of her 2400 crewmen died with her.

On the same day the *kamikazes* scored their first major success, a hit on the carrier *Hancock*, and between 11 and 12 April two more carriers, three battleships and many smaller ships were hit. Although no major warship was sunk the carriers were vulnerable to explosions and gasoline fires among the aircraft parked on deck and in the hangar. The six British carriers present were all hit but continued to operate largely because of the protection conferred by their armored decks.

The most disturbing revelation was the discovery that light anti-aircraft guns lacked stopping power against *kamikazes*. Supplies of the new 'variable-time' or proximity fuze were rushed to Okinawa in May, to enhance the killing-power of anti-aircraft fire, and bombing raids against Japanese airfields were stepped up.

By the end of May the stalemate on land was broken, and as the ground troops extended their hold over the island, the need to keep large numbers of ships off the beaches dwindled. In all 36 Allied warships were sunk and 368 damaged, nearly all by *kamikaze* attacks, and the Allied land and naval forces lost 12,500 killed and 35,000 wounded.

Casualties among the defenders were heavy, 120,000 killed or committed suicide, and the civilian population of the island suffered heavily as well. Taken with the fearful cost of capturing Iwo Jima, these figures suggested that the planned invasion of the Japanese home islands would be even more costly. Although the arguments for dropping the atomic bomb were already strong, Okinawa and Iwo Jima provided proof of how expensive the invasion of Japan would be.

The 250,000-ton tanker *Esso Cambria*, a massive 1141 feet long.

THE MODERN ERA

The Korean War

When forces of the Communist People's Republic of North Korea crossed the border to begin a full-scale invasion of the neighboring Republic of Korea (South Korea) on 25 June 1950, the United States government assumed that it was the precursor of an all out war with Communist China and the Soviet Union. President Truman ordered naval and air support of the South Korean defenders, and the Seventh Fleet was ordered to prevent the Chinese Communists on the mainland and the Nationalists in Formosa (Taiwan) from attacking each other. The US was also able to win support in the United Nations for a multi-national force to be sent to help the South Koreans but clearly America would need to take the leading role.

It was a bad time for the US Navy, with only one aircraft carrier in the Far East, and the whole future of naval air power under strong threat from air force lobbyists who insisted that money should be diverted to strategic bombers. Yet the 27,000-ton *Valley Forge* proved that she could provide much more effective support to the South Koreans,

and faster. The Air Force's B-29 bombers in the Western Pacific were only trained for strategic nuclear bombing, and the President had ruled out the use of nuclear weapons. The standard F-80C Shooting Star fighters based in Japan could only stay for 15 minutes over South Korea, *if* they kept to their economical height of 15,000ft or more.

The *Valley Forge* was soon joined at Okinawa by the British light carrier HMS *Triumph*, and the joint Task Force 77 launched its first strike on 3 July, hitting the North Korean capital Pyongyang and nearby Haeju without loss. Until airfields could be established ashore, capable of operating US Air Force fighters and ground support aircraft the naval pilots bore the brunt of interdicting North Korean supplies and movement of troops.

The Commander in Chief of US and UN forces, General MacArthur, planned to outflank the enemy invasion forces by landing at Inchon, on the west coast near Seoul, the capital of South Korea. By September the forces attacking the Pusan Perimeter (Pusan

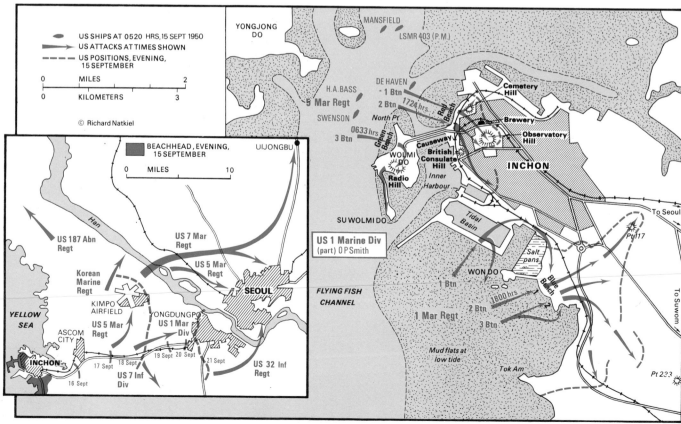

being the vital southern port through which all reinforcements came) had been held off and the invasion could go ahead. It was a large operation involving 230 ships and a Marine division of highly trained amphibious forces. Once the Marines established a bridgehead on 15 September the enemy forces withdrew, and two days later the vital Kimpo airfield was captured. Seoul fell on 27 September and by early October 1950 the Marines had been joined by the other UN forces which had advanced from Pusan and were ready to take the offensive and march across the 38th Parallel into North Korea.

Over-confidence now led the UN forces into more complex and risky operations. An attempt to repeat the Inchon success at Wonsan on the east coast of Korea ran into trouble when the amphibious forces were held up by a huge minefield. When the troops finally got ashore on 25 October they were two weeks behind South Korean forces, who had already liberated the city by conventional means. In spite of this Wonsan became a major supply port, compensating for the poor state of the roads.

As UN forces raced up through North Korea the Chinese became extremely nervous and on 14 October the first Chinese air attack was delivered, and on 1 November the first MiG-15 jet fighters crossed the Yalu River and fired on a flight of USAF

Mustangs. Communist Chinese ground forces also poured across the border from Manchuria, and the carrier aircraft were now ordered to do their utmost to reduce the flow of men and supplies. Allied troops trapped near the Yalu River, at the Chosin Reservoir had to be evacuated, as well as large numbers from Hungnam, Chinnampo, Wonsan and even Inchon, in all nearly 300,000 soldiers and civilian refugees.

Thereafter until armistice talks began in July 1951 the aircraft carriers and surface ships offshore continued their classic missions of interdiction and gunfire support. Only one operation was unusual, the attack on the Hwachon Reservoir. This important target had been attacked several times, including a land assault by US Rangers and high-level bombing by B-29s. Finally the US Navy was asked to take a hand.

The first effort, by six Skyraider aircraft from the light carrier *Princeton*, hit a sluice gate with a dive-bombing attack. Next day, 1 May 1951, the *Princeton* launched eight Skyraiders and 12 Corsairs, the Skyraiders each carrying a single 22-inch torpedo set for surface running. One torpedo failed to explode and one ran out of control but the remaining six ran true and destroyed the dam.

A feature of the naval war was the support from the British and British Commonwealth

Above: The battleship USS *Iowa* off the Korean coast during a bombardment mission, 30 May 1952.
Above left: Military installations and stores are burned ashore as the UN forces evacuate Wonsan before the Chinese advance, 7 December 1950.

navies. The British carrier *Triumph* was relieved in October 1950 by her sister HMS *Theseus* and then in April 1951 by HMS *Glory*. In September 1951 the Australian light carrier HMAS *Sydney* took over, establishing a record for this class of ship by flying 89 sorties in one day and 147 sorties in two days.

The Korean War was fought strictly in World War II terms, without nuclear weapons but with more advanced aircraft than had been available in 1945. Naval tactics and equipment were, however, generally little more advanced than they had been five years earlier. Nonetheless, without the flexible and constant support of seapower there is little doubt that the ground forces of the United States and her UN allies would have been defeated. In the face of constant predictions about instant nuclear exchange the pattern set by the Korean War has been repeated ever since, and as a result the US Navy's insistence on retaining its fleet of big carriers has been vindicated many times over.

The Suez Crisis

The rise of Arab nationalism and its hostility to Israel caused unceasing tension in the Middle East in the years after the Second World War. The British hoped to continue to control the Suez Canal, but the overthrow of King Farouk of Egypt in 1952 lessened British influence over Egyptian affairs. When in 1955 President Nasser of Egypt announced that the Canal would be closed to Israeli ships and that ships using Eilat on the Red Sea would be fired on by Egyptian artillery, Israel's interests began to be seen as close to those of Britain. The French government was angry about Egyptian help for Algerian rebels and also had an interest in the Suez Canal, and thus by an unhappy chance all three countries had reason to look for ways of unseating Nasser.

The Egyptian President in the meantime had approached Great Britain and the United States for large loans to build a new Nile dam at Aswan, but when he was offered money without military aid he announced that he would seek aid from the Soviet Union. The result was a declaration by London and Washington that they would withdraw financial aid for the Aswan Dam.

Nasser's riposte was to nationalize the Suez Canal, an action which struck hard at British post-Imperial sensitivities and alarmed France and Israel as well. The three countries decided in secret to co-ordinate military action against Egypt, Israel beginning hostilities on 29 October 1956 on the pretext that she was preventing Nasser from closing the Canal. The British and French then announced that they would occupy the Canal Zone to prevent either of the belligerents from damaging the Canal.

The military operations went comparatively smoothly. A French force including the battleship *Jean Bart* and two cruisers captured the destroyer *Ibrahim el Awal* off Haifa *before* the Anglo-French ultimatum had expired, but resolved the diplomatic embarrassment by handing the prize over to the Israelis. The cruiser HMS *Newfoundland* sank a frigate in the Gulf of Suez on the night of 31 October, but shortly afterwards the frigate *Crane* was mistakenly attacked by Israeli aircraft, and she was forced to shoot one down.

The Royal Navy and French Navy carried out the classic tasks of supporting the amphibious landings, but the British light fleet carriers *Ocean* and *Theseus* made a unique contribution to naval history. Hurriedly converted to assault carriers, their helicopters

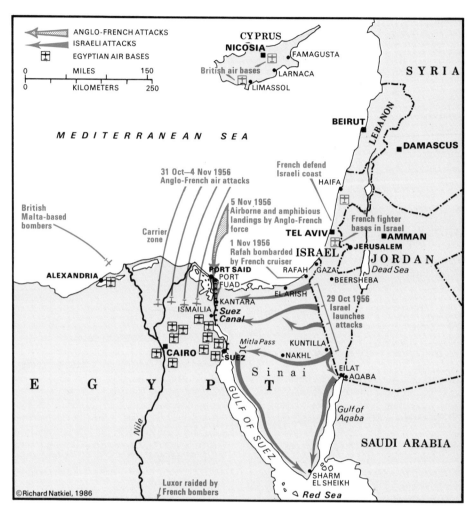

enabled the Royal Marine Commandos to make the first ever helicopter-borne assault.

The alleged aim of the Anglo-French military intervention was clearly defeated when Nasser gave the order to block the Canal. A total of 51 obstructions, ranging from scuttled ships to demolished bridges put the Canal totally out of action, necessitating an enormous salvage operation under UN control subsequently.

Neither the British nor the French can have anticipated the political consequences of their hasty intervention. The United States in particular was outraged, but Britain also forfeited an enormous amount of goodwill in the Arab world by her connivance with France and Israel. The humiliating Anglo-French withdrawal in December, under American and UN pressure destroyed whatever prestige either country had gained from

the defeat of Egypt's armed forces. The political crisis which followed left both countries deeply divided. Even those who had supported military action could not deny that the Anglo-French action had driven Nasser even further into the arms of the Russians, and it was to be 20 years before Anglo-Egyptian relations were restored to anything like harmony.

The Vietnam War

Although American equipment had been supplied in large quantities to the French during their war against the Vietminh in the 1950s, the first formal US involvement began in August 1964, when the destroyer *Maddox* was attacked by North Vietnamese motor torpedo boats. The US Government was determined to support South Vietnam against the invasion from the North, and this 'Gulf of Tonking Incident' was the starting point of outright hostilities.

A second attack a few days later merely confirmed American suspicions that their naval forces were under serious threat, and on 5 August air strikes were launched by two carriers. During the next eight years carrier aircraft of the Seventh Fleet (Task Force 77) flew thousands of sorties against troop concentrations and communications between North and South, the carriers' operating areas being known as Yankee and Dixie respectively for attacks on targets in the North and South. On the ground the US Marine Corps fought long and hard: 12,936 marines were killed and 88,589 were wounded.

A feature of the southern part of what was then South Vietnam is the maze of waterways and irrigation canals crisscrossing the countryside. Like the French before them

the Americans extemporized a large number of shallow-draft fighting vessels to deny the Vietcong forces free use of the waterways. These craft fought many fierce battles at point-blank range.

In 1968, in response to repeated demands for heavy gunfire support, the battleship *New Jersey* was recommissioned to serve on the 'gunline.' She was to fire more than 3000 rounds of 16-inch and 7000 rounds of 5-inch ammunition before the end of that year. She was recalled to the USA the following year but several 8-inch gunned cruisers were kept in commission to meet demands for gunfire support.

Apart from very occasional gunfire from coastal batteries and ineffectual attacks by aircraft the ships lay offshore without fear of serious harassment. The carriers worked very hard to keep up the rate of sorties and several deck accidents caused serious damage. Their escorting cruisers and large destroyers performed a vital role in controlling air traffic, distinguishing neutral civil aircraft from friendly and hostile military contacts. The small number of attacks by North Vietnamese aircraft were dealt with by Combat Air Patrol (CAP) aircraft from the carriers and by missiles from the air defense ships.

Above: Flight deck activities aboard the nuclear aircraft carrier USS *Enterprise* during the last days of South Vietnam.

On shore the marines distinguished themselves by their defense of Khe Sanh, followed by the bitter fighting around Hue during the Tet Offensive. In the recriminations which followed after the war it was usually forgotten that the marines and their South Vietnamese allies inflicted such a severe defeat on the Vietcong that the Communist irregulars never took the field again, and had to be replaced by North Vietnamese regular troops.

After President Nixon's announcement of the first troop withdrawals in June 1969 the intensity of naval operations fell off sharply. The marines were withdrawn steadily as the process of 'Vietnamization' was put into effect. Three USMC divisions left by the end of that year, and by April 1971 the only naval combatant unit left was Light Attack Squadron Four, equipped with counter-insurgency aircraft.

Before the ceasefire in January 1973 the US Navy had transferred large numbers of river craft and a number of escort-sized warships to the South Vietnam Navy, but the 'Vietnamization' was applied too late to stem the tide of defeat. With some 145,000 North Vietnamese troops controlling roughly a third of South Vietnam, and no threat of attack from American aircraft or helicopters there was little the defenders could do but retreat before the Communist advance, which had hardly stopped for the ceasefire.

The last act of the tragedy was the evacuation of the US Embassy in Saigon on 30 April. Conforming to their tradition of 'first in, last out,' the last US troops to leave were marine embassy guards, lifted to safety from the roof as looters ransacked the lower floors of the building.

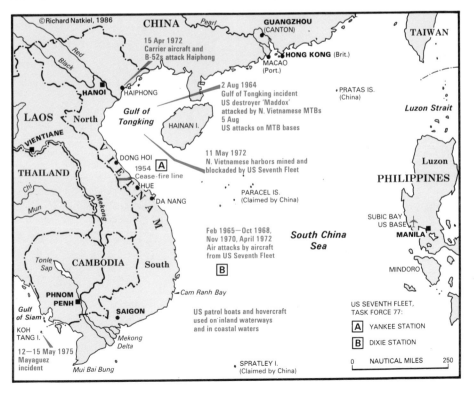

The World of Oil

Since the Second World War the developed nations' use of energy has been rising steadily. Throughout the 1950s and 1960s the world's shipyards built larger and larger oil tankers, culminating in the ULCCs or Ultra Large Crude Carriers of 500,000 tons and more. These huge vessels draw so much water that they cannot enter normal harbors, and take on or discharge their cargoes of crude oil at ocean terminals, and spend all their working careers shuttling between such terminals.

In 1960 five of the chief oil-producing nations, Iran, Iraq, Kuwait, Saudi Arabia and Venezuela formed OPEC, the Organisation of Petroleum Exporting Countries in an attempt to prevent the powerful international oil companies from keeping prices down. By 1970 OPEC had succeeded in pushing prices up, but in 1973 it overreached itself by forcing through a very steep rise in prices. The recession in the Western economies which had previously been protected came to pass with frightening rapidity, but there was a knock-on effect throughout the world. The countries of the Third World found that without the developed world able to buy their raw materials, they lacked the means to finance development loans or buy oil of their own. In the advanced economies there was a general increase in prices, caused by the direct or indirect dependence on energy for most forms of production. As prices rose output in many important sectors declined, followed by a decline in oil imports.

OPEC members were hit badly by the decline in their oil exports. The energy-consumers turned to alternative forms of fuel, particularly coal, natural gas and nuclear power, and fostered non-OPEC sources of oil. The luckiest countries in this respect were those in Northwest Europe, particularly Great Britain, the Netherlands and Norway, which opened up new oilfields in the North Sea.

The effect of the upward trend in oil prices had its effect on all navies. There is now great emphasis on economy of machinery, and many navies have found it necessary to restrict large-scale exercises to save fuel and money. The trend towards gas turbines in place of steam machinery has given way to all-diesel or combined diesel-and-gas turbine plant in many new designs.

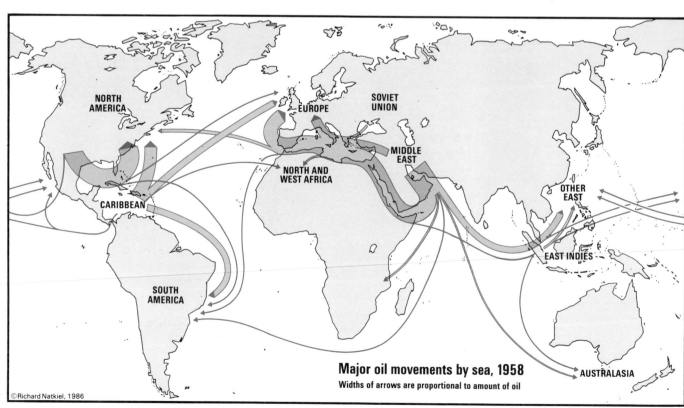

Major oil movements by sea, 1958
Widths of arrows are proportional to amount of oil

Above: Sheikh Yamani of Saudi Arabia, one of the most influential of the Arab oil ministers, during an OPEC meeting in 1979.
Left: The massive bulk of the Shell tanker *Latirus*, 278,220 tons, typical of the super-tanker breed which now dominates the trade in oil.

The most feared eventuality, a war in the Persian Gulf, proved not to have the disastrous effect on oil-supplies which most experts feared. Iraqi aircraft, including French-built Super Etendards armed with Exocet anti-ship missiles have repeatedly attacked foreign tankers in the vicinity of Iran's Kharg Island oil terminal, damaging many but not so far cutting off the trade. In most cases the missiles have crippled the tankers without setting fire to their cargoes of crude oil, which tend to absorb the energy of missile-hits. The war began in 1980 and shows little sign of ending whether by a negotiated peace or by one or other side winning militarily.

The shrinking oil market had catastrophic effects on the world tanker market. Shipyards which in the 1960s and 1970s had been specially equipped to build nothing but super-tankers found their newest deliveries being towed away and laid up immediately. The older small tankers have all been relegated to the scrapyard but the steady climb in tanker size has stopped.

With their deep draft super-tankers can only navigate safely in deep channels, and the risk of wide-scale pollution is constant. The ships themselves are unwieldy and cannot maneuver out of trouble, and to make matters worse there was a series of structural failures in Japanese-built tankers, caused by metal fatigue.

The irony of today's world is that OPEC's problems can only be removed if world trade recovers to its pre-1973 levels, and that that fall in trade was caused directly by OPEC's increase in oil prices.

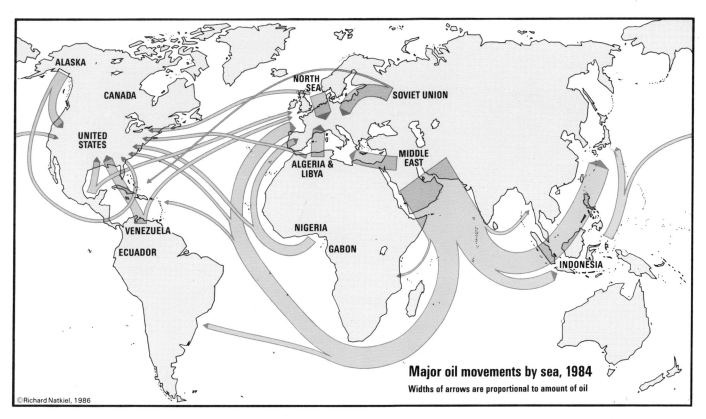

Major oil movements by sea, 1984
Widths of arrows are proportional to amount of oil

©Richard Natkiel, 1986

237

The Middle East Flashpoint

The West's reliance on Middle East oil, combined with territorial rivalries in the Horn of Africa, makes the Middle East a constant source of friction and threatens to drag the Super Powers into conflict.

The oldest quarrel stems from the foundation of Israel as an independent nation in 1948. There have been four Arab-Israeli wars since then, each one resulting in humiliation of the Egyptians, Jordanians and Syrians. In the 1956 war the British and French became embroiled, but there is little doubt that the Israelis would have triumphed without their help. The Six-Day War in 1967 was a crushing victory over the Egyptians in the Sinai Desert, but at sea the destroyer *Eilat* became the first victim of modern anti-ship missiles when she was sunk by 'Styx' missiles off Port Said. The 1973 Yom Kippur War was notable for the appearance of Israeli missile boats, and in two separate actions the new *Sa'ar* class boats and their Gabriel missiles inflicted severe losses on the Syrian and Egyptian missile boats.

Russian intervention in the guerrilla war in Eritrea caused shivers of apprehension in the West, but apart from a few naval bombardments there was little direct intervention. Despite the low-key Soviet presence, the 'Horn of Africa' continues to cause concern to the Western naval powers as it dominates crucial approaches to the Arabian Sea and the Indian Ocean.

The long-feared Gulf War broke out in 1980 between Iraq and Iran, but in spite of numerous attacks on oil tankers by Iraqi and Iranian aircraft the oil continues to flow. Both sides operate sophisticated equipment and although lack of spares must have caused problems they seem to have an inexhaustible supply of weapons.

Other complications are an insurrection in Oman and the Soviet invasion of Afghanistan in 1979. The cauldron continues to seethe, but it is worth noting that a precarious peace has been preserved in the region, against all predictions. Not even the laying of mines in the Gulf of Suez in 1984, apparently carried out by Libya to harm Egyptian commerce, sufficed to provoke open hostilities. An international mine countermeasures force was hurriedly sent to Egypt, and Soviet-made mines were found by a Royal Navy minehunter but in spite of the blame being laid at Libya's door no further action was taken.

After the Gulf War the most destructive conflict is the long-running civil war in the Lebanon, which has devastated this once prosperous country. An Israeli invasion has been followed by American landings and bombardments and the landing of international troops to try to separate the warring factions but nothing has stopped the murderous strife.

Despite their loudly repeated sympathies for the various combatants in the Middle East neither the Americans nor the Soviets are willing to risk a major war to decide any of the Middle East disputes, which seem doomed to continue with varying intensity for the foreseeable future.

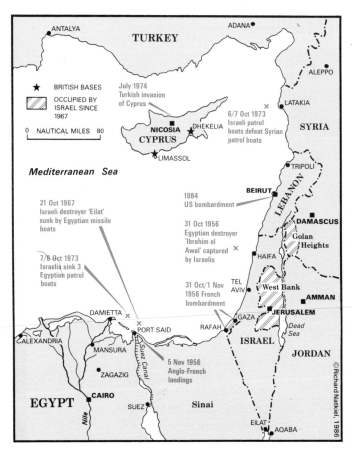

GREECE
CRETE
TURKEY
Caspian Sea
SOVIET UNION
CYPRUS
LATAKIA
SYRIA
TEHERAN
24 Dec 1979
Soviet invasion
of Afghanistan
Mediterranean Sea
LEBANON
BEIRUT
DAMASCUS
Tigris
BAGHDAD
Iran-Iraq war
Sept 1980 -
ESFAHAN
IRAN
AFGHANISTAN
ALEXANDRIA
TEL AVIV
AMMAN
JERUSALEM
ISRAEL
JORDAN
IRAQ
Euphrates
KHORRAMSHAHR
BASRA
ABADAN
KUWAIT
SHIRAZ
BANDAR ABBAS
Strait of Hormuz
PORT SAID
CAIRO
Suez Canal
Gulf of Aqaba
Arab-Israeli wars
1948-49, 1956,
1967, 1973
1983-85
Attacks by Iraqi
and Iranian aircraft
on oil tankers (mainly
at Kharg Island)
KHARG I.
The Gulf
1984
Libyan mines
Gulf of Suez
SHARM EL SHEIKH
BAHRAIN
QATAR
ABU DHABI
Musandam Peninsula
Gulf of Oman
MUSCAT
EGYPT
U.A.E.
Ra's al Hadd
RAS BANAS
MEDINA
RIYADH
SAUDI ARABIA
OMAN
MASIRAH I.
Red Sea
JIDDAH
MECCA
PORT SUDAN
Nile
1970's
Russians bombard
Eritrean separatists
Undefined
THAMARIT
KURIA MURIA IS.
SALALAH
SUDAN
OMDURMAN
KHARTOUM
YEMEN ARAB REPUBLIC
SANA
PEOPLE'S DEMOCRATIC REPUBLIC OF YEMEN
Arabian Sea
MASSAWA
DAHLAK IS.
Eritrea
TAIZ
White Nile
Blue Nile
ETHIOPIA
Lake Tana
ADEN
PERIM I.
Bab el Mandab
Gulf of Aden
SOCOTRA
(S. Yemen)
★ RUSSIAN BASES
☆ US FACILITIES
DJIBOUTI
BERBERA
SOMALIA
0   NAUTICAL MILES   250
©Richard Natkiel, 1986

Left: Following the spectacular success of the Israeli Army's attacks in the Sinai during the Six Day War in 1967, an Israeli gunboat enters the harbor at Sharm El Sheikh.
Right: British Royal Navy divers at work during operations to clear the blocked Suez Canal in 1974.

The Falklands War

The Argentine seizure of the Falkland Islands (las Islas Malvinas) on 2 April 1982 took place at a time when the British Royal Navy was under threat of cuts imposed by the new Secretary of State for Defence, John Nott. Despite warnings from the Royal Navy that the ice patrol ship *Endurance* was a cost-effective reminder to Argentina not to press her claim to the islands with excessive force, she was listed for early scrapping. At the same time the ruling military junta in Argentina was under internal pressure from popular unrest at economic problems, and when they saw what appeared to be the first sign that Britain was at last prepared to withdraw her claim to the islands, they decided that the time had come to use force to accelerate the process and at the same time divert public attention to an external issue.

Both sides paid dearly for their miscalculations. The British government, outraged at what they saw as a violation of international law, immediately dispatched a powerful task force to repossess the islands, while a divided group of senior Argentine military officers tried to fend off or escape the consequences of their actions by haphazard diplomatic efforts. One by one the diplomatic initiatives collapsed, as they came up against two hard facts: the British regarded the islands as theirs legally, and the Argentine military junta's precarious prestige could not survive a climb-down.

We now know that the junta finally accepted that hostilities were inescapable when on 1 May a single RAF Vulcan bomber flew from Ascension Island to bomb the runway at Port Stanley. Believing that the British intended to bomb Buenos Aires, the Argentine high command gave permission for two naval Super Etendard aircraft to launch a missile strike against the British next day, in the hope that a severe loss would force the British task force to withdraw. A small British detachment had already recaptured South Georgia, 800 miles beyond the Falklands, but the facilities there could not support a fleet, and on the advice of Admiral Anaya the junta believed that the British would soon be forced back to Ascension.

The Super Etendard sortie was launched but was abandoned when the two aircraft failed to rendezvous with their tanker, but in the meantime the nuclear hunter-killer submarine HMS *Conqueror* had found the old cruiser *General Belgrano* steaming just outside the Total Exclusion Zone which the British had proclaimed around the islands. With some units of the task force already on the south-western side of the islands, and two Exocet-armed destroyers escorting the cruiser, Admiral John Woodward and his superiors at Fleet HQ, Northwood, decided that the *Belgrano* task group was a threat and, after consultation with the British government, *Conqueror* was given permission to sink

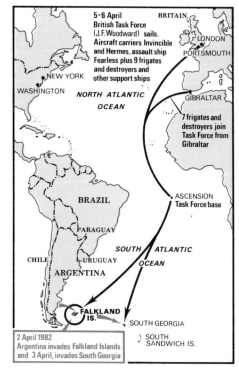

her. Some 350 of the Argentinian crew went down with the ship or succumbed to exposure before they could be rescued.

Two days later the Super Etendards made another sortie and this time one of their AM-39 Exocet missiles hit the air defense destroyer *Sheffield*. A fierce fire took hold and about five hours later the fire parties abandoned the ship. In fact the gutted hulk stayed afloat for another six days but when the weather worsened she was scuttled.

Contrary to Argentine predictions the British did not withdraw, and during the next 17 days Sea Harrier strike aircraft and individual ships probed the defenses, bombarding Port Stanley's airfield, sinking any Argentine ships still in the Exclusion Zone and 'inserting' SAS and SBS forces ashore. On the night of 15 May a raid on Pebble Island destroyed aircraft and fuel dumps, and incidentally confused the defenders

Left: A feature of the British effort to retake the Falklands was the use of ships converted from their normal civilian uses. One of the best known of these was the cruise liner *Canberra*, shown here during a refueling operation, which became a troop transport with a minimum of conversion work.

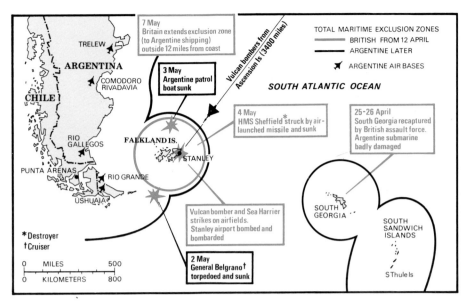

about the point of assault. At dawn on 21 May the main land forces under Major General Jeremy Moore RM landed at San Carlos on the western side of East Falkland. They had achieved the ideal amphibious landing, taking the defenders by surprise and not losing a man.

After a week to consolidate the troops broke out of the bridgehead and captured Goose Green, but the speed of advance was hampered by lack of heavy-lift helicopters. Air attacks by Argentine Air Force Mirage fighter-bombers and Navy Skyhawks had sunk two frigates and damaged a number of ships in San Carlos Water, culminating in a massive series of raids on 25 May. Once again the Super Etendards were in action and their Exocets crippled the big transport SS *Atlantic Conveyor*. In the fire which engulfed her three Chinook and 12 Wessex helicopters were destroyed, as well as a vast quantity of military stores.

With only one Chinook surviving to carry the largest loads to the forward battle zone the decision was made to economize on carrying capacity by getting the Marines and Paras to make their way to Port Stanley on foot – the epic 'yomping' and 'tabbing' (as the soldiers' slang described it) which outflanked the Argentine defenses. Thereafter the pressure on Port Stanley was inexorable, marred only by a setback at Bluff Cove on 8 June. In a rash attempt to speed up the advance two landing ships, *Sir Galahad* and *Sir Tristram* moved detachments of the Welsh Guards into Bluff Cove in daylight. There they were caught by Skyhawks which set both ships on fire. In the confusion some 50 soldiers died and the *Sir Galahad* was so badly damaged that she was subsequently scuttled.

While the troops tightened their grip on Port Stanley the task force continued to supply them with their munitions and supplies, and the two carriers *Hermes* and *Invincible* flew off constant Sea Harrier strikes. On 31 May the Argentines made their last attempt to break the naval stranglehold. A force of six Skyhawks and two Super Etendards with their single remaining Exocet missile attempted to sink the *Invincible* but ran into a well prepared defense. The destroyer *Exeter* shot down two Skyhawks and in the confusion the Etendards were forced to make their attack at maximum range. The pilot who fired the Exocet mistook the still smoldering hulk of the *Atlantic Conveyor* for a carrier, and thus wasted the last of these deadly weapons.

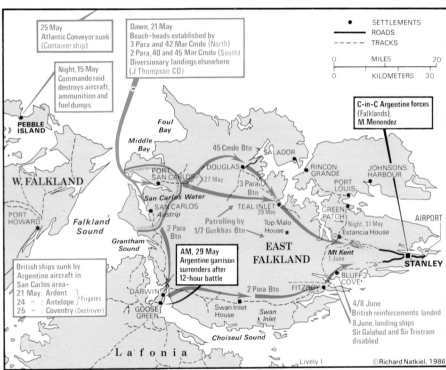

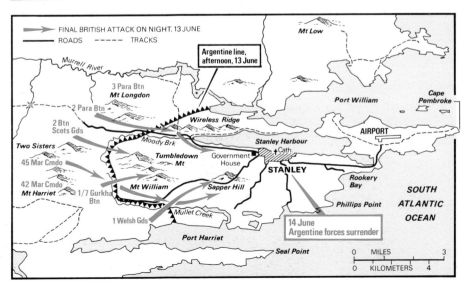

Above: Admiral Woodward, commander of the British Task Force.

The last major naval engagement was on the night of 11 June, when the destroyers *Exeter* and *Glamorgan* bombarded the Port Stanley defenses. As they moved out to sea an Exocet missile mounted on shore was fired at them. Fortunately the *Glamorgan* was alert and turned her stern to the approaching missile to minimize any damage. The missile did not explode but wrecked *Glamorgan's* helicopter hangar and after auxiliary engine compartment, killing 13 and injuring 14 men.

Port Stanley surrendered on 14 June. Casualties had been remarkably light, roughly 250 British and 1000 Argentines, about 75 percent lower than the British had estimated at the start of the campaign. The long-term future of the Falklands remains unsure but to prevent another Argentine attack the British have left a powerful garrison in the island and have built an airport capable of handling wide-bodied transport aircraft. Port Stanley's harbor facilities were also improved to permit RN warships to spend the winter 'down South.' The strategic value of the islands now obscures any considerations about the welfare of the 1800 inhabitants.

Not only the Royal Navy but other Western navies learned important lessons from the Falklands. The danger from sea-skimming missiles was already known but the need to deploy electronic countermeasures promptly was not widely understood. Nor was the risk from smoke in a damaged ship appreciated; new designs emphasize preventing smoke spreading and the elimination of materials which generate toxic smoke. Designs of anti-missile guns were under development before 1982 but now they are widely used.

On the positive side the British Sea Harrier STOVL (short take off/vertical landing) aircraft proved a match for Mirage IIIs capable of flying at twice the speed, and their heroic air defense decimated the Argentine Air Force and Navy strikes sent against the task force. The Argentine Air Force was handled bravely but failed to drive away the British; the Navy was handled very badly, and after the sinking of the *General Belgrano* returned to harbor.

The British devoted considerable energy to countering the threat from submarines, but out of four boats available to the Argentines one was already stripped for scrapping, one was sunk while running reinforcements into South Georgia and a third was laid up with machinery trouble. Claims were made that the fourth, the *San Luis* had torpedoed HMS *Invincible* with a 'dud' torpedo, but the submarine captain's own testimony revealed that he fired three torpedoes in 34 days, two at surface escorts and one at a submarine, all apparently at long range and without success. British submarines proved a major deterrent to Argentine surface forces, and also played a useful role in landing and recovering SAS and SBS patrols.

Below left: Argentinian 'near miss' in San Carlos Water.
Below: A Sea Harrier hovers above the landing pad on the *Atlantic Conveyor*. Both the British and US Navies are looking at ways to carry out similar conversions to container ships in the future.

Maritime Resources in the 1980s

Since 1977, when the International Conference on the Law of the Sea ruled that countries bordering on the sea have rights to minerals and fisheries off those coasts, the areas of national jurisdiction have changed dramatically.

The basic rights of free passage remain unchanged, although some states now insist on a 12-mile limit to their sovereignty, rather than the formerly preferred 3-mile limit. What has been created is the concept of an Exclusive Economic Zone (EEZ), an area in which the country bordering on that area has rights to the fishing, and any oil and minerals to be found. Any other nation wanting to exploit those rights may only do so with express permission from the sovereign state but normal shipping may pass through.

Problems arose immediately in narrow seas, for it is almost impossible to extend 200-mile limits when a near-neighbor is doing exactly the same. Thus Argentina immediately extended her claim to the Falklands (Malvinas) to include South Georgia, and a similar argument with Chile over the Beagle Channel brought the two countries to the point of war. Another point of friction is Sakhalin, an island which once formed part of the Japanese home islands but is now occupied by the Soviet Union.

Many areas were never in serious dispute before 1977 because they were considered worthless but today the immense value of offshore resources is recognized everywhere. Even without oil and natural gas, fisheries and whaling provide much needed food and

Above: Oil production and service platforms in the British sector of the North Sea, typical of the way continental shelf resources are being exploited.

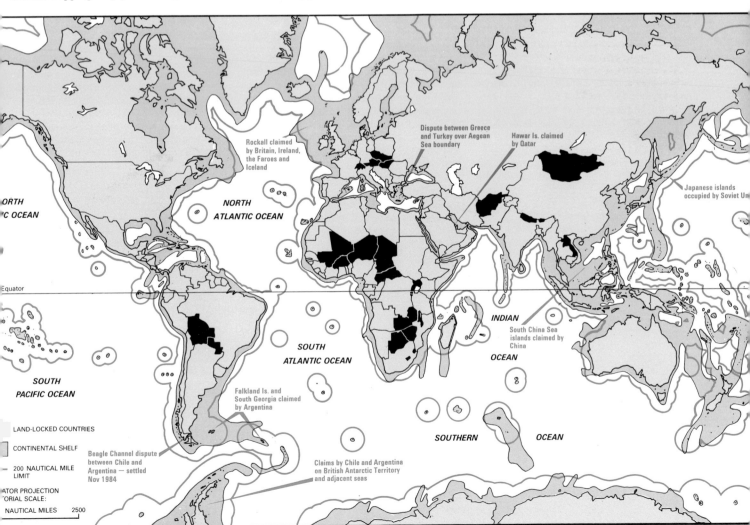

Rockall claimed by Britain, Ireland, the Faroes and Iceland

Dispute between Greece and Turkey over Aegean Sea boundary

Hawar Is. claimed by Qatar

Japanese islands occupied by Soviet Un

NORTH ... C OCEAN

NORTH ATLANTIC OCEAN

Equator

INDIAN

South China Sea islands claimed by China

SOUTH ATLANTIC OCEAN

OCEAN

SOUTH PACIFIC OCEAN

Falkland Is. and South Georgia claimed by Argentina

SOUTHERN OCEAN

LAND-LOCKED COUNTRIES

CONTINENTAL SHELF

200 NAUTICAL MILE LIMIT

Beagle Channel dispute between Chile and Argentina — settled Nov 1984

Claims by Chile and Argentina on British Antarctic Territory and adjacent seas

ATOR PROJECTION
ORIAL SCALE:

NAUTICAL MILES   2500

29 NOV 1984: CHILE GRANTED SOVEREIGNTY OVER PICTON, LENNOX AND NUEVA. BOUNDARY SOUTH OF CAPE HORN UNCHANGED

0   N MILES   100

RIO GALLEGOS
Strait of Magellan
CHILE
Tierra del Fuego
USHUAIA
STATEN I.
NUEVA
PICTON
LENNOX
Beagle Channel
Cape Horn

CLAIMED BY CHILE
CLAIMED BY ARGENTINA

0   NAUTICAL MILES   2000

ARGENTINA
CHILE
FALKLAND IS. (Brit.)
S. GEORGIA (Brit.)
To Britain
Antarctic Circle
Unclaimed   To Norway
South Pole
ANTARCTICA
To Australia
To Australia
To France

GREEK-TURKISH BOUNDARY
CONTINENTAL SHELF CLAIMED BY TURKEY

0   NAUTICAL MILES   200

BULGARIA
ISTANBUL
Sea of Marmara
SAMOTHRACE
Aegean Sea
LESBOS
TURKEY
IZMIR
ATHENS
CHIOS
SAMOS
GREECE
KOS
Crete
RHODES

ISLANDS OCCUPIED BY THE SOVIET UNION IN 1945, CLAIMED BY JAPAN PENDING A FINAL PEACE TREATY

0   NAUTICAL MILES   200

SOVIET UNION
Sakhalin
Sea of Japan
YUZHNO-SAKHALINSK
ETOROFU
La Perouse Strait
KUNASHIRI
SHIKOTAN
HABOMAI IS.
Hokkaido
SAPPORO
JAPAN   *PACIFIC OCEAN*
Honshu

fertilizers, and the possible value of 'nodules' of minerals on the seabed has only recently come to be appreciated.

One example is the tiny uninhabited rock north-west of Ireland known as Rockall. When it was formally annexed in the 1950s nobody questioned the right of Great Britain, who claimed to want a firing range for guided missiles. Only when offshore oil started to be found in the late 1970s did it occur to Denmark, Iceland and the Republic of Ireland that Rockall should belong to them.

Since the creation of exclusive economic zones numerous warships have been allocated to patrol the new zones, and for this task new types of offshore patrol vessels (OPVs) have been built or converted. They carry only light armament but many have sophisticated communications and position-fixing equipment to enable them to keep track of law-breakers. Foreign fishermen frequently fish in prohibited areas or use nets with too small a mesh, both offences which deplete fishing stocks, so fishing craft must be visited and examined. Countries which have seen their fish stocks depleted are particularly anxious to husband and rebuild these precious resources, and fines for transgressions are heavy.

Most of the disputes are settled by nego-

tiation and arbitration but occasionally the adversaries prefer more violent means. It was a dispute over Libya's attempt to close the Gulf of Sirte to international shipping which led to the destruction of two Libyan aircraft by the aircraft of the carrier USS *Nimitz* in 1981.

Below: **One aspect of the competition for maritime resources has been disputes over fishing rights. This picture shows a British trawler (right) and an Icelandic gunboat during the 'Cod War' in 1972.**

The NATO Alliance

The differences between the United States and the Soviet Union which were visible at the Yalta Conference in February 1945 were exacerbated by the end of hostilities, and Stalin decided to consolidate the Soviet Union's hold over Eastern Europe. In 1947 pro-Russian governments were set up in Bulgaria, Czechoslovakia, Hungary, Poland and Romania. Nor did the process stop there; an attempted Communist takeover of Greece started at the end of 1947, and in April 1948 the Soviets threatened to incorporate all three western sectors of Berlin into the new German Democratic Republic, which was finally established in October 1949.

It is easy to argue now that Stalin may not have been ready to launch a Third World War, or that he felt threatened by the American monopoly of nuclear technology, but the brutal repression of democratically-based governments and wholesale subversion, culminating in the heartless attempt to starve out West Berlin, thoroughly alarmed Western Europe, Great Britain and Canada, so that when the United States Government proposed a North Atlantic defensive treaty to 'contain' the Soviet Union, it found a willing audience.

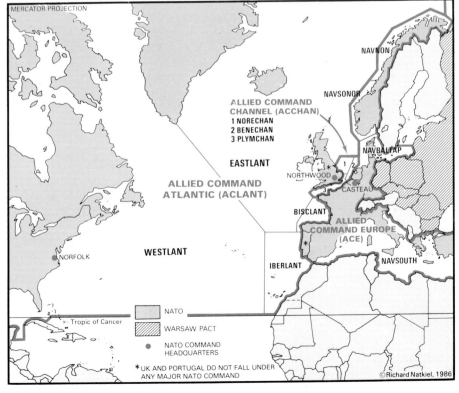

Above: The battleship *New Jersey* and the frigate *Meyer Kord*. Although built during World War II, the *New Jersey* has been refitted with modern weapons and serves with the US Pacific Fleet.

The North Atlantic Treaty Organization (NATO) was set up as a defensive alliance in 1949, on the presumption that an attack on one was an attack on all. A Supreme Headquarters of the Allied Powers in Europe (SHAPE) was set up at Fontainebleau in France, with a Supreme Allied Commander Europe to command the ground forces and a Supreme Allied Commander Atlantic (SACLANT) with responsibility for naval operations throughout the North Atlantic.

The operational area of NATO's naval forces is limited by the Tropic of Cancer to the south. SACLANT, always an American admiral, exercises command through a series of subordinate NATO commands such as C-in-C Eastern Atlantic (CINC-EASTLANT) who is always a British Royal Navy Admiral, Commodore Baltic Approaches (COMBALTAP) etc. National forces are allocated to NATO at an agreed level, but individual ships are rotated, so that it is impossible to talk of a 'NATO fleet.' In recent years, however, permanent forces have been established to improve cohesion and training: a Standing Naval Force Atlantic (STANAVFORLANT) composed of escorts, and its counterpart, the Standing Naval Force Mediterranean (STANAVFORMED), and a Standing Naval Force Channel (STANAVFORCHAN), made up of minesweepers.

The most impressive achievement of NATO's naval organization has undoubtedly been the creation of a common-language signalling system; ships in a multi-national force now talk to each other and operate under a truly international command structure. Less obvious is NATO's continuing drive to achieve standardization, not only of weaponry but such basic items as couplings for refuelling hoses. Many would say that NATO's greatest contribution to the good of the alliance has been the spread of expertise and experience, from the bigger and more experienced operators down to the lesser navies.

The sophisticated level of cooperation now being achieved is demonstrated by the NATO Frigate Requirement for 1990. Known as NFR 90, this is an ambitious

scheme to design a common frigate to meet American, German, British, Dutch and Italian needs for an ocean escort after the year 1990. The original objective, a single design capable of being built in large numbers, has undergone considerable modification as time passes, but the NFR 90 team should achieve at least a common hull which can accept a range of NATO-approved weapons and sensors, varied to suit each navy's needs.

In the Mediterranean command is exercised by C-in-C South (CINCSOUTH), with his HQ at Naples. Although the alliance has lost some of the drive which characterized its early days, it has proved itself strong enough

Above: **The British carrier** *Illustrious* **operates Harrier jump jets and Sea King helicopters and is one of the most powerful ships in the present-day Royal Navy.**

to survive a war between two member-states, Greece and Turkey. Nor has it inhibited individual states from pursuing their own national aims when necessary. Many of its senior planners, both serving and retired, claim that the Tropic of Cancer is too restrictive a boundary to NATO's operating area, but political support for such a widening of the alliance's sphere of operations is at best lukewarm.

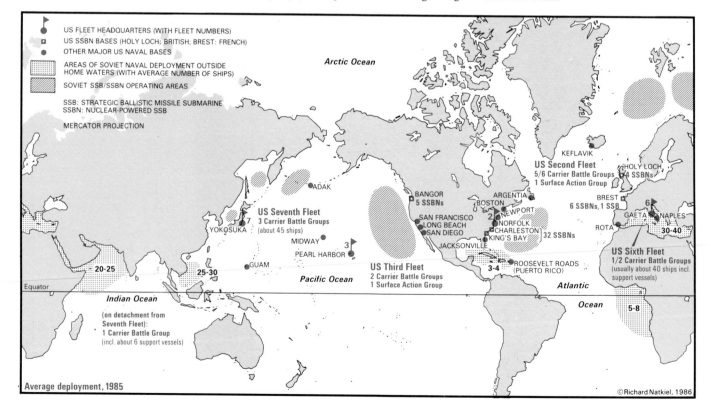

US FLEET HEADQUARTERS (WITH FLEET NUMBERS)
US SSBN BASES (HOLY LOCH; BRITISH; BREST: FRENCH)
OTHER MAJOR US NAVAL BASES
AREAS OF SOVIET NAVAL DEPLOYMENT OUTSIDE HOME WATERS (WITH AVERAGE NUMBER OF SHIPS)
SOVIET SSB/SSBN OPERATING AREAS

SSB: STRATEGIC BALLISTIC MISSILE SUBMARINE
SSBN: NUCLEAR-POWERED SSB

MERCATOR PROJECTION

Arctic Ocean

KEFLAVIK

US Second Fleet
5/6 Carrier Battle Groups
1 Surface Action Group

HOLY LOCH
4 SSBNs

ADAK

BANGOR
5 SSBNs

ARGENTIA
BOSTON
NEWPORT
NORFOLK
CHARLESTON
KING'S BAY

BREST
6 SSBNs, 1 SSB

6
GAETA NAPLES

US Seventh Fleet
3 Carrier Battle Groups
(about 45 ships)

YOKOSUKA

7

SAN FRANCISCO
LONG BEACH
SAN DIEGO

32 SSBNs

ROTA

30-40

MIDWAY

3

JACKSONVILLE

PEARL HARBOR

US Third Fleet
2 Carrier Battle Groups
1 Surface Action Group

ROOSEVELT ROADS
(PUERTO RICO)

US Sixth Fleet
1/2 Carrier Battle Groups
(usually about 40 ships incl.
support vessels)

20-25

25-30

GUAM

Pacific Ocean

3-4

Atlantic

Equator

Indian Ocean

(on detachment from
Seventh Fleet):
1 Carrier Battle Group
(incl. about 6 support vessels)

Ocean

5-8

Average deployment, 1985

©Richard Natkiel, 1986

The Rise of the Soviet Navy

Since the end of the Second World War the growth of the Soviet Navy has been the most dramatic single phenomenon in maritime affairs. In 1945 the US Navy, even without the substantial fleets of its allies, had unquestioned superiority over the Soviet Navy, but since the early 1970s that superiority has been seriously eroded, to the point where the growth of the Soviet Navy is seen as a serious threat to Western seapower.

The Soviet Navy was in a very poor state in 1945. Its shipyards and supporting factories were in ruins, while the mighty fleet planned by Stalin before World War II had largely been destroyed to avoid capture. Clearly Stalin perceived the need to rebuild the navy as soon as possible, but the priority had to be given to the army, who would bear the brunt of any Western assault. The navy's role was seen to be coastal defense, with a view to preventing hostile forces from approaching

the Soviet heartland, and thereby turning the Army's flanks.

The Soviet fleet therefore built in considerable haste a force of motor torpedo boats and light escorts to protect inshore waters, and a force of small (coastal) submarines and medium-sized submarines to deny the approaches to hostile forces. Meanwhile the shipyards and dockyards were being rebuilt and brought up to date, partly with the help of captured German technology. No attempt was made to build a battlefleet but a large program of cruisers was started in the late 1940s, with a view to interrupting Western seaborne commerce.

Stalin's death in 1953 brought an end to this plan, for shortly after his arrival on the scene, the new ruler Nikita Khrushchev initiated a radical change of policy. In 1956 he replaced Stalin's appointee with Admiral Sergei Gorshkov as Commander in Chief.

Under this dynamic officer's leadership large building programs were stopped and the fleet was purged of elderly pre-war veterans.

Gorshkov and his planners were worried about the preponderance of Western aircraft carriers, but recognizing the appalling difficulties in trying to build a comparable fleet of carriers, they turned to long-range missiles as a means of countering Western seapower. The first *raketny kreyser* or 'rocket cruisers' appeared in 1962, powerful ships intended to destroy aircraft carriers and other surface combatants by means of long-range surface-to-surface missiles. What was even more significant was that these ships were clearly intended to operate on the high seas. Clearly Gorshkov had approval at the highest level to move away from the purely coastal role envisioned in the 1950s.

Substantial resources were devoted to the anti-carrier role, and the next major step was

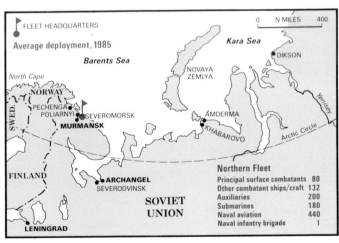

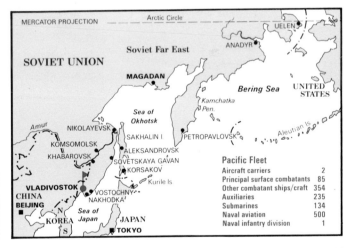

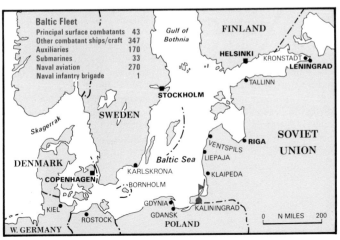

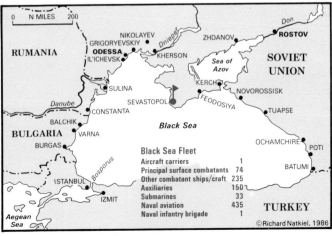

© Richard Natkiel, 1986

to devise a means of firing anti-ship missiles from submerged submarines. The new strategic plan worked, to the extent that the US Navy has given up any idea of using carrier-launched bombers to attack Soviet land targets with nuclear weapons. A large investment has also been made in nuclear attack submarines to interdict American power-projection in time of war.

The biggest single problem for the Soviets continues to be the speed with which the United States can deploy advanced technology. When the US Navy first deployed the Polaris submarine-launched ballistic missile system in the mid-1960s the Soviet Union had no alternative but to develop its own version. Only then did Soviet priorities begin to switch from anti-carrier tactics to anti-submarine tactics.

To extend anti-submarine warfare capability from waters near the coasts of the Soviet Union to mid-ocean it was necessary to build two helicopter carriers, the *Leningrad* and *Moskva*. These were of limited value, and they were followed by four much larger hybrid cruiser-carriers, the *Kiev* class. These 40,000-tonners deploy not only anti-submarine helicopters but also VSTOL strike aircraft. In the early 1980s it was revealed by Western intelligence that a 70,000-ton nuclear carrier is under construction. Progress has been slow, but the existence of this large combatant confirms the intention to create a large surface fleet capable of at least denying certain areas of ocean to Western forces. Admiral Gorshkov retired at the end of 1985 but his successor, Admiral Chernavin, seems likely to continue the existing programs.

The Soviet navy remains an enigma. There is evidence of considerable technical ability but equally convincing evidence of a con-

Above: The Soviet research ship *Kosmonaut Yuri Gagarin* mainly operates in support of the Soviet space program.

siderable shortfall in practical experience of the exercise of seapower. A regrettable tendency on the part of Western intelligence to over-estimate Soviet capability, and particularly to 'worst-case' the West at the same time as 'best-casing' the Soviets has led to alarmist and misleading claims about the Soviets overtaking the West. In fact the '600-ship Navy' program initiated by the Reagan Administration headed off any likelihood of the Soviets overtaking the US Navy in either quantity or quality. On the other hand, the powerful Soviet Northern and Pacific Fleets have put an end to the West's monopoly of the exercise of seapower.

Maritime Trade in the 1980s

In the 1980s the principal shipping routes remain unchanged from those of earlier in the century but the whole pattern of world-wide shipping has been changed by the impact of air travel.

The big ocean liner has disappeared from the North Atlantic and the Pacific, and such big passenger ships as remain in service operate as cruise liners, taking passengers to such exotic vacation areas as the Caribbean and the Greek Islands. There is no longer any requirement for scheduled passenger and mail services from Europe to South Africa or Australia; in today's busy world no traveller can afford the time needed for a long ocean passage.

The virtual extinction of scheduled passenger traffic led many to predict that air transport would take over entirely from shipping but the expected takeover has not happened. The reason lies in the fact that although passengers are best handled by aircraft, heavy cargoes are not. Crude oil and grain, for example, cannot be handled in economic quantities by transport aircraft. This conundrum affects the projection of military power as well. To cite one vivid example: in the 1973 Yom Kippur War between Israel and Egypt and Syria, the United States had to use its Air Force's entire fleet of C-5 Galaxy transport aircraft to deliver 50 tanks to Israel, whereas one ship carried replacement 105mm ammunition for the entire Israeli tank force.

Aircraft, then, did not drive big ships from the oceans as predicted, but another far-reaching development has totally transformed the pattern of world shipping. Containers are standard-sized steel cargo-carrying units intended to be pre-packed with cargo, then shipped by rail or road to ports, where they are then loaded onto specially designed container ships. The idea behind container shipping is to avoid expensive 'breaking bulk' of cargoes at either end of the voyage. Containers can be speedily loaded and unloaded by gantry cranes, eliminating the need for warehouse storage and reducing opportunities for theft or accidental damage.

The specialized container ships are, of course, restricted to using port facilities tailored to handle the big ISO (International Standards Organisation) containers. This has driven away the old general-purpose cargo carrier, the 'tramp' which went from port to port picking up cargoes wherever she could. But container ships are only economical to operate on fixed routes between container terminals, and so the general-purpose cargo vessel has found a new role, 'feeding' and distributing cargoes to lesser ports.

Specialization is now a permanent part of the shipping scene, with giant tankers shuttling from oil-producing areas such as the Arabian Gulf to refineries in Europe and America, and carriers of grain and ore performing similar missions for other bulk cargoes. A variant on the container theme is the 'Roll-on Roll-off' or Ro-Ro ship, which embarks large road vehicles, some towing containers between ports to speed distribution by road.

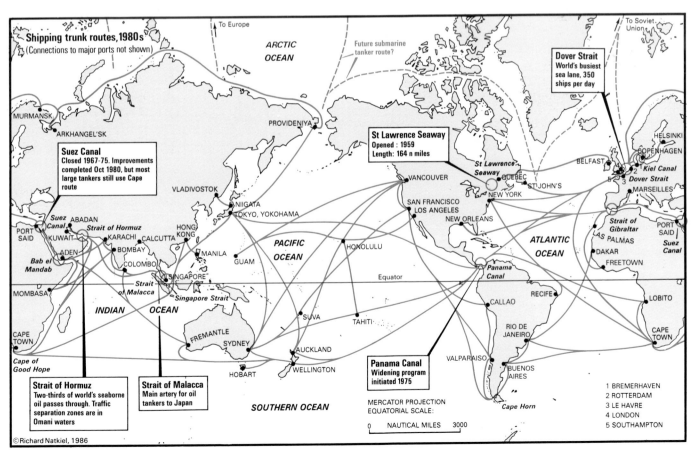

The former indifference to maritime trade shown by the Soviet Union is now a thing of the past. Across the world's shipping routes Soviet merchant ships of all types compete with Western and non-aligned shipping, undercutting freight rates and earning much-needed foreign currency for the Soviet economy.

Another phenomenon of the 1980s is a growing lawlessness on the high seas, reminiscent more of the nineteenth century. Tankers in the Straits of Hormuz have been attacked indiscriminately by both Iraqi and Iranian aircraft during the Gulf War, and anonymously-laid mines have damaged shipping in the Gulf of Suez in recent years. Although the Western powers take limited action to protect their shipping against such outrages the machinery for international intervention shows no sign of being created.

Although the world for a time seemed to be drifting into two camps, one Western or non-aligned and the other Communist or Soviet-dominated, the pattern emerging in the mid-1980s is different in major respects. The real division which is emerging is between the rich nations of the world and the so-called Third World of poor nations. The rapid rise of oil prices in the 1970s showed that the developed nations had become too reliant on oil, but it also showed the fragility of Third World economies; if the rich nations became impoverished they would no longer be able to buy the Third World's raw materials and agricultural produce. Another development has been the growing importance of trans-Pacific trade between the countries of the Pacific rim – a development reflected in the projection chosen for the accompanying map with the Pacific at the center.

This new set of factors makes the future uncertain, but maritime trade remains the central nervous system of all the major trading nations, without which nothing can function.

Above right: A typical container ship, the 18,500 ton *Contender Argent* of the Sea Containers' fleet.
Right: With the rise of the container ship the traditional ports in many countries have been overtaken by new purpose-built facilities. The photograph shows the container terminal at the British port of Felixstowe.

GLOSSARY

Cross references to other entries are noted in *italic* type.

ABDA Command: American-British-Dutch-Australian, a command organisation set up by these four countries to control operations against the Japanese in the East Indies in World War II, soon superseded in the light of early Japanese success.

AMC: Armed Merchant *Cruiser*, a merchant ship, most commonly a passenger liner, converted in wartime for patrol duties.

ANZAC: Australia and New Zealand Army Corps, originally a formation established for the Gallipoli operation in 1915 but subsequently used to describe troops of either nation.

Asdic: The submarine detection apparatus now generally known as *sonar*, originally from Allied Submarine Detection Investigation Committee, an Anglo-French organisation established in 1918.

ASV: Air-to-Surface-Vessel, the official designation of various British types of airborne radar.

Bark (also **barque**): A three-masted sailing vessel square rigged on fore and main masts, lateen rigged on the mizzen mast.

Battle turnaway: A maneuver employed by the German fleet in World War I, involving a nearly simultaneous 180 degree turn by each ship in the *line of battle*.

Battlecruiser: A variant of the *battleship* equally well-armed but faster because less heavily armored.

Battleship: A warship of the largest class. The term derives from the related expressions *ship of the line* and *line of battle(ship)*.

Beam: Either (1) the width of a ship or (2) to the side, rather than ahead or behind.

Blackwall frigate: A type of merchant ship built in Britain in the early 19th century.

Caravel: The type of ship most commonly used by the great Spanish and Portuguese explorers of the 15th and 16th centuries. They had no standard size or arrangement of sails but generally had three masts and were between 80 and 100 feet long.

Carronade: A short-barrel cannon of heavy caliber widely employed by the British Navy around the time of the Napoleonic Wars, from the foundry at Carron, Scotland, where they were first made.

Chronometer: In maritime navigation a ship's *longitude* can be calculated by comparing local time, which can be checked by astronomical observation, with Greenwich mean time. A very accurate clock or chronometer is needed for this method and the first examples were produced by John Harrison in the mid 18th century.

Clipper: A type of fast merchant sailing ship, faster than previous designs, widely built in the mid 19th century. With a large crew and a small cargo capacity they were expensive to operate and were soon overtaken by steam.

Codenames of Major Operations

    Anvil: Allied invasion of southern France, 1944. Because of a suspected breach of security this was changed to *Dragoon*.

    Dragoon: see *Anvil*.

    Drumroll: German submarine attack on shipping off US East Coast, 1942.

    Dynamo: Dunkirk evacuation, 1940.

    Husky: Invasion of Sicily, 1943.

    Neptune: The naval component of the Normandy invasion in, 1944.

    Overlord: The overall plan for the Normandy invasion, 1944.

    Pedestal: The last major convoy operation to bring supplies to Malta, 1942.

    Roundup: The overall Anglo-American plan for the European theater in WWII, calling for a build-up of forces for an eventual full scale invasion of western Europe.

    Sealion: The abortive German plan for the invasion of Britain, 1940.

    Shingle: The Allied landings at Anzio, 1944.

    Torch: The Anglo-American invasion of North Africa, 1942.

    Watchtower: The US landings on Guadalcanal, 1942.

    Wilfred: The British plan to land in Norway, 1940.

Cog: The characteristic North European merchant vessel of the Middle Ages.

Contraband: In maritime law those articles of a warlike nature which a belligerent nation can prevent reaching an enemy by way of neutral shipping. In modern times contraband has been judged to include virtually any commodity.

Convoy: A group of merchant ships sailing together, (usually) escorted by friendly warships.

Coppering: Covering a wooden ship's underwater surface with thin sheets of copper to prevent the formation of marine growths which would damage the ship's structure and slow its sailing.

Corvette: Originally a small sailing warship designed for scouting and patrol duties, the term was revived during World War II to describe the smallest class of anti-submarine escort.

Crossing the 'T': A battle maneuver in which one line of ships crosses ahead and at right angles to the enemy line enabling all the ships of the first unit to concentrate their fire on a few of the enemy.

Cruiser: In the sailing ship era synonomous with *frigate*. In the modern era a warship of the size next smaller than a *battleship* ranging roughly from 5000-15,000 tons.

Dead reckoning: The method of calculating a ship's position by attempting to measure course and speed. This is inaccurate because it is difficult to take into account winds and currents which affect speed over the ground as opposed to speed through the water.

Destroyer: A type of warship smaller than a *cruiser* designed to protect larger warships and merchant ships from submarine or torpedo boat attack.

Dreadnought: A general term for the type of *battleship* built by all navies following the launch of HMS *Dreadnought*, the first of the type, in 1906. Previous battleships had carried a combination of light, medium and heavy guns. Dreadnoughts discarded the medium calibers for an 'all big gun' arrangement which made control of long-range shooting easier.

Escort carrier: An aircraft carrying warship smaller than the standard or fleet aircraft carrier. Normally used for supporting landing operations or for anti-submarine work.

Fighting Instructions: The standing orders laid down by the British Admiralty governing the conduct of battles. Introduced during the seventeenth century to counteract the indiscipline of many fleet and ships' commanders of the time, revised forms continued in use until Napoleonic times and often had the effect of preventing tactical initiative in battle.

First rate: During the eighteenth century most navies introduced systems of classifying or 'rating' warships by size. The Royal Navy had six 'rates', first rates being the largest. In 1800 a first rate was a ship of 100 or more guns.

Frigate: In the sailing ship era a warship of 30-40 guns, faster than the larger *ships of the line* and used for patrol or scout duties. The term was revived during World War II and is still current for the class of general purpose warship smaller than the destroyer.

Galleass: A type of warship designed to be a compromise between the sail-powered *galleon*, suited for long journeys and bad weather, and the oared *galley*, for battle maneuverability and speed.

Galleon: A type of ship developed in the late fifteenth century with better sailing qualities than previous designs because of the removal of the high forecastle previously usual.

Galley: An oared fighting ship used mainly in the Mediterranean from the earliest times to the end of the 18th century. Galleys carried a fairly simple arrangement of sails for long passages but would use only oars in battle.

Galliot: A smaller type of *galley*.

Grand Fleet: The main, home-based, British fleet of World War I.

Great Marianas Turkey Shoot: The name given by men of the US Navy to the Battle of the Philippine Sea (1944) because of the ease with which many Japanese aircraft were destroyed.

High Seas Fleet: The main German fleet in World War I.

Huff-Duff: From the initials HF/DF for High Frequency Direction Finder, the type of radio direction finders introduced by the British during World War II to help track submarines by their radio reports. Because these could be made small enough to fit in escort ships operating with convoys they were an important anti-submarine weapon.

In ordinary: A modern equivalent might be 'mothballed'. In the sailing ship era it was the practice to take warships out of service between campaigns and remove and store much of their equipment. Such ships were said to be 'in ordinary'.

Ironclad: The early term for an armored warship, from the initial practice of fitting iron plates over the main wooden structure of the ship.

Latitude: One of the co-ordinates used to describe a position on the surface of the earth. Latitude describes the position north or south of the equator and for navigators can be calculated by measurement of the midday altitude of the sun. (see also *Longitude*)

Leeward: The direction to which the wind is blowing at sea or the side of a ship sheltered from the wind. The opposite of *windward*.

Lend-Lease: The arrangements enacted by the US during WWII to give military and other aid to allied nations without expecting any immediate payment.

Letter of marque: A commission or permit issued by a government or monarch to the captain of a privately-owned ship allowing the ship to act against enemy vessels. Without a letter of marque such conduct would legally be piracy. In fact letters of marque were widely abused and their owners often little better than pirates.

Line of battle/Line ahead: The 'single file' formation adopted almost universally from the mid 17th century for a fleet going into combat. Only the larger vessels would take a place in the line hence the terms *ship of the line* and (line of) *battle-ship*.

Longitude: See also *latitude*. Longitude describes the position east or west of the prime meridian, a notional north-south line running through Greenwich in England. Longitude can be calculated if an accurate clock is available to compare local time with Greenwich time. While latitude could be calculated relatively easily it was not until the development of the *chronometer* that it became possible to make an accurate check of a ship's position during a long voyage. Longitude can also be calculated with the help of observations of the moon but accurate tables for this method were not produced until the eighteenth century also. Other methods have since been developed.

Monitor: From the USS *Monitor* (1862), a type of warship in which a gun turret or turrets would be fitted on a raft hull. Because of their small superstructure such ships were difficult to damage in battle but they were equally very vulnerable to heavy weather.

Mulberry harbors: Two artificial harbors constructed by the Anglo-American forces to support the Normandy Invasion in 1944.

NATO: North Atlantic Treaty Organisation, an alliance established in 1948 to co-ordinate Europe and North America's defense against potential Soviet aggression.

OPEC: Organisation of Petroleum Exporting Countries.

Orders in Council: The administrative devices used by British governments at various times to legalise departures from normal peacetime practice as in blockade or seizure of foreign shipping.

Panzerschiff: Literally armored ship, a type of vessel built in Germany in the 1930s and designed to circumvent the strictures of the Versailles Treaty which ended World War I which aimed to restrict the fighting power of future German warships. In part because illegal details of their construction were concealed from foreign observers the *panzerschiffe* seemed to be particularly powerful for their small size and were hence known as 'pocket battleships.'

Port: The left side of a ship or that direction.

Quadrant: Any of several types of navigational instrument used for measuring the altitude of a celestial body. The sextant, available since the mid eighteenth century, superseded the quadrant and is still used in navigation.

Q-ships: In an attempt to counter U-Boat losses during WWI the British fitted concealed armament to a number of merchant ships hoping that submarines could be lured into making an attack on the surface and be destroyed. Such ships were Q-ships but the tactic was by no means an unqualified success.

Ram, ramming: A ram is a sharp reinforced spur fitted on the bows of a ship, often partly or completely underwater, which can be driven into an enemy vessel to hole it and sink it.

Roaring forties: The area of the southern oceans between 40 and 50 degrees South, known, particularly in the sailing ship era, for the strong prevailing westerly winds.

SAS: Special Air Service.

SBS: Special Boat Service.

Seabees: From the initials CB for Construction Battalion, members of the US Navy during WWII who accompanied amphibious operations in the Pacific and built base facilities ashore wherever landings were made.

Ship of the line: see *line of battle*.

Sonar: A device for detecting a submerged submarine (see also *Asdic*), the name being derived from SOund Navigation And Ranging.

STOVL: see *V/STOL*.

Starboard: The right hand side of a ship or that direction.

Tokyo Express: The name given by US Marines and seamen to the Japanese ships which made night passages with supplies to the Japanese forces fighting on Guadalcanal in 1942.

Torpedo boats: Any of various types of vessel built from the time of the development of the torpedo in the late 19th century and armed principally with that weapon. Torpedo boats ranged in size from small launches to vessels almost of destroyer size and could pose a threat to the largest and most powerful ship.

Unrestricted submarine warfare: The situation prevailing when submarines were ordered to sink merchant ships of an enemy without enquiry regarding the nature of the cargo carried and without offering passengers or crew any warning before the attack. Before the advent of the submarine, International Law laid down that before a merchant ship was sunk, the attacking warship had first to make sure that the cargo was of a warlike nature and also to make provision for crew and passengers to reach land safely.

V/STOL: Vertical/Short Take Off and Landing also *STOVL* and other variants.

Washington Naval Treaty: An agreement made by the principal naval powers in 1922 and extended at London in 1930 to limit the size and numbers of warships in various classes that each power could build or maintain. The treaties became widely disregarded as WWII approached.

Windward: The direction from which the wind is blowing. Opposite of *leeward*.

Wolfpack tactics: The tactics developed by the German U-Boat command in the early part of WWII for making attacks on convoys. Before the development of more sophisticated forms of radar in the middle years of the war it was particularly difficult to detect a submarine on the surface at night. The U-Boats therefore aimed to penetrate inside the convoy formation on the surface at night, sink a few ships and escape in the resulting confusion. The US Navy later developed a modified form of this tactic for operations against the Japanese in the Pacific.

INDEX

Page numbers in *italics* refer to illustrations

ABDA Command, World War II 208, 209-10
Aboukir Bay, Battle of, 1798: 86, 90
Abyssinia 140, 170
*Achilles,*HMNZS, light cruiser 177, 178
Acre, bombardment of, 1840: 106
Actium, Battle of, 31 BC: 17, 18
Admiral Graf Spee (panzerschiff) 177-8, 183
Admiralty (British) 62, 104, 105, 148, 151, 154,
   157, 162, 180, 182, 183
   Fighting Instructions 60, 71, 75, 80
Aegates Insulae, Battle of, 241 BC: 15
Agamemnon, HMS, battleship 158
Agricola, Gnaeus Julius 18
Agrippa, Marcus Vipsanius 17, 18
air transport 249
Ajax, HMS, light cruiser 177, 178, 192
Akagi, carrier 214
Alabama, Confederate raider 117, *118*
Alabama, USS, Battleship *171*
Alaska 139
Alcibiades *13*, 14
Alexander, the Great 9, 10
Alexandria 20, 32, 106, 170, 192
   bombardment of, 1882: 125
Alexius Comnenus, Emperor 29, 30
Alfred, King 27
Algeria, Algerians 99, 102, 140, 191, 234
Algiers 102, 194
   bombardment of, 1816 102
American Civil War 55, 110, 111, 117-22, *118,*
   120-21, 127, 139
American colonies 46, 69, 80-82, 111, 127
American Revolution 74, 80-82
Amherst, Major General Jeffery 73
amphibious operations 158, 174-5, 195, 196, 200,
   202, 224, 234, 241
Amundsen, Roald 104
Anglo-Dutch Wars
   First, 1652-4: 59-60, *60*
   Second, 1664-7: *56,* 61-2, *61-2*
   Third, 1672-4: 64-5, *64-5*
Angospotami, Battle of, 405 BC: 14
Antarctic exploration 77, 104
Arabi Pasha 125
Arabs 19, 20, 21, *21,* 34, 54, 234
Arctic Convoys, in World War II 174-5, 197-9, *198*
Arctic exploration 27, 105
Argentina, Argentine forces 240-42, 243
Arginusae, Battle of 406 BC: 14
Ark Royal, HMS, carrier 190, 192
Atahualpa, Inca ruler 43
Athens, Athenians 11-12, 13-14
Atlantic, Battle of 183-8, 200
Augustus, Emperor 17, *17,* 18
Australia 99, 110, 126, 170, 207, 210, 211, 218
   discovery and exploration of 52-3, 77
Austria-Hungary 127
Austrian navy 123-4, 148

Baffin, William 51
balance of power policy 99
Balboa, Vasco Nunez de 43
Baltic Sea 116, *116,* 180
   Baltic Trade 46, 81, 91
   Swedish Empire and the Baltic 58
Baltimore 97, 98
Barclay, Capt Robert 97
Barents, Willem 51, *51,* 111
Barents Sea, Battle of, 1942: 197-8
Barham, Admiral Lord 93, 93-4
Barham, HMS, battleship 192

Battle of the Masts, 655: 21
Bayeux Tapestry 28, *29*
Beachy Head, Battle of, 1690: 66, *67*
Beatty, Vice Admiral Sir David 151, 152, 156, 157,
   160, 160-62
Belfast, HMS, cruiser 199
Bellinghausen, Thaddeus Fabian von 104
Bey, Admiral Erich 198
Bismarck, battleship 185, 189, *190*
   sinking of 189-90
Bismarck Archipelago 219
Black Sea 113, 114-15, *114-15,* 116, 158
   Black Sea Trade 10, 14, 32
Blake, Admiral Robert 59, 60, *60*
blockade
   in Napoleonic Wars 86, 88, 93
   in War of 1812 96
   in American Civil War 117, 118
   of Central Powers in World War I 148
Blücher, SMS, 156, 157, *157*
Bomarsund fortress, Baltic Sea 116, *116*
Borough, Stephen 51
Boscawen, Admiral Edward 73, 75-6
Bouvet, French battleship 158
Boyne, Battle of the, 1690: 66
Bradley, General Omar *202*
Breslau, and *Goeben,* pursuit of 150
Brian Boru, King of Munster 27
Britain
   end of Roman Britain 24
   commercial expansion of 54, 69
   in American War of Independence 80-82
   see also England, Great Britain
Brock, General 97
Brueys, Admiral François 90
Bucentaure, 80-gun ship 95
Buchanan, Admiral Franklin, CSN 122
Burma 208
Burrough, Admiral H 193
Byng, Admiral John 71-2, *72*
Byzantium 18, 24, 26, 29, 30, 31, 32
   Maritime Empire of 20-21

Cabot, John 45
Calabria, Battle of, 1940: 191
Calder, Sir Robert 93
Callaghan, Rear Admiral D J, USN 216-17
Camperdown, Battle of, 1797: 86
Canada 51, 70, 72, 72-4, 75, 76, 77, 96, 97, 99, 126,
   139
Canada, HMS, battleship *163*
Canberra, SS *240*
Cannae, Battle of, 216 BC: 16
Canopus, HMS, battleship 153, 154, *154*
Cape Artemision, Battle of, 480 BC: 11
Cape Barfleur, Battle of, 1692: 66-7
Cape Engaño, Battle of, 1944: 227
Cape Finisterre, action off, 1805: 93, *93*
Cape Matapan, Battle of, 1941: 192
Cape of Good Hope 40, 46, 77, 78, 87, 170
Cape St Vincent, Battle of, 1797: 86, 89, 90
Capellan, Baron van de 102
Caroline Islands 170
Carthage, Carthaginians 9, 10, 15-16, 21
Catesby Jones, Lieutenant ap, USN 98
Cavour, Count 115
Cervantes, Don Miguel de 48
Cervera, Admiral Pascual 130-31
Challenger, HMS 104
Chancellor, Richard 51
Charles II, King 61
Charles V, Emperor 54
Chauncey, Captain Isaac, USN 97
Chesapeake Bay, Battle of, 1781: 80
Chesma, Battle of, 1769: 79
China, Chinese 19, 34, 40, 107, 109, 126, 140
   and Mongol Empire 36, *36,* 37
   Commercial Empire in 14th-17th centuries 37
   conflict with Japan 109, 128, 134
   navy 128
   Opium Wars and China Trade *107,* 107-9, *109*
chronometer (Harrison's) 77
Churchill, Winston 146, *147,* 158, 180, 191
Clerke, Captain James 78
clipper ships *107,* 110, 127
Clive, Robert 70
Cnut, King 27
Cochrane, Vice Admiral Sir Alexander 96, 97, 98

Cockburn, Rear Admiral Sir George 96
Codrington, Admiral Sir Edward 103
Collingwood, Admiral Lord 94, 95
Collinson, Captain Richard 105
colonial empires and expansion 69-70, 99, 126,
   140, 170-71
Columbus, Christopher 41-2, *41, 42*
combined operations 74, 158 *see also* amphibious
      operations
commerce raiders 177
   in American Civil War 117-18, *118,* 127
   in World War I 148
   in World War II 177, 185, 189
Conflans, Admiral de 76
Constans II, Emperor 20-21
Constantinople 20, 21, *21,* 26, 31, 34, 79
Continental System 86, 95
convoys 148, *166,* 166-8, 183-8
   Arctic convoys in World War II 197-9, *198*
   in Mediterranean in World War II 192-3
Cook, Captain James 73, 77, 77-8, *78,* 104
Copenhagen, Battle of, 1801: 91, *91,* 93
Coral Sea, Battle of, 1942: 211-12, *212,* 213, 215
Cordoba, Admiral Don Jose de 89
Cornwall, HMS, armored cruiser 154
Coronel and Falklands, Battles of, 1914: 153-4,
   154
Cradock, Admiral Sir Christopher 153
Crete 8, 21, 192
Crimean War 113-16, *113-16*
Crusades *22-3,* 30-31, *31,* 32
Cuba 41, 127, 130-31, 132, 139
Cuddalore, action at, 1782: 83
Cumberland, HMS, heavy cruiser 177, 178
Cunningham, Admiral Sir Andrew *175,* 191, 192
Curzola Island, Battle of, 1298: 32
Cutty Sark, clipper ship 110
Cyprus 31, 48

Dahlgren, Rear Admiral John A, USN 117
Dampier, Captain William 46, 52, *53*
Danes 25, 27, 28
Dardanelles 158
Darius I 11, *11*
Davis, Jefferson 117
Davis, John 43, 51
Deane, Richard 60
de Lesseps, Ferdinand 139
Demosthenes 13
Denmark 58, 61, 86, 90, 93
Derfflinger, SMS 156, 160, 162
de Ruyter, Admiral Michiel 61, 62, 64-5
de Ruyter, cruiser 209
d'Estrées, Comte 65
Deutschland (later *Lützow*), *panzerschiff* 177, 178
Dewey, Commodore George, USN 132, *132*
de With, Witte 59, 60
Dias, Bartholomeu 40
Discovery, HMS 78
Dogger Bank, Battle of, 1915: 156-7
Dogger Bank Incident, 1904: 136
Dönitz, Admiral Karl 179, 183, 184, 186, 187,
   188, 198
Doorman, Admiral Karel 209
Doria, Lamba, Luciano, Pietro 32
Dorsetshire, HMS, cruiser 190
Douglas, Captain Charles 81
Drake, Sir Francis 45, *45,* 49
Dresden, SMS, light cruiser 153, 154
Drocour, Chevalier de 73
Duke of York, HMS, battleship 199
Duncan, Admiral Viscount 86
Dundas, Vice Admiral 116
Dunkirk, evacuation of 182
Dupleix, Joseph François 70
d'Urville, Dumont 104
Dutch *see* Holland
Dutch East India Company 40, 46, *46,* 52, 53
Dutch East Indies 52, 53, 99, 207, 208, 210
Dutch West India Company 46

Eagle, HMS, carrier 191, 193
East Africa 40, 55, 126, 170
East India Company, 40, 69, 70, 90, 107
Ecnomus, Battle of, 256 BC: 16
Egypt, Egyptians 8, 17, 20, 103, 106, 125, 140,
   170, 234, 238, 249
Eighty Years War, 1568: 46
Eisenhower, General Dwight D 200, *202*

Elizabeth I, Queen 45, *48*
Endeavour 77
England, English 35, 41
   American colonies 46, 69, 80-82, 111, 127
   Anglo-Dutch Wars 59-65
   Danes, Saxons, Vikings in 27
   English Succession War, 1688-91: 66-7
   European trade of 33
   exploration by 45, 51, 77-8, 105
   Norman Conquest of 28
   rivalry with France 69-76, 80-83, 86-91, 93-5
   rivalry with Spain 49, 59
   slave trade and 54, 68
   see also Britain, Great Britain
Enterprise, USS, carrier WWII *175*, 206, 214, 215, 216
Enterprise, USS, nuclear carrier *235*
Ericsson, John 119
Eritrea 140, 170, 238
Europe
   Liberation of in WWII 188, 200-203, *200-203*
   national rivalries in 1900: 140
   recovery from Dark Ages 29, 30, 32
Exclusive Economic Zones 243, 244
Exeter, HMS, heavy cruiser 177, 178, *178*, 209, *209-10*
Exmouth, Admiral Lord 102, *102*

Fabius, Quintus F Maximus 16
Falklands, Battle of, 1914: 153-4, *154*
Falklands War, 1982: *240*, 240-42, *242*
Farragut, Vice Admiral D G, USN 117, 121, 122
Ferdinand and Isabella, of Spain 41, 42
Ferdinand Max 123-4
Fighting Instructions, RN 60, 71, 75, 80
fireships 50, 64, 67, 79
Fletcher, Admiral Frank USN 212, 214, 215
Formidable, HMS, carrier 192
Fort McHenry, action at, 1812: 97
Four Days Fight, 1666: 62, *62*
Foxe, Luke 51
France, French 34, 35, 41, 55, 65, 106, 112, 125, 134, 234
   colonial development 46, 54, 69, 76, 99, 109, 140, 170, 207, 235
   exploration by 45
   in American War of Independence 80, 81
   in World War II 182, 183, 191, 194, 200
   navy in twentieth century *148*, 158, 176, 191, 194, 234
   rivalry with Britain 69-76, 80-83, 86-91, 93-5, 99, 140, 170, 176
   Southern France, invasion of, 1944: 202
Franklin, Sir John 105
Fraser, Admiral Sir Bruce 198-9
Frobisher, Sir Martin 49, 51
Furious, HMS, carrier 193
Fuso, battleship 226

Gabbard Bank, Battle of the, 1653: 60
Gallipoli Campaign 158
Gama, Vasco da 40
Genoa, Genoese, 16, 33, 34, 35, 89
   struggle with Venice 31, 32, 34
Germany 33, 34, 126, 128, 134, 197, 207, 245
   colonial possessions 132, 140, 170, 176
   navy in WWI 132, 148, 151-4, 156-7, 160-69
   navy in WWII 177-90 *passim*, 196, 198, 200
   scuttling of fleet in 1919: 169
Gibraltar 71, 89
Gilbert and Ellice Islands 208, 219
Glasgow, HMS, light cruiser 153
Glorious, HMS, carrier *180*, 181
Glorious First of June battle, 1794: *84*, 88
Gloucester, HMS, light cruiser 192
Gneisenau, SMS 153-4, *154*
Gneisenau, WWII battlecruiser 180, 181, 185, 189
Goeben and *Breslau*, pursuit of, 1914: 150
Goldsborough, Admiral, USN 119
Golden Hind (ex-*Pelican*) 45, *45*
Good Hope, HMS, armored cruiser 153
Goodenough, Commodore, RN 152
Gordon, General Charles G 109
Gorshkov, Admiral Sergei 247, 248
Goto, Rear Admiral 215
Grasse Count de 80, 81, 82
Graves, Rear Admiral Thomas 80, *80*
Great Britain 99, 126
   and Egypt 125, 140, 234

and Far East 134, 207, 208, 210, 211
   colonial empire 140, 170, 176
   in American Civil War 117, 118
   in Revolutionary and Napoleonic Wars 86-91, 93-5, 96
   in War of 1812: 96-8
   in World War I 148, 164
   in World War II 182, 200, 202
   North Sea oil and 236
   see also Britain, England
Great Migrations of Nineteenth Century 126, 127
Greece, Ancient 8-14 *passim*, 29
Greece, modern 103, 192, 246
Greek fire 20, 21, *21*
Greenland 26, 27, 51
Greer, USS, destroyer 187
Grenville, Sir Richard 48
Guadalcanal, Battles for 215-17, *216*, 218
Guam 139, 220, 222, 223
Guiscard, Robert 29
gunnery 81, 89, 124, 131, 157, 169, 177
gunpower 48, 49-50, 82, 89, 96, 113, 115, 229
Gustavus Adolphus, of Sweden 58

Hakluyt, Richard 45
Halsey, Admiral W, USN 219, 223, 224, 226, 227
Hampton Roads, Battle of, 1862: 119-20, *120*
Hannibal 15-16
Hanseatic League 33, 46
Harold II (Godwinson) 28, *29*
Hart, Admiral T C, USN 208
Hartford, USS, screw corvette 121, *121*, 122
Harwood, Commodore Henry 177
Hawaii 78, 139, 205
Hawke, Admiral Lord 76, *76*
Hawkins, John 45, 49
Heligoland Bight, Battle of, 1914: 151-2
Henry VII 35, 45
Henry, Prince, the Navigator 40
Heraclius, Emperor 20, *21*
Hermes, HMS, carrier 241
Hiei, battleship 216, 217
Hipper, Admiral Franz von 156, 157, 160-62, *162*
Hiryu, carrier 214
Hobson, Lieut Richmond P, USN 130
Holland 86, 89, 102, 182, 207, 236
   Anglo-Dutch Wars 59-62, *60-62*, 64-5, *64-5*
   colonial empire 43, 46, 52, 53, 69, 99, 207, 208, 210
   trade in 17th Century 52-3, 54
Holland, Vice Admiral Lancelot E 189
Holmes, Captain Sir Robert 61, 62
Hong Kong 107, 208
Hood, Rear Admiral Sir Horace 162
Hood, Admiral Sir Samuel 81, 82
Hood, HMS, battlecruiser 189, 190
Hornet, USS, carrier 216
Houston, USS, heavy cruiser 209
Howard, Lord, of Effingham 49, 50
Howe, Admiral Lord 88
Hudson, Henry 38, 51
Hughes, Admiral Sir Edward 80, 82-3

Iachino, Admiral Angelo 192
Ibrahim Pasha 103, 106, *106*
Idaho, USS, battleship *227*
Illustrious, HMS (1941) carrier 191, 192
Illustrious, HMS, carrier (1982) *246*
Indefatigable, HMS, battlecruiser 160
India 19, 40, 69, 70, *70*, 75, 99, 125, 140
Indiana, USS, battleship 130
Indo-China 109, 140, 170, 207
Indomitable, HMS, battlecruiser 156, 157
Indomitable, HMS, carrier 193
Inflexible, HMS, battlecruiser 154, 158
Invincible, HMS, battlecruiser 152, 154, 162
Invincible, HMS, carrier 241
Iowa, USS, battleship 130
Iran, Iraq 236, 237, 238, 250
Iron Duke, HMS, battleship 162
Ireland, Vikings in 25, 27
Israel, Israeli forces 234, 238, *238*, 249
Italy, Italians 29, 34, 89, 115, 126, 127, 140, 148, 170, 191, 195
   Greek colonies in 10, 15
   invasion of, in WWII 195-6, *195-6*, 202
   navy 123-4, 176, 191, 192, 195-6
   Normans in 29
Ito, Admiral Yugo 128

Iwo Jima 221, 223, *227*, 228-9

Jackson, General Andrew 98
James II 61, 62, 64-5, 66, 67, *67*
Japan 37, 40, 46, 109, 112, 128, 134, 176, 220
   and Mongol Empire 36
   and Russo-Japanese War 134-8, *135*, *137*, 176
   expansion plans 128, 132, 170-71, 205, 215, 218
   Far East conquests in WWII 207-8, 211
   navy 128, 134, *135*, *137*, 138, 176, 191, 205-7, *207*, 209, 211-19, 221-9
Jason and the Argonauts 10
Java, light cruiser 209
Java Sea, Battle of, 1942: 208, 209-10, *209-10*
Jean Bart, French battleship 194, 234
Jellicoe, Admiral Sir John 160, *161*, 162-3
Jervis, Admiral Sir John 89, 90
John, Don, of Austria 48
Joyeuse, Admiral Villaret 88
Jutland, Battle of, 1916: 157, 160-63, *161-3*, 169, 224

Kaga, carrier 214
Kakuta, Vice Admiral 223
kamikaze 36, 221, 227, 228, 229
Kearny, USS, destroyer 187
Kellet, Captain 105
Kent, HMS, armored cruiser 154
Key, Francis Scott 97
Keyes, Vice Admiral Sir Roger 151, *152*, 158, 168
King George V, HMS, battleship 190
Kinkaid, Admiral Thomas, USN 224, 226
Kirishima, battleship 216, 217
Kitchener, Lord 158
Koga, Admiral 219
Kondo, Admiral 214, 217
Korea 128, 134
Korean War 232-3, *233*
Kretschmer, Otto 186
Kublai Khan 36, *36*
Kurita, Vice Admiral 223, 224, 226

La Hougue, Battle of, 1692: 66, 66-7
Lagos, 1759 naval action at 76
Lake Erie, Battle of, 1813: 97
La Lociera, Battle of, 1353: 32
Langsdorff, Captain Hans 178
Leach, Captain J 208
Leahy, Admiral W D, USN 225
Lech, Battle of, 955: 32
Leigh-Mallory, Air Marshal Sir Trafford 202
Leipzig, SMS 153, 154
Lepanto, Battle of, 1571: 48
Lexington, USS, carrier 206, 211, 212
Leyte, Battle of, 1944: 221, 223, 224-7, *225-7*
Lilybaeum, Battle of, 241 BC: 15
Lincoln, President Abraham 117
Lion, HMS, battlecruiser 152, 156, 157, 161
Lissa, Battle, of, 1866: 123-4, *124*
Lord Nelson, HMS, battleship 158
Louis XIV 58, 65, 66
Louisbourg, capture of, 1758: *72*, 72-3
Lowestoft, Battle of, 1665: 61, *61*
Lütjens, Admiral 189, 190, *190*
Lützow, SMS, 162, 163
Lützow (ex-*Deutschland*), panzerschiff 177, 197
Lyons, Admiral Sir Edmund 115, *115*

MacArthur, General Douglas 208, 218, 221, *221*
McClure, Captain Robert 105
McClusky, Lieut Commander, USN 214
McLintock, Leopold 105
Madison, President James 96
Magellan, Ferdinand 43, *43*
Magellan, Straits of 43, 53
magnetic compass 19, 34
Maine, USS, armored cruiser 130, *131*, 132
Makarov, Admiral Stefan 135
Malaya 170, 205, 207, 208
Malta 48, 72, *148*, 191, 192-3, 195
Manila Bay, Battle of, 1898: 132, *132*
Manzikert, Battle of, 1071: 30
Marathon, Battle of, 490 BC: 11
Mariana Islands 170, 220
maritime resources 243-4
Marshall Islands 170, 208, 219, 220
Massachusetts, USS, battleship (1898) 130, 131
Massachusetts, USS, battleship (1942) 194

Medina Sidonia, Duke of 49, 50
Mediterranean 8, 15, 32, 35, 48, 94, 102, 150
    Greek domination of 10, 12
    Roman trade and domination in 15, 16, 18, 24
    trade in 14th and 15th centuries 34-5
    in 18th century 71, 76, 89
    in World War II *191*, 191-3
Mehemet Ali 103, 106
Meloria, Battle of, 1284: 32
Merchant Adventurers 45, 51
merchant shipping
    early types 10, 18, 33
    19th century types, clippers etc 107, 110, 127
    20th century armed ships 148, 185
    in 1980s 249-50
Merrimack, USS, steam frigate 119-20, *120*
Mers-el-Kebir, action at, 1940: 191
Middle East Flashpoint 238, *239*
Midway Island 139
    Battle of, 1942: 212, *213*, 213-14, 218
Mikawa, Vice Admiral 215
Milne, Rear Admiral David 102
mines 122, 135, 148, 158, 166, 168, 180, 238
Minorca 16, 71-2, 76
Mississippi Forts, attack on, 1862: *118*, 121, *121*
Mitscher, Admiral Marc, USN 220, 223, 229
Mobile Bay, Battle of, 1864: 122
Modon, Battle of, 1354: 32
Moltke, SMS 156
Mongol Empire, Japan and 36
Monitor, USS, 119-20, *120*
Monk, 'General at Sea' George 60, 62, *62*
Monmouth, HMS, armored cruiser 153, 154
Monroe Doctrine 140
Montcalm, Marquis de 73
Montgomery, General Sir Bernard *202*
Montojo, Admiral Patricio 132
Moore, Major General Jeremy 241
Moreno, Vice Admiral 89
Morgan, Sir Henry 46, *46*
Munk, Jens 51
Musashi, battleship 224
Muscovy Company 45, 51, 111
Mylae, Battle of, 260 BC: 15

Nagumo, Admiral Chuichi 206, 214, 215
Nakhimov, Admiral Pavel 113, 114
Napier, Vice Admiral Sir Charles 116
Napoleon I 74, 86, 88, 90, 91, 93, 95
Napoleon III 114
Napoleonic Wars 74, 86-91, 93-5, 148
    the world after 99
Nasser, Gamel Abdul 234
NATO Alliance 245-6
Naupactus, Battle of, 430 BC: 13
naval tactics 12, 15, 17, 18, 49, 50, 59-60, 64, 67,
    79, 82, 90, 91, 123, 124, 138, 162, 163, 223
Navarino, Battle of, 1827: 100, 103, 106, 113
navigation 34, 40, *43*, 77, 78
Negapatam, Battle of, 1782: *82*, 82-3
Nelson, Horatio 51, 86, 89, 90, 91, *91*, 93, 94, *95*,
    138
Nevada, USS, battleship *201*, 205
New Guinea 52, 53, 170, 208, 211, 212, 215, 218,
    219, 220
New Jersey, USS, battleship 235, *245*
New Orleans, Battle of, 1814: 98, *98*
New Zealand 52, 77, 170
New Zealand, HMNZS, battlecruiser 152, 156
Nicias, Athenian commander 14
Nile, Battle of, 1798: 90
Nimitz, Admiral Chester W, USN 208, 213, 218,
    225
Nishimura, Admiral 224, 226
Norfolk, HMS, cruiser 189, 199
Normandy, Normans 26, 28, 29
    landings in, 1944: *172*, 200-201, *200-202*
Norsemen, 25-6, 27
North Africa 29, 99, 191-2
    invasion of, 1942: 188, 192, 193, 194, *194*
North Cape, Battle of, 1943: 198-9
North Foreland, Battle of, 1653: 60
North-East Passage 51, *51*, 105
North-West Passage 51, 78, 105
Norway, Norwegians 58, 180, 236
    campaign in, 1940: 180-81, 183
Nürnberg, SMS 153, 154

Ohio, SS, tanker 193

oil, World of *230*, *236*, 236-7, 243, *243*, 244, 250
Okinawa, capture of *221*, *227*, 228-9
Oldendorf, Admiral Jesse, USN 226
OPEC, Organization of Petroleum Exporting
    Countries 236, 237
Opium War and China trade *107*, 107-9, *109*
Oregon, USS, battleship 130, 131
Orion, HMS, light cruiser 192
Orlov, Admiral Alexei 79
Otranto, armed merchant cruiser 153
Otto I, Emperor 32
Ozawa, Vice Admiral 222, 223, 224, 226, 227

Pakenham, General Sir Edward 98
Palmerston, Lord 99, 106
Panama, Panama Canal 139
Parker, Admiral Sir Hyde 91
Parma, Duke of 49, 50
Parrott, Captain Robert, USN 117
Parry, Sir William 105
Paul, Saint 18
Pearl Harbor 219, *219*, *220*
    attack on 138, 171, 187, *205*, 205-6, 207
Pellew, Admiral Sir Edward *see* Exmouth, Lord
Pellion de Persano, Count Carlo 123
Peloponnesian Wars 13-14
Pepys, Samuel 62
Pericles 13
Perry, Captain Oliver Hazard, USN 97
Persia, Persians 10, 11-12, 13, 14, 19, 20, 26
Persian Gulf 40, 237, 238
Perth, HMAS, light cruiser 192, 209
Peru 43, *43*
Philip, of Macedon 10
Philip II, of Spain 49
Philip Augustus, of France 31
Philippine Islands 43, 53, 127, 132, 139, 140, 170,
    205, 206, 208, 218, 221, *221*
Philippine Sea, Battle of, 1944: 220, 221, *222*,
    222-5
Phillips, Admiral Tom 208
Phoenicia, Phoenicians 8-9, *8-9*, 11, 18
Pisa, Pisans 31, 32
Pisani, Vettor 32
Pitt, William 70, 73, 75
Pizarro, Francisco 43
Plataea, Battle of, 479 BC: 12
Pommern, SMS *163*
Port Arthur 128, 134-5, *135*, 136
Port Mahon, Minorca 16, 71, *71*
Porter, Commodore, USN 121
Portland, Battle of, 1653: *60*
Portugal, Portuguese 34, 41, 43
    exploration and trade empire 37, 40
    in Africa 40, 43, 54, 140
    in New World 43-4, 45, 51, 54, 99, 140
Pridham-Wippell, Vice Admiral H D 192
Prien, Günther 179, *179*, 186
Prince of Wales, HMS, battleship 189, 208, *208*
Princess Royal, HMS, battlecruiser 152, 156, 157
Prinz Eugen, heavy cruiser 185, 189, *190*
Puerto Rico 130, 131, 139
Punic Wars 15-16

Quadrant, Davis' *43*
Quebec, capture of 72, 72, 73-4, *75*, 77
Queen Elizabeth, HMS, battleship 158, *159*, 192
Queen Mary, HMS, battlecruiser 152, 160, *161*
Quiberon Bay, Battle of, 1759: *75*, 75-6

Raeder, Admiral Erich 169, 178, *181*, 198
Ramsay, Vice Admiral Bertram 182, *202*
Re d'Italia 123, *124*
Red Sea 19, 40, 55, 170
Regulus, Attilius 15
Renown, HMS, battlecruiser 180
Repulse, HMS, battlecruiser 208
Resolution, HMS, 77, 78
Reuben James, USS, destroyer 187
Rhium, Battle of, 429 BC: 13
Richard I 31, *31*
River Plate, Battle of, 1939: 177-8
Robeck, Admiral John de 158, *158*
Robinson Crusoe (Defoe) 53
Rodney, Admiral Lord 80, 81
Rodney, HMS, battleship 190
Roger I, Roger II 29
Roman Britain, end of 24
Rome, Romans 10, 18, 19, 20, 24

rise of 10, 15-16, 18, 20
Roosevelt, President Franklin D 187, 206, *225*
Roosevelt, President Theodore 132
Ross, Captain James Clark 104, 105
Ross, Sir John 105
Ross, Brigadier Robert 97
Royal Canadian Navy 184, 187
Royal Marines 60, 234, 241
Royal Navy 50, 61, 67, 70, 71, 72, 73, 75, 81-2, 86,
    87, 88, 90, 93, 96, 106, 115, 125, 136, *140*,
    176, *239*, *246*
    in World War I 148, *148*, 150-54, *154*, 156-8,
    160-63, *161-3*
    in World War II 177-9, *178*, 180-81, 184-90,
    191-3, 197, 199, 200, 208, 229
    Fleet Air Arm 190, 191, 192
    policing role 99, 102, 106, 125, 176
    post-1945 operations 234, 238, *239*, 240-42
Royal Oak, HMS, battleship 179, 180
Royal Society 77, 78
Royal Sovereign, HMS, 100-gun ship 95
Rozhdestvensky, Admiral 136-7, 138
Rupert, Prince 65
Russell, Admiral Edward 66, 67
Russia, Russians 58, 91, 112, 127, 140
    in 19th century 109, 113-16, 128
    navy 134, 135-8
    rivalry with Turkey 79, 103, 113, 114
    see also Russo-Japanese War, Soviet Union
Russo-Japanese War 134-8, *135*, *137*
Ryujo, carrier 215

Sadras, Battle of, 1782: 82
St James's Day Fight, 1666: 62
St Lo, USS, escort carrier *226*
St Vincent, Admiral Lord 88
Saintes, Battle of the, 1782: 80, 81-2
Saipan 222, 223, 228
Salamis, Battle of, 480 BC: *6-7*, 10, 11-12, *12*
Samar, Battle of, 1944: 226-7
Samoan Islands 139, 170
Sampson, Rear Admiral William T, USN 130, 131
Santa Cruz, Battle of, 1942: 216
Santiago, Battle of, 1898: 130-31
Saratoga, USS, carrier 206, 214, 215, *227*
Saunders, Admiral 73, 74
Saxons, 18, 24, 27, 28
Scapa Flow 148, 156, 160, 169, 179, 180
Scharnhorst, SMS (WWI) 153-4
Scharnhorst, (WWII) 180, *180*, 181, 185, 189, 198-
    9
Scheer, Vice Admiral Reinhard 160, 162-3, *163*,
    164
Schepke, Joachim 186
Scheveningen, Battle of, 1653: 60
Schley, Commodore Winfield S, USN 131
Schooneveldt, Battles of 65, *65*
Scipio, Publius Cornelius 16
Scotland, Viking raids on 27
Scott, Rear Admiral Norman, USN 215, 217
Sea Power versus Land Power in Revolutionary
    and Napoleonic Wars 86-7
Selkirk, Alexander 53
Sevastopol 114-15, *115*
Seven Years War 70, 71-6
Seydlitz, SMS, 156, 157, 161
Seymour, Admiral Sir Frederick B 125
Sheffield, HMS (1941) 190, 197, 199
Sheffield, HMS (1982) 240
Sherbrooke, Captain Robert 197
Shima, Admiral 224
Shirley, Governor William 73
Shoho, carrier 211, *212*
Shokaku, carrier 211, 212, 215, 223
Sicily 10, 14, 15, 21, 29
    1943 invasion of 195
signals, signalling 157, 161, 162, 246
Sims, Admiral, USN 148
Singapore 208
Sinope, Battle of, 1853: 113, *113*, 114
Slave Trade 42, 43, 54-5, *54-5*, 68, 99
Smith, General Bedell *202*
Sole Bay, Battle of, 1672: *64*, 64-5
Solomon Islands 215, 218, 219
Somaliland 140, 170
Somerville, Vice Admiral Sir James 191
Soryu, carrier 214
South Africa 126, 170
South America 42, 43, 46, 99, 126

South Dakota, USS, battleship 217
Soviet Union 188, 197, 207, 243, 245, 250
   as superpower 176, 238, 245
     growth of navy 247-8, *248*
Spain, Spaniards 34, 35, 40, 43, 48, 86, 89, 132
   in New World 42-3, 43-4, 45, 46, 51, 54, 68, 69,
     70, 72, 76, 99, 140
   in Revolutionary/Napoleonic Wars 86, 89
   Spanish Armada 49-50, *50*
   see also Spanish-American War
Spanish-American War 127, 130-32, *131*, *132*, 139
Sparta, Spartans 13-14
Spee, Admiral Graf von 153-4, *154*
Spragge, Sir Edward 65
Spruance, Admiral Raymond, USN 214, 222-3
Star Spangled Banner, The 97
Stamford Bridge, Battle of, 1066: 28
steam, advent of 110, 115, 127
Stoddart, Rear Admiral 154
Stopford, Admiral 106
Stricker, General 97
Sturdee, Vice Admiral Sir Doveton 154, *154*
submarines 148, 168, 193, 219, 221, 248
   see also U-boats
Suez 8, 23
   1956 campaign 234, 238
   Suez Canal 110, 125, 140, 170, 234, *239*
Suffolk, HMS, cruiser 189
Suffren de St Tropez, Admiral Pierre de 80, 82-3
Suffren, battleship 158
Sunda Strait, Battle of, 1941: 209-10
Superb, HMS, battleship *163*
Surigao Strait, Battle of, 1944: *227*
Sweden, Swedes 26, 33, 180
   Swedish Empire and Baltic Trade 58
Syfret, Admiral 193
Syracuse 29; battle at, 413 BC: 14, *14*

Tagaki, Admiral Takeo 209, 211-12
Taiho, carrier 223
Takahashi, Admiral I 209
Tanaka, Admiral Raizo 215, 217
Taranto, attack on, 1940: 191, *191*, 192
Tasman, Abel Janszoon 52-3, *53*
Tasmania 52
Tassafaronga, Battle of, 1942: 217
Tegetthof, Admiral Wilhelm von 123, *124*
'Terra Australis' 77, 104
Texas, USS 130
Texel, Battles of, 1653, 1673: 60, 65
Tedder, Air Marshal Sir Arthur *202*
Themistocles 11, 12
Thermopylae, Battle of, 480 BC: 11
Thermopylae, clipper ship 110
Tiger, HMS, battlecruiser 156
Ting Ju-ch'ang, Admiral 128
Tirpitz, Admiral Alfred *140*
Tirpitz, battleship 189, 190, 197, 199
Togo, Admiral 135, 137, 138
torpedoes 122, 179, 188, 209, 217
Torrington, Earl of 66
Tourville, Vice Admiral Comte de 66-7
Tovey, Admiral Sir John 190
trade
   Baltic Trade and Swedish Empire 58
   in Ancient World 8-9, 10, 15, 18, 19
   in 14th and 15th centuries 33, 34-5
   in 19th century 99, 110
   maritime trade in 1980s 249-50, *250-51*
   oil 236-7, 249
   Opium War and China trade 107, 109
   Triangular Trade in 18th century 68
   World Trade in 1920s, 176
Trafalgar, Battle of, 1805: 90, 93-5, *95*
Trincomalee, action at, 1782: 83
Triumph, HMS (1653) *60*
Tromp, Cornelius 65
Tromp, Marten 59, *59*, 60
Troubridge, Rear Admiral 150
Tsushima Strait, Battle of, 1905: 137-8
Turkey, Turks 30, 31, 32, 35, 48, 79, 103, 106,
   113, 114, 150, 158, 246
Tyrwhitt, Commodore Reginald 151, *157*

U-Boats
   operations in WWI 148, 160, 164-8, *165-7*, 169,
    182
   operations in WWII 178, 183-8, 197, 198, 200
United States

and China 134, 139
and Middle East 234, 238, 249
and slavery 54-5, 68
and Vietnam 235
as World Empire 132, 139, 170
Civil War *see* American Civil War *main heading*
immigration to 126, 127
in World War I 148, 166-7
in World War II 184, 186-8, 194, 197, 200, 202,
   205-6, 215, 218-21
Pacific Counter Offensive in WWII 218-21
Spanish-American *see main heading*
War of 1812 96-8, *98*
United States Marines 215, 216, 218, 223, 228, 235
United States Navy 176, 247, 248
   in War of 1812 96
   in Civil War 117, 119, 120, 121, 122
   in Spanish-American War 130-32
   in World War II 187, 205-6, 208, 211-9 *passim*
   in Vietnam 235

Valiant, HMS, battleship 161, 192
Van Diemen's Land 52, *53*, 77
Venice, Venetians 21, 31, 33, 34, 35, *35*, 40, 48
   struggle with Genoa 32, 34
Vespucci, Amerigo *44*
Victorious, HMS, carrier 189, 193
Victory, HMS 88, 94, 95
Vietnam War 235, *235*
Vikings 18, 24, *26*, 32
   explorations of 25-6
   in Britain and Ireland 27
Villeneuve, Admiral Pierre de 93, 94, *94*
Vindictive, HMS 168, *168*
Virginia Capes, Battle of, 1781: 80
Vitgeft, Admiral 135-6
Von der Tann, SMS 160

War of 1812: 96-8, *98*
War of English Succession, 1689-91: 66
Warspite, HMS, battleship 180, 192
Washington, General George 80
Washington, DC 96-7
Washington, USS, battleship 217
Wasp, USS, carrier 215, *216*, 223
Weddigen, Otto von *165*
Welles, Gideon 118
West Africa 40, 46, 54, 61, 170
West Indies 46, 54, 55, 68, 80
whaling 27, 104, 111-12, 127, 243
Whitworth, Admiral 180
Wilkes, Lieutenant 104
William III (William of Orange) 66
Willoughby, Sir Hugh 51
Wolfe, General Sir James 72, 73-4
Woodward, Admiral Sir John 240, *242*
World War I 146-7
   Blockade of Central Powers 148
   pursuit of *Goeben* and *Breslau* 150
   Heligoland Bight, Battle of 151-2
   Coronel and Falkland Islands, Battles 153-4
   Dogger Bank, Battle of 156-7
   Gallipoli campaign 158
   Jutland, Battle of *see main heading*
   Crisis of U-boat War 164-8
   Scuttling of German Fleet 169
   aftermath 139, 176
World War II 174-5
   River Plate, Battle of 177-8
   Scapa Flow defenses 179
   Norwegian Campaign 180-81
   Dunkirk 182
   Atlantic, Battle of 183-8, 200
   Bismarck, sinking of 189-90
   Mediterranean, war in 191-3
   North Africa, invasion of *see main heading*
   Italy, invasion of 195-6, *195-6*
   Arctic Convoys in 197-9
   Liberation of Europe 188, 200-203
   Pearl Harbor *see main heading*
   Japanese Conquests in Far East 207-8, 211
   Java Sea, Battle of *see main heading*
   Coral Sea, Battle of *see main heading*
   Guadalcanal, Battles for 215-17, *216*, 218
   Midway, Battle of *see main heading*
   American Counter Offensive in Pacific 218-21
   Philippine Sea, Battle of *see main heading*
   Leyte Gulf Battle *see main heading*
   Okinawa and Iwo Jima, capture of *227*, 228-9

aftermath of 244-6
worms, wood boring 42, 82
Wright, Rear Admiral Carleton H, USN 217

Yalu River, Battle of, 1894: 128, *128*
Yamamoto, Admiral I 205, 211, 213, 214, 218
Yamani, Sheikh *237*
Yamashiro, battleship 226
Yamato, battleship 224, 228-9
Yellow Sea, Battle of, 1904: 135-6, *137*
Yeo, Sir James 97
Yorktown, surrender at 80, 81
Yorktown, USS, carrier 211-12, *213*, 213-14

Zama, Battle of, 202 BC: 16
Zeebrugge, operation at, 1918: 168, *168*
Zheng He, Admiral 36
Zuikaku, carrier 211, 212, 215, 223, 227

Acknowledgments

The author and publishers would like to thank
David Eldred who designed this book, Ron
Watson who prepared the index, Wendy Sacks and
Jean Martin who did the picture research and
Donald Sommerville, the editor. The agencies
listed below kindly supplied the illustrations.

Australian War Memorial: page 226.
BBC Hulton Picture Library: pages 8, 10(both),
11, 13, 16, 20, 31(below), 34(top), 36, 43(below),
46, 47, 52(below), 53, 73, 80, 86-7, 106, 109(top),
112(top), 113, 114, 120(top), 128, 132-3, 134, 135,
140-1(below), 148, 149, 152(below), 157(top
right), 159(left), 160, 161(left), 178, 200.
Bison Picture Library: pages 12(right), 144-5, 181,
183, 196.
Bundesarchiv: page 155(below).
Esso Petroleum Company: pages 230-1.
Archiv Gerstenberg: pages 1, 34(below), 41,
43(top), 44, 45, 51, 52(top), 54(top), 55, 124(top),
141(middle and right), 152(top), 157(top left),
162, 163(below), 165(top right), 166-7,
167(below), 180.
Imperial War Museum, London: pages 4-5,
147(both right), 161(right), 163(top), 164,
165(left), 175(bottom), 179, 190(below), 191, 196,
198, 208, 209, 240, 242(top and below left).
Israeli Government Press Office: page 238.
Library of Congress: pages 42(top), 120(below),
133.
Mansell Collection: pages 2-3, 6-7, 9, 12(below
left), 14, 15, 17, 19, 21(both), 22-3, 24, 26(left),
28-9(Giraudon), 31(top), 38-9, 53(below),
54(below), 72(below), 74-5, 77, 78, 84-5, 94, 98,
100-1, 107, 109(below), 118(below), 129.
MARS, Lincs: pages 112(below), 115(top left),
116, 130(top), 137.
MOD: page 242(below right).
National Maritime Museum, London: pages
42(below), 49, 50, 56-7, 60(below), 61, 62,
63(top), 64, 65(both), 66, 67(both), 69, 70(both),
71, 72(top), 75(below), 76, 82, 87(top left and top
right), 93(both), 102, 112(middle), 115(top right
and below), 140-1(top), 146, 154(below),
159(right), 168. Jacket illustration.
Peter Newark's Historical Pictures: pages
26(right), 35(below), 59, 60(top), 63(below), 91,
95, 121, 124(below), 154(top and middle), 155(top).
Port of Felixstowe: page 250(below).
PPL: page 239.
Sea Containers Ltd: page 250(top).
Shell International Petroleum Company: pages
236, 243.
C & S Taylor: page 246.
TPS/Central Press: pages 147(left), 237.
TPS/Keystone: pages 210, 244.
US Army: pages 194, 195(top), 202-3(top).
US Army – Signal Corps: pages 221, 225(top),
232-3.
US Coast Guard: pages 172-3, 225(below).
US Naval Historical Center: pages 166(below),
213, 222, 233.
US Navy: pages 118(top), 130-1, 171, 190(below),
235, 245, 248.
US Navy/National Archives: pages 174, 175(top),
195(below), 201, 202-3(below), 205, 207,
212(both), 216(both), 219, 220, 224, 226-7, 228,
229(both).